D1034148

FROM TROY TO ENTEBBE

Special Operations in Ancient
and
Modern Times

Edited by

John Arquilla

University Press of America, Inc.
Lanham • New York • London

Copyright © 1996 by
University Press of America,® Inc.
4720 Boston Way
Lanham, Maryland 20706

3 Henrietta Street
London, WC2E 8LU England

All rights reserved
Printed in the United States of America
British Cataloging in Publication Information Available

Library of Congress Cataloging-in-Publication Data

From Troy to Entebbe : special operations in ancient and modern
times / edited by John Arquilla.
p.   cm.
Includes bibliographical references.
1. Special operations (Military science)--Case studies.   2. Raids
(Military science)--Case studies.   I. Arquilla, John.
U262.F76   1995   355.4'22--dc20   96-45702 CIP

ISBN 0-7618-0185-5 (cloth: alk. ppr.)
ISBN 0-7618-0186-3 (pbk: alk. ppr.)

⊖™The paper used in this publication meets the minimum
requirements of American National Standard for information
Sciences—Permanence of Paper for Printed Library Materials,
ANSI Z39.48—1984

The smaller the unit
the better its performance.

-- T.E. Lawrence

To the memory of Trevor Dupuy

Contents

Preface

Special operations, though most commonly associated with the period from the Second World War to the present, have a long, rich tradition that reaches back deeply into history. This volume provides a representative sampling of instances of raiding and the *coup de main* from antiquity to the Cold War. In addition to expanding the temporal perspective on special operations, these readings conceptualize them as going well beyond the function of hostage rescues, the activity upon which so much popular, and even scholarly, attention is focused. This broad approach allows for thorough analysis of such issues as the importance of surprise, the need for integration between general purpose and special forces, and the overall impact of irregular and commando operations on war outcomes.

The readings in this anthology incorporate relevant examples drawn from classics of historical fiction, such as Tolstoy's rendering of Russia's first war in Chechnya during the 19th century, and Lartéguy's searing tale of French post-war counterinsurgency in Algeria. Also, several eyewitness memoirs are excerpted, including a critical episode from T.E. Lawrence's desert campaign during World War I, and the World War II operations of the Special Boat Service in the Mediterranean, along with

Milton Miles's inventive and highly effective efforts against the Japanese in occupied China. These selections, along with the other historical pieces included in this reader, help to form a broad, general picture of special operations, and of those who prosecute them.

Nevertheless, it must be noted that the historical and literary perspectives afforded in these selections are designed to encourage analysis rather than to paint comprehensive pictures of special operations in the various eras under examination. Keeping this principally didactic mission in mind, I have limited my own observations to the extent of sketching an analytic framework in the introductory chapter, one that may be used to help generate insight and understanding of the historical episodes that follow. The readings are thus allowed to speak, quite eloquently, for themselves.

Acknowledgments

This book has grown out of my experience in teaching the history of special operations over the past few years, and I am deeply indebted to my students, from whom I have learned much. I also gratefully acknowledge the support and assistance of Jennifer Duncan, Michelle Harris, Annie Howard, Hannah Liebmann, Gordon McCormick, Carlo Medina, and E. Panholzer, whose various efforts have contributed so much to the successful completion of this project.

Thanks are also owed to a number of publishers for granting permissions to use these readings:

"The Wooden Horse" and "The Sack of Troy" from *The Siege and Fall of Troy* by Robert Graves. Copyright © 1962 by International Authors N.V. (Netherlands Antitles). Used by permissions of Doubleday, a division of Bantam Doubleday Dell Publishing Group, Inc.

"The Damage Done by This Corsair" and "The Wind Commands Me Away" from *Sir Francis Drake*. Copyright © 1972 by G.M. Thomson. Used by permission of William Morrow and Company, Inc.

"The Impérieuse" from *The Sea Wolf*. Copyright © 1978 by Ian Grimble. Used by permission of Random House UK, Ltd.

"The Raid on St. Francis" from *Northwest Passage* by Kenneth Roberts. Copyright © 1936, 1937 by Robert Kenneth. Used by permissions of Doubleday, a division of Bantam Doubleday Dell Publishing Group, Inc.

"Struggle for the South" from *The American Revolution* by Fred Cook. Copyright © 1959 by Forbes, Inc. Used by permission of American Heritage Magazine, a division of Forbes, Inc.

"Wars With the Barbary Pirates" from *The Little Wars of the United States.* Copyright © 1968 by R.E. Dupuy and W.H. Baumer. Used by permission of Hawthorne, New York.

"How the Legion Began" and "The Legion Fights in Algeria" from *The French Foreign Legion.* Copyright © 1955 by Wyatt Blassingame. Used by permission of Random House, New York.

"Military Means, Political Ends" from *Why the Confederacy Lost.* Copyright © 1992 by Archer Jones. Used by permission of Oxford University Press, London.

"Total War and an Election" from *The Civil War* by Bruce Catton. Copyright © 1961 by Forbes, Inc. Used by permission of American Heritage Magazine, a division of Forbes, Inc.

"Trapped by a Q-Ship ..." from *Raiders of the Deep* by Lowell Thomas. Copyright © 1928 by Doubleday, a division of Bantam Doubleday Dell Publishing Group, Inc. Used by permissions of Doubleday, a division of Bantam Doubleday Dell Publishing Group, Inc.

"The Raid Upon the Bridges" from *Seven Pillars of Wisdom* by T.E. Lawrence. Copyright © 1926, 1935 by Doubleday, a division of Bantam Doubleday Dell Publishing Group, Inc. Used by permissions of Doubleday, a division of Bantam Doubleday Dell Publishing Group, Inc.

"The Coup de Main at Eben Emael" and "The Blood-Bath of Crete" from *The Luftwaffe War Diaries* by Cajus Bekker, translated by Frank Ziegler. Translation copyright © 1967 by Macdonald & Co. Used by permissions of Doubleday, a division of Bantam Doubleday Dell Publishing Group, Inc.

"A British Commando Attempt to Capture Rommel," "The British Raid on Tobruk," and "Brandenburgers in Action Behind the Front" from *The Foxes of the Desert.* Copyright © 1962 by Paul Carell. Used by permission of Doubleday.

Chapters 16-18 from *Raiders From the Sea.* Copyright © 1990 by John Lodwick. Used by permission of the U.S. Naval Institute, Annapolis, Maryland.

"A Very Private War" from *Lonely Vigil.* Copyright © 1977 by Walter Lord. Used by permission of Penguin Viking, New York.

"The Road to Myitkyina" from *Eagle Against the Sun.* Copyright © 1984 by Ronald Spector. Used by permission of The Free Press, an imprint of Simon & Schuster Inc., New York.

"Chinese Pirates and the SACO Dragon" from *A Different Kind of War.*

Copyright © 1968 by Milton E. Miles. Used by permission of NAL Dutton, a division of Penguin.

"The Leap of Leucadia" from *The Centurions.* Copyright © 1960 by Jean Lartéguy. Used by permission of Les Presses de la Cité, Paris.

"Entebbe" from *The Arab-Israeli Wars.* Copyright © 1982 by Chaim Herzog. Used by permission of Random House, New York.

Introduction

There has been a tremendous interest in special operations and military elites in recent years; and a very substantial literature has arisen covering primarily the period from the Vietnam War to the present. These studies have keyed on narrative[1] or, when of a more analytic bent, have analyzed high-level political questions.[2] The focus on recent events has created a rich body of knowledge concerning still-applicable tactics and military techniques, while considerations of strategic policy effects may prove of inestimable use to decision makers.

However, some gaps remain. First, there has been a tendency to neglect the treasure trove of older case studies of special operations, which may prove useful sources of insight and understanding. Second, keying on either the tactical level or upon questions of national policy has left, mostly unexamined, crucial issues pertaining to the nature, course and impact of special operations in the realm of conflict. This volume seeks to redress matters, drawing upon a diverse set of literary and historical writings as the basis for gaining a deeper appreciation of special operations.

In order to justify the inclusion of cases from periods long before the creation of modern "special forces" organizations, it is necessary to work with a broad definition of special operations, conceiving of them as that class of military (or paramilitary) actions that fall outside the realm of conventional warfare during their respective time periods. This places significant emphasis on the *coup de main* by small forces whose aim is to achieve very substantial effects upon the course of a war or international crisis. Thus, Rogers's deep strike against St. Francis during the French and Indian Wars qualifies as an early example of special operations. However, the definition also allows for the inclusion of more protracted campaigns in which small forces are used, either independently, or in concert with regular (or other irregular) forces to achieve larger aims. Marion's campaign during the American Revolution provides an arch-typical example, as do Cochrane's raids in support of Spanish guerrillas during the Napoleonic Wars.

This definition, while capturing the essential spirit of special operations, avoids some of the problems posed by requiring that they be performed by "specially trained, equipped, and organized" forces,[3] or that they must fall into the category of the one-shot *coup de main*.[4] Instead, many special operations are prosecuted by regular forces doing quite exceptional things. Nevertheless, on many occasions, raiders constitute a *de facto* elite attack force, as can be seen by the great warriors chosen to ride in the Trojan Horse, or in the rigorous training and distinctive attire of Rogers Rangers. By looking beyond the *coup de main,* one can also see that protracted operations often have both substantial military and political effects. T.E. Lawrence's Arab insurgency during World War I is perhaps the best-known of these longer-term special operations; but one can see this in other cases as well. For example, Merrill's Marauders played a key military role in the campaign to liberate Burma during World War II; and also, as Ronald Spector notes, did much to meet Stilwell's political need to induce Chinese forces to remain active in the campaign.

In the twenty excerpts that follow, the reader will have the opportunity to benefit from the perspectives afforded by a number of different national traditions in special operations. Britain is well-represented, with readings spanning from Drake's harassing and pre-emptive exploits against imperial Spain to the Special Boat Service's campaign against the Axis in the Aegean and Adriatic Seas during World War II. Special operations can be found at the heart of French involvement in Algeria, as depicted in the readings pertaining to its entry, and century-later exit, from this troubled North African state. The American special operations tradition considered in this volume keys primarily upon the formative experiences of the French and Indian Wars, the Revolution and the Civil War, concluding with an analysis of General Joseph Stilwell's ruthless use of his elite U.S. forces in the brutal struggle for Burma against the Japanese. Finally, there are readings covering Russia's special operations in its first counterinsurgency in Chechnya, dating from the mid-19th century, Germany's unique contributions to the advancement of doctrine, particularly air assault by forces of varying sizes, and Israel's peerless rescue at

Entebbe.

This exposure to the approaches to special operations taken by differing strategic cultures allows the reader to engage in fruitful comparative analysis across cases. For example, the linear Russian approach to fighting the Chechens, so compellingly depicted by Tolstoy in *The Raid,* contrasts sharply with the far more irregular tactics undertaken in Algeria by, first, the French Foreign Legion and, later, the paratroops. Unsurprisingly, the staid Russian operations achieved far less in the field than the imaginative French raiding tactics. However, as Tolstoy points out, a great deal of care was given by the Russian officers to avoid any violations of the rules of engagement,[5] a task simplified by their straightforward operational plan. The French, on the other hand, engaged in a desperate twilight struggle against zealots whom they inevitably brutalized in order to achieve their counterinsurgent goals.

In the end, despite their balky approach, the Russians ended up subduing Chechnya (a lesson for the present?), while the more ethically questionable methods employed by the paras led to the unraveling of overall French policy toward Algeria. This observation implies the often very substantial linkage between special operations, at even the lowest levels, to consequences for high state policies.[6] The brief excerpt from Lowell Thomas's *Raiders of the Deep* offers another twist on this point, explaining how the lowly Q-ship had profound strategic effects by inducing, this time the adversary, to violate the existing laws of war. For it was fear of falling victim to these British decoy vessels, of which hundreds were built during World War I,[7] that pressured German U-boat captains to eschew surfacing to confront and warn merchant ships and, instead, to sink them by torpedo attack without warning. This shift in commerce raiding tactics created a great deal of international opprobrium, with which the Kaiser's government never adequately dealt.[8]

Opportunities for comparative analysis across cases abound, as will be suggested in the discussion of key issues that follows. However, it is important to note that intra-case analysis is also amply encouraged by these readings, a process guided by the need to investigate questions relating to the type, scope and conditions for success of special operations. For example, a critical analysis of the Trojan Horse mission might lead one to conclude that this was a heedlessly complicated, risky operation to which, a careful reading of Graves will show, good alternatives existed. Why, for example, didn't the Greeks infiltrate the city through the drainage tunnel that they had discovered, and used previously for purposes of stealing the Palladium, a wooden temple statue of Athena? This would have reduced the risks of having to wait for a long period in their horsey "hide sight," hoping that the Trojans would drag them inside the city's walls. Also, why were only two men of the nearly two dozen raiders assigned to take care of opening the gate to let in the regular Greek forces? Were they thwarted, the others in the party would have been killed or captured before reinforcements came to their aid.

Mention of the Greeks and the probably apocryphal tale of their fatal "gift horse" highlights the presence of a significant literary component in this reader. Four excerpts come from classics of historical fiction. They have been chosen for inclusion both because of their lucid exposition and their illumination of important analytic issues in special operations. They also help in the process of "rounding out" the notion of the *coup de main* and counterinsurgency actions as military phenomena whose histories lie well beyond the experiences of Vietnam and other Cold War conflicts. Indeed, the readings from Tolstoy and Lartéguy evoke both a sense of the timelessness of guerrilla warfare tactics; but of timeliness, too, in that present-day Chechnya and Algeria are once again important low intensity battlegrounds. That the Russians pursue a similar linear approach to that of their forebears, and the Algerian government has so quickly resorted to the harsh measures characteristic of their former colonial masters, leaves one with a profound, sad sense of *déjà vu.* When Roberts's account of the raid on St. Francis, from *Northwest Passage,* is added to the other literary pieces, one can see clearly what Monsarrat meant when he wrote that good fiction had to be "a true story because that is the only kind worth telling."[9]

As for the "true stories" that make up the other readings, four are from memoirs of high literary quality, particularly Lawrence's dolorous rendering of a raid undertaken principally to please Allenby, and Lodwick's zestful account of the fits the Special Boat Service gave the Germans and Italians. Two excerpts come from lively biographies of Drake and Cochrane; and the other ten derive from various corners of the secondary historical literature. All were selected on the basis of their relevance to and clarity in exposition of the analytic issues whose study is the object of this volume.

All the readings are, in many ways, both less and more than what one might expect. First, they can in no way be considered comprehensive treatments of their subjects. The reader may, if prompted by these excerpts, wish to obtain further knowledge of these cases, and will certainly have to go elsewhere for detailed histories of the various events described. On the other hand, each of these readings does a bit more than most accounts of special operations, in that these excerpts all place them within the context of the larger currents of conflict in which they occur. A particularly good example of this is provided by Cook's account of the campaign in the South during the American Revolution. His narrative alternates between describing the activities of Marion's raiders and Greene's regulars, interweaving them so as to provide the reader both with a clear sense of overall operations and of the crucial importance of well-integrated irregular forces to the ultimate victory at Yorktown.

The integration of special and conventional operations constitutes perhaps the most important analytic issue highlighted by these readings. Time and again, one sees success or failure hinging entirely upon the smooth coordination of regulars and raiders. Aside from the example from the American Revolution, the ancient Greeks and modern Germans also reflect this insight clearly. For, had Agamemnon not responded with alacrity to the fire signal to sail back from behind the isle of Tenedos to storm Troy, Odysseus and his small raiding force would have been hacked to pieces and the gates would have stayed closed. Similarly, Assault Detachment Koch would have withered away had follow-on forces of the *Wehrmacht* not arrived to reinforce them at Eben Emael in 1940. These tactical examples aside, the readings on the Barbary Wars and the Coastwatchers address the issue of integration from a strategic campaign perspective as well.

The linkage between poorly integrated operations and defeat appears clearly also, with Confederate operations in the Civil War providing the counterpoint to the magnificent success won by Marion and Greene during the Revolution. Interestingly, the southern tradition in irregular warfare appeared, at first blush, to be carried on in high style by the likes of Nathan Bedford Forrest and John Mosby. As Archer Jones and Bruce Catton point out, these raiders tied up significant portions of the Union Army for long periods of time. However, higher-level commanders appeared to have little sense as to how to incorporate these matchless forces into their campaign plans. Hood, for example, decided to defend Atlanta by sending his raiders on far-flung harassing missions, while assuming the offensive with his outnumbered regulars. The result was that he softened the overall impact of Forrest's operations by dispersing them so widely, and dissipated his own field army in attritional battles with Union regulars. Robert E. Lee, who viewed commando-type operations as "an unmixed evil," also sought continually to take the tactical offensive with regular forces, a costly and ultimately disastrous strategy for the outnumbered Confederate Army.

These readings should prompt critical analysis of Southern strategy, and might lead one to suggest an alternative that would have kept Rebel regulars on the defensive while raiding forces carried the offensive burden. This would have husbanded scarce resources and prevented the North from achieving the aims of its attritional "Anaconda" plan. Jones's notion of the importance of viewing strategy in terms of either its raiding or persisting character may also prove a useful general model for thinking about the integration of special and regular military operations over the course of campaigns and wars. A particularly useful case for analysis, in this regard, is Lawrence, who moved almost faultlessly between raiding and persisting.

In addition to the issue of integration, a number of other key analytic points are illuminated by the readings. They may be broken down into either abstract, often definitional, or more specific functional issues. With regard to the former category, aside from helping to refine a basic definition of special operations, these excerpts can also be used to generate insights into their varied nature. That is, special operations can be seen to have both strategic and tactical dimensions, and may be protracted or short-term. Almost all such missions may have similar structural characteristics, along the lines of the "approach-assault-escape" phases described by Israeli General Shlomo Gazit in the context of his discussion of rescue operations.[10]

The value of articulating a more nuanced view of special operations lies in the ability to extract deeper understanding from events. For example, awareness of the dual tactical-strategic dimensions of special operations allows one to see that what is necessary for success at one level may create problems at the other. Lartéguy's paras succeed tactically, but their very brutality acts to undermine overall French policy toward Algeria. Russian tactical bumbling in Chechnya nevertheless got the strategic message of firm commitment through to the insurgents. The Q-ships that Thomas describes, which actually sank very few U-boats during World War I,[11] unwittingly forced a profound change in the nature of the commerce raiding campaign. The reader, if alert to these nuances, will find similar instances in many of the other readings.

Typological matters aside, there are a number of other conceptual issues to address. First, with regard to the conditions for success or failure of special operations, how important is surprise? The answer to this question depends on how fully one defines the concept. For the purposes of these readings, one should think of it as having a triune nature. Surprise can be achieved strategically if the adversaries have no idea that the raiders are operating against them. Drake's preventive raid at Cadiz, which delayed the Armada's invasion plans for a year, and gave Britain the chance to muster sufficient defensive forces, caught the Spaniards totally unawares, a perfect example of strategic surprise. Surprise is tactical if there is no warning, or insufficient response to warning, of a specific attack arising during a period of either open hostilities or rising tensions. Cochrane's many raids on the Languedoc coast during the Napoleonic Wars lacked strategic surprise, as the French knew, in general, where he was and what he was doing. Despite this limitation, Cochrane continually found ways to obtain tactical surprise, principally, by knocking out enemy semaphore signalling stations, so that warning of his immediate presence could not be relayed. Finally, surprise can be doctrinal, if the opponent doesn't understand *how* the raiders are attacking. The first-time use of gliders as a form of air assault, at Eben Emael in 1940, provides the best example of a new doctrine affording a significant surprise effect. The power of a new doctrine is especially well-highlighted in this case, because the Belgian defenders actually had both strategic and tactical warning of the attack, as Bekker's account from *The Luftwaffe War Diaries* shows.

Interestingly, analysis of these readings will lead one to conclude that special operations can succeed quite often despite the loss or absence of strategic surprise. Indeed, most of the special operations described in this reader fall into the category of not having this "highest" level of surprise, yet they succeed because of the maintenance of tactical surprise. On the other hand, few endeavors prevail after the loss of tactical surprise, as one may observe from the problems faced by Russian troops in Tolstoy's *The Raid,* and the collapse of the British commando attempt to kidnap Rommel after losing its initial tactical surprise advantage. The advantage of having a new doctrine, such as glider-borne assault, is profound. Nevertheless, it is important to observe that this last dimension of surprise falls very much under the category of a "wasting asset." That is, what works well the first time because of its novelty may soon lose its luster as familiarity and the development of countermeasures improve the defenders' chances. The Germans certainly found this out in the bloody fight for Crete, the description of which rounds out the Bekker reading.

The foregoing discussion of the various aspects of surprise should lead to some refinement of the notion that special operations must have total surprise in order to succeed, because they invariably entail fights between tiny raiding forces and heavily armed, more numerous defenders. Instead, these readings point out that special operations often retain a very substantial amount of robustness, even after the loss of significant elements of surprise. The key may lie in maintaining "relative superiority" during an operation, as has been argued in a recent scholarly examination of this question.[12] According to this hypothesis, the operation may go ahead with good chances for success as long as raiders continue to predominate at the point of contact.

While maintaining some form of surprise is important in achieving relative superiority over an adversary, and thus good chances for success, one must remain careful not to exaggerate the causal impact of single variables. For example, Confederate commandos under Forrest and Mosby consistently achieved surprise, of all varieties, in their operations. Nevertheless, their lack of integration with the operations of Rebel regulars led to the failures of their campaigns. Thus, at the very least, the integration issue must be weighed, in addition to the factor of surprise, in the mix of variables that form the necessary conditions for success. Indeed, whether one refers to the *coups de mains* at Troy and Eben Emael, or to more protracted operations such as Marion's or Merrill's, integration and close coordination with general purpose forces remain crucial to success.

To round out this discussion of structural/organizational factors, one must first revisit the question of the need for elite forces to mount special operations and the various bureacratic and organizational considerations that grow from this issue. As previously mentioned, this anthology reflects many instances of special operations being undertaken by regular forces. However, careful examination will reveal that the protagonists in these readings, even when very "regular" in appearance and training, do indeed constitute elites. Odysseus took only the best of the Greeks with him inside the Horse. Though Drake and Cochrane worked with ordinary seamen, they imbued them with special skills in amphibious warfighting that gave them a profound edge over their enemies. Miles, in World War II China, worked with an odd assortment of regulars. Of course, many instances from the readings also show the creation of explicitly separate elites. Rogers, for example, trained, dressed and organized his Rangers along completely different lines from either the British regulars or the colonial militias.

These latter examples, which also include the British Special Boat Service and Long Range Desert Group, and the French Foreign Legion and Paratroops, become particularly interesting in terms of the bureaucratic political "pulling and hauling" that so often takes place over them. Eliot Cohen elucidated a number of problems that might arise from this phenomenon. He identified the possibilities that such elites might spark intra- and interservice rivalries, induce political or high military leaders either to overuse or misuse these forces, and that the commandos might politicize themselves, undermining healthy civil-military relations.[13]

Though not the focus of Roberts's narrative, the issues of both politicization and bureaucratic infighting are both present in the excerpt concerning the raid on St. Francis. The notion of military elites developing separate political agendas is well exposed in the speech that Major Rogers gives regarding his postwar plan of forming his own country, which would have both elements of democracy and authoritarianism, clearly mirroring the organization of his Rangers. As to bureaucratic squabbling, one must read closely to find that, while General Amherst supports Ranger operations, General Gage does not. Gage, responsible for resupplying and covering the last stage of the Rangers' retreat, sends a subordinate, Stephens, who has little intention of helping the raiders during the "escape" phase of their operation. This leads to a narrowly averted disaster, and Amherst's court-martial of Stephens. About the situation, the good general muses: "All the Stephens's of the world ought to be shot, and the Rogers's ought to have statues."

The other clear example of politicization is provided by Lartéguy's paras who, when not fighting, are dreaming of leading a *putsch* that will bring down the French government back home. On this point, of course, one must not fail to mention Lawrence's growing political awareness, and his effort to turn the Arab insurgency into a movement to liberate the nomads from colonial control. Indeed, this case points out the connection between special operations in support of insurgents and the tendency to move toward revolutionary warfare, whose aim is the wholesale overthrow of the existing political order.[14]

Of bureaucratic politics, there are a multitude of cases. The most interesting examples come from Lawrence's candid admission that the raid upon the bridges grew out of the need to do *something* to maintain Allenby's support of the Arab Revolt, and from Carell's brief discussion of the origins of the Tobruk raid. In this latter case, one can see how a simple idea about infiltrating the Afrika Korps supply center by truck in order to blow up its petrol reserves grew, with each new set of eyes that saw the plan, to a combined sea-air-land assault that would also destroy the enemy's communications infrastructure, free prisoners and disable a tank repair and recovery factory. Trying to conquer all, the raiders achieved virtually nothing, at grievous cost in planes, ships and men.

With regard to the matter of overusing or misusing special operations forces, the fate of Merrill's Marauders illuminates both problems. Quite simply, as Spector relates, Stilwell kept them continuously in the field for far too long, giving them missions that, while integrated with his plans for his regular forces, compelled the raiders to fight regular pitched battles. This over- and misuse of elite forces led to very high attrition and, though, they succeeded tactically on the "road to Myitkyina" (pronounced *mitch' in uh*), they were soon rendered inoperative.

To some degree, the sorry end of the Marauders may be attributed to the callousness of "Vinegar Joe" Stilwell toward them. However, he had reasons for keeping them in the field, and for using them in conventional roles. First, he faced the political need to field American ground forces in order to demonstrate commitment to his fellow coalition members, particularly the forces of Chang Kai-Shek. Second, the Marauders were among the most reliable forces under his command, and thus were the logical candidates to undertake the most difficult tasks, especially those that required sustained conventional fighting. Lest one think that overuse or misuse grows only out of the misunderstanding of the higher command, or from Machiavellian calculations of high policy, it is necessary to refer to Cook's discussion of the brilliant Marion-Greene partnership. How is Marion rewarded for his inspired guerrilla efforts? Greene, out of the best intentions, assigns the "Swamp Fox" and his small band a front-rank position in the assault on British defensive positions at Charleston!

Finally, to close out this brief overview of the definitional/structural issues engaged in these readings, it is important to point out that special operations don't always call for offensive action. Despite the common view of the commando raid as a fast-paced, irresistible mission designed to bowl over the opposition, many special operations consist of far more prosaic activities, though they are as important as their flashier counterparts. The third vignette from Carell's narrative of the North African Campaign in World War II depicts the role of the elite Brandenburgers in the period after the battle of El Alamein. These commandos performed a series of vital defensive chores during the two-month period in which the Afrika Korps was driven back nearly a thousand miles, helping to consolidate a defensible perimeter in Tunisia. They mined roads, provided observation for Axis artillery, attacked communications and, in many other ways, slowed the Allies down. So successful were they that the bridgehead was consolidated sufficiently to allow the Afrika Korps to resume the offensive at Kasserine Pass, where a stunning defeat was inflicted upon the as yet unblooded American expeditionary forces.

Other excerpts also point out the variety of defensive chores taken up by special operations. Miles's memoir of the irregular campaign he led in World War II China, which remained defensive in nature for over a year, includes such activities as rescuing downed pilots and attacking Japanese command and control centers so as to slow down their offensive operations. If one considers also that special operations, even when tactically offensive, may be designed to serve *strategically* defensive purposes, one may add several more examples to the list of these sorts of special operations. Certainly Drake's preventive raid on Cadiz was aimed at slowing down Philip's offensive"Enterprise of England," and Rogers's attack on St. Francis grew out of the need to deter further depredations against American colonists in the vulnerable western part of New York during the French and Indian War. During the Civil War, Mosby's operations clearly served defensive strategic purposes, though, in the West, Forrest's remarkable successes as a raider were never integrated into a defensive plan, but rather were treated as loosely related adjuncts to the costly, failed offensives of General Hood. On balance, though, there is much evidence of special operations of the defensive variety, both tactical and strategic, suggesting that the scope of utility for them is quite broad, as opposed to being narrowly confined to support for or integration with strategically offensive actions.

With regard to what one might call "functional" issues, the readings that follow give ample opportunity to explore three key areas: counterleadership targeting, partisan warfare and operations aimed at achieving a form of "information dominance."[15] The first important concept relates to the role of special operations in counter-leadership actions; that is, the effort to deny the adversary a smooth-running command and control system by killing, capturing or wounding the opposing high commander.

The first episode related by Carell, of the commando attempt to kidnap Rommel, provides an arch-typical example of this type of operation. Another key aspect of this case is its timing, which coincided, within a few hours, with the start of Operation Crusader, General Auchinleck's offensive to relieve the siege of Tobruk in November of 1941. Despite this careful integration with the operations of regular forces, designed to obtain maximum benefit from upsetting enemy command and control, all came to naught as Rommel was not at home at the time. However, had the commandos been imbued with a somewhat broader notion of their mission, they would have realized that incalculable damage could have been done to German logistics, which were controlled from Beda Littoria, the site of the raid. As matters turned out, some disruption occurred, but not enough to prevent the Afrika Korps from meeting Crusader head-on. Since the British won a narrow victory in the ensuing battles, throwing

Rommel temporarily out of Cyrenaica, one can only hypothesize that a more successful raid would have magnified the chances for and effects of a British victory.[16]

The second key functional issue to consider involves irregular warfare, particularly the efforts either to counter insurgents or to lead them in battle. Both of these dimensions of so-called "low intensity conflict" find description in several readings. Two approaches to counterinsurgency are described, by Tolstoy and Lartéguy, both of which have received some previous attention in this introduction. For purposes of their analytic value in expositing the functional issue of the role of special operations in quelling revolts, one may need to compare and contrast their respective approaches, and to consider the types of war-making they represent.

The key point of comparison between the two revolves around the issue of linearity. Tolstoy's rendering of the raid on the Chechen insurgents depicts a very sequential process, from the mustering of the forces to their straightforward (and loud) approach to the village and, finally, to their return, by the same route, punctuated by a very conventional deployment against the harassing rebel forces. Lartéguy, on the other hand, evokes a far more nuanced view of how to deal with rebels. The "lizards" behave in very unexpected fashion, striking here and there, following up hard intelligence leads decisively, if also brutally. Their operations tend toward a nonlinear approach, though the French paras do have logistical and manpower limitations that force them into some traditional operations, leading to, among other things, the ambush featured in the reading.

At this point, one might argue that, based on comparative analysis, the nonlinear French approach appears inherently superior to the imperial Russian efforts. However, there remains the nettlesome problem of the powerfully negative effects of the paras' use of brutality to gain vital intelligence. What use is a good counterinsurgency doctrine if it causes political disaster? The answer to this dilemma is, perhaps, to perform some further comparative analysis. But this time, instead of looking across cases of Russian and French experiences, there may be merit in engaging in a comparison of the paras with the earlier experiences of the French Foreign Legion in 19th-century Algeria, as reported by Blassingame. This reading, though simple and quite short, also reflects a very nonlinear approach to counterinsurgency. However, instead of following a strategy largely composed of raiding, the Legion also engaged in a very considerable amount of "persisting," which made all the difference in defeating Abd-el-Kader.

The Legion's treatment of the insurgents also contrasts with the behavior of the paras a century later. On this point, it is important to note that atrocities did occur in the first Algerian conflict, though, as Douglas Porch has noted, "the French behaved with no greater brutality abroad than did other colonial powers..."[17] Thus, while the French may have committed as many, if not more, brutal killings of Algerians in the earlier conflict, they were not out of step with international practices in counterinsurgent/colonial warfare. In the second Algerian revolt, though, the paras' behavior clearly violated the moral ethos of the time, causing considerable international outcry and undermining domestic political support for the government's policy of trying to hold on to Algeria. One can see the difference symbolically, in the treatment of the rebel leaders. Abd-el-Kader surrenders voluntarily, having been progressively hemmed in by the Legion's persisting strategy of blocking his lines of communication and logistics, while Si Lahcen, a former comrade of the paras from the Indochina War, is gunned down by them, providing a chilling counterleadership angle to their strategy. There is much insight to draw from Blassingame's narrative, and one will be well served to examine the first French campaign in Algeria in greater depth.[18]

The reverse side of the issue of irregular warfare, the role of special operations in support of insurgency or even of revolutionary warfare, is perhaps even better covered in this reader. Cochrane's exploits demonstrate the manner in which commando raids can assist guerrillas by distracting the occupying forces, and compelling their dispersion. Indeed, as Grimble points out, Cochrane was so convinced of the powerful effects of his endeavors in simultaneously weakening the French and strengthening the guerrillas, that he argued vociferously (but unsuccessfully) that the Peninsular campaign could be waged along strictly irregular lines, at low cost. One should consider this as an alternative to the costly six-year-long campaign waged by the Duke of Wellington's regulars, in loose conjunction with the guerrillas. Was Cochrane right? For a variety of reasons, some bureaucratic, others political and strategic, he wasn't given even modestly larger resources with which to demonstrate the operational value of his theory. However, in his later career in South America, he did prosecute this grander view of amphibious special operations in several of the wars of liberation waged against Spain, all of which concluded successfully.

Two other insurgencies are featured. First, Dupuy and Baumer, in their account of the Barbary Wars, describe a fascinating expedition led by William Eaton and supported by a platoon of Marines, one designed to apply coercive pressure on the Tripolitan pirates to release the American hostages they held, and to cease and desist their depredations on U.S. flag vessels. Though the operation was mounted with minimal material support, its initial successes moved the pirate leader Karamanlis to give in to American coercion (which featured a financial "carrot" in addition to Eaton's military "stick").

The second reading, in T.E. Lawrence's elegant prose, describes one campaign in the long Arab revolt that he fomented and led. Despite some revisionist assessments that have tended to downplay his military skills and the value of his contributions to the campaigns against the Turks,[19] one can see clearly his close integration with Allenby's overall campaign, and the remarkable effects that he had on his Arab minions. Finally, whatever operational effectiveness his forces demonstrated must have been quite troubling to the Turks, as they felt compelled to divert large forces to protect their lengthy, vulnerable rail and telegraphic lines of communication from the raiders' depredations.[20]

The third functional issue addressed in many of these readings relates to the role of special operations in providing informational advantages for one side during a crisis or conflict. In this context, it is important to define information in terms of both its content and with regard to the conduits by which it is transmitted. An example of protracted special operations aimed specifically at achieving information dominance in the first, or "message" dimension, is provided by Lord's account of the Coastwatchers during the 1942-43 campaign in the Solomon Islands. Time and again, these irregulars gave early warning of Japanese air and naval movements, enabling the U.S. Marine "Cactus Air Force" on Guadalcanal to muster and deploy in time to thwart their attacks. Of the second type of information control, the dominance of the information "medium," or means of transmission, one should consider Cochrane's systematic raids on French coastal signalling stations, his disruption of which paved the way for his startling run of successful raids along the Languedoc coast.

Sensitivity to the aforementioned definitional, structural and functional issues should enrich the study of the readings that follow, helping to place special operations in better perspective as a key element across the broad spectrum of types of conflict. There remains now only the need to make one final admission, and one suggestion. First, as this volume deliberately looks to the past for present insight, and considers operationally strategic issues rather than either tactics or grand strategy, one should also note that it scarcely touches on the rescue mission as a form of special operation. Admittedly, the representative case excerpted herein, the Israeli rescue at Entebbe, is probably the best rescue ever conducted. Nevertheless, this traditionally important type of special operation, the subject of so much popular and scholarly attention,[21] has been relatively neglected in this reader. This has not been done to denigrate the importance of rescues, but rather to avoid having a too narrow focus on special operations. Their varied nature cries out for a broader perspective and, in the literature and history of earlier special operations, there is indeed only a small emphasis on rescues as an aspect of raiding. Therefore, the relative lack of attention to rescues should be viewed less as an attempt to downplay them, and more as an effort to provide "equal time" for the many other fascinating aspects of special operations.

Finally, it is imperative to suggest that the role of leadership be analyzed throughout these readings. The human factor can be seen as crucial in all of them, from Odysseus's bold, innovative planning, to Rogers's indomitable will to succeed; and from the wonderful chemistry between Marion and Greene to the uncoordinated efforts of Hood and

Forrest, Lee and Mosby and, in some respects, between Stilwell and Merrill. These cases all suggest that individuals have played a determining role in the success or failure of special operations, and will continue to do so.

If this is true, then what types of commando leaders should be developed? For all his cleverness, Odysseus showed that this trait of his also encouraged"sharp" practices of dubious probity. Drake showed tremendous technical skill and strategic vision, but insufficient concern for the political consequences of his actions, which may actually have precipitated Philip's grave displeasure with England. Khlopov, for all his solid soldiering qualities, showed too little imagination in his approach to fighting the Chechens. Forrest never lost a fight, but fought too often without larger strategic purposes in mind, being driven more often by the hatreds that dominated his dark, slave trader's soul. Lawrence inspired his Arab supporters, but was wracked with self-doubts that sometimes led him to bad decisions. Miles was a wonderful manager, but much less of a true warrior. Where can one turn for an appropriate leadership model for special forces?

Based on those leaders described in this reader, minus the abovementioned, who suffer from a variety of problems, one is nevertheless still left with a rich menu from which to choose. There is Cochrane, who never allowed his grander visions of how to wage the Peninsular War to stand in the way of paying close attention to operational details, as well as to the welfare of his men. Rogers, for all his intractability, turned to the positive side of this character limitation, coming to personify the indomitable spirit that drove his Rangers to achieve the near impossible, again and again.

Finally, there are also a several middle-level and even junior officers featured in many of the readings who may form, with their courage, skill and resourcefulness, a composite image of the optimal type of special operations leader. From the Barbary Wars, there are Stephen Decatur who, as a naval lieutenant, led the successful raid on Tripoli harbor, and Presley O'Bannon, a Marine platoon leader who commanded the field maneuvers of a large, polyglot insurgent force. From World War II, there are two more candidates, beginning with German paratroop Captain Koch, whose dash and determination in command of the brilliant glider assault at Eben Emael did so much to enable victory in the campaign of 1940 in Western Europe. His reputation is not at all diminished by his needless death in the invasion of Crete, a campaign that gives yet more evidence that higher commanders are often tempted to overuse their elite forces. Another remarkable example of leadership is provided by Donald Kennedy, the extraordinary Coastwatcher on New Georgia Island in the Solomons, hundreds of miles behind Japanese lines. A deliberate man, Kennedy combined a very unusual application of a persisting strategy along with his raiding operations. He created a "forbidden zone" into which Japanese could never leave once they entered. The need to police this security area drove Kennedy to fight, on his slender resources, something of a full-scale guerrilla war, which he waged with great success, in addition to performing his intelligence functions.

Having these many sterling examples from which to choose, however, shouldn't lead one to discard the flawed characters mentioned. For they have their merits as well. Who wouldn't want Odysseus to lead the way out of some tight spot, or desire to have Khlopov at his side in a stern fight? The key may be to have these sorts of leaders ahead or beside, never behind one. But then, in special operations, no one leads from the rear. Not successfully.

Notes

1. Ward Just, *Military Men* (New York: Alfred A. Knopf, 1970); Francis J. Kelly, *U.S. Army Special Forces, 1961-1971* (Washington, D.C.: Government Printing Office, 1973); and Roger A. Beaumont, *Military Elites* (New York: Bobbs Merrill, 1974) are good examples of narratives that provide general surverys of the period. Heather David, *Operation Rescue* (New York: Random House, 1971); and Benjamin F. Schemmer, *The Raid* (New York: Harper and Row, 1976) relate the tale of the raid on the Son Tay prisoner of war camp outside Hanoi. The Mayaguez rescue attempt has also been well chronicled. See Roy Rowan, *The Four Days of Mayaguez* (New York: Dutton, 1975); and Thomas D. Des Brisay, *Fourteen Hours at Koh Tang* (Washington, D.C.: Government Printing Office, 1975). Finally, the Desert One fiasco in Iran has also been thoroughly recounted, from such firsthand memoirs as Charlie Beckwith and Donald Knox, *Delta Force* (New York: Random House, 1983), to more detailed operational studies, of which Paul B. Ryan, *The Iranian Rescue Mission: Why It Failed* (Annapolis: Naval Institute Press, 1985) remains the most comprehensive. More recent special operations in Grenada, El Salvador, Panamá and the Gulf War have yet to generate an equally well developed narrative literature, though Greg Walker, *At the Hurricane's Eye: U.S. Special Operations Forces from Vietnam to Desert Storm* (New York: Ivy Books, 1994) makes a game effort to cover the entire period.

2. Lucien S. Vandenbroucke, *Perilous Options: Special Operations as an Instrument of U.S. Foreign Policy* (New York: Oxford University Press, 1993) is the best example of this, as he also combines lively renderings of specific incidents with insightful analysis. Other thoughtful, policy-relevant studies include F.R. Barnett, B.H. Tovar, and R.H. Shultz, eds. *Special Operations in U.S. Strategy* (Washington, D.C.: National Defense University Press, 1984); Ross S. Kelly, *Special Operations & National Purpose* (Toronto: Lexington Books, 1989); and John M. Collins, *Special Operations* (Washington, D.C.: National Defense University Press, 1994). Finally, Eliot Cohen, *Commandos and Politicians: Elite Military Units in Modern Democracies* (Cambridge: Harvard University Center for International Affairs, 1978) considers some of the political effects of having an organizationally distinct special operations force.

3. This is the prerequisite for an operation to be considered "special,"

according to the U.S. Department of Defense, Joint Chiefs of Staff, *Publication 1, Department of Defense Dictionary of Military and Associated Terms* (Washington, D.C.: Government Printing Office, 1979).

4. Vandenbroucke, *Perilous Options,* p. 3 adopts this view of special operations, contending that "[m]ost such undertakings are daring yet minor operations meant to achieve limited military objectives. Occasionally, however, a country will mount such a strike to achieve major foreign policy goals."

5. That there was a great sensitivity to the issue of "noncombatant immunity" is reflected in Lieutenant Alanin's alert response when he heard cries coming from behind a hut. Fearing that a child was being murdered, he ran to intercede, only to find that it was a goat being slaughtered by his troops. Of course, the fact that this good officer believed his troops might kill a civilian could lead one to infer that Tolstoy was making a subtle point about the occurrence of atrocities during the war to conquer Chechnya. After all, his deep devotion to pacifism grew out of his first-hand experiences in this conflict. Perhaps Tolstoy saw things there that fostered his revulsion to war.

6. The external effects of special operations on national-level policy is a key concern addressed in Vandenbroucke, *Perilous Options.* This theme is also considered in Cohen, *Commandos and Politicians.*

7. Bernard Brodie, *Sea Power in the Machine Age* (Princeton: Princeton University Press, 1944), pp. 309-12, provides a lucid discussion of the role and effects of Q-ships, suggesting also that forcing U-boats to attack by torpedo reduced their effectiveness by causing them to expend their ordnance more quickly, reducing their time patrolling the sea lanes. Of course, the fact that this

8. As Brodie put it (*Ibid.,* p. 309): "The threat did force the Germans to adopt form of attack that was least advantageous to themselves and at the same time extremely offensive to the sensibilities of neutrals, particularly the United States."

9. Nicholas Monsarrat, from the introduction to *The Cruel Sea* (New York: Alfred A. Knopf, 1951), p. 3.

10. See Shlomo Gazit, "Risk, Glory, and the Rescue Operation." *International Security,* 6/1:111-135 (Summer 1981).

11. Brodie, *Sea Power in the Machine Age,* p. 309, notes that only 13 were sunk by Q-ships.

12. William McRaven, *SPEC OPS: Case Studies in Special Operations* (Novato, CA: Presidio Press, 1995).

13. See Cohen, *Commandos and Politicians,* especially pp. 53-80.

14. James H. Billington, *Fire in the Minds of Men: Origins of the Revolutionary Faith* (New York: Basic Books, Inc., 1980) explores these connections in some depth using, among others, the example of Polish revolutionary insurgency for several decades after Poland had been partitioned out of existence in the late 18th century. See especially pp. 166-72.

15. For a general discussion of this phenomenon, see John Arquilla, "The Strategic Implications of Information Dominance." *Strategic Review,* 22/3:24-31 (Summer 1994).

16. Though not as closely integrated with a specific campaign plan, the successful American effort to assassinate Yamamoto, mastermind of Japan's amphibious blitzkrieg in the early months of the Pacific War, had profound strategic and psychological effects on the future course of the conflict. The classic account of this special counterleadership operation is Burke Davis, *Get Yamamoto* (New York: Random House, 1969). Carroll V. Glines, *Attack on Yamamoto* (New

York: Orion, 1990) reflects the insights provided by more recently released information, and also engages the interesting issue of the American government's concerns over the legality of the assassination attempt. While U.S. forces were ultimately given permission to go ahead, there was some high-level debate about the propriety of such actions. Similarly, as Carell notes, the question of possibly killing Rommel was at least addressed at the command level, though there is little evidence of delay or reluctance to authorize and effect the mission.

17. Douglas Porch, "Bugeaud, Galliéni, Lyautey: The Development of French Colonial Warfare," in Peter Paret, ed., *Makers of Modern Strategy: From Machiavelli to the Nuclear Age* (Princeton: Princeton University Press, 1986), p. 381.

18. It is interesting to note that Alexis de Tocqueville, who made so many sage observations about the United States of the mid-19th century, also wrote with equal perception on the situation in Algeria. For a good synopsis of his views, see Melvin Richter, "Tocqueville on Algeria," *Review of Politics,* 25:361-93 (July 1963). Douglas Porch, *The French Foreign Legion: History of the Legendary Fighting Force* (New York: HarperCollins, 1991) provides an excellent general history of the Legion that addresses in great detail its involvement in Algeria.

19. As Cohen puts it in *Commandos and Politicians,* p. 19: "The truth--that Lawrence's campaigns contributed little to Turkey's defeat--has yet to tarnish his legend." Cohen's view is supported by others, notably Hugh Trevor-Roper, "A Humbug Exalted," *New York Times Book Review,* November 6, 1977, p. 1; and Elie Kedourie, "The Real T.E. Lawrence," *Commentary,* 64:49-56 (July 1977).

20. Howard Sachar, *The Emergence of the Middle East, 1914-1924* (New York: Alfred A. Knopf, 1969) assesses the impact of Lawrence's operations as militarily useful, and argues that the insurgency he led had a profound influence on the awakening of Pan Arab political consciousness, the effects of which continue to be felt today. Other thoughtful studies of Lawrence, which generally conform to Sachar's thesis, are: B.H. Liddell Hart and Robert Graves, *T.E. Lawrence to his Biographers* (New York: Doubleday, 1963); John E. Mack, *A Prince of Our Disorder* (Boston: Little, Brown, 1978); Jeffrey Meyers, ed., *T.E. Lawrence: Soldier, Writer, Legend* (New York: St. Martin's Press, 1989); and Jeremy Wilson, *Lawrence of Arabia* (New York: Macmillan, 1990). See also Robert Asprey, *War in the Shadows: The Guerrilla in History* (New York: Morrow, 1994), pp. 179-191 for a penetrating analysis of the revolt in the desert, Lawrence's crucial role, and the importance of the campaign to overall British success.

21. On this point, it should be noted that three of four cases examined in Vandenbroucke, *Perilous Options,* are rescues, a class of mission that clearly dominates his view of the realm of special operations.

Chapter 1

Origins

Special operations have been present from the earliest stirrings of organized conflict, a point well made, from a literary perspective, by chroniclers of the Trojan War. The often key role of the *coup de main* in determing the outcome of war is particularly well illustrated in this case. For, in the absence of a successful commando action to open the gates of Troy from within, the Greeks would surely have given up their ten-year siege and gone home.

Despite the enormous suffering of the Trojans, the attacking forces, operating far from home, had serious logistical difficulties that threatened their ability to sustain operations. Over the course of the war, the need to forage, ever further afield, necessarily brought them into hostile contact with Troy's neighbors, who resented the Greeks' depredations. This pattern of interaction led a number of nearby city-states, including the countrymen of Aeneas, as Graves notes, to become active allies of the Trojans. These reinforcements shifted the battlefield balance against the gradually dissipating Greek army, prompting the decision to venture all on a gambler's final fling.

That the ploy succeeded had as much to do with Trojan laxity as Greek inventiveness. Indeed, the failure to heed the warnings of Cassandra and Laocöon provides a classic (no pun intended) example of the breakdown that so often occurs between the receipt of information about a threat and the taking of an appropriate response. In this regard, the Greeks took great care to allay the fears and suspicions of their opponents, including the major move of evacuating their entire field army in support of what might be characterized as the one of the most cunning psychological special operations ever conceived.

Robert Graves

The Wooden Horse

The war dragged on. New allies came to King Priam's help, including the Amazon Queen Penthesileia from Armenia, who killed King Machaon and three times drove Achilles himself off the field. Finally, with Athene's help, Achilles ran her through. Memnon, the negro King of Ethiopia, accounted for hundreds of Greeks, including Nestor's eldest son, and almost succeeded in burning the Greek ships; but Great Ajax challenged him to a duel, which was rudely interrupted by Achilles. He ran up, brushed Ajax aside, speared Memnon, and threw the Trojans back once more.

This proved to be Achilles' last victory, because when that night he met Polyxena by private arrangement in Apollo's temple, she wormed out of him his most important secret. Polyxena was sworn to avenge her beloved brother Hector, and there is nothing a beautiful girl cannot make a man tell her as a proof of love. He revealed that when Thetis dipped him in Styx water as a child, to make him invulnerable, she had tightly held his right heel, which stayed dry and unprotected.

They met again next day at the same place, to confirm his promise that, after marrying Polyxena, he would so arrange matters that the Greeks went home without Helen. King Priam had insisted on his offering a sacrifice to Apollo and taking an oath at the God's altar. Achilles came barefoot and unarmed; but two of Priam's sons, whom he sent to represent him, were secretly plotting murder. Prince Deiphobus embraced Achilles, in pretense of friendship, while Paris, hiding behind a pillar, shot at his heel. The barbed arrow, guided by Aphrodite, wounded him mortally. Though Achilles snatched firebrands from the altar and struck vengefully at Paris and Deiphobus, they got away; and he killed a couple of temple servants only.

Odysseus and Great Ajax, who suspected Achilles of treachery, had crept after him into the temple. Dying in their arms, he made them swear that when Troy fell they would sacrifice Polyxena at his tomb. Paris and Deiphobus returned to fetch the body; but Odysseus and Ajax beat them off in a stiff fight and brought it safely back.

Agamemnon, Menelaus and the rest of the Council shed tears at Achilles's funeral, though few ordinary soldiers regretted the death of so notorious a traitor. His ashes, mixed with those of Patrocles, were placed in a golden urn and buried in a lofty barrow at the entrance to the Hellespont.

Thetis awarded Achilles' arms and armour to the bravest Greek leader left before Troy; and to embarrass Agamemnon, for whom she felt a deep scorn, appointed him the judge. Odysseus and Great Ajax, having successfully defended his corpse against the Troyans, came forward as rivals for this honour. But Agamemnon feared the anger of whoever lost so valuable a prize, and sent spies by night to listen under the walls of Troy and report what the Trojans themselves thought.

The spies crept up close, and after awhile a party of Trojan girls began to chat above them. One praised Ajax's courage in lifting Achilles's corpse on his shoulders and taking it through a shower of spears and arrows. Another said: "Nonsense, Odysseus showed far greater courage! Even a slave-girl will do what Ajax did, if given a corpse to carry; but put weapons in her hand, and she'll never dare use them. Ajax used that corpse as a shield, while Odysseus kept our men off with spear and sword."

On the strength of this report, Agamemnon awarded the arms to Odysseus. The Council knew that he would never have preferred him to Great Ajax if Achilles had been alive—Achilles thought the world of his gallant cousin. Besides, the spies understood no Phrygian, and were probably prompted by Odysseus. Yet no one dared say so.

In a blind rage, Ajax swore revenge on Agamemnon, Menelaus, Odysseus, and their fellow-Councillors. That night Athene sent him mad and he ran howling, sword in hand, among the flocks he had captured in raids on Trojan farms. After immense butchery, he chained the surviving sheep and goats together, hauled them to camp, and went on with his bloody work. He chose two rams, cut out the tongue of the largest, which he mistook for Agamemnon, and lopped off its head. Then he tied the other to a pillar by the neck and flogged it unmercifully, screaming abuse and shouting: "Take that, and that, and that, treacherous Odysseus!" At last, coming to his sense, and greatly ashamed of himself, he fixed the sword which Hector had given him upright in the ground, and leaped upon it. His last words were a prayer to the Furies for vengeance. Odysseus wisely avoided this danger by presenting the armour to Achilles's ten-year-old son Neoptolemus, who had just joined the Greek forces and, like his father at the same age, was already full-grown. His mother had been one of the princesses among whom Thetis hid Achilles at Scyros.

Calchas prophesied that Troy could be taken only with the help of Heracles's bow and arrows, now owned by King Philoctetes. Odysseus and Diomedes sailed to fetch them from the small island off Lemnos where Philoctetes was still marooned. Even after nine years, his wound smelt as badly as ever, nor had the pain grown less. Odysseus stole his bow and arrows by a trick; but Diomedes, not wishing to be mixed up in so dishonourable an affair, made him restore them, and persuaded Philoctetes to come aboard their ship. When they landed at Troy, Machaon's brother cured him with soothing herbs and precious stone called serpentine.

No sooner was Philoctetes well again than he challenged Paris to an archery duel. Paris shot first, and aimed at his enemy's heart, but the arrow went wide—Athene, of course, saw to that. Philoctetes then let loose three arrows in quick succession. The first pierced Paris's bow-hand, the next his right eye, and the last his ankle. He hobbled from the fight and, though Menelaus tried to catch and kill him, managed to reach Troy and die in Helen's arms.

Helen was now a widow, but King Priam could still not bear the idea of restoring her to Menelaus; and his sons wrangled among themselves, each wanting to be her husband. Helen then remembered that she had been Queen of Sparta and Menelaus's wife. One night a sentry caught her as she was about to climb down a rope from the battlements; whereupon Deiphobus married her by force--an act which disgusted the entire royal family.

Jealous quarrels between Priam's sons grew so fierce that he sent Antenor to discuss peace terms with the Greeks. But Antenor had not forgiven Deiphobus for having helped Paris to murder Achilles in Apollo's own temple, a sacrilege which Priam left unpunished. He told Agamemnon's Council that he would betray Troy if they made him King afterwards and gave him half the spoils. According to an ancient oracle, he said, Troy would not fall until the Palladium, a legless wooden image of Athene, some four feet high, had been stolen from her temple on the Citadel. As it happened, the Greeks already knew of this prophecy through Helenus, who was madly jealous of Deiphobus's marriage. So Antenor promised to hand over the Palladium when Athene's two favourites, Odysseus and Diomedes, had entered Troy by a secret way he would show them.

That night, Odysseus and Diomedes set out together and, following Antenor's instructions, cleared away a pile of stones under the western wall. They found that it hid the exit of a long, wide, dirty-water pipe leading straight up to the Citadel. Antenor's wife Theano, warned what to expect, had drugged the temple servants; so that Diomedes and Odysseus met no trouble at all once they reached the top by a hard, filthy climb. To make sure the servants were not shamming sleep, they cut their throats and then returned the same way. Theano lowered the Palladium down after them, and put a replica in its place.

Diomedes, being higher in rank, carried the Palladium strapped to his shoulders, but Odysseus, who wanted all the glory for himself, let him go ahead and then stealthily unsheathed his sword. The rising moon peered large and bright over a crest of Mount Ida, throwing the shadow of Odysseus's upraised sword-arm in front of Diomedes. He spun around, drew his own sword, disarmed Odysseus, tied his hands behind him, and drove him forward with repeated kicks and blows. Back in the Council Hut, Odysseus protested violently against Diomedes's treatment. He claimed to have unsheathed his sword because he heard a Trojan coming in pursuit. Agamemnon counted too much on Odysseus's help not to agree that Diomedes must have been mistaken.

Athene now inspired Odysseus to think of a stratagem for getting armed men into Troy. Under his directions, Epeius the Phocian, the best carpenter in camp though a fearful coward, built an enormous hollow horse out of fir planks. It had a concealed trap-door fitted into the left flank, and on the right a sentence carved in tall letters: "With thankful hope of a safe return to their homes after nine years' absence, the Greeks dedicate this offering to Athene." Odysseus would enter the horse by means of a rope-ladder, followed by Menelaus, Diomedes, Achilles's son Neoptolemus, and by eighteen more volunteers. Coaxed, threatened and bribed, Epeius was forced to sit by the trap door, which he alone could open quickly and silently.

Having gathered all their gear together, the Greeks set fire to their huts, launched the ships, and rowed off; but no farther than the other side of Tenedos, where they were invisible from Troy. Odysseus's companions already filled the horse, and only one Greek was left in the camp: his cousin Sinon.

When Trojan scouts went out at dawn they found the horse towering over the burned camp. Antenor knew nothing about the horse and therefore kept quiet, but King Priam and several of his sons wanted to bring it into the city on rollers. Others shouted: "Athene has favoured the Greeks far too long! Let her do what she pleases with her property." Priam would listen neither to their protests nor to Aeneas's urgent warnings.

The horse had been purposely built too large for Troy's gates, and stuck four times even when these were removed and some stones pulled away from the wall on one side. With strenuous efforts the Trojans hauled it up to the Citadel, but at least took the precaution of re-building the wall and putting the gates back on their hinges. Priam's daughter Cassandra, whose curse was that no Trojan would ever take her prophecies seriously, screamed: "Beware: the horse is full of armed men!"

Meanwhile two soldiers came across Sinon, hiding in a turret by the camp gate, and marched him to the Royal Palace. Asked why he had stayed behind, he told King Priam: "I was afraid to sail in the same ship as my cousin Odysseus. He has long wanted to kill me, and yesterday nearly succeeded."

"Why should Odysseus want to kill you?" asked Priam.

"Because I alone know how he got Palamedes stoned, and he doesn't trust my discretion. The fleet would have sailed a month ago, if the weather hadn't been so bad. Calchas of course prophesied, just as he did at Aulis, that a human sacrifice was needed, and Odysseus said: 'Name the victim, please!' Calchas refused an immediate answer, but some days later (bribed, I suppose, by Odysseus) he named me. I was on the point of being sacrificed, when a favourable wind sprang up, I escaped in the excitement, and off they went."

Priam believed Sinon's tale, freed him and asked for an explanation of the horse. Sinon answered: "You remember those two temple servants who were found mysteriously murdered on the Citadel? That was Odysseus's work. He came by night, drugged the priestesses, and stole the Palladium. If you don't trust me, look carefully at what you think is the Palladium. You'll find that it's only a replica. Odysseus's theft made

Athene so angry that the real Palladium, hidden in Agamemnon's hut, sweated as a warning of disaster. Calchas had a huge horse built in her honour, and warned Agamemnon to sail home."

"Why was it made so huge!" asked Priam.

"To prevent it from being brought into the city. Calchas prophesied that if you succeeded in this, you could then raise an immense expedition from all over Asia Minor, invade Greece, and sack Agamemnon's own city of Mycenae."

A Trojan nobleman named Laocoön interrupted Sinon by shouting: "My lord King, these are certainly lies put into Sinon's mouth by Odysseus. Otherwise Agamemnon would have left the Palladium behind as well as the horse." He added: "And by the way, my lord, may I suggest that we sacrifice a bull to Poseidon--whose priest you stoned nine years ago because he refused to welcome Queen Helen?"

"I don't agree with you about the horse," said Priam. "But now that the war has ended, let us by all means regain Poseidon's favour. He treated us cruelly enough while it lasted."

Laocoön went off to build an altar near the camp, and chose a young and healthy bull for sacrifice. He was preparing to strike it down with his axe, when a couple of immense monsters crawled from the sea and, twining around Laocoön's limbs and those of the two sons who were helping him, crushed the life out of them. The monsters then glided up to the Citadel, and there bowed their heads in honour of Athene--a sight which Priam unfortunately took to mean that Sinon had told the truth, and that Laocoön had been killed for contradicting him. In fact, however, Poseidon sent the sea-beasts at Athene's request: as a proof that he hated the Trojans as much as she did.

Priam dedicated the horse to Athene, and although Aeneas led his men safely away from Troy, suspecting any gift of the Greeks and refusing to believe the war ended--everyone else began victory celebrations. Trojan women visited the Scamander for the first time in nine years, gathering flowers by its banks to decorate the horse's wooden mane. They also spread a carpet of roses around its hooves. A tremendous banquet was got ready at Priam's palace.

Meanwhile, inside the horse, few of the Greeks could stop trembling. Epeius wept silently in utter terror, but Odysseus held a sword against his ribs, and if he had heard so much as a sigh would have driven it home. That evening, Helen strolled along and took a closer look at the horse. She reached up to pat its flanks and, as though to amuse Deiphobus who came with her, teased the hidden occupants by mimicking the voices of all their wives in turn. Not being a Trojan, she knew that Cassandra always spoke the truth; and also guessed which of the Greek leaders would have volunteered for this dangerous task. Diomedes and two others were tempted to answer "Here I am!" when they heard their names spoken, but Odysseus restrained them and even had to strangle one man in the process.

Worn out by drinking and dancing, the Trojans slept soundly, and not even the bark of a dog broke the stillness. Helen alone lay awake, listening. At midnight, just before the full moon rose, the seventh of the year, Sinon crept from the city to light a beacon on Achilles's tomb; and Antenor waved a torch from the battlements. Agamemnon, whose ship lay anchored close offshore, replied to these signals by lighting a brazier filled with chips of pinewood. The whole fleet then quietly landed.

Antenor, tip-toeing up to the wooden horse, said in low tones: "All's well! You may come out." Epeius unlocked the trap door so noiselessly that someone fell through and broke his neck. The rest climbed down the rope-ladder. Two men went to open the City gates for Agamemnon; others murdered the sleeping sentries. But Menelaus could think only of Helen and, followed by Odysseus, ran at full speed towards Deiphobus's house.

The Sack of Troy

Odysseus had undertaken to spare the life of any Trojans who offered no resistance; but, while respecting Antenor's mansion, on the door of which was chalked a leopard's skin design, his companions silently broke into all other houses and stabbed their occupants as they slept. Agamemnon's troops followed the example. Hecuba and her daughter fled to a sacred laurel-tree which overhung Almighty Zeus's altar. She kept tight hold of old Priam's arm to prevent him from fighting. It was only when Neoptolemus ran up and butchered their youngest child, splashing the altar with blood, that Priam broke away and seized a spear. Neoptolemus at once speared him and dragged his headless corpse off the Achilles's tomb, where he left it to rot unburied.

Prince Deiphobus, who was a magnificent swordsman, struggled for his life against Odysseus and Menelaus on the stairs of his palace, and would have killed them both, had Helen not stolen quietly down and stabbed her hated new husband between the shoulders. Menelaus, though intending to cut Helen's throat, realized that she still loved him and, sheathing his sword, led her safely back to the ships.

Cassandra stood in Athene's temple clutching the wooden replica of the stolen Palladium. Little Ajax caught her by the hair, crying: "Come, slave!" But she clung so tightly to the image that he had to bring it along, too. Later in the day, Agamemnon claimed Cassandra as his prize of honour and, to please him, Odysseus put the story about that Little Ajax had grossly insulted Athene by mishandling her priestess. To avoid being stoned to death, like Palamedes, Little Ajax took refuge at Athene's own altar and swore that Odysseus was lying once more. Nevertheless, Athene herself punished Little Ajax's violence: for when his ship was wrecked on the way home to Greece, she borrowed one of Almighty Zeus's thunder-bolts and struck him dead as he scrambled ashore.

Agamemnon's people plundered Troy for three days and nights. Then they divided the spoils, burned the houses, pulled down the walls, and sacrificed immense numbers of cattle and sheep to the Olympians. Andromache had been given as a slave to Achilles's son Neoptolemus; and the Council discussed what should be done with young Scamandrius. Odysseus recommended the wiping out of all Priam's descendants, on the grounds that Heracles made the Trojan War possible by foolishly sparing Priam at the same age; and Calchas obligingly prophesied that Scamandrius, if left alive, would avenge his father and grandfather. Since everyone else shrank from so horrible a deed, Odysseus grimly flung the child over the battlements.

The Council also discussed Polyxena's fate: Calchas's view was that she should be sacrificed at Achilles's tomb, in accordance with his dying wish. Agamemnon protested. "Enough blood has been spilt--the blood of old men and infants, as well as of fighters. Dead princes, however famous, have no claim upon the living." But two Greek Councillors who had not got as much treasure as they hoped at the distribution of spoils, shouted that Agamemnon said this only to please Polyxena's sister Cassandra, and make her a more submissive prisoner. After a good deal of heated argument, Odysseus forced Agamemnon to give way. Polyxena was therefore slaughtered on Achilles's tomb, in sight of the whole army. Young Neoptolemus beheaded her with an axe. "May you meet the same fate as I!" were her last words.

Favourable winds sprang up, and the Greek fleet was soon ready for launching. "Off we sail at once, while the breeze holds!" cried Menelaus.

"No, no," said Agamemnon. "We must first sacrifice to Athene."

"I owe the Goddess nothing," grumbled Menelaus. "She defended the Trojan Citadel against us far too long!"

The brothers parted on bad terms, and never saw each other again.

It remained to murder Polydorus, a child of Hecuba's old age, sent by her, a few years before, to safety in Thrace, where King Polymnestor reared him as though he were his son. Agamemnon's envoys now required Polymnestor to kill the boy, offering as payment a vast sum in gold and the hand of his daughter Electra. Fearing that to refuse would mean disaster, Polymnestor accepted the gold but, rather than break faith with Hecuba and Priam, killed his own son, Polydorus's playmate, in the envoys' presence. Seeing the King and Queen plunged in grief, and not knowing the secret of his own birth, Polydorus was so mystified by the murder that he went to consult the Delphic oracle. He asked Apollo's priestess: "What troubles my parents?" She answered: "Why are you not troubled yourself? Is it a small thing that your city has been burned, your father left unburied, your mother enslaved?" Polydorus returned in anxiety to Thrace, where he found nothing changed since his departure. "Can Apollo be mistaken?" he wondered. Then the Queen told him who his parents really were.

Hecuba had indeed been enslaved by Odysseus. He was about to sail off with her, but she heaped such hideous curses on him and the other cruel, lying, treacherous Greek leaders, that he decided to kill her. However, she transformed herself by magic into a fearful black bitch, and ran around howling so dismally that everyone fled in terror and confusion.

Antenor never became King of Troy as he had been promised, nor got any share in the spoils; but Menelaus generously took him, his wife Theano, and their four surviving sons aboard his ship. They settled first in North Africa, then in Thrace, and finally colonized the islands of Henetica, now Venice. He also founded the town of Padua. The one other Trojan hero who escaped was Aeneas: from Dardanus, his city near Mount Ida, he had seen the distant flames of Troy and, crossing the Hellespont, took refuge in Thrace. The Romans say he eventually wandered to Italy, and there became Julius Caesar's ancestor.

Troy lost its importance, since the Greeks were at last able to enter the Black Sea freely and trade with the East. A few landless, houseless folk settled in the city ruins. Aeneas's grandson Ascanius ruled them; but it was a poor kingdom. And a generation later, Zeus taking Hera at her word, destroyed the three cities, Mycenae, Argos and Sparta, which she loved best.

Calchas traveled southward through Asia Minor to Colophon, where he died (as an oracle had warned him) on meeting a rival who could foretell the future better than himself. This was Apollo's son Mopsus. A large fig-tree grew at Colophon, and Calchas tried to shame Mopsus by challenging him: "Can you perhaps tell me, dear fellow-prophet, how many figs grow on that tree?" Mopsus, closing his eyes, because he trusted to inner sight rather than to calculation, answered: "Certainly: first ten thousand figs, then a bushel of figs according to the measure used in Aegina, carefully weighed--and, yes, one single fig left over." Calchas laughed scornfully at the extra fig; but when the tree had been stripped, and the fruit weighed and counted, Mopsus proved exactly right.

"To come down from thousands to lesser quantities, dear fellow-prophet," said Mopsus. "Can you perhaps tell me how many piglings that fat sow will produce, and when they'll be born, and of what sex they'll be?"

"Eight piglings, all male, and she'll have them within nine days," answered Clachas at random, hoping to have left Colophon before his guess could be checked.

"I believe that you're in error," said Mopsus, again closing his eyes. "I prophesy that she'll have no more than three piglings, only one of them male, and that they'll be born at midnight tomorrow, not a minute earlier."

Mopsus was right, and Calchas died of shame--Apollo's punishment for the many bad guesses he had made to please Agamemnon and Odysseus.

From Robert Graves, *The Siege and Fall of Troy,* (New York: Doubleday, 1962), pp.78-94.

Chapter 2

Raiding in the Age of Sail

From the fall of Troy to the end of the Middle Ages, naval technology changed very little. Galleys had sails, but relied principally upon oar-power for propulsion; and sea fights often resembled land battles, once the combatants came within grappling range. During this period, a great deal of raiding went on from the sea. The Periclean strategy in the Peloponnesian War, for example, relied heavily upon a protracted special operations campaign of pinprick raids against the Spartans and their allies. Later on, after the fall of the Roman Empire, the Vikings would raise raiding to a science, and incorporate also some elements of "persisting," as their occupations of Normandy and Sicily, and settlement of Russia, attest. Perhaps the most sustained raiding occurred, though, in the long twilight struggle between Islam and Christendom in the Mediterranean. For centuries, both parties preyed on the shipping of the other, sometimes sparking larger conflicts, as in Suleiman's costly (and unsuccessful) mid-16th century invasion of Malta, which aimed to put an end to the activities of the Knights of St. John operating from the island.

Within a few years of Suleiman's defeat, Sir Francis Drake launched his remarkable career. He was a master mariner and naval strategist who took full advantage of the marriage of gun and sail that revolutionized sea power and led to the many voyages of discovery and conquest that made Europeans the masters of the world for so long. Yet he also exhibited a particular talent for amphibious raiding, and for leading irregular forces on land. The tradition of special operations that he began had a powerful influence on British strategic thought; and one can see, in such conflicts as the Seven Years' War (1756-1763), an almost Periclean approach to raiding as a means of wearing down the enemy. Later, during the Napoleonic wars, Lord Cochrane's campaign along the Languedoc coast represents the zenith of this form of protracted special operation. His success, using such slender resources, hints at the possibilities of even larger gains had he received even modestly greater material support.

G.M. Thomson

The Damage Done by this Corsair

> It seems as if Nature had destined [the Spaniards] to occupy the West Indies to enrich the industrious who could not live there.''
>
> *Thomas Jefferys*

Cartagena, lying on the eastward side of the Gulf of Darien, was one of the richest prizes on the coast of Spanish South America. The city was an important commercial centre, although lacking the historical prestige of Santo Domingo. It was correspondingly hard to attack. This was due, not so much to the fortifications which the Spanish had built, as to the natural strength which geography had conferred.

Cartagena was built on a sandbank between a steamy mangrove swamp which enclosed two sides of the town and a long lagoon which covered the third side. the fourth side faced the open sea but could not be approached by ships. The lagoon was divided into an outer basin and an inner harbour by a spit of land which thrust southwards to within two ship's lengths of the mainland. At this point, where a narrow channel joined the two basins of the lagoon, a fort stood on guard with sixteen guns. When danger threatened, a chain could be drawn across. At the closed end of the lagoon to the north the promontory which formed it was joined to the town by a causeway, the Caleta, a hundred and fifty yards wide.

Unless there was a surprise attack, or an overwhelming preponderance of force on the English side, Cartagena should have been held easily enough. There was no surprise and, in numbers at least, the two sides were evenly matched. The Governor of the city, Don Piero Fernandez de Busto, had three weeks' warning that Drake was on his way. Thereupon the Governor ordered military exercises to be carried out every day and sowed the foreshore with poisoned stakes. Across the Caleta he built a breast-high stone barricade in which a gap was left open for mounted patrols to go in and out. Heavy guns were brought up into position here. At its seaward end, this barrier degenerated into a mere line of wine-butts filled with earth. Other preparations for defense were made. For instance, the women retired to the hills outside the town and all images were hidden from 'the bestial fury of the heretics.'

In the inner harbour were stationed an armed galleass and two galleys, the *Ocasion* and *La Napolitana*, which could bring an enfilading fire to bear should the English attempt an attack along the causeway. These ships had a hundred and fifty professional arquebusiers on board under a distinguished soldier, Don Pedro Vique Manrique, general in command of all the coastal defence of the Spanish Main. Apart from these regular troops, the Governor had at his disposal 50 lancers, 450 arquebusiers, 100 pikemen, 20 Negro musketeers and 400 Indian archers.

Against these defenders, Drake could not expect to land an assault force numbering as many as a thousand. Battle casualties and, far more, disease, had cut down the numbers of combatants available to him. And, in fact, sickness was still at work in the fleet. Hardly a day passed but the burial service was to be heard on the deck of one vessel or another. Flags were dipped and a new small scratch was made on morale. For that reason alone, Drake was in a hurry.

The ships sailed along the coast, within range of the Cartagena guns. It was 9 February, Ash Wednesday, and the Governor had just received a new warning of the impending onslaught. It came by a vessel fresh from Spain which also brought the good news that, in a week's time, the latest galleon to reinforce the Indies Squadron would arrive. This news heart-ened the local population at the time when Drake's show of force gave them a chance to estimate, and even over-estimate, the strength that was coming against them. Drake, ignoring two shots from the land batteries, was rowed at his leisure along the seafront in a small boat. What impressed the spectators most, however, was that he was dressed all in black. The English ships were draped in the same funeral colour. What was the reason for this? Mourning? It is possible, although no personage of note is known to have died. More likely, the black emblems were a signal to the Cimarrons. If so, the signal was seen and answered.

The English ships anchored at the Jews' Cape in the outer basin a mile from the entrance to the inner harbour. That same evening Drake put his infantry ashore on a beach from which they could march through wooded country to the Caleta. Meanwhile he kept the defence in a fever of doubt about what he meant to do. His fleet was placed as if it was about to break through into the inner harbour, and Frobisher was detached, with the pinnaces, to carry out a diversion against the fort covering the entrance.

Drake had heard an important piece of news. Two Negro fishermen, heirs of the old Cimarron alliance, had slipped aboard the *Bonaventure* to warn him about the poisoned stakes on the foreshore. He passed the information on to Carleill and the other leaders of the attack. As dusk closed in the soldiers on the beach formed up, waist-deep in the water. Command of the vanguard was divided between the Irishman Sampson, who led the pikes, and Goring (English), who led the musketeers. The main battle was under the Sergeant-Major, Anthony Powell, and the rear was commanded by another Welshman, Captain Morgan.

Captain Wynter, although a sea officer, had joined the landing party. In his eagerness for a fight he had bartered his ship for Captain Cecil's company of foot. He marched with the rest. Overall command was assigned to Carleill.

Among the defenders of the city there was something that fell short of unanimous enthusiasm for the battle. Complaints were heard that the rich were looking after their own safety. The soldiers wanted a rise in pay. Don Pedro Vique heard with disgust of one citizen who, after boasting of his courage, had fled disguised as a woman. When Governor Busto addressed the soldiers he was greeted with disloyal murmurs. Finally, however, the defenders of the city marched out to do battle with colours displayed and drums and fifes making music. To this martial incitement was added the support of the spiritual arm. The bishop, Don Fray Juan de Montalvo, whose sermons were much admired, marched with all his prebendaries and priests, armed with rapiers and halberds. So, too, did Fray Bartolomé de Sierra, prior of the Dominican monastery, and Fray Sebastian de Garibay, of the Franciscan friary. There was thus no lack of reminders, brown-robed or black, that the Church militant was involved in this business. Encouraging as this may have been, it was somewhat less so to men who believed, as the defending force seems to have done, that they were about to meet nine thousand English infantry--or just ten times as many as Carleill had under his orders.

His soldiers marched in the darkness towards the town holding to the seaward shore of the Caleta, knee-deep in the water. Thus they were clear of the poisoned stakes, while they were hidden by the ridge of the Caleta from the guns of the two galleys in the harbour.

Just two miles short of the town, the English infantry had a brush with Spanish horsemen. Frobisher, in his pinnace, a mile and a half farther south, may have heard the sounds of this clash, for at that moment he opened fire on the fort. It was hot work, at close range. The pinnace of the *Primrose* had her rudder shot away. The top of her mainmast was hit and oars were struck out of men's hands as they rowed.

About this time, the main actions was going briskly forward in the first light of dawn. Carleill, carrying a partisan, put himself at the head of the vanguard and led the onrush against the line of wine-butts on the shore. His musketeers fired a volley. As the smoke cleared, pikemen passed through their ranks and ran, stumbling, cursing and cheering, along the beach towards the defences. There was a scrambling, vicious little skirmish in which the English had the advantage of longer pikes and heavier armour, the Spaniards being accustomed in hot climates to fight in quilted cotton jackets. Even so, casualties were heavier among the English owing to the effectiveness of the Spanish guns. For a moment, indeed, the attack wavered. Then the wine-butts were overturned and the Spanish seaward flank was broken. Among the defenders the alarming rumour spread that the town had already fallen and that they should flee to avoid being surrounded and massacred.

One Spaniard stood his ground, Cosme de Blas, the standard-bearer, a stout fighter who killed two Englishmen with the spearhead of his banner. Then Carleill felled him with a stroke of his partisan and snatched the standard. All the English officers were bloodily in the thick of the business. Sampson, brandishing his sword at the head of his pikesmen, was wounded. Goring met in single combat the Spanish commander of the section, wounded him and made the man his prisoner. Wynter, who had apparently become separated from his company, fought at Carleill's side. Now that the main defense line had been broken there was nothing between the English and Cartagena but routed Spaniards. Already, says a Spanish authority, the Indian cowmen had fled.

One attempt was made, however, to rally the defence. Don Pedro Vique, commander of the galleys, rode forward with twenty lancers. "Fight for your Spanish blood and Catholic faith!" he shouted. But the appeal came too late to save the day. The cavalry galloped off to the town and from that moment Don Pedro devoted himself to the fate of his galleys, which he ordered to be removed to safety. Here again misfortune fell on the Spaniards. A soldier, distributing gunpowder on the *Ocasion*, was careless in his work. A powder barrel exploded and the *Ocasion* caught fire. The slaves abandoned their oars and escaped, those of them who were Turks giving themselves up to the English. In the meantime, the chain across the harbour mouth had been removed so the second galley, *La Napolitana*, could escape. In their haste to be off, however, the crew ran the galley ashore and the soldiers aboard leapt on to the land and disappeared. In disgust, Don Pedro gave orders that *La Napolitana* should have her cargo unloaded and be burnt.

Fighting from one barricade to another, the English came at length to the main square of the town, where they met a desperate resistance in front of a new and still unfinished church. The firing of a big cannon shook down part of the church wall. Its collapse seems to have induced a wave of defeatism. The garrison fled southwards out of the city over a bridge and into the country beyond. About the same time the Governor, who had retired to a village near by, ordered Pedro Mejia, holding out in the fort against Frobisher's guns, to withdraw.

Cartagena had fallen at a cost in English lives which, in the circumstances, was not excessive. Perhaps thirty were killed. The worst blow to Drake came soon after the fall of the town. His old comrade-in-arms,

Captain Tom Moone, was killed. Moone had heard a sentry posted in a church tower in Cartagena call out that two small craft were entering the inner harbour. At once, he, along with Captain Varney, and John Grant, master of the *Tiger,* went off in two pinnaces to investigate. The Spaniards ran their boats aground and made off into the bushes. While the English were taking over the abandoned boats, a blast of musket fire came from the snipers hidden among the trees. Moone and Varney fell dead.

On the second day, the city was given over to the looters. The official English story is that, as at Santo Domingo, the booty fell far short of the men's expectations. The Spaniards say that treacherous Negroes betrayed to Drake where they had hidden their valuables and that the plunder amounted to about 250,000 ducats. On the whole, the picture of crestfallen British soldiers and seamen baulked of their prey, in this prosperous colonial city, can be looked on with some skepticism. It is not in the least likely that, on this occasion or any other, the amount of the loot declared on the returns to the Customs bore any relation to the real value of the "import." Human nature is what it is.

What is certain is that the hope of plunder, illusory or otherwise, helped to give special bite to the English onset. Long afterwards, Raleigh, comparing the poor performance of English troops in the bogs of Ireland with their verve and pertinacity in the Caribbean fighting, ascribed the difference to the profit motive lacking in the former: "No man makes haste to the market where there is nothing to be bought but blows."

Thanks to his Negro allies, Drake's intelligence was good. Thanks to his own talent, the attack was shrewdly planned so as to divide the Spanish defence effort. It may be admitted, too, that the Cartagena defence was ill-organized. It was plainly absurd to keep the two royal galleys immobile in harbour. This was pointed out in a sharp memorandum written next year by no less a personage than the Duke of Medina Sidonia, first grandee of Spain. Some years later, after a far greater disaster to Spanish arms, the Duke himself was to be the target of criticism. In the meantime, he enjoyed all the advantages of the untested critic.

After the Cartagena failure, Don Pedro Vique was arrested and sentenced to death. This was later commuted to life imprisonment. To the general accusation of incompetence were added allegations of fraud. Don Pedro's private life was far from spotless. But he had one advantage. His brother was the Bishop of Majorca who employed his influence successfully to free Don Pedro from his cell in the Castle of Pensicola, on the Valencian coast. In fact, Don Pedro could not fairly be blamed for the poor display made by his galleys. He had wanted to go out and meet the enemy in the open sea but had been overborne by the population, who felt that he was proposing to desert them.

While the occupying troops busied themselves with digging for hidden jewellery, insulting church images or--most horrifying of all to the Spanish clergy--listening to "the tenets of Luther" being preached on the terraces of the Governor's residence, Drake settled down to the serious business of war. When Bishop Tristan de Oribe, at the head of a delegation, arrived to discuss the matter of ransom he found the Englishman in a furious temper. Drake had just come upon a letter from the King of Spain in which he was described as "a corsair."

The English commander refused even to talk about money until the bishop had a apologised for this insult to one whose flag ship flew the royal standard of England. At length, simmering down, he demanded 600,000 ducats. The bishop made an offer of 100,000 which Drake dismissed as derisory. Negotiations continued in the usual dilatory way until Drake, losing patience, gave orders for the systematic destruction of the town. He had one good reason for haste.

He has been criticised by historians for not holding Cartagena once it was in his hands. On the map, it seems to be just the base he needed in the Caribbean. But Cartagena had allies stronger than the galleons of King Philip: the anopheles mosquito and the bacillus of yellow fever. Set amidst its swamps, it was an unhealthy city on an unhealthy coast, much troubled by the Calenture, an infection which the inhabitants attributed to the evening air, La Serena. Two centuries later, an English author sombrely remarked that "a person of a humane disposition" considering the dire effects of the climate of the Indies, especially on the English, "cannot help deploring the insatiable desire that carries such crowds to these countries." The steady drain by sickness on the strength and morale of the expeditionary force induced Drake to settle for a ransom only ten per cent above the first Spanish offer. In addition, he claimed 1,000 crowns as the price of sparing a monastery situated a quarter of a mile outside the town. The fort at the harbour mouth he blew up.

Before agreeing to these terms he had asked his officers if they thought they could hold the town. The soldiers' answer was a reluctant "Yes," conditional on the Navy guaranteeing to give protection against the fleet which was known to be on its way from Spain. What the sea officers believed can be deduced from the fact that the English fleet departed soon afterwards. They returned, however, when "the New Year's gift," the galleon Drake had taken at Santo Domingo, was found to be sinking.

This return caused a renewed panic among the townspeople. But Drake wanted only the use of their ovens to bake biscuit. A few days after he sailed, the Spanish rescue fleet arrived at Cartagena, greeted by bitter sarcasm from the inhabitants, who sneered at "Spanish help--an old ass laden with lances lacking steel heads."

The whole of the Caribbean area was by this time in a state of nervous hubbub in which the wildest rumours gained credence: twenty thousand Englishmen were coming to conquer the New Kingdom of Granada! The entire black population had joined the invaders, who had later massacred them, lest they should again change sides! The Indians in Santa Marta had risen in revolt! Horrific stories like that kept nerves on edge.

But Drake had by this time so few men fit to fight that any idea of an attack on Panama was perforce abandoned. This was discouraging, for it meant giving up all thought of "the stroke for the treasure and full recompense of our tedious travails." But there was no alternative. Havana was another possible objective.

With the Negroes, Indians and liberated galley slaves, of whom he had gathered in all five hundred of both sexes aboard the ships, he contemplated establishing a settlement in the area with a fortified harbour which could serve as a base for later English operations. But this project, too, was reluctantly given up because of a strong, persistent and adverse wind.

He had one more task to attempt before sailing for England. He would pay a visit to the English settlement which, under Raleigh's inspiration, had been founded at Roanoke in Virginia. Perhaps--it is by no means unlikely--he intended to reinforce it with the ex-slaves and Negroes he had taken aboard at Cartagena. By the middle of May, then, the fleet was skirting the coast of Florida sniffing out, on its way to the north, any Spanish forts from which attack on the young English colony might be launched.

From a Portuguese pilot, faithless to the Spaniards as were so many of his kind, he picked up useful information: the Spaniards had established a base at San Agustin in Florida at the place where Jean Ribault's Huguenots had been massacred. Drake resolved to find it and attack it. The first clue to its position was given when a beacon was seen from the sea standing high on four masts. Drake put a party ashore and marched inland with them along the bank of a river. Carleill, Morgan and Sampson went on reconnaissance in a rowing skiff. They could find no trace of the Spaniards. Then they heard a sound which arrested every movement and caught every breath short. Someone was playing on a fife a tune they knew, the tune which every good Protestant in Europe called "William of Nassau"--the Prince of Orange's song. Solemn and heavily charged with emotion, the notes, to which Sainte Aldegonde's poem of patriotic defiance of Spain had been set, were eerily arresting and meaningful beside that creek in Florida. It was the most anti-Spanish air in the world . . . Somewhere close by was a friend.

Following the sound, they tracked the fife-player down. He was Nicholas Borgoignon, a French prisoner, who had spent six years in Spanish hands. He had exciting tales to tell of the gold, rubies and diamonds which could be found in the Appalachian mountains by those who, at the price of hatchets presented to the Indians, were permitted to look for them. With the Frenchman as their guide, Drake and Frobisher, along with Carleill and some captains of foot, advanced in skiffs and pinnaces to San Agustin.

They found a newly built fort, built of massive tree-trunks set upright. On top was a platform on which fourteen brass cannon were ranged side by side. In a chest they came upon the garrison's pay, amounting to £2,000.

But although the fort was deserted, the enemy was close at hand. When snipers fired from the trees, Anthony Powell, second-in-command of the English infantry, leapt on a horse the Spaniards had left, saddled and bridled, and rode off in pursuit. The pursuit did not last long. Powell was shot in the head and when he fell, was stabbed to death. After that, the English took fewer risks. They demolished the settlement and the fort. Tools and implements which might be of use to colonists were carried off.

Drake was now on his way to Virginia. Anchors were dropped at the entrance to Charleston Harbour, six hundred miles north of San Agustin, and search parties were sent out to look for the English colony. In the end, it was found that Ralph Lane, the Governor, had built a fort on Roanoke Island. It seemed, however, that Lane had no great confidence in the future of the colony. When Drake realised this, he offered Lane a choice between being taken home by ship along with his colonists and having his needs supplied. Lane chose the latter and was sent a 70-ton ship and two pinnaces. They were apparently not enough to restore morale and, when the new ship was lost in a hurricane, Lane insisted on being shipped home. Thus, rather tamely, ended the first English attempt to settle in the New World.

Drakes's fleet arrived in Portsmouth on 28 July 1586. It had been absent just ten months and it had achieved moral and political results out of all proportion to its material consequences. Only in one respect had it fallen short of the hopes of its backers. Money. After a careful audit of the spoils, it was found that the shareholders must be content with a dividend of 15 shillings in the pound. The expedition had cost just under £60,000 to send out. It came back with valuables worth about the sum, including two hundred and forty brass cannon. It had released many galley slaves, a hundred of whom, Turks, the Queen sent to the Grand Signior, whom she was cultivating for military and commercial reasons. Of the declared plunder, the ships' companies, as was their due, took a third--£6 a head, plus anything that might have found its way into their sea-chests.

Looked on as a commercial enterprise, then, the raid on the Indies was hardly a triumph. The only hope that it might be one had vanished when Drake missed the treasure fleet--"the cause best known to God"--by twelve hours, a misfortune which he bemoaned to the Lord Treasurer on his return. But, without some extraordinary stroke of luck, an expeditionary force of 2,300 men and more than twenty ships could not be expected to pay its way. Only in the dreams of Elizabethan Treasury officials can war be conducted as a business.

Drake's voyage of 1585-6 was conceived as a stroke of policy, an act of war. Its ultimate purpose--in which it failed--was to bring Philip to the negotiating table. What it accomplished was to expose the weaknesses inherent in the imposing but overextended Spanish power and to do so at a time when its might seemed most overwhelming. With insolent ease, four of Spain's colonial settlements had been taken and pillaged. "We have neither artillery nor powder, neither arquebuses nor men experienced in war." The complaint of Santo Domingo was echoed by Cartagena: "The damage done by this corsair amounts to more than 400,000 ducats. The English have left this city completely destroyed and desolate." The Venetian ambassador in Madrid, Gradenigo, reported that Lisbon and Castile were in an uproar over Drake's depredations, and that the King, in a panic, had, on Easter Monday, called the Marquis de Santa Cruz into secret consultations at the Escorial. The Seville fleet of fourteen ships was to reinforce the men already at Lisbon. The trouble was, said the ambassador, that the Seville troops were the mere dregs of the population, released convicts and the like, many of whom had already deserted. In Spain, it seemed, the ranks were filled by much the same types as in England.

The King irresolute, finances embarrassed, Drake--a humane man it appeared, on the testimony of men he had taken prisoner--at large again, bound for God knows where! Was it any wonder that the bankers on whom Philip depended for his flow of cash showed a disagreeable lethargy in the matter of fresh loans. For how credit-worthy was a monarch who had been unable to defend his most important overseas possessions? About this time Gritti, the Venetian ambassador in Rome, heard that the Pope had been impressed by Drake's successes in the Caribbean. He thought the King of Spain would do well to hurry up. Was Philip's health all right? His Holiness was worried about it. The King's gout was apparently troublesome. Well, well, he was entering on his sixtieth year and it was notorious that the house of Austria died young.

Drake now moved in a haze of glory. Gossips in the London taverns said that the Queen meant to make him a peer. The French Ambassador sent copies of his portrait to the dukes of Joyeuse and Epernon and other favourites of Henri III. From Paris, where Mendoza had established his listening post, a stream of anti-Drake rumours was directed towards King Philip. The Queen, he was told, had not received a groat from the proceeds of the voyage; the soldiers had taken all the booty. On the other hand, the sailors were said to be discontented with results because Drake had kept everything to himself--apart from 50,000 ducats which he had sent to Leicester. The truth was that Mendoza's intelligence service was no longer quite as accurate as it had been when he lived in London.

In one respect, the raid on the Indies had been costly. Seven hundred and fifty men had lost their lives in it, most of them as a result of disease. It was more than thirty per cent of the force that had sailed from Plymouth and it included distinguished captains like Anthony Powell, Tom Moone, Fortescue, Bigges, Cecil, Hannam and Grenville.

A fortnight after Drake's return to England, Anthony Babington was arrested. The long-drawn-out and perilous drama of Mary Stuart's life had entered its ultimate crisis and with her execution, which followed six months later, the final obstacle was removed to a full-scale attack upon

England by the King of Spain. Already commercial and financial interests were urging war on the Catholic monarch as the only way of ending the insulting and troublesome forays which were undermining the pride, peace and power of his empire. Now a victory over the island freebooters and their perfidious queen, if it were gained, would not be for the profit of the Scottish queen who was, after all, a Frenchwoman, a Guise princess. In making herself a martyr for the Catholic faith, Mary did something else which won Philip's approval. She bequeathed to him her most precious heirloom, the succession to the English throne. For months he had been adding galleon to galleon and gun to gun in the hope that the mere rumour of his growing strength would bring Elizabeth to reason. In much the same way, the Queen had thought that her undeclared war might induce a mood of accommodation in the stiff-necked Hapsburg. Instead, the drift towards war had become a current of growing power and speed.

With lamenting Spanish colonists and burning cities behind him and the cheers of the Portsmouth mob in his ears, Drake can hardly have expected in that late summer of 1586 to spend a long time in idleness ashore. The great clash was at hand, to which, as an instinctive man of action, he looked forward with supreme confidence. In the meantime, he was to write, in blood and fire, on Philip's own coast, a new preface to the main theme.

The Wind Commands Me Away

'Drak est en mer vers la coste de Hespaigne.'
(Drake is at sea on his way to the coast of Spain.')
Claude de l'Aubespine, French Ambassador
in London, March 1587

On 2 April 1587 Drake put to sea anew. He had been just eight months at home. They had been eight months of plans and counter-plans, projects that had been prepared and then abandoned, alarms and calms. During that time, he had crossed to Holland to try to persuade the Dutch to take part in a new assault on Portugal in aid of Dom Antonio, that eternal Pretender. But the Dutch did not trust the steadfastness of Queen Elizabeth's resolution far enough to fall in with an English scheme. Nothing came of the proposal.

Where all was confusion and frustration, where the Queen seemed to have raised indecision to a principle of statecraft, one grim certainty rose out of the swirl: Mary Stuart was dead, with all that implied for Spanish policy and Catholic propaganda. The first news of the Scottish queen's execution had arrived from Mendoza at the Escorial on 23 March, just thirty-three days after the event it reported--and just a week before Sir Francis Drake sailed out of Plymouth Sound.

All controversies were now resolved or, if not resolved, evaded. His orders were clear, or clear enough. He was to distress Spanish ships within their harbours, capture their seaborne supplies and do all he could to "impeach the drawing together of the King of Spains's fleets out of their several ports" to the main base of Lisbon, where the ships were to assemble under the Marquis of Santa Cruz. No assignment could be plainer. It is true that, a week after Drake departed, the Privy Council in London drafted a fresh set of instructions based on the Queen's alleged belief that she could detect in the King of Spain a new spirit of conciliation. Drake was therefore not to force his way into any Spanish harbour, attack any Spanish town or "do any act of hostility upon the land." However, a pinnace, sent from Plymouth with the revised orders, failed to overtake Drake's fleet, which was hardly surprising since he had nine days' start.

Whether the new instructions were ever seriously intended to reach the Queen's admiral may be doubted. The episode is too reminiscent of Elizabeth's tortuous behaviour over the execution of Mary Stuart. On that occasion, Secretary Davidson was threatened with the gallows and Lord Treasurer Burghley was pursued with "marvelous cruel speeches, calling him traitor, false dissembler and wicked wretch," and all because they had arranged for the execution of a woman whose death sentence the Queen had signed! The belated dispatch might help to clear her of responsibility should Drake go too far and King Philip lose his temper. And, since it could not arrive in time, it would not frustrate any practical benefits from the expedition.

Drake was, all through that period of international crisis, in an exalted frame of mind, aware of sense of mission, touched as he thought by divine approval and, with the meek arrogance of the religious, liable to view opposition to his will as akin to apostasy. He was on the brink of his most brilliant campaign and what shone out before long as an inspired audacity in action is to be seen already in the fervour of his letter to Walsingham on the day he sailed:

'The wind commands me away. Our ship is under sail. God grant we may so live in His fear as the enemy may have cause to say that God doth fight for Her Majesty as well abroad as at home . . . Pray unto God for us that He will direct us the right way; then we shall not doubt our enemies, for they are the sons of men.'

Here, obviously, was the religious enthusiasm that belonged to the age.

But was there not something else, too, older and even more profound? "The wind commands me away. Our ship is under sail." In the joyous lilt of these sentences there is something that Drake shared with all the sea rovers: Columbus, Leif Erikson, Ulysses himself. The thrill of escape from queens, statesmen, domestic concerns, and the cramping letter of the law, into the infectious anarchy of the sea. He knew that he was at the height of his powers; he did not doubt of success.

Considering the task ahead, a challenge to King Philip in his own waters, the fleet which Drake led out of Plymouth was none too numerous. But it was powerful: four ships of the Queen's, including Drake's old flagship, the *Elizabeth Bonaventure*; four other ships which he and his business associates had contributed; a ship of the Lord Admiral's; and eight which nineteen London merchants, prominent in the privateering business, had supplied. There were, also, six pinnaces, likely to be useful in any inshore work. It was, then, a composite fleet partly owned by the state, partly private, as in the case of most naval adventures of that period. Drake had as his second-in-command William Borough, a Devon man like himself, a regular naval officer with a gallant record at sea in the Baltic; Borough was respected among the graver navigators for his *Discourse of the Variation of the Compass*. He was six years older than his admiral. Captain Robert Flick, member of the Drapers' Company, nominee of the City of London, was vice-admiral of the fleet. Aboard were ten companies of infantry under Captain Anthony Platt. These soldiers were to carry out one of the most gallant exploits of the campaign that lay ahead.

Somewhere off Lisbon, Drake picked up the news from Flemish merchantmen that Cadiz harbour was packed with ships. On 19 April he called a council of war at which he gave perfunctory attention to the views of the others, having already made up his mind what he was going to do. William Borough, in particular, was shocked by this unconventional way of conducting a war, "wherein," as he complained by letter to Drake at the time, "we have served but as witnesses to the words you have delivered; or else you have used us well by entertaining us with your good cheer. . . and we have departed as wise as we came." He was even more dismayed by the outcome of these "assemblies," as he called them. Drake announced that he was going into Cadiz Bay at once; they were all to follow him and destroy what shipping they found there. The scheme had a splendid simplicity more appealing to one who had known the results of surprise onsets in the Pacific than to a prim naval technician like Borough.

The harbour defences of Cadiz were reasonably strong. The topographical lay-out of the port resembled a funnel which first narrowed and then opened out again into a basin shaped like a retort and roughly four miles across. This was the inner harbour. The city of Cadiz straddled a detached spit of land, an island, although joined to the mainland by a bridge. This protected the harbour from the open water. On its seaward side it rose cliff-like out of the water. In order to make their way into the harbour, ships must sail through a narrow channel, skirting dangerous shoals and coming under the gunfire of a castle which had been built fifty years earlier as a protection against the Algerine corsair, Barbarossa. (This fortress was less dangerous than it looked.) In addition, there was in attendance a pack of galleys under an experienced officer, Don Pedro de Acuña, which had been detained in port by high winds. Among the shoals of confined waters like this, the oar-driven, shallow-draught galley, with its complete command over speed and direction, should enter into its own. Coming in under the land, Drake might lose the wind and would then be at the mercy of the galleys' rams. On the other hand, he had more gun-power in the *Elizabeth Bonaventure* than there was in the whole galley fleet.

He went in to attack at four o'clock in the afternoon, his ships flying French or Flemish colours. As he did so, two galleys put out from Port St. Mary on the distant side of the bay. They wanted to know his business. The *Bonaventure* made towards them at once, her guns blazing. At the same time, she and her consorts hoisted the Cross of St. George. The galleys sheered off out of range. Drake ordered his helmsman to bring the ship's head round so that it was pointed towards the harbour. He could see, to his satisfaction, that sixty sail of merchant ships were alongside the quays.

They had been loading or unloading. Many of them lacked their sails, which had been removed because these were foreign ships which had been commandeered by the Spanish authorities and, if given the opportunity, might desert King Philip's service. Most of them were waiting for their artillery, at that moment on its way by sea from Italy. At the sound of Drake's guns, all this mass of shipping was thrown into the wildest confusion. Everything that could move on the water cut its cables and bolted for safety. The smaller boats hurried across the shoal water to Port St. Mary. Half a dozen Flemish cargo boats made for the inner harbour.

To the citizens the invasion of their harbour came as a complete surprise. They had been passing the afternoon agreeably, and now there were these unknown ships suddenly crowding into the bay--for what purpose had they come to Cadiz? The noise of guns, rolling across the water and echoing back from the farther shore, made that only too plain. The Governor sent the women, children and old people to the citadel. But the citadel gates were firmly shut in the faces of the refugees, and more than a score of them were crushed to death before the commander of the fortress relented. Citizens picked up what arms they could find, forgetting in their haste to lock their doors against looters. Soldiers were dispatched to the point of rock where the channel between the outer and the inner harbour is narrowest. And a message was sent across the bay to the Duke of Medina Sidonia who, as the most important magnate in the province, was expected to organize the rescue of the city. As soon as he received it, the Duke dispatched fast couriers to Seville and Jerez, ordering those towns to send reinforcements to Cadiz. Then he set off for the scene of action.

Meanwhile, in Cadiz Bay, ten galleys of Pedro de Acuña's command rowed out, as was their duty, and launched themselves at the beam of the incoming English fleet. They ran into the broadsides of four Royal Navy warships, sailing across their bows. The English shot struck them before their own bow guns were within range of the invading ships. With all decent speed, the galleys left the scene either for the inner harbour or for the shelter of the guns of Cadiz fortress. The shipping in the outer harbour could now be pillaged or destroyed at the convenience of the English. There was one exception, a Genoese argosy of 700 tons, loaded with cochineal and logwood and, since it carried forty guns, a match for any two ships in Drake's flotilla. What is more, it was willing to fight.

Naval gunfire in the sixteenth century was notable for noise and smoke rather than for accuracy. *"Il fait plus de peur que du mal"* ("It causes more fear than damage"), as Montluc said, scornfully. And even if that remark is put aside as exaggerated, guns were certainly inaccurate and the effective range was modest. Beyond two hundred yards--the range of a musket--a cannon was useless. As for accuracy, the windage of a gun, i.e., the difference between the diameters of the bore and the bullet, was by no means uniform. For those reasons, there was more banging than blasting in the average sea-fight of the time. Besides, a wooden ship is very hard to sink.

However, a close-up duel in a sheltered harbour provided ideal conditions for the naval gunners of the time. After a good deal of pounding, the obstinate Genoese, firing her brass guns to the last, went down. She was mourned by the victors, who hated to see forty good cannon lost. Meanwhile, the English ships that were not involved in this main engagement were busy with those other cargo boats that had not been able to reach the inner harbour. Burning some and towing off others--it was a congenial task which the guns of the coastal batteries hardly disturbed. When night fell, the outer port of Cadiz was under a heavy pall of smoke through which ships, burning like torches, reeled crackling towards the shoals.

Drake ordered Captain Flick in the *Merchant Royal* to anchor with the London squadron out of reach of the Cadiz guns, near the entrance to the inner harbour. He himself with the Queen's ships kept a watch on the galleys. Borough urged that the fleet would now clear out. But Drake would have none of it. He had not finished with Cadiz yet. Apart from anything else, he had still nothing to take home to the shareholders. The ships spent the hours of darkness uneasily at anchor, where they lay.

On the Spanish side the alarm went up after midnight that an English landing was imminent near the bastion of St. Philip. It was low tide; a cold, damp night. The sentries strung out along the shore depended on the light given by blazing tar barrels. One of Acuña's galleys had run aground and the noise made by her crew as they worked to get her off was mistaken on shore for the coming of an English assault party. However, good news came: at the bridge that joined Cadiz to the mainland a guard of arquebusiers was in position, while a relief force was hurrying on its way from Jerez.

The people who had taken refuge in the citadel recovered their courage and went to church to give thanks for their deliverance. Those who had left their houses unlocked went back, expecting the worst. But nothing had been touched. This in a town teeming with Moors, slaves and suchlike untrustworthy elements, was thought to be indeed miraculous.

At daybreak, Drake took his flagship closer to the inner harbour, where he knew there lay a fine galleon belonging to the Marquis of Santa Cruz, commander-designate of the fleet with which King Philip was proposing to invade England. This ship had lately arrived in Cadiz from the shipyards on the Biscay coast to take on her cannon; she was laden with wine. Two galleys were on guard over her and the other merchantmen which had taken refuge from the attack of the previous evening. Drake collected a flotilla of pinnaces and boats and led them into the attack.

Before long, Santa Cruz's galleon was surrounded by a swarm of little craft and her decks were overrun by English boarders. Resistance was soon at an end. Having taken the ship, they looted it thoroughly; having looted it, they set it on fire. Other ships that could be reached were similarly treated. There was a ship about to take on spices, nails, horseshoes, etc., for a voyage to the Indies. Four ships were loaded with victuals for the King of Spain's armada at Lisbon. Some of these were sunk; some were fired; some were towed away.

When Drake went back to his flagship he left the inner basin of Cadiz harbour filled with the reek of burning ships. In the *Bonaventure* he found Borough, his second-in-command, shaking his head over the recklessness of the morning's work. After a time Borough set off in his boat to return to his own ship. What followed is in some doubt. Borough's story is that, while he was absent looking for Drake, his ship, the *Golden Lion*, came under fire from a shore gun, and the master began to warp it out towards the open sea. At this point, seeing the *Lion* dangerously isolated, the galleys darted out from their sheltered position behind the shoals of Port St. Mary. Drake, who observed that his vice-admiral was in some danger, moved seven ships to his support. Borough then anchored in the harbour mouth. (Drake's opinion was that his vice-admiral, who had taken no pains to hide his disapproval of the whole operation, was keeping his ships out of trouble.) Borough claimed later that he posted them there to beat off the galleys should they attack the main fleet. What is certain is that there was a clash of temperament between the two men and that Drake became convinced that Borough was disloyal to him.

But now the work was finished. Twenty-four ships, perhaps as many as thirty, had been taken or destroyed. Considerable damage had been done and little had been suffered. Five unlucky sailors whose craft had trailed too far behind the main fleet on the way in had been snapped up by galleys. The master gunner of the *Golden Lion* had his leg broken by a shot from a shore cannon. And that was all. But now it was time to leave, with drums beating and trumpets sounding in strident derision from the English ships. At that point, one of those dangerous situations arose to which sailing-ships were subject when they operated in closed waters. Hardly had Drake hoisted the signal to withdraw than the wind died.

This was a possibility against which Borough had all the time been warning Drake. His ships were now immobile, in a landlocked harbour. And Cadiz had been reinforced. At the moment when the calm fell on the sea, the Duke of Medina Sidonia, answering frantic appeals for help, marched into the town with three hundred horse and three thousand foot. Encouraged by the arrival of this nobleman, Cadiz prepared to avenge itself for the affront it had suffered. Culverins were brought down to the foreshore. Fireships were made ready and sent out on the ebbing tide to annoy the invaders.

And there were the galleys. Now, if ever, was their opportunity. But they could do nothing. Again and again they darted into the attack but were beaten off by the English broadsides. Watchful officers and experienced crews had hauled the ships into the right alignment for firing. "I assure your honour there is no account to be made of his galleys," wrote Thomas Fenner to Walsingham. "Twelve of her Majesty's ships will make account of all his galleys in Spain, Portugal and all his dominions within the straits."

The fireships likewise were coolly fended off by longboats and sent on their way towards the shoals, where they ran aground and burned out. Drake remarked jovially, "The Spaniards are doing our work for us by burning their own ships." The shore guns did no damage. About two o'clock in the morning, the weather changed. The cheeks of Drake and his captains were freshened by a wind that had blown up from the land and, in a few minutes, was filling the sails of the fleet. He stood out to sea, past the Cadiz fortifications, unharmed by the fire of their batteries. He beat off the galleys, which, dogged but ineffective, sought to embarrass his escape and, in the open sea, at a moment when the wind had died once again, darted in with a last futile onslaught.

After the attack, too, had been beaten off, Drake and his ships lay at anchor outside the town. He tried to negotiate with the galley commander an exchange of his prisoners against English galley slaves. But although there were courteous talks, on a matter of this kind no Spanish officer was prepared to do business. There was, in any case, no lack of other and more urgent things to think about. Drake wrote an exultant dispatch home. Then he set sail for Cape St. Vincent, shadowed as he went by two caravels, acting on instructions from Medina Sidonia.

On the first Sunday after the departure of the English, the people of Cadiz held a solemn procession of gratitude to the convent church of San Francisco. They had good reason to be thankful: the English had not killed one civilian in the town.

One reason why Drake went to Cape St. Vincent was that he had just heard that one of the most redoubtable of Spanish admirals, Juan Martinez de Recalde, marked down to be second-in-command of the Enterprise of England, was to be found in those waters. But, apart from that incentive, the Cape had a strategic importance clear to anyone from a glance at a map. There it was, a hundred and fifty miles west of Cadiz, a pivot as it were where the Portuguese coastline, which had been running east and west, suddenly turned due north. All the Spanish shipping coming from the Mediterranean to reinforce or to supply the Armada assembling in Lisbon must sail round the Cape. No more convenient station, therefore, could be found for an English fleet charged, as Drake's was, with the task of impeding Spain's war preparations. So, although as it turned out Recalde with his squadron had been warned in time and had fled to the security of Lisbon, Drake found enough to occupy him at Cape St. Vincent. So long as he was on station there, with his powerful fleet, only a major formation of heavily armed galleons could fight its way past him from Cadiz or the Mediterranean to the main Spanish base at Lisbon.

About this time, King Philip, who had been confined to bed with gout which had gone to his knee, and who had been bled twice, felt well enough to get up. He was much distressed by the news from Cadiz, especially as he knew that all Spain expected some counter-action from him. "The Spanish say that the King thinks and plans while the Queen of England acts," the Venetian ambassador reported. "These injuries inflicted by Drake will raise many considerations in the minds of other princes . . ." But what was Philip to do? And what, if there was truth in this rumour that a second English fleet was waiting for the troopships that were bringing to Spain the Sicilian *tercio*? What a relief to hear that Medina Sidonia had arrived at Cadiz and had taken a grip of the business there! Now he ordered the Duke to leave the city and raise troops to be ready to meet the new attack that was expected at any moment. "I should be more worried about the situation," he wrote, "if you were not in charge."

At sea, Drake had decided that it was not enough to cruise about off Cape St. Vincent. It was necessary to establish a shore base where ships could be cleaned and watered. And there, a few miles south and east of Cape St. Vincent, at Sagres on the Algarve coast, was a natural harbour, protected by a castle on the cliffs above it. Drake resolved to attack the castle and lay hands on the anchorage.

He had been painfully impressed by what he had seen and what he had picked up from talkative prisoners about the scale of King Philip's preparations. "Prepare in England," he wrote to Walsingham, "strongly and most by sea. Stop him now and stop him ever." To John Woolley, the Latin Secretary, he wrote a letter on the same day, scrawling in haste a postscript, "Cease not to pray continually and provide strongly to prevent the worst."

Ships were being built in Mediterranean ports; guns were being shipped from Italy; Don Diego de Pimentel's Sicilian *tercio*, the fortune of which had been such an anxiety to King Philip, had now arrived at Cartagena, within the straits. So long as Drake's ships remained on station off Cape St. Vincent, Philip's galleons could not be concentrated and Pimentel's soldiers, ear-marked to be a spearhead of the invasion of England, would be compelled to make their way overland to Lisbon. This, in due course, they did, by forced marches.

After hovering about off the Algarve coast and snapping up two Dunkirk flyboats laden with Spanish goods, Drake had tried and failed to surprise the fortified port of Lagos.

Now he resolved to attack the redoubtable castle at Sagres, famous in the history of the sea as the hermitage of Henry the Navigator, the Portuguese prince who more, perhaps, than any man, launched the age of discovery. It was over this attack that Drake broke finally with his restive second-in-command, William Borough, who considered the whole operation crazy, contrary to the instructions which the Lord Admiral had given them and launched by the commander-in-chief without proper consultation with his senior officers. Drake dealt with the dissident officer with his usual vigour. In the heat and sweep of action, Drake was a dangerous man to cross; suspicious, despotic, intolerant and unjust. But if that was Drake at his worst, the assault on Sagres, like the dash and fury of the Cadiz raid, showed him at the top of his form. Borough was unlucky to collide with him at such an hour. Perhaps--indeed, it is likely--Borough meant only to recall the proprieties of the naval service, to offer the sound advice which had not been invited. But he had shared his misgivings with his subordinates; his doubting spirit had infected his ship and to that extent Drake's passionate charge of disloyalty against this veteran naval officer was justified. Borough was deprived of his command and made a prisoner in his own ship, "expecting daily when the admiral would have executed upon me his bloodthirsty desire as he did upon Doughty." And Drake landed with eight hundred men at Cape Sagres. His purpose was to storm the castle, a task which, on the face of it, seemed incredible. On three sides cliffs fell a sheer two hundred feet to the sea; on the fourth side, a wall forty feet high and surmounted by battlements impeded the advance of an attacking force.

Through the scattered fig trees, bowed by the wind that always blows up there, past the almond trees with their ashcoloured branches, up to the heights where rare juniper bushes raised their dark pylons. After that climb the sweating English could look down on windmills and the sea that stretches out towards Africa.

Drake took command of the assault. After the failure at Lagos, he had little confidence in the spirit of his subordinates. He had infinite confidence in himself. In helmet and corselet, with targe and sword, he climbed at the head of the troops up the steep slope to the castle gate. There, after a preliminary exchange of musket fire, he demanded the surrender of the garrison. When this was rejected, he called up the pitch and faggots which, in the absence of cannon or explosives, were his only hope of destroying the gate. Under fire from four flanking towers in the wall, he took part in piling and firing the faggots. It was hot work: two of the storming party were killed, many were wounded. But Drake's musketeers kept up a steady covering fire which had miraculous good fortune.

After two hours a trumpet sounded from the castle. A parley! The commander had been badly wounded by two musket balls. The garrison of a hundred and ten men asked terms of surrender, which Drake conceded, generously. He had won a victory which astonished everybody--except himself. For in his mood just then, it is probable that only a repulse would have surprised him. He was now master of the Sagres anchorage, from which a fleet could command the exit from the Mediterranean. This he meant to use as his shore base while denying it to the Spanish ships that were accustomed to call there on the way to and from Gibraltar. He set about dismantling the castle, tumbling its eight cannon over the cliffs into the sea, from which they were salvaged by his longboats and carried off. Neighbouring strongpoints were treated in the same way.

While these demolitions were taking place ashore, the rest of the fleet had been carrying out savage destructive raids against the local shipping and fisheries. Nets were taken and burnt; forty-seven caravels taking barrel-hoops and such-like stores to the Armada at Lisbon were seized. In the evening, the ships came back to Sagres and took off the infantry who had been finishing their task of demolition at the castle. One of the captured flyboats, an exceptionally fast sailer, was sent off to England with dispatches for the Queen and Walsingham; two other flyboats were sent home with the sick. Drake suggested to Walsingham that he should be reinforced. Six more of the Queen's ships "of the second sort" would, he said, enable him to prevent the Spanish forces from uniting and, "in my poor judgment, will bring this great monarchy to those conditions which are meet." A great matter had begun but "the continuing unto the end until it be thoroughly finished yields the true glory ... Haste!" Having sent this message home, Drake set sail for the mouth of the Tagus where, behind powerful shore batteries, Santa Cruz was waiting for supplies of every kind, guns, ammunition, biscuits, men, to reach him, and plagued by a stream of orders from his gout-stricken master.

Having inspected the situation, and reflected, Drake decided that Lisbon, the second richest city in Europe, was too hard a nut to crack. Not only was the estuary lined by impressive forts, but the approach along the narrow, winding fairway of the Tagus was an operation for which special pilots were normally required. And Santa Cruz, supervising the defence of the port from St. Julian's Castle, had a squadron of galleys at his orders. Drake, coming to anchor on 10 May outside the river bar, could see them, their oars out, ready to strike the water. He sent a message to Santa Cruz by two Hamburg merchantmen bound for the port to say that he was waiting for the galleys to come out. The galleys did not budge. Then he suggested an exchange of prisoners to Santa Cruz. When the Marquis replied that he had no English prisoners, Drake, who did not believe him, said that in that case he would sell his prisoners to the Moors and use the money to buy the release of Englishmen held in slavery by the Moslem. There being nothing for him to do outside Lisbon, he sailed back to Sagres to clean his ships and give his men shore leave.

Meanwhile, King Philip from his sickroom at Aranjuez was trying to control the situation. His doctors, who disagreed among themselves about the treatment for his gout, were unanimous in thinking that he should not be encouraged to work. It was useless. Philip insisted in grappling with a crisis which, changing hour by hour, usually made nonsense of his orders. First, Medina Sidonia, in command at Cadiz, was to embark the soldiers of Pimentel's *tercio* in galleys and dispatch them to Lisbon. Then, hearing that Drake was no longer hovering outside the Tagus bar, the King issued new orders. He decided that the Englishman must have sailed off to attack the infinitely precious treasure fleet due to arrive from the Indies. That being the most likely peril, Santa Cruz, Recalde and Medina Sidonia were to make rendezvous at Cape St. Vincent and, acting together, save the treasure from the pirate.

Then the news reached Philip that Drake had turned up again off Cape St. Vincent. Santa Cruz was brought into consultation and gave it as his opinion that Drake's purpose could only be to prevent a junction of the Cadiz and the Lisbon fleets. Philip agreed, and ordered Pimentel's troops to make for Lisbon overland by forced marches. At this juncture, however, the authorities in Cadiz announced that they would be ready in a week's time to attack Drake with sixty ships. In his perplexity, the King fell in with this idea. But, to be sure that Cadiz was capable of carrying out its plan, he sent Don Alonso de Leyva to report. Leyva, an exceptionally brilliant soldier, who had charmed the King into making him Captain-General of the Sicilian galleys and then Captain-General of the Milanese Cavalry, sent back gloomy news. Cadiz was quite capable of dealing with Drake. Philip was recasting his plan once more when a new presage of disaster reached him.

Drake, as if on a sudden impulse, had set off westwards into the ocean. Watchers on the coast saw his ships disappear, one by one, below the horizon. This made no kind of strategic sense at all but, then, the Cadiz expedition, like other episodes in this strange half-war between England and Spain, was only in part a military undertaking. It was business, too. Very much so, as Drake knew better than most men. He remembered how, only a year earlier, his prestigious raid on the Indies had been followed by complaints: the speculators had been paid a dividend of only 15 shillings in the pound. As one who was himself an investor both in the Indies expedition and in this new one, he had a personal interest in the commercial side of the venture.

So, when he picked up the information, probably somewhere on the Portuguese coast, that an immensely valuable cargo boat was on its way home from Goa, he set off to snatch it. A whole year's harvest of the Portuguese settlements in Asia was expected to reach the Azores in the carrack *San Felipe*. With luck, he should be able to intercept it, thus winning favour in the eyes of the Queen, the City merchants and the poor mariners to whom one prize was worth many weeks of vigil off Cape St. Vincent. And so it fell out.

Although he lost contact with the London squadron in a heavy gale, and with the *Golden Lion* in which Borough was held prisoner, Drake, with the Queen's ships and three others, one of which was his own, met the *San Felipe* off the Azores. By that time he had been sixteen days on the way from Cape St. Vincent. The big Portuguese carrack, on the last leg of her voyage from India, invited Drake's flagship to declare her nationality, but this she declined to do until the *San Felipe* was within range of her guns. After that, there was a brisk exchange of fire between the *Elizabeth Bonaventure*, a flyboat and a pinnace on the one hand, and the *San Felipe* on the other. In this engagement, the Portuguese had the worst of it; with six dead and many wounded and with the English ready to send boarders at any moment, the captain of the *San Felipe* struck his colours.

In all the records of privateering down to that June day, there had never been such a prize. The pride of the Portuguese merchant marine, laden with all the spices, silks, china, jewels and gold she could conveniently carry! Sir Horatio Pallavicino, a Genoese who had settled in London, was said to have offered £100,000 for her cargo, as was sourly reported by Mendoza to King Philip. Mendoza was probably not far wrong because he had a spy in Plymouth that year, a Fleming, who brought the news over by fishing boat to the French coast. The official valuation of the *San Felipe* and her cargo was £114,000. What it was in reality, heaven knows.

A fortnight after taking her, Drake sailed triumphantly into Plymouth Sound. He had been at sea for less than three months, in which time he had done a great deal of damage to Spanish shipping, more to Spanish credit and most of all to Spanish pride. The Portuguese mourned the loss of their best merchant ship and swore that they were worse off now than they had ever been under kings of their own. Among the Spanish public the conviction grew that Drake worked in collaboration with a familiar spirit who told him where and when to strike. It is, indeed, clear that he had excellent intelligence about Spanish shipping movements, probably obtained from disaffected Portuguese.

While Drake was on his way home with £40,000 of prize money for the Queen and £17,000 for himself, Santa Cruz had been able to find crews to man a punitive fleet, which was now scouring the seas round the Azores for signs of Drake. When at last the old Spanish admiral gave up the hunt, and came fuming back to Lisbon, he had made up his mind on one important question: there would be no attack on England that year.

The Cadiz raid had a sequel which Drake found less than satisfactory. Not long before the capture of the *San Felipe*, he had been enraged to hear that the crew of Borough's ship, the *Golden Lion*, had mutinied and, defying Captain Marchant, whom Drake had put over them, had stood away before the wind for England. Rather risk the anger of the Queen than certain death in the company of this madman, Drake! Marchant had left the ship, convinced, as he told Drake, that the real source of the trouble was to be found in Borough, then a nominal prisoner on his own ship. Drake, who probably did not need much convincing on the score, called a court-martial which duly passed sentence of death, *in absentia*, on the officers of the runaway ship, chief of whom was, of course, Borough. On his return to England, Drake presented the case against his vice-admiral before the Council, then in session at Lord Burghley's country house. To the Queen, who was staying there at the time, he brought a fine casket of jewels which had been turned up when the *San Felipe* was being searched at Saltash.

Drake had, as usual, no doubt at all that right was on his side. And, indeed, the *prima facie* case against Borough was a substantial one. Out of vanity and pique, as it seemed, he had dragged a foot in the crisis of battle. Later, when he had been deprived of his command, he had allowed himself to be brought back to England as a passenger by mutineers who shared his lack of confidence in the fleet commander. However it was regarded, the episode lacked the dignity expected of a member of the Navy Board and Clerk of the Ships. But, as it proved, Borough was in luck. He returned to England at a time when the Queen and Burghley were inclined to think or, at least, to hope that war after all could be avoided or postponed. Walsingham wrote despondently to Leicester: he had never seen the Queen so little inclined to war. The Duke of Parma, who was encouraging this mood of optimism among the Queen and her councillors, let it be known that he greatly disliked Drake's actions, which might turn King Philip from thoughts of peace.

In the same week as Borough's case came before the Council, Burghley wrote to Parma's London agent, explaining that only contrary winds had prevented Drake from receiving later instructions which would have kept him off Spanish soil. As it was, the Queen was very much annoyed with him. The case of the stolen carrack was, however, on quite a different footing. There could be no question of disgorging any of the prize money which Drake had brought home. He pointed out that it would go only a small part of the way to recompensing the Queen and her subjects for the losses they had suffered at Spanish hands.

From Borough's point of view the important thing was that the Queen, while taking her share of the loot from the *San Felipe*, was blaming Drake for the landing at Cape Sagres which Borough had criticised. So Borough, favoured by a change of wind in the Council chamber, was not hanged as his admiral had proposed; he even received his share of the *San Felipe* money and, in due course, was promoted. And this during days when a grave view was being taken of mutiny by the Council! Recently it had ordered the Lord Mayor of London to deal severely with some conscripts who had refused to obey Captain Sampson's orders. They were to be tied to carts and flogged through the streets from Cheapside to Tower Hill. There they were to be set on a pillory and have each an ear cut off. But a more tolerant attitude was taken towards the supposed offence of a distinguished naval officer.

Drake may well have resented it that the decision of his court-martial was overturned by Burghley. He persisted in his belief that Borough had, by his behaviour in the crisis at Cadiz, endangered the whole operation. He told the Queen so when she sought his advice during the tense months before the Armada came. But whatever Drake's inner feelings, he swallowed his annoyance. He had more important things to think of than his quarrel with an elderly and pedantic sailor. As for Borough, he did not suffer too severely in career or reputation as a result of his quarrel with Drake. During the Armada campaign of the following summer he commanded the *Bonavolio*, the only galley in the English fleet. His service was confined, however, to the Thames estuary at a distance from his enemy; when it was all over, he busied himself with handling another matter, "getting a good wife," in which apparently he was successful.

From G.M. Thomson, *Sir Francis Drake,* (New York: Morrow 1972), pp. 183-215.

Ian Grimble

The Impérieuse

At Wimbledon House near London there lived a rich West Indies merchant named Joseph Marryat, who was a Member of Parliament and also colonial agent for the island of Grenada. These activities brought him into contact with Admiral Sir Alexander Cochrane, who had been appointed to the West Indies station after his promotion; Andrew Cochrane Johnstone, the former governor of Dominica and now Member of Parliament for Grampound; and their nephew the Member for Westminster.

Marryat was blessed with a family of fifteen sons and daughters of whom one, named Frederick, showed Cochrane's youthful desire to go to sea. Like Cochrane, Frederick Marryat met strong opposition from his father until his persistence finally won him his heart's desire. At the age of 14 he made the same journey by coach to his ship that Cochrane had made when he was 3 years older: such a journey as he described graphically in one of his novels, and a far longer one than Cochrane's for it took him all the way to Plymouth. In his novel the Captain is aboard the coach also, as Cochrane may well have been, since he was appointed to the *Impérieuse* on 23 August 1806 and the 14-year-old midshipman joined her to begin his first voyage under his hero's command on 23 September. At the moment when Cochrane was reaching the zenith of his skill as a seaman, his character and career were to be studied and chronicled by the most outstanding and popular naval writer the English language had ever known.

Midshipman Marryat joined a happy and enthusiastic crew. The men whom Cochrane had been driven to impress by force to serve in the *Pallas* all clamoured to be taken aboard the *Impérieuse.* But since she was a much larger ship, Cochrane also had to post an advertisement on the dockyard walls to attract the extra hands required:

> **Wanted.** Stout, able-bodied men who can run a mile
> without stopping with a sackful of Spanish cobs on
> their backs.

From the applicants he was able to pick and choose until he had made up his complement of 284 men, including thirty-five marines. Guthrie the surgeon, who had held the helm of the *Speedy* when the *Gamo* was captured, was still serving the Cochrane but now he had an assistant. Another midshipman who joined with Marryat was Houston Stewart, who would become an Admiral one day; while the Master's Mate, the Honourable William Napier, was destined to be Britain's first ambassador to China. 'A giant amongst us pigmies,' Marryat recalled him, 'one of the best navigators in the service, he devoted his time and talents to those who wished to learn. At the same time as he laughed and played with us as children, he ensured respect; and although much feared, he was loved much more. . . . Well do I recollect the powerful frame of Napier with his claymore, bounding in advance of his men and cheering them to victory.' There was, in fact, a strong Scottish element aboard; but Marryat also found Henry Cobbett there, nephew of Cochrane's English radical friend.

Frederick Marryat's story of his naval service opens with the latest stroke Cochrane was to suffer at the hands of that old rogue Sir William Young, the Port Admiral at Plymouth. Whether or not he was carrying out instructions from officials of his own stamp at the Admiralty, he forced the *Impérieuse* to sail before she had been properly serviced in the dockyards. 'How nearly,' wrote Marryat, 'were the lives of a fine ship's company, and of Lord Cochrane and his officers, sacrificed to the despotism of an Admiral who *would* be obeyed.'

For the 14-year-old boy making his first trip to sea it was a frightening experience. 'The signal for sailing was enforced by gun after gun; the anchor was hove up and with all her stores on deck, her guns not even mounted, in a state of confusion unparalleled from her being obliged to hoist faster than it was possible she could stow away, she was driven out of harbour to encounter a heavy gale. A few hours more would have enabled her to proceed to sea with security, but they were denied. The consequences were appalling; they might have been fatal. In the general confusion some iron too near the binnacles had attracted the needle of the compasses; the ship was steered out of her course. At midnight, in a heavy gale at the close of November, so dark that you could not distinguish any object however close, the *Impérieuse* dashed upon the rocks between Ushant and the Main. The cry of terror which ran through the lower decks; the grating of the keel as she was forced in; the violence of the shocks which bore her up and carried her clean over the reef will never be effaced from my memory.'

Admiral Young became Sir Hurricane Humbug in Marryat's novels, while Cochrane himself is drawn to the life as Captain Savage in *Peter Simple*. 'A sailor every inch of him. He knew a ship from stern to stern, understood the character of seamen and gained their confidence. He was besides a good mechanic, a carpenter, a rope-maker, sail-maker, cooper. He could hand reef and steer, knot and splice; but he was no orator. He was good tempered, honest and unsophisticated, with a large proportion of common sense and free with his officers.' Many others who knew him were to confirm that this man who could be so rancorous in his public life was by nature affable, courteous in his manners and considerate. His reported speeches provide the best evidence that he often ruined a good argument by his way of presenting it.

Marryat also drew attention to another quality that Cochrane demonstrated on so many occasions. 'I never knew anyone so careful of the lives of his ship's company as Lord Cochrane, or any who calculated so closely the risks attending any expedition. Many of the most brilliant achievements were performed without the loss of a single life, so well did he calculate the chances; and half the merit he deserves for what he did accomplish has never been awarded him, merely because, in the official despatches, there has not been a long list of killed and wounded to please the appetite of the English public.'

It would be hard to find any other commander, either on land or on sea, who possessed this particular gift in such an eminent degree as Cochrane did: and naturally it was the men who shared with him the dangers of active service who were so deeply impressed by it, not the civilian parasites of the war game. For instance, Jahleel Brenton, who had commanded the *Speedy* before him and whose own services were to make him a Knight of the Bath, a Baronet and a Vice Admiral. 'Bold and adventurous as Lord Cochrane was,' Brenton noted particularly, 'no unnecessary exposure of life was ever permitted under his command. Every circumstance was anticipated, every caution against surprise was taken, every provision of success was made; and in this way he was enabled to accomplish the most daring enterprises with comparatively little danger and still less actual loss.'

The chorus of praise from those best able to assess his qualities heaps coals of fire on the men who spent their time denigrating his character—an occupation that has still not ceased. Sir Jahleel's brother Captain Edward Brenton's comments have a particular interest because he published the first biography of Admiral St. Vincent, and might have yielded to prejudice against the critic of Old Jarvie. But on the contrary, he added his own illustrations of Cochrane's wonderful gift.

'No officer ever attempted or succeeded in more arduous enterprises with so little loss. Before he fired a shot he reconnoitred in person, took sounding and bearings, passed whole nights in the boats, his head line and spy glass incessantly at work. Another fixed principle of this officer was never to allow his boats to be unprotected by his ship, if it were possible to lay her within range of the object of attack. With the wind on shore he would veer one of his boats in by a bass hawser (an Indian rope made of grass, which is so light as to float on the surface of the water). By this means he established a communication with the ship, and in case of reverse the boats were hove off by the capstan, while the people in them had only to attend to the use of their weapons.' Such were the feats of ingenuity and seamanship that inspired the future Captain Marryat to write his tales of naval adventure.

He recalled the thrill of his first experience of the sea, so different from Cochrane's placid initiation among the Norwegian fjords. 'The cruises of the *Impérieuse* were periods of continual excitement from the hour in which she hove up her anchor till she dropped it again in port. The day that passed without a shot being fired in anger was with us a blank day. The boats were hardly secured on the booms than they were cast lose and out again. The yard and stay tackles were for ever hoisting up and lowering down. The expedition with which parties were formed for service; the rapidity of the frigate's movements day and night; the hasty sleep, snatched at all hours; the waking up at the report of the guns, which seemed the only key note to the hearts of those on board; the beautiful precision of our fire, obtained by constant practice; the coolness and courage of our Captain, inoculating the whole of the ship's company . . . when memory sweeps along those years of excitement, even now my pulse beats more quickly with the reminiscence.' Such was life aboard the *Impérieuse* when she sailed to join the fleet of Admiral Collingwood in the Mediterranean in September 1807, after Cochrane's interlude at the hustings of Westminster. She travelled in state, having a convoy of thirty-eight merchantmen to escort, some to Gibraltar, the remaining fifteen as far as Malta. Warned by past experience both offensive and defensive, he ran no risks with the ships under his protection, but fired repeatedly at stragglers to bring them back into position.

Of all the Admirals with whom he ever came in contact, there was none for whom he expressed such unqualified admiration as Collingwood; and the respect between these two men, so utterly unlike in character, was mutual. Vice Admiral Lord Collingwood had taken over the command at Trafalgar after the death of Nelson, and had since been appointed to the extraordinarily difficult task of blockading the French fleet in Toulon and stamping out both enemy trade and piracy. He had not revisited his home since 1803, and as his health declined he made repeated requests for leave to do so. But the government found him so irreplaceable that he was kept in harness until he died aboard his ship off Port Mahon in 1810. He opposed the use of flogging and the press-gang, and he treated his crews with such kindness that they called him 'father.'

At a time when communications were slow it was a perpetual problem for Collingwood to determine which ships should be respected as friendly, and which attacked as enemy ones. Officially all ships not flying the British ensign could be regarded as hostile, but a government directive of January 1807 laid down that British commerce was to be safeguarded as far as possible. To promote this, licences were issued to vessels that smuggled British manufactures into foreign markets; which increased the confusion and gave rise to widespread abuses. Cochrane soon had disquieting evidence of them. Soon after he had deposited the remainder of his convoy at Malta he encountered a Maltese privateer off Corsica named the *King George*. She was heavily armed, and in fact a £500 reward had been offered for her capture. Cochrane sent three unarmed boats to enquire her business. Furiously, he informed Collingwood of what followed:

'I am sorry to inform your Lordship of a circumstance which has already been fatal to two of our best men, and I fear of thirteen wounded, two will not survive. These wounds they received in an engagement with a set of desperate savages collected in a privateer, said to be the *King George* of Malta, wherein the only subjects of his Britannic Majesty were three Maltese boys, one Gibraltar man, and a naturalised Captain; the others being renegadoes from all countries, and great part of them belonging to nations at war with Britain.' They had allowed Cochrane's crew to come alongside, under the command of Napier, who was among the wounded, before receiving them with 'a volley of grape and musketry discharged in the most barbarous and savage manner, their muskets and blunderbusses being pointed from beneath the netting close to the people's breasts. The rest of the men and officers then boarded and carried the vessel in the most gallant manner. The bravery shown and exertion used on this occasion were worthy of a better cause.'

Worse was to follow. Somebody with a financial interest in the *King George* brought his influence to bear on that sink of iniquity, the Maltese Court of Admiralty, and a license was produced under which Cochrane was fined for having interfered with what was described as a British vessel. Marryat described the fight for the *King George* in his most famous novel,

Mr. Midshipman Easy, and he recalled elsewhere: 'I never at any time saw Lord Cochrane so much dejected as he was for many days after this affair.'

The system of granting licences to ships that traded in the Mediterranean not only gave raise to genuine confusion, it also offered a huge temptation to dishonesty. For so long as some merchant vessels received the privilege of passes, the authorities who granted them were bound to be exposed to attempts to bribe or influence them. There was also the question of whether a pass was genuine. This was the next difficulty that Cochrane encountered, when Collingwood appointed him to the command of the Corfu squadron whose responsibility was to enforce the blockade off the Ionian islands. He was to succeed Captain Patrick Campbell, an officer who was only a year older than Cochrane, and who would also reach the rank of Admiral.

It was the first time Cochrane had ever been appointed to the command of a squadron, and the commission reflects Collingwood's confidence in him. Cochrane sailed from Valletta early in December and arrived off Corfu to discover that preparations for the transfer of the command had not been completed in the squadron there. Disliking inactivity, Cochrane obtained leave from Campbell to reconnoitre north of Corfu and there, to his surprise, he encountered thirteen merchantmen sailing along the blockaded coast as confidently as if they had been British vessels. Cochrane singled out the three nearest for inspection, and discovered to his further astonishment that each carried a pass from Captain Campbell. Cochrane sent them to Malta for examination by the Court of Admiralty.

Whether or not it had been proper for Captain Campbell to issue those passes, the action he took when he heard what Cochrane had done was not merely an ill-mannered breach of professional etiquette but a grotesque over-reaction for anyone with a clear conscience. Without waiting to discuss the matter with the officer who had come to succeed him, he immediately sent a ship to Admiral Collingwood with a letter complaining that Cochrane's want of discretion rendered him unfit to be entrusted with a single ship, much less with the command of a squadron. As a comment on another officer of about the same age and seniority, this would appear impertinent even if that other officer had not been Cochrane: but such backstairs libel was by no means uncharacteristic of those times. Nor can it be taken as evidence of guilt any more than Campbell's subsequent promotion to the rank of Admiral is evidence that he acted with invariable good sense or integrity.

Collingwood recalled Cochrane without any preliminary enquiry. Homesick, his health ebbing away, his days harassed by a hundred problems, he acted in a typically constructive and conciliatory manner. He was bound to have heard already of Cochrane's reputation for insubordinate and quarrelsome behaviour. It was as a loner that he had become a legend in this war, and Collingwood perhaps blamed himself for not having given him the right appointment in the first place. He wasted no

time now over an angry confrontation between his two Scottish subordinates—particularly since news had just arrived that Russia had declared
war on Britain as Napoleon's ally. He did not even discuss with Cochrane
the grounds for his recall, but expressed his confidence in him by sending
him back to Malta to revictual his ship and thence to harass enemy shipping
off the coasts of France and Spain in total independence. With such an
exciting prospect, Cochrane easily forgot his disappointment that he
would not command a squadron after all, especially an inactive squadron
whose only responsibility was to blockade a few frigates.

There followed the marvellous climax to Cochrane's services in the
British Navy, remembered so vividly by Marryat that 'even now my pulse
beats more quickly with the reminiscence.' The dawn strike after a night
of preparation; the daylight chase under billowing sails; the boarding
party's scuffle on deck; the exploration of holds stacked with merchandise
and munitions; the prizes carried off for adjudication; such was the
ceaseless round of activity, upon which Cochrane was later to reflect: 'One
ship well officered and mannered is more effective than two of the opposite
description and will cost less to the nation. The true strength of the navy
is not in a multitude of ships, but in the energies and alacrity of officers and
crews.' His exploits in the *Impérieuse* have been studied ever since as the
supreme example of the truth of this axiom.

One of the tasks he undertook was to destroy the coastal fortifications
on the islands of Majorca and Minorca. The ship's boats that he had sent
in on one occasion returned after failing to assault the enemy position. At
the gangway Cochrane turned to the coxswain and asked:

'Well, Jack, do you think it impossible to blow up the battery?'

'No, my Lord, it's not impossible,' he replied. 'We can do it if you will
go.'

Cochrane immediately leapt into the cutter and ordered the assault
party to return to the shore, where he and his men made good the
coxswain's words.

On 31 May the *Impérieuse* sailed into Gibraltar for a much-needed
overhaul, and she had hardly arrived when Cochrane heard news of vast
import. Napoleon had attempted to place his brother Joseph Bonaparte on
the throne of Spain, and the country had risen in revolt. It was the signal
for Wellington to land at Oporto and begin the Peninsular war which ended
with his triumphant entry into Paris. From Admiral Collingwood Cochrane
received instructions that he was to give the Spaniards all the assistance in
his power in their resistance to French rule. As Cochrane returned east
along the coast he must have wondered what sort of reception he would
receive from people to whom he had been such a menace hitherto. He need
not have worried. As soon as his frigate reappeared amongst his erstwhile
enemies with British and Spanish colours flying, delighted officials rowed
out to make him welcome, and received him ashore as though El Cid had
arisen from his centuries of sleep to fight for them again. They knew the

value of their new ally from harsh experience. The man who had captured the *Gamo* was now on their side.

Cochrane concentrated his attention on the province of Catalonia, all the principal strongholds of which remained in French hands, and thus began an association with a foreign people that was to be the most satisfactory of his entire career. The Catalans were scarcely less distinct from the Spaniards than the Basques who bestrode the other end of the Pyreneean frontier with France. At frequent periods in their history they had lived under French rule, and they possessed the spirit of independence innate in all frontier peoples. To this day their somewhat ugly and abrupt speech is markedly different from Castilian Spanish; their abundant folklore is all their own; their churches are filled with their rich and original arts. History and geography have combined to give them a character that a Lowland Scot such as Cochrane could salute as much resembling his own.

'The Catalans made capital guerilla troops,' Cochrane recalled, 'possessing considerable skill in the use of their weapons, though previously untrained. A character for turbulence was often attributed to them; but in a country groaning under priestcraft and bad government the sturdy spirit of independence, which prompted them to set the example of heroic defence of their country, might be, either mistakenly or purposely—the latter the more probable—set down for discontent and sedition. At any rate the descendants of men who, in a former age, formed the outposts of the Christian world against Mahomedism in no way disgraced their ancestors, and became in the end the terror of their enemies. One quality they predominantly possessed, patience and endurance under privation; and this, added to their hardy habits and adventurous disposition, contributed to form an enemy not to be despised—the less so that they were in every way disposed to repay the barbarities of the French with interest.' These were the kind of people Cochrane understood and liked and knew how to lead. The partnership began in mutual esteem and was quickly cemented by success.

The principal stronghold of Catalonia was the great seaport of Barcelona, less than a hundred miles from the French border. As it was garrisoned by French troops, Cochrane could do no more than hearten the inhabitants by sailing to a point just out of range of the shore batteries, hoisting British and Spanish colours, and firing a salute of 21 guns. As he did so, he could see the inhabitants crowding excitedly on the housetops and gathering in the public squares, while French cavalry and foot-soldiers were hastily dispersed to intimidate the menacing crowds. From the coastal batteries began a cannonade which merely sent jets of water flying in the air between the *Impérieuse* and the shore. Not knowing how effective the French military presence in Barcelona was, Cochrane made one further gesture to stimulate its citizens. He hoisted British colours over French, and then Spanish colours over French, to the sound of an additional salvo. Then, seeing that a civilian uprising in the capital was out of the question, he departed to explore the situation in the neighbouring towns, and particularly along the road which linked them all to France.

Since the interior was rendered unsafe by guerillas, this road was the indispensable supply route for the French garrisons. So now Cochrane flung himself into the novel trades of engineer and instructor of guerillas, while he maintained the *Impérieuse* as a floating battery, ever ready to bombard any who should attempt to use the road. First he landed with a party of his crew to blow up bridges and dislodge overhanging rocks with gunpowder until the road was blocked. Then he trained local Catalans to continue the same task, which they did with glee. So long as the *Impérieuse* remained at hand to fire on those who attempted to repair the damage, the supply route to Barcelona remained completely blocked.

But Cochrane was called away by intelligence that a French General was approaching with a strong force to augment the garrison at Barcelona. He determined to take possession of the fort of Mongat before the enemy could reach it and hastened there, only to discover that the French advance party had occupied the fort already. There followed the first combined operation in which British seamen and Catalan guerillas together executed one of Cochrane's impromptu master-strokes. There was a band of 800 of these patriots lurking in the neighbourhood, who eagerly agreed to storm the fort of Mongat with British support. But first Cochrane took the precaution of blowing up the road between Barcelona and Mongat so that the separated French forces would be unable to lend one another assistance; then, as the French general still advanced from the other direction, he went ashore to reconnoitre the ground from a hill above the fort. Finally he returned to bring the *Impérieuse* close inshore for the bombardment.

As always, he combined speed with precision and attention to detail, and these precautions proved too great a strain for the impatient Catalans. He had not yet returned with his party of marines when they dashed up a hill to assault a French outpost. The enemy troops hung out flags of truce, but the guerillas would have none of it: they continued their impetuous charge to storm the position, whose defenders maintained a ragged, desultory fire behind their flags to keep the Catalans at bay. Cochrane on the other hand signalled his acceptance of the truce as soon as he had leapt ashore, and was immediately conducted to the castle. He found the troops in it drawn up on either side of the gate, and the French commandant hurried towards him not to allow his Catalan allies to enter with him, and saying that he would surrender to Cochrane alone. He and his soldiers had reason to be thankful that Cochrane exercised such a magnetic influence over the guerillas, for they outnumbered his marines by over twenty to one and yelled for vengeance upon the hated occupiers of their land. And the recorded horrors of the Peninsular war tell what that vengeance might have been like. As it was, the French suffered no more than the abuse of Catalans as Cochrane escorted them to the boats which would carry them to the safety of the *Impérieuse*. He also carried off four brass field pieces and threw the iron guns over their parapets before blowing up the fort of Mongat.

It was the first of the outstanding services of a wholly novel kind that Collingwood reported to the Admiralty with mounting encomiums. There the despatches were filed away in stony silence to await the day when generations of seamen would be trained from the example of his methods, while further generations would be inspired by the same story as it was related by Captain Marryat. And in his old age Cochrane himself could reflect: 'It is wonderful what an amount of terrorism a small frigate is able to inspire on an enemy's coast. Actions between line-of-battle ships are no doubt very imposing, but for real effect I would prefer a score or two of small vessels well handled to any fleet of line-of-battle ships.' Prophetic words.

As a result of the severance of the coastal route from France to Barcelona, achieved by a single frigate, the French troops were compelled to march to the Catalan capital by a circuitous inland route on which they were exposed to the ferocity of the guerillas. The feelings of the Catalans had been further enraged by the steps which the French had taken to repair the coast road. They had not only rounded up the local country people to shift the great blocks of stone, but they had forced them to fill up the holes with everything moveable that they possessed, even their agricultural implements, furniture and clothes. Then, in an attempt to frighten them out of blocking the road again, they had sacked and burned every home in the neighbourhood. The only consequence, of course, was to inspire the Catalans to more furious resistance, and provoke them into more horrible atrocities whenever French soldiers fell into their hands.

By blocking the road and capturing the fort of Mongat, Cochrane had fulfilled the threat he had made off Barcelona a month before when he had hoisted the flags of Britain and Spain over that of France. By mid-August in 1808 the *Impérieuse* had passed beyond the cliffs of the Spanish frontier with France, and lay in the bay of Marseilles. It was Cochrane's intention to destroy another vital means of enemy communication, the signal stations that relayed information about British naval activities up and down the coast, as well as their own military secrets. It was a game that some of his men had learned to play on France's Atlantic seaboard, and they returned to it with enthusiasm.

They demolished their first station without opposition on the 16th, and the following day Cochrane despatched ninety men in boats to attack another on an island in the delta of the river Rhône. Its defenders fled, and the station was demolished with such ease that Cochrane sent the same party to blow up a third the same afternoon. This time they were not only met with a running fire of musketry but bogged down in mud up to the knees as they waded through the swamps of that gigantic estuary at the end of a tiring day. And it is a measure of the fitness and enthusiasm they had attained under their indefatigable Captain's leadership that when they returned 4 hours later, caked with mud and not a man missing, they had accomplished their task.

Without delaying for even a night's rest, Cochrane sailed down the coast through the darkness to surprise his next victims before any warning could reach them. Only when he found their stations guarded by troops did he stay his hand in order not to endanger the lives of his men. But during one night raid he only pretended to retire when his boats were showered with grape shop as they rowed towards the beach. He waited until he judged that the enemy would be off-guard, confident that they had frightened the intruder away, then he personally led his men back, blew up the signal station, and took them along the shore to surprise the battery that had fired on them earlier. Napier was there with his claymore, and Gilbert, the assistant surgeon, who far preferred ploys of this kind to hanging about in the *Impérieuse* waiting for the rare occasion when he and Guthrie had an operation to perform on the table of the midshipmen's mess.

As soon as the men in the battery became aware that the pest had returned—which the explosion from the signal station told them—they opened fire again. But they naturally assumed the assault party was hurrying back to the sea, and so they fired into the darkness in the wrong direction until those leaping figures pounced on them and silenced their guns.

Among these were two brass 24-pounders, which Cochrane was preparing to carry back to his ship in the first light of dawn when the silence was once more broken, this time by a solitary warning shot from the *Impérieuse*. The look-out in the frigate, peering landward through the ebbing darkness, had detected movement which appeared to be that of cavalry advancing over a nearby hill. Although Cochrane could not know the exact nature of the emergency, he could guess that the earlier firing would have alerted French troops in the neighbourhood. But he did not abandon his brass guns: he and his men redoubled their efforts to roll them down to the shore on captured barrels of powder, and they were already being manhandled into the boats by the time the enemy horsemen reached the beach. As usual Cochrane had provided in advance for just such an emergency, by mounting 9-pounder guns in his boats to cover a retreat under attack. The cavalry were kept at bay by these guns while the remainder of the men leapt aboard and the weary oarsmen pulled them out of range. There was only one casualty and it was not achieved by a Frenchman. Seaman Hogan had a box of powder secured to his waist which caught fire as the fusses were lit, blowing him to bits. The rest of the party reached the safety of their ship at 7 o'clock in the morning 'somewhat fatigued by the night's adventure', as Cochrane conceded.

The British gained a long-term advantage from these operations, through the care Cochrane took to deceive the enemy over the fate of their code books. On each occasion when he destroyed a signal station he found the time to scatter all the papers in them in a half burnt condition, in such a way as to convince the French that these books had also been destroyed in the fire. He forwarded them to Admiral Collingwood who was able to read all the information in the enemy semaphores about the movements of French and British ships from the promontory of Italy northwards, simply because nobody thought necessary to alter the code.

While Cochrane returned to report to Collingwood where he lay blockading the French fleet in Toulon harbour, the tale of his achievements leaked far beyond the implacable files of the Admiralty, and his fellow-countryman Walter Scott was the first to give it to the world. 'Lord Cochrane during the month of September 1808, with his single ship, kept the whole coast of Languedoc in alarm—destroyed the numerous semaphoric telegraphs, which were of the utmost consequence to the numerous coasting convoys of the French, and not only prevented any troops from being sent from that province into Spain, but even excited such dismay that 2000 men were withdrawn from Figueras to oppose him, when they would otherwise have been marching farther into the peninsula. The coasting trade was entirely suspended during this alarm; yet with such consummate prudence were all Cochrane's enterprises planned and executed that not one of his men were either killed or hurt, except one, who was singed in blowing up a battery.' Poor Seaman Hogan was more than singed: but Cochrane's autobiography, which records his fate, was not published until long after Walter Scott's death.

In the stern cabin of his flagship off Toulon Admiral Collingwood received Cochrane for the last time, to enjoy his personal account of these phenomenal successes; then despatched him to continue his operations in complete independence. But shortly after the *Impérieuse* had returned to the waters of Marseilles she fell in with the *Spartan* commanded by Jahleel Brenton, and the two captains decided to try some team work. The results were of the kind that heartened the ailing Collingwood to write: 'The activity and zeal of those gallant young men keep up my spirits, and make me equal to bear the disagreeables that happen from the contentions of some other ships. Those who do all the service give me no trouble; those who give the trouble are good for nothing.'

In view of the recurrent failure of personal relations between Cochrane and men of the same profession and social order—Lieutenant Beaver who had brought him to a court-martial, the French officer who challenged him to a duel, Captain Campbell who libelled him behind his back—this new, voluntary partnership with an officer 5 years older than himself and slightly senior in rank is of particular interest. Jahleel Brenton proved in the end to be a more distinguished sailor than either Beavor or Campbell, and he was not jealous of his junior's well-earned fame. He fell in with Cochrane's methods in the most co-operative manner, so that their first combined attack in a signal station defended by troops was an entire success.

The practice it gave them in using two ships and separate contingents of marines enabled them to carry out a more complicated operation at Vendres with even greater precision. The coast where this port lay was defended by shore batteries, cavalry, infantry and even armed peasants. The exploit began as usual with the destruction of a defended signal station followed by a night assault on one of the batteries. Seamen reinforced the marines as they carried the fortification by assault, spiked the guns, destroyed their carriages and blew up the barracks, with such speed that they had embarked again by the time an overwhelming body of troops arrived on the scene with cavalry and artillery.

As they sailed along the coast, only just out of range of the enemy guns, they saw the troops, massing everywhere, determined not to be caught napping again. So this time Cochrane and Brenton decided they would alter their tactics by luring the cavalry away before they got on with their main job. The stratagem was just such a lark as Cochrane loved, and no doubt his men did too. The ships' boys of both the *Spartan* and the *Impérieuse* were dressed up in the scarlet jackets of the marines and despatched in the small boats and the rocket boats to a point well to the right of the real target, as though they intended to make a landing there. Sure enough, as this miniature armada rowed down the coast a body of cavalry set off to receive them. The two frigates meanwhile moved in towards the town they had selected for attack, and although they were hit by the guns from the shore batteries they held their fire until their own broadsides could take full effect. The bombardment continued for an hour, but it did not bring the cavalry back since it was clearly not here that the assault was planned: this was merely a diversion while the marines made their assault farther up the coast.

Then suddenly the real marines were landed in the larger boats that had been kept in reserve for the purpose. As soon as they touched the shore the enemy fled from their guns. While they were being destroyed the enemy cavalry could be seen galloping back to their defence. What these horsemen could observe was that the landing-party was still ashore; the guns were silent; the two frigates now lay close inshore. But they were in far too great a hurry to repair their mistake to evaluate this situation—until they came within musket range of the ships and were mown down by grape shot. Those who retained their saddles fled out of range, leaving the marines to return to the *Spartan* and the *Impérieuse* as though from a spell of shore leave. The ships' boys too rowed back to their ships after their delightful outing in scarlet uniforms.

Jahleel Brenton's co-operation had enabled Cochrane to demonstrate how much more he would have been able to achieve with a squadron than with a single frigate, and Collingwood was not slow to read the same lesson to the Admiralty. 'Nothing can exceed the zeal and activity with which his Lordship pursued the enemy. The success which attends his enterprises clearly indicates with what skill and ability they are conducted, besides keeping the coast in constant alarm—causing a general suspension of trade, and harassing a body of troops employed in opposing him.' Collingwood might have saved his ink.

Cochrane returned to destroy coastal shipping, signal stations and shore batteries on the Spanish side of the frontier on 15 November 1808. The army of occupation there had enjoyed a respite of over 3 months which it was time to terminate. When he sailed back into the bay of Barcelona he discovered that the French were still maintaining themselves uneasily in one quarter of the city, molested by the Catalan peasantry, and he gave them what cheer he could by firing into this sector. He was interrupted 4 days later by news that the enemy were endeavouring to capture the frontier fortress of Rosas, the key to the coast road to Barcelona, and at once sailed there to enact the spectacular finale of his service in the Mediterranean. In it he passed beyond the functions of a naval leader of marine commandos to play the part of a besieged garrison commander.

He arrived at a moment of extreme emergency. The Catalan freedom fighters awaited the approach of an army of 6000 Italian troops in the French service. In an attempt to stiffen their resistance the gallant Captain West of the *Excellent*, a frigate with almost twice the armament of the *Impérieuse*, had flung every man he could spare from his ship into the two principal strongholds of Rosas—the citadel in the town and Fort Trinidad beyond it. This formidable and picturesque fortification climbed up the cliffs from the sea and Cochrane's own description of it can scarcely be improved upon. It was constructed, he found, 'with walls some 50 feet high. Behind this and joined to it rose another fort to the height of 30 or 40 feet more, the whole presenting the appearance of a large church with a tower 110 feet high, a nave 90 feet high, and chancel 50 feet. The tower having its back to the cliff as a matter of course sheltered the middle and lower portions of the fortress from a fire of the battery above it.' This battery had already been established by the French on cliffs behind the fort that were even higher than the tower, but although they subjected the tower to a sustained bombardment they found it to be bomb-proof and therefore could not assail the lower portions of the fort beyond.

The citadel of Rosas was in more immediate danger. Captain West had set his marines to work to make it as defensible as possible and they had defended it with great gallantry against French assault despite its wretched state of repair. The French troops were busy digging entrenchments and bringing up guns with which to batter the citadel into submission when Captain West was superseded by Captain Bennett of the *Fame*, another frigate as well armed as the *Excellent*. But neither of these officers could contribute more than a few dozen men to the defense of Rosas, and the most they hoped to achieve was to retain possession of the two key-points in the hope that a Spanish relieving army would appear before those 6000 Italian troops. When no such help came Bennett withdrew his marines as West had done, and it was immediately after this policy of disengagement had been carried out that Cochrane sailed into the wide semicircle of Rosas bay.

For him to adopt a course that had been abandoned by the future Admiral of the Fleet Sir John West and Captain Richard Bennett, both senior officers and each possessing far superior resources to those of the *Impérieuse*, was virtually to convict them of an error of judgment. At the very least Bennett might have restrained Cochrane on the grounds that he would be entering a death-trap. The wind also exercised a restraining hand, for the *Impérieuse* found herself becalmed almost as soon as she entered the bay: but Cochrane immediately had himself rowed ashore in a gig to make his own appraisal and then returned to lay his plan before Captain Bennett, and found him as co-operative as Jahleel Brenton had been. Bennett did not return himself to take part in the defence of Rosas, but he allowed his junior to embark on the courageous and hazardous attempt.

The wind freshened as Cochrane rowed back to his ship, enabling him to use his favourite weapon—speed. His principal concern was to bring what relief he could to the beleaguered citadel until Spanish troops should arrive to relieve it and to this end he had made a careful study of the positions of the French batteries that were bombarding it and of the trenches that surrounded it. In the rising wind he brought the *Impérieuse* to a range of 600 yards, from which he fired with such effect that the firing of the battery guns was interrupted and the enemy troops were impeded in their digging operations.

At the same time he prepared to re-occupy Fort Trinidad, and the entire operation was executed with such despatch that he had obtained possession of the fort with fifty of his seamen and all his marines the very day after Captain Bennett had evacuated it, before the French could make a move to anticipate him. It was still possible to enter the nethermost of the chain of forts from the beach in perfect safety, but by this time the enemy battery on the hill above their topmost tower had already made a dangerous breach in it. However, the elevation of the guns in this battery was such that the hole was well up the tower wall—as though it were the great west window in Westminster Abbey, as Cochrane explained so graphically. He had brought ashore no guns with which to fire back at the battery on the hill. He concentrated instead on making Fort Trinidad impregnable against attack.

The hole in the tower happened to breach its wall just above a strong stone arch which vaulted the interior 50 feet above its base. Cochrane set his men to smash this arch so that if the enemy should reach the breach they would face a yawning chasm, and as he surveyed his man-trap other devices crowded into his inventive mind. 'I got together all the timber at hand and constructed a huge wooden case, exactly resembling the hopper of a mill—the upper part being kept well greased with cooks' slush from the *Impérieuse*, so that to retain a hold on it was impossible. Down this, with the slightest pressure from behind, the storming party must have fallen to a depth of fifty feet and all they could have done if not killed would have been to remain prisoners at the bottom.' The skeleton crew aboard his ship must have wondered what on earth their Captain would be up to next as they consigned their greasy refuse to Fort Trinidad, and it would not be long before they received their next surprise.

Catalan patriots, seamen and marines entered with gusto into these hectic preparations for an attack, and presently they were joined by a contingent of fifty Irishmen serving with the Spanish forces. In relative safety they repaired the breach as fast as it was widened by French bombardment, but Cochrane himself was hit in the face by a splinter of stone which forced his great nose right back into the cavity of his mouth and caused him intolerable pain. Guthrie the surgeon was summoned to restore it to its original prominence, but to the garrison of Fort Trinidad their commander must have presented a fearsome appearance, with his two black eyes and smashed nose.

After providing for the immediate danger of an assault through the hole in the tower, Cochrane prepared for the contingency of an emergency evacuation. He placed powder in the tower with a train lasting ten minutes, and explosives to demolish the bottom end of the chain of fortifications as soon as the last boat-load of men should have left the shore. Then surveying his handiwork, almost as an afterthought, he invented barbed wire. He ordered ship's chains and a pile of fish-hooks to be brought from the *Impérieuse*, and festooned the chains across the man-trap in the tower so barbed with the fish-hooks that no man caught in them could hope to free himself before he was shot.

During the two days that were spent in making these preparations the French had not been idle on their hill above the tower. First they installed a second battery there which enabled them to enlarge their breach faster than the defenders could repair it. They seem to have had second thoughts because they suddenly launched a night attack, not against Fort Trinidad, but on the town of Rosas.

Captain West, who had begun the defence of these two positions, still kept his 74-gun frigate the *Fame* in company with the *Impérieuse* in the wide bay. Although he was little more than a year older than Cochrane he had obtained his captaincy nearly five years earlier. He nevertheless exhibited the same generous and unselfish patriotism as Jahleel Brenton and Richard Bennett had done in giving his support to the operations of his brilliant junior. The *Fame* now accompanied the *Impérieuse* as she sailed into close range once more, and the two frigates reopened fire on the besiegers. From his fort Cochrane was able to study the enemy's gunnery. 'The practice of the French when breaching the walls of Rosas was beautiful. So skillfully was their gunnery conducted that, to use a schoolboy similitude, every discharge "ruled a straight line" along the lower part of the walls. This being repeated till the upper portion was without support, as a matter of course the whole fell in the ditch, forming a breach of easy ascent.' By dawn the French were in possession of Rosas, just before an army of 2000 Spaniards arrived for its relief. As Cochrane recalled bitterly, 'six hours earlier would have saved the town, the preservation of which was the only object in retaining the fortress'.

But it was not in Cochrane's character to relinquish his foothold without a struggle, even when the Spanish army tamely disappeared back into the hills. The French were now able to bring four more batteries from Rosas to the hill overlooking Fort Trinidad and through the growing din of their bombardment the little garrison waited for the inevitable assault. Twice there was silence as the French ceased firing to offer terms of honourable surrender under flags of truce: twice they were refused.

Cochrane had evidently decided that Frederick Marryat was now old and mature enough to include among his garrison troops, though he could scarcely have dreamed that by doing this he had brought his chronicler with him. Three days after the fall of Rosas the 16-year-old midshipman stood on watch, peering through the dawn mists. As usual the wakeful Cochrane was on the prowl. 'The Captain came out and asked me what I was looking at. I told him I hardly knew; but there did appear something unusual in the valley, immediately below the breach. He listened for a moment, looked attentively with his night-glass, and exclaimed in his firm voice but in an undertoned manner, "To arms! They are coming." In three minutes every man was at his post; and though all were quick there was no time to spare, for by this time the black column of the enemy was distinctly visible, curling along the valley like a great centipede; and, with the daring enterprise so common among the troops of Napoleon, had begun in silence to mount the breach.'

Cochrane gave them particular credit for their silence as they placed their scaling ladders against the walls and 1200 men gathered beneath them. The defenders also made no sound and in this breathless hush of expectancy the first enemy soldiers reached the rim of the breach and saw by the first light of dawn that horrifying chasm with its greased hopper and the barbed chains. At first they could not retreat because their comrades were pressing up the ladders behind them, and so about forty men were swept off their perch by the defenders' fire. Cochrane was looking through the sights of his musket at the officer who stood on the parapet, sword aloft, leading his men. It was a sight reminiscent of the courageous Captain of the *Minerve*, alone on his quarterdeck, who had raised his hat to Cochrane in tribute. 'I never saw a braver or a prouder man,' thought Cochrane to himself, and lowering his musket he shouted to the Frenchman that he was not meant to be shot down like a dog, and was at liberty to return down the ladder. At this the officer 'bowed as politely as though on parade and retired just as leisurely'.

Lest any more should be tempted to scale those ladders, Cochrane now ignited the devices he had prepared with his customary foresight for their discouragement. These were shells suspended from ropes on the outer walls, and to the horror of their explosion was added a hail of hand grenades and musket fire. The dense mass of troops at the base of the tower wavered for a few minutes longer, then they retreated amidst the raucous cheers of the defenders. There were far too many dead bodies to carry away, but Cochrane watched with admiration as they risked their lives to take their wounded comrades with them.

He left the fort himself to bury the French dead, taking with the burial party Midshipman Marryat who commemorated this startling experience in *Frank Mildmay*. Although this was a novel, Marryat's account has always been accepted as an exact description of what occurred that morning below the walls of Fort Trinidad. While the British seamen were digging graves for the corpses the French began to fire at them and Cochrane at once ordered his men to run back to the fort. But 'he himself walked leisurely along through a shower of musket balls'. Marryat described Cochrane a the bravest man he ever met in his life, but such people can be disquieting company. 'As his aide-de-camp I felt bound in honour, as well as duty, to walk by the side of my Captain, fully expecting every moment that a ball would hit me where I should have been ashamed to show the scar. I thought this funeral pace after the funeral was over confounded nonsense, but my fire-eating Captain never had run away from a Frenchman, and did not intend to begin here.'

The resistance of Fort Trinidad not only held down vastly superior forces of French troops; it also prevented these men from concentrating on the reduction of the citadel of Rosas, which still held out despite the capture of the town. But Cochrane was dealing with no novices in the art of war. After their failure to assault his fort they turned all their batteries on the citadel until all at once the boom of their guns was succeeded by an ominous hush, which told Cochrane that the defenders of the citadel were negotiating terms of surrender. As this would release the entire French strength to concentrate on Fort Trinidad and perhaps prevent its garrison from escaping, Cochrane thereupon ordered immediate evacuation.

In the bay of Rosas the *Fame* and *Impérieuse* had been joined by the frigate *Magnificent* of 74 guns. At a signal from the fort all three moved towards the landing-place and the first boats were rowed to the shore under the protection of their guns. The French had read Cochrane's signals and they kept a close watch on the movements that followed. Presently they ceased their fire from the batteries above the tower and despatched a contingent of troops to capture the fort at the moment when Cochrane was despatching his men by rope ladder from the nethermost tower to the boats that awaited them on the beach. Here they were safe from the enemy, protected by the higher ramparts of the fort. It was only as they rowed out into the bay that they ran the gauntlet of the enemy batteries. Cochrane sent the Catalan troops down the ladders first because they had served longest in the fort. Next followed the men from the Irish brigade, while the marines and seamen of the *Impérieuse* were the last to leave. Then the fort was empty except for Cochrane and a gunner, who went to light the trains that would blow up the fort from end to end.

The French troops could by now have reached the breach in the tower, but they had such experience of Cochrane's lethal devices that they hung back warily. It was as well for them that they did, for the first explosion blew up the tower they had been breaching while the garrison was clambering aboard the British ships. Unfortunately the shock affected the portfire which ought to have set off the second explosion so that Cochrane's plan to demolish the fort entirely was frustrated. When the French had waited long enough to satisfy themselves that the lull did not presage another of his infernal tricks they made their entry at last. As Cochrane sailed out of the bay of Rosas he had the mortification of seeing the *tricolore* flying from Fort Trinidad.

But he had held it from 24 November until 5 December after it had been judged untenable, had repelled the assault of an immensely superior force with the loss of three men killed and three seriously injured, and had evacuated his garrison of three nationalities without a single casualty. Trained exclusively as a sailor, he had achieved one of the most exemplary combined operations in British naval record.

Collingwood rammed this down Admiralty throats in despatch after despatch. He told them on 14 December, before he had yet received Cochrane's detailed report: 'Captain Lord Cochrane has maintained himself in possession of Trinity castle with great ability and heroism. Although the fort is laid open by the breach in its works, he has sustained and repelled several assaults, having formed a sort of rampart within the breach with his ship's hammock, cloths, awnings etc. filled with sand and rubbish. The zeal and energy with which he has maintained that fortress excites the highest admiration. His resources for every exigency have no end.' Evidently he had not yet learnt of the chance invention of barbed wire, as a new and terrible weapon of war.

Cochrane's report of 5 December reached him at the speed of sail after he had written those words. 'The citadel of Rosas capitulated at twelve o'clock this day. Seeing, my Lord, farther resistance in the castle of Trinity useless and impracticable against the whole army, the attention of which had naturally turned to its reduction; after firing the trains for exploding the magazines, we embarked in the boats of the *Magnificent, Impérieuse*, and *Fame*.' Those terse words reveal the speed with which he had made and executed his decision to evacuate.

Admiral Collingwood forwarded them with the footnote: 'The heroic spirit and ability which have been evinced by Lord Cochrane in defending this castle, although so shattered in its works, against the repeated attacks of the enemy is an admirable instance of his Lordship's zeal.' With unintentional irony he added, it 'will doubtless be very gratifying to my Lords Commissioners of the Admiralty'.

While the Commissioners of the Admiralty concealed their gratification behind a wall of silence, the Spanish government in Gerona gave Cochrane the first of the encomiums he was to receive from so many foreign countries throughout the world. In so doing it made the common mistake concerning Cochrane's identity as heir to a Scottish chiefship. 'This gallant Englishman has been entitled to the admiration and gratitude of this country from the first moment of its political resurrection.' The Spanish gave a special reason for their gratitude. 'The extraordinary service which we owe to his indefatigable activity, particularly this city and the adjacent coast, in protecting us from the attempts of the enemy, are too well known to be repeated here. It is sufficient eulogium upon his character to mention that in the defence of the castle of Trinidad, when the Spanish flag hoisted on the wall fell into the ditch under a most dreadful fire from the enemy, his Lordship was the only person who, regardless of the shower of balls flying about him, descended into the ditch, returned with the flag and happily succeeded in placing it where it had been.'

Why was the lesson of Rosas and of Cochrane's other operations on the enemy coast so completely lost on the British High Command? Perhaps if Admiral Collingwood had lived to return home he might have succeeded in enlightening those who controlled the direction of the war better than written despatches could do. As it was, these were addressed to William Wellesley-Pole, brother of General Wellington and First Secretary of the Admiralty. He was in regular correspondence with his brother in Spain, and it was only natural that he should have shared the general preoccupation with the military commitment of Britain in the Peninsula. It took Walter Scott, that Tory patriot, to point out as vigorously as any radical could have done the monumental harm caused to the war effort because the Tory war cabinet would not learn the lesson of Cochrane's career.

'The event might have been different had there been a floating army off the coast—the whole of the besieging force might then have been cut off. Of the errors which the British government committed in the conduct of the Spanish war, the neglect of this obvious and most important means of annoying the enemy and advantaging our allies is the most extraordinary. Five thousand men, at the disposal of Lord Cochrane or Sir Sydney Smith, or any of those numerous officers in the British Navy who have given undoubted proofs of their genius as well as courage, would have rendered more service to the common cause than five times that number on shore, because they could at all times chose their points of attack, and the enemy, never knowing where to expect them, would everywhere be in fear and everywhere in reach of the shore in danger.'

Ever since the letter Cochrane had written to Admiral Thornborough from the golden *Pallas*, he had been exploring the immense possibilities of such a strategy on paper, as well as experimenting with it in action as often as he could find an opportunity. He continued to do so when he returned to his routine duties off the Spanish coast after sailing away from Rosas. On one occasion he pounced on an army of no less than 5000 men who were marching along the coast road in the course of a foraging expedition, and scattered them into the interior with extraordinary loss. On another he went ashore to learn what he could from watching a battle between 40,000 Spanish troops and a French army of 10,000 and what he learnt was plenty. The Spaniards were routed and he barely escaped capture as he hurried back to his ship. Admiral Collingwood continued to brief William Wellesley-Pole at the Admiralty without the slightest effect.

Finally Cochrane decided to return home as his own advocate, and applied for leave to do so. 'My reasons for the application were various, the ostensible grounds being the state of my health, which had in reality suffered severely from the incessant wear and tear of body and mind to which for nearly two years I had been exposed.' But he also admitted that 'my chief motive for wishing to return to England was that during our operations against the French on the Spanish coast I had seen so much of them as to convince me that if with a single frigate I could paralyse the movements of their armies in the Mediterranean—with three or four ships it would not be difficult so to spread terror on their Atlantic shores as to render it impossible for them to send an army into Western Spain'. Half a century later he made a more stupendous claim for this strategy than had never been used. 'Had this permission been granted, I do not hesitate to stake my professional reputation that neither the Peninsula war nor its enormous cost to the nation from 1809 onwards would ever have been heard of.'

By the time he wrote that in his old age he had employed his strategy with a success unparalleled in naval history, so that nobody could say it was an extravagant claim although it was far too late to prove whether or not he was right.

It was not merely as a naval hero that Cochrane sailed home to Plymouth, but as a Member of Parliament for Westminster eager to resume his seat 'in order to expose the robberies of the Admiralty Courts in the Mediterranean, the officials of which were reaping colossal fortunes at the expense of naval officers and seamen, who were wasting their lives and blood for official gain'. Their colleagues in Whitehall struck first: 'In place of approbation I was reproached for the expenditure of more sails, stores, gunpowder and shoot than had been used by any other captain in the service'.

From Ian Grimble, *The Sea Wolf*, (London: Blond and Briggs, 1978), pp.71-93.

Chapter 3

The Early American Tradition

While Britain's continental strategy during the Seven Years' War employed substantial elements of raiding, it was in the wide-open North American theater that irregular warfare truly came into its own. Here something that looked, in terms of organization and training, like distinct special operations forces, began to emerge. In the raid on St. Francis, Rogers' Rangers performed a successful strike on enemy forces deep behind the lines held by the regulars, even though they were detected early on, and pursued all along the elliptical course that marked the approach and return phases of their operation. Their success, despite the substantial loss of surprise, may be explained by the pace of their operations, which succeeded in keeping one step ahead of the French ability to order and organize countermoves.

Soon after this experience, during the Revolution, American forces demonstrated a penchant for protracted guerrilla warfare in the remarkable campaign in the South, which was won, and won freedom for the colonies, despite the absence of victory in open battle against the British. This facility for irregular warfare would be demonstrated again soon in the clash with the Barbary pirates who, even in the 19th century, still pursued their predations against Christendom (or at least against those Christians who neither paid tribute nor posed serious threats against them). William Eaton's odd insurgency, though eventually called off when the Tripolitan government acceded to American demands for the release of hostages, provides a clear example of the use of special operations in support of a diplomatic strategy of coercion.

Kenneth Roberts

The Raid on St. Francis

Rogers hitched up his leggins and settled his black infantryman's hat more firmly on his head. "Why," he said, "that's not bad! Things might be worse--lots worse! I could take Quebec with a hundred and forty-two men as good as this! We'll keep the same order. Stockbridge Indians in advance: Lieutenant Turner's detachment in the rear."

After what we had been through, the Indian trail along the high bank of the river was as easy to travel as a post-road. The trees were enormous: the undergrowth long since killed down. Beneath our feet was packed earth and brown pine needles, springy to the touch. If I could have had a decent dinner in me, in place of the few scrapings of corn meal that my pouch had yielded, and if there had been no Frenchmen following on our heels, I think I might really have enjoyed that hurrying march down the St. Franics.

The long line of men in ragged buckskins and green Scotch caps slipped through the darkening forest as noiselessly as owls on the hunt.

It was nearly night when Rogers, finding a tall pine from which to make an observation, gave the order to halt. He was on his way up the tree before the file-closers had come in.

We stared up the tree after him. The detachment gathered around it, their upturned faces blobs of pallor in the dusk. He came sliding and scratching down and dropped among us like a big cat. He straightened his clothes and dug pine needles from his neck. "Well," he said, we're there! I can see the fires, not three miles away. It's the town!"

It was the fifth day of October--the twenty-second day of our journey from Crown Point. We had been twenty-two days without fires; without cooked food; without dry blankets; without shelters over our heads; without clean clothes. And this was the campaign my father, over a months ago, had characterized as being almost over.

Rogers, it seemed to me, could go beyond the limits of human endurance; and then, without rest, buoyantly hurl himself against the fiercest opposition of Nature or man, or both. There was something elemental about him--something that made it possible for men who were dead with fatigue to gain renewed energy from him, just as a drooping wheat-field is stirred to life by the wall of wind that runs before a thunder-storm.

We'd no sooner made camp that night than he called for Lieutenant Turner and Ensign Avery; and the three of them moved silently off into the darkness, Rogers leading at a gait so sharp it was a sort of inaudible run.

He left one order behind him. "Make 'em sleep," he told Ogden. "They're going to need it!"

Sleep, for me, I thought, was out of the question, for I was in a turmoil over the thought that in a few hours we would be fighting. There was no possible way to escape it; and I suspected that I was already as good as dead. I saw with dreadful clarity what a fool I had been about everything, and wished to God I had stayed home, content with an orderly existence. Of what use to me was my foolish, youthful desire to paint, and how would my knack for drawing and for color benefit me when I lay scalped and mangled in a Canadian forest? If I had stayed at home, where I could see Elizabeth's eyes darting amused and sidelong glances at me: where I could have sat comfortably in our warm kitchen on a frosty morning and watched my mother pouring flapjack batter . . .

Sergeant Bradley shook me to consciousness. "Come on," he was saying. "Come on! The Major's back. Everything's all right! Come on: we're going to attack!"

The moon, almost full, touched the tall trees with silver and gave us a faint light, even in the blackest shadows. All around me I could see men moving; hear straps being tightened; ramrods being drawn and rapped home again. "What time is it?" I asked Bradley.

"Time to get up! Come on, for God's sake. The Major's going to talk to us."

I collected my equipment and felt myself all over to be sure I had everything--orderly book, bayonet, hatchet, flints, bullets, powder, blanket, knife, cup, fork, salt, razor, soap. The soap was little smaller than when I had left Crown Point, but when I sniffed at it, wondering whether I'd ever have another opportunity to clean myself, Bradley pulled at me impatiently, pressing me toward a tight-packed throng of men. They had a steamy, animal smell--a smell of wet buckskins, musky bodies, oily hair. Over their shoulders I could see the blue-green glow of a sulphur spunk shining on Rogers' big nose and thick lips. He was comparing his compass with Ogden's and Dunbar's. When he looked up, the spunk threw shadows over his eyes and the hollows of his face, giving it the look of a grinning death's head.

"Everybody accounted for?" he asked.

There was a muttering of "all present" from the sergeants.

"All right," Rogers said. "Now pay attention! Lieutenant Turner and Ensign Avery went with me to look at the town. It's stretched along the high bank, just the right size and position for an attack, and the trail leads straight to it. Everything's in our favor--even the wind. It's in the west, and the dogs can't get our smell."

"Good thing for the dogs," somebody muttered. The men tittered with the sound of wind stirring dry leaves.

Rogers seemed not to hear. "We went up trees and watched 'em. They haven't got a sentry out--not one! They've been dancing nearly all night. They were dancing when we came away at midnight--howling and whooping and having a hell of a time. Maybe they're drunk, but don't count on it."

From the mass of Rangers before him there rose a pleased murmuring.

"Now bear this in mind," Rogers went on. "We can't waste time! We got to work fast and get away, because they'll be after us like hornets. We're under orders to wipe out this town, so see you do it! There's only one way to do it and that's to kill 'em dead! Don't let a damned Indian get away, provided he's big enough to fight. But for God's sake don't kill any of our own Indians, and don't kill any white captives. Our own Indians have white stripes painted around their bodies, and the tops of their heads are painted white. As for captives, there'll be some around; so keep your eyes open and don't make mistakes."

He paused. There was something so peculiarly exciting about those thick accents of his that I found myself shaking. His voice grew harsher. "Our food's gone. So's our clothes. We'll need food and clothes if we expect to be alive this time next week."

His sulphur spunk flickered and went out, and his face disappeared as though it had been that of a grinning demon who, having warned us, had vanished into the realm of disembodied spirits, but his voice went on. "Don't forget how they treated Phillips and Crofton. If we don't wipe 'em out now, they'll go down into New England and skin our people alive, the way they always have."

There was a moment of silence, as heavy as the forest gloom around us.

"Here's the way we'll do it," that thick voice continued. "We'll move up to the edge of the woods and wait for daylight. Captain Ogden's detachment and Captain Jacobs' Indians will attack the right of the town. That's the downstream end, and downstream's the way they'll run if they get the chance."

Everything was planned, as neat as a pin. We were to move out of the woods in a long line, Captain Ogden, Captain Jacobs, Lieutenant Farrington and Lieutenant Grant leading; in the center, Lieutenant Dunbar, Lieutenant Turner and Ensign Avery; in the rear, Lieutenant Jenkins, Lieutenant Campbell and Lieutenant Curgill. When Rogers whistled, the officers and their sergeants were to break down the doors of the houses; and the rest of us, ten paces back, were to wait for the Indians to come out. One man from each detachment was to hunt out a kettle, find food to fill it, take the kettle to a common center, and get the food to cooking as soon as possible.

Rogers himself would be at the downstream end of the town--in case anyone wanted him, he said. Prisoners were to be brought to Lieutenant Dunbar, who would halt his detachment at the drum.

I asked Jesse Beacham what he meant by the drum. Jesse said patiently that when I got where we were going, I'd probably see something that looked like a drum, because if Rogers spoke of anything, you could usually depend on seeing it when you got there.

"Ready," Rogers said. "As they've got no sentries out, we'll travel single file. We'll use no flankers and no advance scouts. Keep in touch with the man in front. That's all. Come on."

I heard Ogden call for Sergeant Bradley, who took me by the knapsack and pulled me forward. Someone caught the slack of my buckskin shirt and shuffled after me, and hands fumbled at me as we moved off past men who whispered irascibly and breathed hard.

The hurrying of the men along that dark and narrow lane between the trees caused a rubbing, whispering, hissing sound that might have been made by a gargantuan serpent. They seemed to flicker through the patches of moonlight like specters.

I felt a stirring in the still, cool air--the stirring of approaching dawn; and at last, on that faint and frosty breeze, I caught the scent of wood-smoke.

Ogden, standing in the path, stopped us. "Dump your packs." We put our blankets, our knapsacks and everything we could spare in compact piles beside the path; then squatted in the trail, working our bayonets over our musket-sights.

The moonlight on the treetops had dimmed, now, and the shadows around us were pallid in a ghostly light--the light of false dawn. In that ghostly light Captain Jacobs and his Indians, crowded close behind us, had the look of dismembered phantoms. Because of the white paint upon them, they seemed like human lobster-buoys, bobbing silently in the murk. I could faintly see the other detachments; hear them dump their packs and adjust their bayonets.

Somewhere in front of us I heard the strident crowing of a rooster.

The false dawn had passed and the shadows were blacker than before. Not far from us a dog barked mournfully, perfunctorily. The men whispered and muttered, fearful that the barking might arouse the sleeping town. I wanted to speak to Jesse Beacham about that dog, but I knew that if I did, my teeth would chatter. I was cold and hungry; worst of all, I was afraid: afraid of the dog: afraid of what lay before us: afraid of being afraid. The dog, as if dissatisfied with his first attempt, barked again--a bark lugubrious beyond belief--and Jesse Beacham sighed shiveringly. It came to me that Jesse was as hungry and cold and afraid as I.

Then I realized that real dawn was coming upon us, and I saw Rogers and Ogden, gray figures against dark tree trunks, staring out at a clearing that began to be revealed before us.

Rogers looked up at the sky: then came back to us, and Sergeant Bradley rose to meet him. "You'll take the downstream end," Rogers said. "Don't make a noise, and don't let 'em get away." He moved along the recumbent line, which was still strung out in single file along the trail, and I saw Lieutenant Farrington, Lieutenant Dunbar, Lieutenant Grant, rising one by one to take his orders: then lying down again.

The mist in the clearing was thin. It rolled up like smoke from the bed of the river, billowing slowly; and through it, as through a veil, we saw the houses of St. Francis. They were strewn along the river bank, on each side of a church with a skeleton steeple, in which hung a bell. Some of the cabins were made of logs and some of planks, like the homes of white men; but they stood at odd angles, as if each one had been pushed a little out of position, so that they had the unreality of houses seen in a dream. It was hard to realize that out of this miserable line of hovels had come the painted demons who had terrorized all New England for a century: that it was in this very town that young Richard Nason and little Sarah Nason, ancestors of mine, had lived for years as captives.

The place looked deserted--dead. Nothing moved in the clearing or near the houses, and that look of deadness was heightened by the frost that lay whitely on every roof as well as on cultivated patches in the clearing. The patches were little farms--corn fields; melon and pumpkin patches. In some were piles of pumpkins.

Rogers came back, loosened his hatchet in his belt, picked up his musket; then swung his arm, scythe-like. The white-smeared Indians, the whole long line of green-clad, bearded men, rose to their feet and began to run into the clearing.

At every step I took, I expected the doors and windows of that misty village to fly open: to spout fire against the long thin line of Rangers running toward it.

The noise we made seemed loud enough to wake the dead. Our feet crunched the frosty ground: our powder-horns and shot pouches thumped and rattled at our hips.

What I was doing seemed familiar, as if I had often done this very thing; and it came to me, as I ran, that it was like the final stealthy race to reach a river bank before hidden ducks leaped out of range.

There was a pink streak in the eastern sky, and by its pale light, as we ran panting on, I could see poles before the black cabins--poles with hairy discs hanging from their tips; and I could smell the place. It had a rank but pleasant odor, as of herbs mixed with grease, sweet-grass and wood-smoke. The strip of ground before the houses was as hard and level as the roadway in a city: as smooth as a dance floor; and I understood that it was indeed a dance floor, where the Indians danced. In its center stood a drum, made of a tree trunk as big around as a washtub and almost shoulder-tall.

The windows of the houses were unglazed: some were black holes: others were covered with paper on which were painted fish, birds, animals. Skins lashed to frames leaned against the walls. The hairy discs on the poles, I now saw, were scalps, and there were hundreds of them, moving gently in the dawn breeze. I wondered if the scalp of Crofton's brother was among them.

We ran on and on across the clearing, our eyes fixed upon that line of dark houses on the river bank, expecting each moment that Indians would burst out of the doors and that fire would leap at us from the windows. I was near the head of our people, and with those who were to attack the far end of the village. We passed the flimsy little church with its skeleton steeple: we passed the cabins beyond the church, and came abreast of the last buildings at the lower end of the town. A skinny black dog with a yellow face ran out at us. His hackles rose and his lips drew back over his teeth, but before he could even snarl, a thrown hatchet struck his head and he fell on his side, his legs jerking.

The whole line had stopped, crouching, their muskets ready. Rogers, ahead of us, whistled through his fingers--a whistle that cut our straining ears like a knife. And then, toward the silent houses, raced the lieutenants and sergeants, while Jacobs and his Stockbridge Indians dodged among the cabins like shadows. Directly before me I saw a low log house with the river running dimly behind it. Sergeant Bradley and Lieutenant Farrington threw themselves against the rough door of that house; the door broke from its hinges with a splitting crash.

Then, almost in the same instant, the whole village seemed to erupt with yells, crashes and screams. From the doorway smashed by Bradley and Farrington there came stumbling an old Indian with a blanket tied around his waist; he tripped on the blanket and fell. Bradley sank a hatchet into the small of the brown back, then jumped to one side.

Out through the doorway burst three squaws, their faces contorted. Bradley thrust his foot before them and they fell in a heap. A well-sized Indian boy, trying to leap over them, fell too, and Farrington was on his back like a cat. I saw white eyes roll upward in the twisted, copper-colored face: then Farrington's hatchet cut down through them.

The squaws, covered with blood, scrambled to their feet. Bradley caught two by the arms, rammed his bayonet through their upper garments and rushed them, whimpering, behind our waiting line. The other ran like a frightened duck, toeing in.

Two faces showed in the doorway, and Jesse Beacham's musket roared in my ear. One of the faces vanished: the other, half shot away, came slowly into full view: the body beneath it sank forward across the threshold.

A girl and two boys squirmed around it as it fell and ran toward us, dodging from side to side, as if hunting a hole. One of the boys was almost the size of my brother Odiorne. When Crofton's musket swung toward him, I pushed it away and caught the boy.

He was greasy and like an eel in my hands, writhing and twisting to break my hold, but I dropped my musket and got him between my knees, where he squirmed and bucked so hard that it seemed impossible one boy could move in so many directions at one time. Crofton stood before me, looking for an opportunity to sink his bayonet in the writhing red body.

"Too young," I said. "Prisoner."

Crofton stared wildly at me; then turned back to watch the doorway. I rapped the base of the boy's skull with my fist; and when he lay still, I picked up my musket, took him by the arm and dragged him to Dunbar's detachment.

Dunbar's men were in a ring around the drum, and Dunbar himself stood upon the drum, giving orders. Pressed close to the drum were squaws, covered with dirt, their clothes half torn off: a few young girls, one wholly naked: another boy. They were huddled on the ground, not moving or making a sound, and not one looked toward the bedlam beyond.

I threw the boy at the feet of one of Dunbar's Rangers: then ran back to my own detachment.

The strip of pink in the eastern sky had turned to a brilliant red, and in its rosy light the darting movements of the Rangers seemed purposeless, like the erratic scuttling of water-beetles on a placid pond. The rattling of their muskets was as rapid as the crackling of twigs in a newly-lit fire, and overhead everywhere drifted layers of gunpowder smoke turning pink in the sunrise.

Two more Indians lay on the ground before the end house when I got back, one a woman--a squaw. Crofton, his face crimson, was shouting like a madman: "There's more of 'em! I saw 'em! I tell you I saw 'em!"

Captain Ogden took him by the arm and shook him; then ran forward and into the house. From within came the sound of two shots, almost together. Ogden backed out again, stepped to one side for shelter, drew the ramrod from his musket, reached for his powder-horn: then leaned against the wall, looking down at his side. The hand that held the powder-horn was covered with blood, and when Bradley and Crofton ran to him, he coughed and sat down heavily. Upon that, both Bradley and Crofton swung away from him, but only to spring into the doorway from which he had emerged.

From the dark interior came a sound of agonized choking: then a sickening pounding and a muffled musket shot.

Then Lieutenant Grant came running from behind the house, shouting, "They're getting away! They're going down river in canoes!"

Jesse Beacham and I ran around the house and down the bank of the river, and although we went as fast as our legs could take us, Rogers was ahead of us, and his voice rang out, not thick, but high and keen. It brought Captain Jacobs and a dozen white-barred Stockbridge Indians tearing after him like a pack of wolves; and behind us I could hear others running and shouting.

The St. Francis at this point was deeper than where we had crossed, and the water ran smooth and brown, with a glassy look. Sunrise was full upon us, and on the shining river was mirrored the blazing colors of the trees on the opposite bank. Black heads moved slowly on this gaudy stream, making for the further shore; and lower down were five canoes, driving swiftly toward the shadowy north. In one were six Indians, paddling raggedly: in another four. The canoes lurched and wobbled from the overhasty paddle strokes of the naked red men. The three hindmost canoes were small ones, and the savages in them, having no paddles, were paddling with their hands and singing a wild, defiant song.

Rogers dropped to his knee and fired. In the leading canoe an Indian stood upright, stumbled backward and fell sideways against the paddlers in the stern. The little craft made an abrupt curve and overturned, and its six passengers disappeared in a flurry of yellow foam.

Along the bank Rangers began to follow the canoes, and around me others were kneeling and firing. I heard them calling their shots. "I'll take the one coming out on the bank," Jesse said. His musket jetted smoke, and an Indian who had reached the shallows of the farther shore stopped where he was. His head fell forward, and his legs, floating, slowly swung downstream.

I heard myself saying, "Good shot!"

"That's three I got," Jesse said mildly. "I got a nice one while you was hauling that boy away--pretty a shot as ever I made. Just caught a flash of him between the houses--snap shot, from the hip."

From between the middle fingers of his left hand he dropped a ball in his musket and smoothly pressed it with his ramrod, staring eagerly downstream at a head that moved at the apex of a wedge of riffles--riffles that were flame-colored from the reflection of the young maples. I raised my musket and drew a bead on the head. It was easy, like dropping a slow-flying partridge. The head plunged under water: the tip of the wedge of ripples became a swirl: the man's whole back came to the surface, rolling sluggishly, and I was aware, with a dully horrified astonishment at myself, that I felt the same satisfaction I'd often felt in seeing a partridge fold up in mid-flight.

The banging of muskets was continuous. Abreast of us, where heads had moved across the gaily colored stream, there were dark bodies floating, face downward. The singing had stopped, and of the five canoes, four were empty, half-full of water, broadside to the current. In the fifth, one man, kneeling, paddled desperately with both hands, while spouts of water shot upward from the surface beyond him.

Jesse shook his white head. "Those fellers must be excited! I wisht we was down there. I'd like to get just one more."

The paddler half rose to his feet and seized the gunnles with both hands. One of he gunnles went under water, and as the canoe overturned I saw that it threw out a squaw with a baby upon her breast. She'd been lying full length in the canoe, and perhaps she was already dead, for she made no effort to swim, but disappeared at once. The male Indian rolled twice, like a porpoise, and it seemed to me he was vainly trying to dive for the woman, or to swim under water; he came up once, but not again.

Then I heard Rogers shout, recalling the men who'd gone along the bank; and turning, I saw the lifting disc of the sun clearing itself above the line of shattered cabins. Jesse Beacham blinked, as if awakened by the golden light. The shadows of the Rangers near us stretched out across the trampled, frosty grass, gigantic though cast by human mites. Everything except the wide sun and the long shadows seemed to have shrunk and become small.

Lieutenant Turner and Lieutenant Farrington were standing with Rogers, who swung his arm at us and shouted angrily, "Get those men back here! Call 'em back to the drum! I want this detachment paraded!"

We started back toward the houses, running.

"Towne!" the Major called. "I want you! You'll be needed when we examine the prisoners.

The smooth dance-ground before the houses was littered with the bodies of Indians, and the houses themselves seemed to have aged immeasurably in the half hour since we had started across the clearing-- unbelievably it was only half an hour since then. Their doors stood open or were broken down: the paper at the windows hung in strips: fragments of cloth and buckskins trailed across the thresholds: blankets and household goods were strewn around them. The poles erected before each cabin stood at drunken angles or lay flat, and in the brilliant light of the newly risen sun, St. Francis was squalid beyond belief.

Clumps of Rangers stood before the dwellings, eating from Indian bowls and staring watchfully at the roofs and upper parts of the cabins; for we knew that a few Indians were still hidden in the shadow cellars and shallower lofts. Among the dead moved other Rangers, prodding at bodies with bayonets, looking for silver bracelets, and peering intently at dusky faces to be sure that they were dead. Still others were busy wrapping strips of cloth around their lower legs, fitting themselves with moccasins, drawing Indian leggins over tattered buckskins. Behind us burned a circle of fires, each one tended by a Ranger; and over each fire hung a steaming kettle--a sight which made my stomach squeak for food.

Around the drum, herded like sheep by Dunbar's men, were twenty-five women and children. For the most part the women wore short skirts of blue cloth, and blue cloth upper garments that came to their thighs. A few carried brats with dirty noses. The naked girl had somehow clothed herself, and the boy I had cracked on the head and dragged away from Crofton was hunkered down against the drum with another smaller boy, both staring slackmouthed at Ogden, who sat, stripped to the waist, on the ground nearby.

On Ogden's ribs were the double purple bruises of a bullet-hole, and beside him sat Bradley sopping a piece of white strouding in a kettle and pressing it to the two wounds.

The next day, the third of our retreat, the trail vanished in a bog, not as bad as the one in which we had spent nine days after leaving Missisquoi, but bad enough. There were deadfalls all through it, and masses of young growth that whipped at us whenever we moved.

Through this bog the river curved in enormous loops, and somehow Rogers felt where they were without seeing them. It is true that he kept four Stockbridge Indians ahead of our line with orders to report any alteration in the river's course, and it is also true that he had Captain Stark's rough map, drawn from the vague memories of his captive days. The loops were indicated on that map, but Stark hadn't remembered just where they were. Rogers anticipated them.

There was something animal-like about the manner in which he always took the proper turning: always knew when he had gone the proper distance. I shall always think he possessed an instinct the rest of us didn't have--the same instinct that infallibly brings a dog home, no matter how winding the trackless course he follows.

When Rogers turned us at right angles to the river and sent us splashing and stumbling to the westward, I had complete faith in him. When, at the end of three hours of struggling, we found ourselves once more looking out over the brown and turbulent St. Francis, it seemed an everyday occurrence instead of the miracle that it really was.

To put down those words, "three hours of struggling," is easy; but I could write forever without learning how to describe the endlessness of those three hours: the aching legs; the twig-whipped face and hands; the trickling sweat that stung my eyes; the recurring anger at the tree-trunks which lay with hellish ingenuity in the path, the under-water holes and trenches that tortured our blistered feet; the little sticks that crawled beneath belt and collar to rub the sweaty skin; the perversity with which knapsack and musket snagged themselves on stumps and branches; the dodging and bending to escape the clutching undergrowth; the eternal necessity of hurrying on and on and on; the never-absent knowledge that close on our heels were men whose sole object in life was to put bullets through us--to sink hatchets in our brains.

No one can know these things who has never fought his way through a pathless forest, with enemies behind him, immensity before him, and a sackful of corn between him and starvation.

So at the end of three hours of struggling we came to the river again, and slept that night on dry land, which we couldn't have done unless Rogers had led us across the bend.

Some of the nights of our retreat aren't clear to me. They lose themselves in each other, as sequential nightmares blend indistinguishably into one horrible dream. The third night I remember clearly because it was the night Jennie Coit attached herself to Ogden, and the night Rogers figured out for us how much corn we could allow ourselves to eat a day.

We had no sooner stopped, settled our packs and muskets, got out our handfuls of corn and gone to crunching them, when I heard Jennie's voice, harsh and hoarse, say something in the Abenaki language, and I thought, from her tone, she was saying something unpleasant. A moment later she ran in among us, with Konkapot after her.

In the bright light of the moon, her face looked pale blue; her yellow hair green. She was furious.

Rogers had gone down the line as soon as we stopped, to make sure everything was all right; so Sergeant Bradley stepped forward as acting commander of the detachment. "What the hell you doing?" he asked Jennie. "Get back where you belong!"

I'm going to see Captain Ogden," she said, "going to fix his bandage."

"We got two Indian boys looking out for Captain Ogden," Bradley told her. "If the Major finds you up here, you'll lose your hair."

With her lips Jennie made an unladylike noise; stepped quickly past Bradley and started for Ogden. Bradley caught her by the arm and jerked her back. As she turned, she swung her fist, catching Bradley on the ear with the sound of a rock hitting a bag of walnuts. He let her go and staggered back, pawing at the side of his head. She darted to Ogden, and I saw her kneeling beside him, holding him up and fumbling with his shirt.

"Well," Jesse Beacham said mildly, "she's getting rough, aint she?"

Bradley walked after her, stood looking down at Jennie and Ogden, then turned to Konkapot. "All right, Konkapot," Bradley said, "don't worry about this mink. We'll let the Major tend to her. You go on back and tell Captain Jacobs the Major'll look after her."

Jennie had Ogden's shirt off by then, and crouching over him she unwrapped his bandage, making mothering sounds. When she'd got it off, she began to knead the flesh about his wounds gently, and she was doing this when Rogers returned. Moving without a sound, he came close behind her and just stood there, watching her.

Then she rose to her feet, with the bandage in her hand, and bumped against him and recoiled, as from a stone wall.

"Who sent you up here?" Rogers growled.

"Who do you think sent me?" she snarled. "Not those foul old strumpets I have to march with!"

"Nobody else, either!" Rogers said. "When I want women around me, I send for 'em! Don't start raising hell with these men of mine or I'll turn you loose in the woods."

"Go ahead!" she cried. "Go ahead and turn me loose! I didn't ask to be brought, did I? I'd rather take a chance with Mohawks or looservees than with you and your men! Turn me loose and turn Captain Ogden loose, too, why don't you, so I can take care of him! Maybe I could find him a cow moose to lick his bullet holes. If he stays with you, there won't be nobody or nothing bother with 'em—only maggots. Look at this!" She thrust Ogden's bandage almost against Rogers' face and shook it at him. "Look at it! Why don't you have him tended to? Who changed that bandage last? I did, last night! It ought to be changed three times a day, so it don't dry on him. He ought to be washed! "

"These Indian boys can wash him," Rogers said.

"You're a liar! No wonder they call you Wobi madaondo! Those boys never washed themselves or anything else in their lives! They wouldn't know how to! They're lousy, both of 'em, and so's Captain Ogden, probably, from leaning on 'em. Look at 'em in the morning and see if they aren't. He's got to be stripped and cleaned, and he's got to have his bandage washed. Get out of my way, you big spider, so I can tend to him!"

She pushed past Rogers and stamped off toward the river through the moonlit brush. Rogers thrust a thick finger under his black hat and scratched his head: then went closer to Ogden. "We'll have to look out for that girl, Captain," he said. "I don't believe she's much good."

"She's pretty handy," Ogden said faintly. "I guess I *would* feel better if she fixed that bandage three times a day, like she said."

"Well," Rogers said reluctantly, "I'll let her move up and fix it, but when she's fixed it, send her back to her mother. I don't want her around the other men. Somebody'll get into a fight over her."

Ogden just whispered, "How far is it to Memphremagog?"

"Ask the girl," Rogers said. "She's going to take care of you." He laughed indulgently. "Memphremagog! Doesn't anybody think about anything except Memphremagog?"

Jennie came back, went down on her knees beside Ogden and lifted him so that he leaned against her shoulder.

She looked up at Rogers. "Why don't you tell him how far it is?" As she spoke she was binding the white strouding around Ogden's two bullet-holes. Still holding him against her shoulder, as a mother holds a sick child, she slipped his buckskin shirt over his head and put his arms in the sleeves for him. Then she picked up his knapsack, unstrapped it, peered within and shook her head. "You've been overeating! How much of that corn did you eat today?"

Ogden looked a little ashamed. "I had two handfuls. I got pretty hungry. I guess it was maybe losing blood that made me want so much."

"It doesn't make any difference what makes you want it," she cried. "You can't have it! You can have one handful of corn a day. One handful: understand?"

"You talk like a fool!" Rogers said.

Jennie leaped to her feet and shook her fist at him. "Tell him how far it is to Memphremagog! It's not knowing what to expect that drives anyone crazy—Frenchmen behind us, nobody knows where; Memphremagog ahead of us, nobody knows how far! I'd tell him if I knew! I'd be telling him all the time, if I stayed with him--yes, and that's where I'm going to stay!"

Rogers stared at her with protuberant eyes. "Lord, but you're noisy!" he said, and sat down a few feet away, took a handful of corn from his knapsack and began to eat, making smacking noises with his thick lips.

"Bring me the book," he called to me; and by the light of the moon he began to study the map I had copied long, long ago--on the night before we struck into the spruce bog from the shores of Missisquoi Bay. Afterward, he lay on his back, staring up at the shafts of moonlight that pierced the trees above us, and I could see that he was moving his lips as if he were reading. Ogden had fallen asleep; and Jennie, sitting beside him, looked down at his face intently. She no longer seemed bold and hard, but helpless and gentle, though I knew she was neither; yet I knew, too, that the rest of us had ceased to exist for her. Yesterday we had been potential prey: today we were potential nuisances who were like to interfere blunderingly with her care for the sick man.

Rogers gave the book back to me. "Here, write down what I tell the sergeant, so there won't be any misunderstanding about it."

He whistled to Bradley, who came to him, covertly eyeing Jennie.

"How much corn you used, Sergeant?" Rogers asked.

"About half," Bradley said, "I guess my knapsack's half full still."

"That won't do," Rogers said, "You're using too much. So's everybody else. We only made eight miles today."

"Well," Bradley said, "that only leaves us forty miles to go, doesn't it?"

Rogers' face looked wooden. "I've been going over Stark's map. Sometime tomorrow, probably, we'll strike pretty bad going. I don't believe this command can make a great many miles a day from now on. The going'll mostly be up hill."

"We could split up and hunt for food," Bradley said.

"Not here we couldn't," Rogers told him quickly. "There's only one way to go, and that's along the banks of this river. Anybody that leaves the river any distance won't get back, and would likely get scalped before long. We've got to stick together till we're past Memphremagog."

Bradley looked doubtful. "I'll tell 'em to eat less." And somewhat unnecessarily, I thought, he added, "They're right hungry."

"Can't help it! They're to do as I say, or they'll be a hell of a lot hungrier! Tell 'em to divide their corn into six parts—six, say, or seven or eight— and not to eat more than one of the parts every day, no matter how hungry they get! If they can eat less than that, they'd better."

"I'll tell 'em Major. There's another thing, though. They're all arguing about how far it is from here to the Ammonoosuc, where you said there'd be food. They keep talking about it all the time. Not knowing nothing about how far it is, they're making some pretty wild guesses."

"Make 'em stop it!" Roger ordered. "I'll tell 'em how far it is. It isn't much over a hundred miles, as the crow flies, from the northern end of Memphremagog to the Ammonoosuc. Call it a hundred and ten. That's all it is. I've been over it myself."

"As the crow flies!" Bradley's mouth dropped open. "My God, we aint crows, Major!"

Rogers shrugged his shoulders. "Well, that's how far it is. Only a hundred and ten miles."

His use of the word "only" struck me as characteristic. So far as I could see, he drew no distinctions between small events and large--between great hazards and minor ones. All obstacles, apparently, looked the same to him--perhaps because he meant to surmount them all.

But my knapsack, like Bradley's was only half full of corn. There may have been about three quarts in it; about twelve cups. Twelve cups of corn to get us to Memphremagog, mysteriously distant, and from there a hundred and ten miles to the Ammonoosuc. I felt myself go suddenly hot all over, like a man with a bad tooth just before the blacksmith pulls it out for him with pincers. For I saw that the distance we'd marched on the way to St. Francis must be less than half as far as we had now to go before we could reach the Ammonoosuc and the store of food waiting for us there.

Bradley walked away with his head down. Jennie Coit had lain down beside Ogden and was asleep, one arm across the blanketed figure.

"Damned mink!" Rogers growled. "Sergeant, get her blanket and pack and send it back here. It kind of looks to me as if she wouldn't bother anybody but Ogden for the next few days."

I can't even imagine how Rogers knew we'd strike bad going on the following day; but we did, and by midnight--it was the fourth day--we began to see hills ahead: miniatures of those abrupt hills peculiar to the northern portion of the section now called Vermont. The river grew narrow, racing over a rock-filled bed between steep banks cut with brooks. By noon we were among them, laboring up steep slopes through tangles of undergrowth; slipping down their far sides: clambering up and stumbling down all through the rest of the day.

Rogers gave orders to Lieutenant Solomon and Konkapot, scouting ahead, to shoot a deer, bear or moose if they saw one, but nothing smaller. Our crashing through the undergrowth and our rustling in the dead leaves must have frightened the game away, for there seemed to be none. At night we had heard, high up, the quawking of ducks going south, or the shrill and mournful comments of geese; and nearer at hand the unending exchange of complaints between owls; but during the day we saw nothing; heard nothing save an occasional crow or the far-off, thrice-repeated call of a hungry hawk.

Ogden did well. He walked with his hand hooked in Jennie's blanket strap; and behind him went the Indian boy Billy, pushing at his rump to help him up hills, and holding to his belt to keep him from falling down them. Behind Billy went Bub, carrying Ogden's blanket, knapsack and musket. The group of them, scrambling up hill and down, put me in mind of Sisyphus, forever rolling his boulder up a slope, only to have it slip to the bottom so that he must start all over.

Ogden had the look of a man doomed to everlasting labor. He never glanced to either side: never raised his eyes from the ground before him: just stumbled on, pulled and pushed onward by his tireless shadows. Not only did Jennie help him on: she fed him, washed his bandage and changed it, clipped his hair, sewed up the rents in his clothes--all within the five-minute halts that we still made hourly, to make sure no one straggled. He seemed to have become her one interest in life, and it was plain that she would have given him her clothes if he'd have taken them: her few remaining kernels of corn; would have done anything to get him on and endlessly on.

That day we made fourteen miles; but the fifth day was bad. The hills were higher; the logans between steeper; the brooks more torrential; the boulders in them larger and more slippery. That was the day Ogden, for the first time since he was wounded, looked around to see how the rest of us were doing. It was difficult, a little later, to tell the days apart; but in the early days of our retreat there were distinguishable features that made them easily remembered.

The fifth day--the day Ogden first looked around--was the tenth day of October.

The sixth I recall because to the southward we saw real mountains in our path--sharp, jagged peaks; and because on that day a few men ran out of corn. They were the ones who had looted; and they began trading their loot for food--a wampum collar for a handful of corn: a silver brooch for a cupful.

The seventh, too, I remember, because when, at night, I returned from filling canteens with water, I saw Crofton kneeling in a singular dog-like posture. When I came quietly up behind him, I saw he had drawn something large and round from his knapsack, and was gnawing at it—gnawing and pulling, as a dog wrenches at the gristle on a bone.

"For God's sake, what's that?" I asked.

Crofton gave the thing a quick push into his knapsack and rubbed his mouth with the back of his hand. His push had been too hurried, and the thing rolled out again, like something alive, creeping out to look around. It was a head--an Indian's head.

I can't recall what I said, but Crofton came close to me--so close that I backed away and wanted to run. "It's mine," he whispered. "No harm taking what's mine, seeing what they did to my brother!" He laughed with the bubbling sound that a horned owl makes when it holds a rabbit in its claws.

Yet it struck me at the time that his argument was reasonable. Perhaps my mind was strange because of a month of insufficient, uncooked food--of daily forced marches and wet clothes--of never knowing when the French and Indians might come up with us. At all events, it seemed to me that if Crofton's brother had been horribly killed by Indians, he too had every right to kill Indians horribly and do what he pleased with those he killed. Not until later did I realize that war robs us of our reasoning powers, so that we think and believe strange things.

It was on the day after this, the eighth since St. Francis, that we sighted Memphremagog—a beautiful, narrow lake set among hills and mountains the shape of sharks' teeth: hills so steep they seemed to have been made by a giant beneath the earth's crust, thrusting upward with a stick before the crust was cold.

That day, I then thought, was the darkest we would know. It was the thirteenth of October. But it was only the beginning of a nightmare that even still comes back to set me exclaiming and groaning in my sleep, until strangers wake in other rooms and pound upon the wall.

It was during the forenoon that we stumbled over the shoulder of a hill and sighted Mempremagog through the brown leaves. The day was a weather-breeder if ever I saw one: a brilliant, glittering day, so clear that we could see, in seemingly unending ranks to the southward, a host of sharp toy mountains, bright blue against the pallid, cloudless sky. Across the lake rose even higher mountains, crammed together helter skelter, so that the land was overcrowded with them. We were coming to a terrible country: no doubt of that.

From the murmuring that arose from the scarecrow men behind me, I knew the sight of Memphremagog, to which we had so long looked forward, meant safety, rest, food--chiefly food. There must be fish in it: deer would come to it to feed: its coves, no doubt, were full of ducks in the early morning.

Food had become an obsession with all of us, for now all our knapsacks were as empty as we were. I was lucky; in the bottom of mine there remained a single cupful of corn, and if I dropped a grain, men hunted for it on hands and knees. For days we had lived in hope that when we reached Memphremagog, we would be free of the fear of pursuit: could build ourselves roaring fires, broil trout by the thousands beside them, sleep warm and undisturbed once more.

Marvelously, though Jennie Coit still marched beside Ogden, he needed her support no longer. The Indian boy Billy carried his pack, but he had taken to carrying his own musket, and he held his head up and looked about him as he walked.

To those who marched near him, Jennie had come to seem almost a part of him--so much a part we scarcely noticed her. She seemed content to keep an eye on him, as a dog keeps an eye on his master. When we sighted the lake, she skipped a little, gaily, clapped her hands and said in that harsh voice of hers: "We'll have trout for supper!"

It seemed impossible that the man who routed me from sleep at sun-up on the following morning had been at death's door from starvation and exhaustion only twenty-four hours earlier. Already, before waking us, he had been to the river to make sure the canoe-loads of supplies had set off for the Ammonoosuc. I had the feeling that the man was indestructible—this Rogers of Rogers' Rangers—this paladin who had destroyed St. Francis, had led us into hell and through it and out of it: that this colossus couldn't be killed or beaten. As I saw him then, it seemed to me his determined soul was such that even had his body perished, his ghost would have continued to lead us: would have threshed and fought the way through to bring us into safety.

I knew that now I was to part from him, which for me meant to walk tamely into a tamer world: when I thought of it, it seemed like a parting from glory; for the plain truth is that the Rogers I'd known until now was glorious, nor could I have believed then that under other circumstances he could ever be less, or anything different. Thus, when we're young, or under great stress, do we see the heroes who lead and save us.

"Come on," he said that morning, when he'd wakened me, "I still need you a while." He wore borrowed buckskins, made for a smaller man—which was only natural, since he was bigger than most: bigger, even, than Cap Huff. He and Ogden and Billy and I ate a whole side of bacon, mopping up the grease with our loaves of bread, and washing it down with a kettleful of tea the color of the water in a spruce bog, and it made me feel as though I had swallowed a bag of bullets.

"I'm going to leave Billy here to fatten up," he told me. "When you come back from Crown Point, stop and get him. Take him home and keep him for me. I'm in Portsmouth every few months. When I need him, I'll ask for him. Meanwhile, if you're going to paint Indians, you can start on him. They're all about the same color."

Then, after breakfast, he set to work framing his report to General Amherst. I have heard it said, often, that everything Rogers wrote was written for him: that he was ignorant and illiterate. That isn't so. He was a bad speller--as bad a speller as I ever saw, barring Peter Pond the trader and John Stark's brother William, the two worst spellers in the world. Aside from that, he expressed himself not only fluently and well, but in simple language, which is a gift denied to many writers who are called great. What was more, his thoughts were clear and logical; and considering that he was working in a hurry, and that a meal or two and dry clothes don't make a man whole when horrid day on day and night on night have shattered him, I say that this report was as accurate and comprehensive as could have been made by either of his two great enemies, General Thomas Gage and Sir William Johnson, at their best.

He dedicated eight pages, telling briefly what he had done and what he proposed to do; and what with consulting the notebook of our travels, and correcting here and inserting sentences elsewhere, it was almost noon before he reached the concluding paragraph—"I shall set off to go up the river myself at once, to seek and bring in as many of our men as I can find, and expect to be back in about eight days, when I shall, with all expedition, return to Crown Point. As to other particulars relative to this scout, which your Excellency may think proper to inquire after, I refer you to Captain Ogden, who bears this, and has accompanied me all the time I have been out, behaving very well. I am, Sir, with the greatest respect, Your Excellency's most obedient servant, R. Rogers. No. 4, Nov. 1st, 1759."

When it was finished, he took it from me and immediately went to work copying it. I never knew a man like him for keeping perpetually busy.

All the time he was writing, settlers were crowding in to stand near him and stare. They looked at him as we look at great men: that was plain in their eyes; and I think Rogers had a not unpleasant consciousness of their admiration. He kept at his work till he finished it: nevertheless I could see he was fully aware of the increasing throng of visitors and of their staring. When he finally signed the report, he folded it neatly; then stood up and looked about him with a bright and complacent glance.

"Well, friends," he said, "I suppose you know now that all danger from the Indians is over. Do any of you propose to take advantage of that improved condition?"

Several of them responded deferentially, yet eagerly. They said they thought of moving up river: as far up, perhaps, as the Upper Cohase, which was reputed to be fertile and beautiful.

"Cohase! That's nothing!" Rogers exclaimed, and launched out into a description of Lake George and the country north of the Mohawk River. His voice strengthened, became resonant with enthusiasm as he spoke; and his kindling eye roved over the room. He made us almost see eagles wheeling above majestic mountains; vast stretches of hardwood groves, devoid of undergrowth; the heavenly, unearthly blue of the fairest of all lakes; glass-clear streams packed with pink-fleshed trout; soil sufficiently fertile to cause apple trees to bear the year after planting; meadows carpeted with grass so rich that the cows that fed upon it could yield only cream; corn-stalks as tall as elms; a land of laughter and golden sunlight; of cool summers and mild winters—a terrestrial paradise.

Rogers paced the floor, gesturing, confident and prophetic. There in that wonderland, he told us, he would himself build a State—a little principality—a little Eden. Twenty-five thousand acres he and his officers would ask from the Crown, to begin with; and to that tract, when the war was over, would go his best officers and their families: his best Rangers and their families. Thus within his principality would be built up an army more perfect and more dangerous than had ever before been seen. Those who accompanied him would have not only their own army, but their own governor, their own legislative body, their own laws. All would work together; help one another ; and there in the wilderness would flourish a community of contented, rich and united people, wholly self-supporting and independent of foreign interference. No enemy would dare approach them: they would be safe forever from aggressors and from tyrants. Traders would come from Montreal, from Philadelphia, from all of North America for security, sending goods to the far West and receiving furs in return. It would supplant Albany, Boston, New York as the great clearing house: the great cross-roads of America.

Already this was a Rogers I hadn't known: an orator: a projector of dreams: a schemer: a man of business, blowing vast and brilliant bubbles--a Rogers strange and new to me--but when he stopped, the listening settlers were staring at him with glistening eyes, entranced.

"Jest Rangers goin' to settle it?" a bearded man asked.

"No," Rogers said. "There'd be room for you--room for every honest man who'd be willing to throw in his lot with me. I'd see you got your land on easy terms."

He put his hands on his hips and grinned that half-bashful grin of his. "How many here would go with me?"

I wasn't surprised when all those who hung upon his words--men and women and even the half-grown boys in the back of the room, staring slack-lipped and pop-eyed over the shoulders of their elders--said they'd go. Indeed, I wanted to go myself.

When I woke at dawn the next day, I heard someone already stirring in the bare room where Rogers, Ogden and I had spent the night. It was Rogers. He was on his feet, rolling his blanket and getting it fast to his shoulders; but as I watched him, he paused to set a brown bottle to his lips and drink long and unctuously. He finished his pack, drank again, looked down at us thoughtfully--then went toward the door, and I thought he lurched a little as he walked. His hand was on the latch when Ogden sat up and spoke.

"Not saying good-bye, Major?" Ogden asked. "No further orders?"

Rogers laughed a little more thickly than usual. "You two go to sleep again," he said. "Sleep a couple of days. It's no weather for you to be going overland to Crown Point. I'll just be sitting comfortable in a canoe myself--good place to drink a little, a canoe. You lay up till the weather clears. When you get there, just tell the General I'll be back here in about eight days." Then, as casually as though he were only going around the corner, he left us, and we heard him calling to Bellows to fill the empty flask. After that there came to us the sound of his footsteps outside, tramping across the frozen slush of the parade, and finally there was the distant sound of his voice, thick and loud, as he went down to the river. So, for that time, he passed from our ken.

He was right, as usual, about the weather; and we should have waited till it cleared before we set off for Crown Point. But Ogden--with Jennie Coit in his mind, I knew--insisted on starting that morning. We made miserable work of the comparatively safe and short journey through snow and rain and slush and mud. The truth is we were sick men, and by nightfall of the first day's march my legs had swelled horrifyingly. Ogden's legs swelled too, and one of his wounds was giving him trouble again.

Five days and nights it took us to cover those fourscore miles; the frigid lemon-colored glare of a November sunset shone in our faces when, on the 7th, I stood again on the bank where Hunk Marriner, McNott, Konkapot and I had stood, seven weeks before, looking across to the broad hook of Crown Point.

It was a desolate-looking place now. The ramparts of the new fort were dusted with snow, like lemon frosting on a giant cake, the tents gleamed coldly yellow in the declining sun, and the countless pointed spruces on the heavy hills beyond were powdered with an icy coating.

While we waited for the bateau to ferry us across, Ogden was consumed by a fever of impatience. He couldn't stand still, but limped up and down, fumbling with his accouterments, feeling his bristly chin; and when at last we were in the bateau, he was as fidgety as a caged fox: jumping up to stare toward the shore; shifting his powder-horn and cartridge box, only to shift them back at once, scratching himself; clearing his throat; staring about as if the place were strange to him; ignoring the bateau-man's questions; talking to me at random.

When the bateau touched shore, he blundered up the bank like a blind man. Officers stopped to stare open-mouthed at us; but he walked past them as if they didn't exist. If they had stood in his path, I have no doubt he would have tried to walk straight through them. His trembling eagerness to reach the fort and the general's markee was like that of a man half-dead with thirst hurrying toward water.

Amherst's markee was at the near end of the parade ground within the towering earthen ramparts. It was a double one--two big square tents placed close together, with a connecting corridor--and flanked on either side by two others, one for aides and one for the adjutant. In front of all three stood sentries so magnificent in their uniforms that I, part emaciated, part swelled, and clothed in a kind of ragged patchwork given me by charitable kind settlers at Number Four, wished myself elsewhere.

They wore scarlet coats with white belts whose buckles shone like gold, brilliant canary-yellow waistcoats, breeches so white that they were dazzling, and black gaiters that came above their knees. On their powdered heads were high, pointed hats with glittering regimental badges, and around their necks were stocks made of shining black leather. I had never dreamed that anything could look so beautiful and at the same time so coldly repellent.

Ogden hobbled to the closed flap of the middle tent, said "Message for General Amherst," and started in. Both sentries dropped their bayoneted muskets across the entrance. One of them snorted. The other said "Go over to the adjutant's tent first."

Then out of the tail of my eye I saw the sentries in front of the other two tents looking at us with an air of amused contempt; and my shame at my disreputable appearance vanished.

Ogden stepped back a pace from the crossed muskets and looked the two men up and down. They stopped smiling.

"You're lucky today," Ogden said. "I'll only ask you to announce me. Captain Ogden of His Majesty's Rangers, returning from St. Francis with despatches for General Amherst from Major Rogers. Go ahead! Read it out!"

The two sentries rattled their muskets and brought their hands up in a smart salute. Their faces were as red as their scarlet jackets: their backs so straight that their noses seemed to point to the sky. The sentries at the other tents stared haughtily into infinity. The man who had directed us to the adjutant's tent opened his mouth and bellowed "Captain Ogden of His Majesty's Rangers, returning from St. Francis----"

The flap of the markee was pulled aside to reveal the face of a handsome young officer. "Great Guns!" he shouted. "Stop that racket!" With his eye on Ogden he weakly exclaimed, "Great Heavens!" He held up the tent flap. "Come in here, Captain! That is to say--just a moment! By any chance are you lousy?"

Ogden looked at him distastefully. "Not yet," he said. "Thanks for warning us, but we've got to come in to see the General, even if we *do* get that way."

"What!" The young man stared. "No, no! You misunderstand me! I'll tell the General at once! A most remarkable sight! Fortunate the General's dined! Enough to take away a man's appetite! No offense, Captain! Splendid work! Splendid work!"

He turned toward the inner door of the markee, only to encounter a lean man with beetling brown eyebrows and grooves in his cheeks as deep as though gashed by a chisel. He wore a little tight wig, and over his uniform a loose green coat lined with brown fur. The Aide said "Captain Ogden, General. He----"

The General stopped him and came up close to us. Ogden was standing as rigid as a fence-post. "We're happy to have you back, Captain." He put out his hand.

Ogden relaxed and shook it. "Thank you, General! Thank you, sir." He fumbled in his haversack for Rogers' letter.

Amherst took it and sniffed at it without taking his eyes from Ogden. "Turn around, Captain," he said. "I'd like to have a picture of you, the way you are."

Ogden obediently turned around.

The General whistled softly; then looked at me. "Who's this?"

"Langdon Towne of Kittery, sir," Ogden said. "Acted as secretary to the Major."

"Private soldier or volunteer?" the General asked.

"Volunteer, sir," I said.

"Volunteer," the General repeated. "Ah yes--expedition finished--get your discharge now. Good." Then he sat down on his aide's bench and broke the wax wafer on Rogers' despatch.

"Hm, hm," he grumbled, running his eye over it. "Discovered the town from a tree--hm, hm--first found Indians in a high frolic or dance--hm--surprised the town when all fast asleep--hm, good!--chiefly destroyed--good, good!--destroyed both them and their boats--ha! yes!--set fire to all their houses--by Jove!--killed at least two hundred Indians and took twenty of their women and children prisoners--yes, yes, yes!--retook five English captives----"

He looked up at Ogden. "Interesting thing, Captain. Stockbridge Indian fellow came in last night. Those five captives the Major mentions have arrived at the mouth of Otter River with five Indians. I sent three whaleboats for them at once. They'll be in tomorrow morning."

Ogden made a strangled sound like a loud gasp, and the General looked at him sharply. Outside the sentries rattled their muskets, and through the tent-opening came a gaudily dressed officer, all scarlet, gold and white. As he entered, I caught sight of a throng of soldiers standing nearby, and in the distance others hurrying toward the General's markee.

"Oh, there you are, D'Arcy," Amherst said. "You've been out with the Rangers, so this'll interest you. Here's Captain Ogden, back from St. Francis all dressed up in the latest ranging costume, mostly holes. Thought you might like to have it copied to wear when we march on Montreal."

D'Arcy shook hands with Ogden: then stepped back, as had Amherst, to have a comprehensive view of us. The General's servant came in with a pair of candles. "By Jove!" D'Arcy exclaimed. "By Jove!"

"Quite!" Amherst said dryly. He resumed his reading of Rogers' letter. "Hm. Ah, yes. Found Captain Ogden badly wounded in his body----" He looked up at Ogden. "How'd that happen, Captain?"

"Well, sir, there was some question as to whether one of the houses was empty. I went in to find out, and it wasn't."

"I see," Amherst said. "I see."

He went back to the letter. "Badly wounded in the body--yes, yes--examined prisoners and captives--hm--party of three hundred French and Indians down the river, boats, waylaid, second party of two hundred French and Indians--hm, yes, yes!--return by Number Four--assemble at the mouth of the Ammonoosuc River--ah, yes: a great march: a great march!"

He frowned at Captain Ogden. "Badly wounded in the body, eh?" How did you get through the woods? Did they carry you?"

"No, sir," Ogden said.

"Well," Amherst said impatiently, "didn't you bleed? How'd you keep up?"

"I don't know, sir. I *had* to keep up."

"No doubt," Amherst said blankly. "No doubt." He sighed. "Let's see:

ah, yes: came to Cohase Intervales--yes--put down the river on a small raft to this place--dispatched provisions up river in canoes--why, what's this?" He rose to his feet, fumbling with the letter to find the last page. "Dated Number Four, November 1st. What's he mean by saying he dispatched provisions up river after reaching Number Four? I sent Lieutenant Stephens up river with provisions--provisions enough for all of you! Didn't you find them?"

"No, sir," Captain Ogden said. "Lieutenant Stephens went up, but he came back and brought the provisions away with him. His men heard our guns and--and didn't bother to wait. We found their fire burning. We could hear them firing guns, down river. We fired ours, but they didn't seem to notice." Under his breath he added, "We were pretty near gone."

Amherst's face turned dark red, a blue vein stood out on his forehead. "D'Arcy," he said, "have Lieutenant Stephens put under arrest and confined to his quarters. Have it done immediately." He turned a cold blue eye on Ogden; then added, "No: not confined to quarters. Better put him in the guard house in the fort where he'll be safe from visitors."

D'Arcy clicked his heels together, "Yes, General."

Amherst spoke fretfully to his aide. "John, make a note about Stephens. Life is full of Stephens's. No matter what we do, we're surrounded by Stephens's who can't obey orders. All the Stephens's of this world ought to be shot, and the Rogers's ought to have statues. Write something to that effect, only put properly, John."

The handsome young aide, his lips moving spasmodically, scribbled furiously in a notebook.

The General looked from Ogden to me. "It's customary," he said, "to confer some small reward for a scout of this nature--for one that proves both arduous and successful. Captain Ogden will receive recognition in due course. But at present I'd suggest complete Ranger uniforms— D'Arcy, I'd be obliged if you'd see to that. Complete. All accouterments, D'Arcy. Scotch caps, green strouds, shoulder brooches--all. Gift of His Majesty, so to speak, what?" He glanced at the end of Rogers' letter. "Yes. Behaved very well. Yes, yes. Let's see, Captain Ogden; you reached Number Four the last day of October. You hadn't had much to eat, I take it."

"No, sir. We could crawl, but we couldn't lift a hatchet."

"Mm. So you've come eighty miles since then, in these clothes and through the storm."

"Yes, sir."

"Mm. Legs trouble you?"

"Yes, sir."

"Very well," Amherst said testily. "Come back here tomorrow afternoon when you're clothed and in your right mind. I'll write Major Rogers. Oh, and D'Arcy: have this gentleman"--he pointed to me--"entered on the rolls as an ensign. When he's discharged, let him draw pay as an ensign from September 13th. Now take these gentlemen to your tent and give orders for what they need. They probably need a drink as much as anything."

D'Arcy smiled. "May I have the honor, gentlemen?" He stood aside to let us precede him from the markee. We came out, and there were hundreds of soldiers--Rangers, Provincials, British Regulars in work overalls and in the uniforms of half a dozen regiments--standing at a respectful distance and staring at us. But staring wasn't all they did. They began to cheer and kept on cheering.

From Kenneth Roberts, *Northwest Passage* (NY: Doubleday, 1937), pp. 159-170;171;198-207;285-295)

Fred Cook

Struggle for the South

> *"We fight, get beat, rise, and fight again."*
> General Nathaniel Greene—March 18, 1781

The Revolutionary fighting began in the North and ended in the South. In the first years, the hostilities were mainly in Massachusetts, in New York and New Jersey and Pennsylvania. Except for the futile British attack on Charleston in 1776, the South was quiet, hardly touched by the war. But with the French alliance and the Battle of Monmouth Court House in 1778, everything changed. London decided to try to knock the Southern colonies out of the war and to conquer them.

The first step in the new campaign was taken early in 1779. A British force under General Augustine Prevost moved up the coast from British Florida and entered Georgia. The force was strengthened by British, Hessian, and Tory units brought down the coast in transport ships from New York. The combined army swept through Georgia--Sunbury, Augusta, and Savannah fell, and the military government actually set up a new Georgia legislature loyal to the British Crown.

The patriots had no way of meeting the new threat. Across the Savannah River in South Carolina, Major General Benjamin Lincoln of Massachusetts tried to build up a force of Continentals and militia strong enough to attempt the recapture of Savannah. The task seemed hopeless, for the South was sparsely settled and had nothing like the manpower that had fed the Northern armies. Besides, there was no way of sealing off Savannah from the supplies that the British could ship into it by sea.

Then someone thought of Admiral d'Estaing and the powerful French fleet lying in the West Indies. Word was sent to d'Estaing, and he replied promptly. He would sail for Savannah with a strong fleet of warships and transports carrying more than 6,000 French regulars. Benjamin Lincoln and the Americans were delighted. At last, it seemed, the great alliance with France was about to bear fruit.

On September 12, 1779, d'Estaing arrived off the Georgia coast and began unloading troops for the attack on Savannah. An immediate attack almost certainly would have carried the city, for Prevost and his British army were struggling desperately to repair the ruined old earthworks. But d'Estaing, the prisoner of old-fashioned military custom, did not strike at once. Instead, he sent the British a formal demand to surrender.

The British stalled--and worked frantically on the defenses. General Lincoln, arriving with a small American force, was snubbed by d'Estaing, who seems to have had a knack for making himself disliked by every officer with whom he had to deal. It was not until September 23 that d'Estaing finally broke ground for his siege train, and it was not until October 9, almost a month after his arrival, that a joint attack was launched on the Savannah lines.

By that time, the busy Prevost had made the originally weak defenses truly formidable. The attack was a terrible failure. The British, at a loss of only 100 men of their own, inflicted casualties of more than 800 on the attackers. Among the dead on the American side was the brilliant Pole, Casimir Pulaski.

Lincoln wanted to renew the assault, but d'Estaing had had enough. The crews of his ships were ill, the hurricane season was near, a British fleet might appear at any moment. Offering these excuses, he re-embarked his men and sailed to the West Indies. Lincoln and his little army trudged back to Charleston. Again, as at Newport, the French-American alliance had produced only discord and disaster.

Even worse, the whole affair had served to advertise the weakness of the Americans in the South. The miserable failure of Lincoln and d'Estaing before Savannah practically invited the British to come in force and hammer at a weak spot, and up in New York, Sir Henry Clinton read the message correctly. He abandoned Newport, pulling back 3,000 troops that had been idling there, and early in 1780 set sail for South Carolina.

Avoiding the mistakes that he and Admiral Sir Peter Parker had made in 1776, Clinton did not try to pound his way directly into the city past the harbor forts. Instead, he landed his troops down the coast and began to circle leisurely inland, cutting off Charleston on one side while his fleet blockaded it on the other.

These tactics forced General Lincoln to choose between two courses. He could either fall back from Charleston, drawing Clinton inland, far from the strength of the British fleet; or he could hole up in Charleston and, with his poorly equipped 5,000 try to beat off the attack of Clinton's seasoned 10,000. Lincoln, perhaps influenced by Carolinians who did not want to see their prize city lost, made the wrong decision. He decided to stay in Charleston.

Disaster came swiftly. Lieutenant Colonel Banastre Tarleton, who had landed with his finely trained and well-equipped Tory Legion, smashed into 500 American cavalry under General Isaac Huger at Monck's Corner, some 30 miles from Charleston. Tarleton practically wiped out Huger's force, seized 100 fine dragoon-mounts, and slammed shut the last escape route from Charleston. Clinton drew his siege lines tighter, and his ships bombarded the city. On May 12, 1780, Benjamin Lincoln surrendered with all his army.

More than an army had been lost. The greatest city in the South had fallen. Huge quantities of supplies had been destroyed. Nearly all the patriot leaders of South Carolina, both political and military, had been taken prisoners of the British. The Americans had suffered their worst setback of the war, and Clinton moved quickly to take further advantage of it.

Flying columns spread out over the whole of South Carolina--north to Camden along the Wateree, west to oddly named Ninety-Six, northeast toward the North Carolina border. There was nothing anywhere to stand in their way. The few patriots who tried to fight met with defeat. Colonel Abraham Buford of Virginia tried to make a stand at the Waxhaws near the North Carolina border. Tarleton, with his hard-riding Tory cavalry, cornered Buford in May, 1780. Buford tried to surrender, but Tarleton, perhaps deliberately, misinterpreted his signals, and a horrible butchery followed. Even the wounded received no mercy. From that day on, Tarleton, with his almost womanish good looks and his streak of cruelty, became known to the Americans as "Butcher."

On June 8, 1780, Clinton turned the Carolina command over to Cornwallis and sailed back to New York with 4,500 of his troops. He believed, a bit too optimistically, that the rebellion had been crushed in the Carolinas for all time. As for Cornwallis, he built a chain of forts across South Carolina, then turned to meet a new force coming at him from North Carolina.

A small American army had started south, originally in the hope of relieving the pressure on Lincoln at Charleston. Low in numbers, the troops were high in quality. Among them were the always reliable, always staunch Delaware and Maryland Continentals. These were backed by an infantry-cavalry Legion commanded by the mysterious Frenchman know as Colonel Armand. Leading the force was the huge, physically powerful Baron de Kalb, a soldier of fortune who had come to America with Lafayette in 1777 and had turned into a real patriot. With de Kalb were such capable officers as General William Smallwood and Colonel Otho Holland Williams.

These were some of the best men in the army, but Congress decided that it would not do for de Kalb, a German, to command the only American army in the South. Furthermore, Congress wanted a leader known throughout the land, someone whose name would make the public feel confident of victory. The politicians had always been impressed with Horatio Gates, the victor of Saratoga, and now he was given the command.

Gates took over from de Kalb in late July, 1780, on the Deep River in North Carolina. Some militia had come in, and Gates set out for the South to find Cornwallis. On the way, he met a shabby little troop of South Carolinians, whom he described as "distinguished by small black leather caps and the wretchedness of their attire; their number did not exceed twenty men and boys, some white, some black, and all mounted, but most of them miserably equipped." Their leader was a small, dark man who rarely talked and who limped from a still-healing ankle fracture--Lieutenant Colonel Francis Marion, soon to be know as the "Swamp Fox." Gates sent Marion and his men south to seize the Santee River crossings behind Camden, South Carolina, hoping to cut off Cornwallis' communications with his base at Charleston.

This done, Gates hastened on south, committing many errors along the way. He had a choice of two routes to Camden, where Cornwallis was. The longer of the two routes led through a rich countryside where patriot sentiment was strong; the shorter, through a barren waste where there were no provisions for the army and where the Tories were strong. Gates chose the shorter way. Colonel Otho Williams, one of the most capable officers in the South, pointed out that the army consisted of only 3,000 men, most of these militia and miserably equipped; Gates insisted he led 7,000. When Williams politely tried to show his commander that nearly all units had fallen in number to half strength or less, Gates cried out: "Sir, there are enough for our purpose."

On the night of August 15, Gates sent out his green troops, many of them sick, half-starved, and exhausted, on a night march to surprise and strike Cornwallis.

The British commander, who had not been napping, had exactly the same idea at exactly the same time. His veterans, marching through the night to strike Gates, crashed into Armand's Legion and scattered it. There was some confused fighting in the dark; then Cornwallis drew back and waited for dawn.

Gates still had time to retreat. De Kalb and Otho Williams, who had learned from British prisoners that Cornwallis had some 2,200 veterans at his command, privately expected him to do so, but Gates accepted the view of one officer that it was now too late. "We must fight, then," he said. "To your commands, gentlemen."

The British struck at dawn. The American left and center caved in. The raw, exhausted militia broke and fled from the British bayonets in utter, senseless panic. With the first charge, the Battle of Camden was lost.

Only on the American right, where de Kalb commanded, was there stiff resistance. There the veteran Marylanders and Delawares, a bare 600 troops, stood like a wall of iron, battling the entire British army. For more than an hour, thinking they were winning, they kept up the unequal fight. They charged with the bayonet, reformed, and charged again, rallying always around the huge figure of de Kalb, as around a battle standard. Cornwallis had to call off the pursuit of the shattered militia and throw the bulk of his army at the gallant 600. Then de Kalb was struck down, dying from his eleventh wound of the day. Tarleton's Legion charged, and the Delawares and Marylanders at last were routed.

The wreckage of Gates' army streamed north from their defeat at Camden. Officers like Otho Williams and William Smallwood and Armand stayed with the troops, struggled with them, restored some kind of order. They protected the rear as the beaten columns straggled north to Charlotte, North Carolina. And there at last they caught up with their commander, Horatio Gates.

While de Kalb was fighting and dying, while Williams and Smallwood were trying desperately to hold the command together, Gates had leaped upon a horse and led the way to the rear. He galloped sixty miles before he stopped in Charlotte, a performance that led Alexander Hamilton to remark bitingly that Gates' speed did "admirable credit to the activity of a man at his time of life."

Never had American fortunes in the South been brought so low. The army that Gates had numbered at 7,000 men in mid-August now mustered less than 700. It was in wretched shape, without equipment, arms, blankets, artillery, ammunition, or food. All of South Carolina had been crushed by Cornwallis; even North Carolina and Virginia were menaced.

This was the darkest hour in the South, a moment comparable to the disasters in New Jersey before Trenton. There were only a few bright spots. One was provided by Francis Marion on August 20. A mixed band of British and Tories was convoying a column of Americans captured at Camden back to prison in Charleston. Suddenly, at daybreak, out of the swamps a mounted band burst upon them, struck hard, freed prisoners, and captured the captors. The British and Tories were ashamed to find that they had been overwhelmed by Marion and only 16 followers.

The second blow at British power in South Carolina was far more important. Cornwallis, trying to protect his left flank by cleaning out the western section of the state, sent Major Patrick Ferguson, one of his best officers, into the western mountain country with a force of the western section of the state, sent Major Patrick Ferguson, one of his best officers, into the western mountain country with a force of more than 1,000 Tories. The invasion stirred up the "over-mountain men" of the Watauga settlements, of modern Tennessee, who rallied around their leaders, Colonels Isaac Shelby and "Nolichucky Jack" Sevier, and trapped Ferguson's force on a long, wooded hill known as King's Mountain.

Some 900 of the best-mounted frontiersmen were sent ahead. They tethered their horses and swarmed up the mountain slope to the attack, taking cover behind trees and rocks as they went. All the time they sprayed the crest with deadly rifle fire. Behind this blanket of bullets, they gained the top with slight loss. Then the end came quickly.

Ferguson was shot down. His men were surrounded, and the loss was almost total. Only some 200 men, whom Ferguson had sent out on a foraging expedition before the Battle of King's Mountain, managed to stumble east to Cornwallis and safety.

Staggered by the loss of his left wing, angered by the raids of Marion and Thomas Sumter and Andrew Pickens, Cornwallis changed his plans. He had been thinking of an easy march north to the Potomac. Now he saw that he still had problems in South Carolina, and he went into winter quarters at Winnsboro, well to the west of Camden.

Still, the plight of the Americans was desperate. Even Congress recognized that the army no longer had any faith in Horatio Gates, and it empowered Washington, whose advice previously it had refused to seek, to name a new commander. Washington promptly selected the man he had wanted to see in charge in the South in the first place--his own strong right arm in all the major campaigning in the North, Major General Nathanael Greene.

Greene, a man of great modesty, seems to have had some doubts about his fitness for the command, but he agreed to take it. He succeeded Gates at Charlotte on December 2, 1780, and officers of the Southern army were amazed at the difference one man could make--almost overnight, at that. Colonel William Polk of North Carolina exclaimed that Greene "by the following morning understood [supply problems] better than Gates had done in the whole period of his command!"

Green's task was truly staggering. He had but 2,300 men—and only 800 of these fit for duty. They had only three-days' rations. Clothes were in tatters, shoes lacking. The camps were filthy, badly placed; morale was low. And Green's assignment was to defeat Cornwallis' powerful army and reconquer three states.

The job seemed impossible, but Greene saw strength where another man might have overlooked it. He knew the value of those solid Continentals from Delaware and Maryland. His sound soldier's mind quickly placed the right value on men like Otho Williams; Colonel William Washington, a tested cavalry leader and a distant cousin of the commander-in-chief; Lieutenant Colonel Edward Carrington, an artillery expert who had smashed a British attack at Monmouth; and John Eager Howard, one of the best officers in the Maryland line.

These were leaders on whom a general could rely, and soon two others, even more important, joined Greene. One was a huge figure in fringed buckskin, creaking and groaning with arthritis--the "Old Wagoner," Daniel Morgan. Morgan had been in retirement since 1779, because of his resentment over the failure of Congress to reward his great services with promotion; but he had been made a Brigadier at last and had come out "to crack his whip once more." Also joining Greene was a famous cavalry leader, Lieutenant Colonel Henry "Light-Horse Harry" Lee. Lee brought with him a green-jacketed, helmeted Legion of some 300 finely equipped and trained men.

Greene considered his strengths and his weaknesses and saw the whole picture with the eye of genius. He knew that his army, already discouraged, would rot away if he sat in winter quarters doing nothing. He saw that his army, as a single unit, was too weak to accomplish anything. If Greene kept his force together in one place, Cornwallis could keep his iron grip on all of South Carolina, and could drive on into North Carolina to crush the one army that still stood in his way. To prevent such a move, Greene decided to go against the rules of all the military books. He decided to *divide* his already weak force.

Even now, the move seems almost like madness until one stops and thinks it out the way Greene did. He sensed at once the value of guerrilla leaders, such as Francis Marion. The day after he took command, he wrote Marion at the latter's camp on Snows' Island in the Great Pee-Dee River in South Carolina. Greene pointed out that the guerrillas and the regular army could team up to help each other. The guerrillas could harass Cornwallis with swift raids against his far-flung outposts and long lines of communication; at the same time, Greene's army could pose enough of a threat so that Cornwallis would not risk turning all his power upon the raiders.

It was a new and brilliant idea for the conduct of war in the South, and Greene's first major move as commander was to put it into effect. Instead of attaching Lee's legion to his main army, as another commander almost certainly would have done, he sent Lee south to joint Marion and step up the raids against Cornwallis' supply lines.

Next, Greene daringly divided his own army. The part under his own command he moved just across the South Carolina border to a camp in the Cheraws. The rest, a scant 600 men, he placed under the command of Dan Morgan for a sweep far to the west. Greene hoped that he could tempt Cornwallis into dividing the British forces, and that Cornwallis would send in chase of Morgan a detachment that, just possibly, Morgan might have a chance of beating.

Cornwallis did just what Greene hoped he might do. He sent Tarleton at the head of force of 1,100 men to track down Morgan. The Old Wagoner, kept advised of Tarleton's movements by Andrew Pickens' roving men, picked his battlefield with care. Morgan, too, had a keen military instinct that led him now to throw away the rule book and to adopt new tactics to fit his own situation. He decided to give battle on a park-like tract that had been used by drovers to rest and graze their cattle on the way to market--a place known as the Cowpens, in the very shadow King's Mountain.

Two low hills commanded the pasture. Behind the hills was the Broad River, a deep stream that would cut off all escape if Morgan were beaten. The book said a commander should never invite such disaster, but Morgan reasoned that, with the Broad River at their backs, his militia would *have* to fight. To make sure, Morgan placed the militia out in front, with the veterans of the Continental line drawn up on the first of the low hills behind them, with Washington's cavalry hidden behind the second hill. Before the battle, Morgan went among the militia, commanded by Pickens, and told the men exactly what he expected of them. They were to fire two volleys, Morgan said, and he told them to aim first at the British officers. "Look for the epaulets!" he said. "Pick off the epaulets!" Their two volleys fired, the militia could break and fall back behind the Continentals on the first hill. It was a daring and decidedly different battle plan.

On January 17, 1781, Tarleton drove straight into the Cowpens pasture. The helmet plumes of his dragoons tossed in the wind as they charged into the sights of the militia and riflemen. Fire crackled along the skirmish line, and the dragoons fell back. In the center, the British and Tory infantry charged straight forward. The militia fired once, fired again, then fell back according to Morgan's plan. But Tarleton did not see a plan; he saw only the panicked flight of clumsy Rebels. Rashly, he charged forward with everything he had--and crashed head-on into the solid wall of those Delaware and Maryland Continentals, commanded by John Eager Howard.

There was hard, desperate fighting on the slick, brown grass. Howard, fearing his line was about to be turned, bent it back, and Tarleton, again thinking the Americans were breaking, charged furiously. And again he was surprised. Morgan was there roaring at the men along that shifting line; the ranks steadied, and suddenly the Americans plunged downhill with the bayonet. Tarleton's charge was broken, thrown into confusion, and instantly the battle picture changed.

Pickens' reformed militia, backed up by Kirkwood's Delawares, swept out around the flank of the first hill, circled and struck the British on their left and rear. At the same time, William Washington's cavalry charged around the other side of the hill and smashed into the right rear. Tarleton's whole force was trapped.

In blind fury, Tarleton tried to rally his dragoons, but Washington crashed through them and engaged in a saber duel with Tarleton himself. Washington's horse was wounded, and Tarleton, with a small knot of riders around him, galloped away down the road. Behind him, his men threw down their arms. The patriots had lost 12 killed, 60 wounded; the British 100 killed, 800 prisoners. Virtually all of Tarleton's command was wiped out at the Battle of Cowpens, in what has been called the most brilliant, best-fought action of the entire war.

Cornwallis was shocked, and he lashed out in fury. He started after Morgan, but that clever fighter had lost no time. Immediately after Cowpens, he had turned and fled toward the fords over the Catawba River, 100 hard miles to the northeast. Cheated of quick revenge, Cornwallis prepared for a long chase. He burned all surplus wagons, baggage, supplies, and equipment so that he could move faster, and on January 28, 1781, he set out to catch Morgan and Greene before they could reach the fords over the Dan River leading into Virginia. If he could get to the Dan first, he could cut off the Americans' retreat and force them into battle with his greatly superior army.

But Greene had reacted to the news of Cowpens as swiftly as Cornwallis. He started at once on a march across state to join forces with Morgan and get across the Dan. Greene seems to have had amazing foresight into exactly what Cornwallis would do, and he planned accordingly. He sent Lieutenant Colonel Edward Carrington ahead to snap up every boat on the Dan River, and he called back Light-Horse Harry Lee, who had been raiding with Marion along the Congaree River.

Combining Lee's Legion with Washington's cavalry, some Continental infantry and militia riflemen, Greene formed a rear guard of less than 700 men under the command of Otho Williams. Williams' job was one of the most difficult in war. He had to strike at Cornwallis' advance, led by General O'Hara of the Guards; he had to fight it, halt it, delay it--and yet never fight it so hard that his whole command became involved in a pitched battle or got itself surrounded. Williams carried out his assignment to perfection, while O'Hara lashed out furiously and strained every nerve to pin him down. And all the time this fierce feinting went on, the two main armies raced for the Dan. Sleet stung their faces, then changed to a wet and sticky snow that lay on the roads. Men and horses died of exhaustion. Rations ran out. And still the grueling race went on.

Greene won it, finally, by the narrowest of margins. On February 13, he got his forward lines across the Dan, and by midnight of the fourteenth, the last man of Lee's Legion--the rear guard of the rear guard--was ferried over to the Virginia shore, just as the spearhead of O'Hara's column burst from the woods on the south bank and stared down at the bridgeless flood before them.

Cornwallis had driven Greene out of North Carolina, but what was he to do now? He had lost over 200 men during the long pursuit to the Dan; he had destroyed wagons and supplies--and in the end, all for nothing. He needed to re-equip, so he turned back to Hillsboro, North Carolina. There he issued a call for all loyal Tories in the region to join up, and recruits began to flock in.

Across the Dan, safe after a retreat that had been worth a battle, Greene went right back into action. He did not want Cornwallis reinforced by Tories, and he at once stepped up the guerrilla warfare. Lee's troopers swooped down on Tory formations heading for Hillsboro. Kirkwood's Delawares snapped up supply parties, seized local leaders. Andrew Pickens' men raided day and night. And near Alamance, Lee surprised the mounted company of Tory Colonel Pyle and massacred them with a ferocity that matched Tarleton's bloodiest exploits. Suddenly Tory enthusiasm cooled, and Cornwallis' recruits drained away to a trickle.

Almost at once, Greene went back on the attack with his regular army. Baron von Steuben had sent him some troops from Virginia, and he now had some 4,000 men under his command. About 1,600 of them were Continentals, many never tested in battle. With this new-found strength, Greene went south, the cavalry of William Washington and Henry Lee screening his advance and brushing Tarleton aside. By March 14, Greene had brought his army to a spot he had carefully picked out, during his retreat to the Dan, as a promising battle site.

It was only a dot on the map, with a hill and a brick building know as Guilford Court House. Greene had studied Morgan's tactics at the Cowpens, and the Old Wagoner himself, forced by bad health to leave the army, had written advising Greene to put his militia in the front and center "with some picked troops in their rear to shoot the first man that runs." Greene followed this advice, spotting the militia in the flat woodland approaches to the court house hill, with picked men in a second line behind them, and the cream of his troops in a third line on the crest.

On the fifteenth, Lee's cavalry, raiding south down the wood road, crashed into the British advance. Cornwallis was coming. The British forward lines charged straight up the road toward the court house hill. Greene's North Carolina militia fired the two volleys he had asked of them, but then they broke and fled. Virginians in the second line behind them were entangled in the woods and the fleeing troops; suddenly, panic spread.

O'Hara's Guards drove on with the bayonet, smashed through the second line, plunged on across the crest of the hill, and seized the guns planted there. Then they were met by the counter-shock of John Howard charging headlong with his hardy Delaware and Maryland troops. The veteran Guards were rocked back, split for a moment, and in that moment William Washington led a cavalry charge that pounded over and back again through the shredding British ranks.

Americans and British were tangled in wild fighting all over the slope of the court house hill. Cornwallis, in desperation, wheeled up his artillery. The wounded General O'Hara, understanding his intention, was horrified and pleaded with Cornwallis not to open fire on his own men. But Cornwallis, iron-faced, gave the word to his gunners and turned loose a murderous hail killing friend and foe alike.

This brutal measure saved the day for Cornwallis. The Americans fell back. One final charge by Greene might have taken the field, but if it had failed, it might have cost his army. Greene was never prepared to pay such a price. He knew that, at whatever sacrifice, he must always keep his army intact in the field, ready to fight. And so he ordered a retreat, and Cornwallis was left in possession of the ground around Guilford Court House--left with a technical victory that was worse than defeat. He had taken 1,900 men into action, and he had lost more than a quarter of them in killed and wounded. He was left with an army so weakened that it was in poor condition to fight again, and Greene, who had lost only 78 killed and 183 wounded, was almost as strong as ever.

Cornwallis could only retreat, and he did, taking his battered army off to Wilmington on the coast. There he refitted and set out on the march that was to lead to a little village named Yorktown in Virginia.

Greene had whittled down the main British army and chased it out of the Carolinas. Now the time had come to win back what had been lost. Messages went out to Francis Marion and to Sumter and Pickens. Lee's Legion again rode south. One after another, the British posts, strung out in a T-shape from Charleston to Ninety-Six, came under fierce guerrilla attack. Greene made certain that the guerrillas had a free hand by leading his own army to engage the principal British force, commanded by Lord Rawdon at Camden, South Carolina.

Greene and Rawdon met in battle on April 25, 1781, on a small rise know as Hobkirk's Hill near Camden, almost on the site of the field where Gates had been so disastrously defeated. Greene placed his troops in the familiar Cowpens-Guilford Court House pattern, with the militia out in front, and it seemed for a time that the Americans would be victorious. But some units were mishandled; William Washington rode into the British camp and so overloaded himself with non-combatant prisoners that he was useless when most needed. And again Greene, unwilling to risk all on a final charge, drew off with his army. "We fight, get beat, rise, and fight again," he wrote--a sentence that describes perfectly his entire campaign.

The fights and the beatings were never in vain. Each time they cost the British so heavily that the result, in the end, was victory for the Americans. Lord Rawdon, after Hobkirk's Hill, found himself in very much the same position as Cornwallis after Guilford Court House. He had suffered so heavily that, on May 10, he abandoned Camden, burning a great quantity of military stores, and marched south to try to protect his outposts, now being hammered by Marion and Lee.

This fighting team captured Fort Motte. Then Marion went off to harry the Georgetown area, and Lee with some Marylanders struck at Fort Granby. Greene himself swung west and lay siege to the farthest outpost, Ninety-Six. The siege lasted from May 22 until mid-June, when Lord Rawdon charged up to the fort's relief. Again Greene had to retreat, but again he gained his objective.

Lord Rawdon, finding his lesser posts falling to Marion and Lee, realized he could not hold Ninety-Six. So he burned the post and marched back to Charleston. Even today, the almost complete reversal of British fortunes in six short months seems astounding. In December, 1780, Nathanael Greene had inherited the wreck of an army from Gates; and by late June, 1781, after a campaign in which Greene had not won a single major battle, British power in the Carolinas had been broken, their entire chain of posts had been swept away, and they held securely only the area immediately around Charleston. It was an achievement that still seems little short of magic.

In the tropical heat of a South Carolina summer, Greene rested his marched-out, battle-weary troops in the High Hills of Santee and planned his next move. Lord Rawdon, broken in health and thoroughly disgusted, gave up the British command and sailed back to England. He left a capable officer, Lieutenant Colonel Alexander Stuart, in charge of the British army. Greene, studying these changes, went back to his familiar guerrilla-regular army, two-way attack.

Sumter and Marion and Lee struck at the British supply depot at Monck's Corner, just outside of Charleston. They carried the post and brought off 150 prisoners, 200 horses, and a long string of wagons. Then in late August, 1781, Greene moved out of the High Hills of Santee, crossed flooded plains, and advanced on Stuart's army, camped at Eutaw Springs. Marion and his guerrillas joined the main army and were put in the front line for the approaching battle.

On September 8, 1781, Greene struck. Lee led the attack, crashing into Tory cavalry and infantry that had been sent to feel out the American advance. He broke the enemy and drove them before him in rout. Greene's whole command followed closely and smashed into Stuart's surprised line. The entire British left wing collapsed, the center folded, and British troops took to their heels down the road to Charleston. A major victory seemed in the making, but off on the British right, a tough major named Marjoribanks stood his ground with his grenadiers and light infantry.

He beat off every attack Greene sent against him. William Washington charged with his cavalry and saw his troopers shot down. Greene tried to mass his infantry for a crushing blow, but the Americans now were as out of hand from victory as the British were from defeat. The famished, poorly-clad Americans had entered the well-stocked British camp, and the lure of plunder and rum was too much. They broke ranks.

Stuart sensed the changed situation. He rallied his troops and charged to Marjoribanks' relief. Somehow he reformed a battle line, and Greene knew that he would have to risk his whole army in one all-out charge if he were to dent it. Again Greene refused the gamble. Once more he drew off, this time leaving the British in possession of the battlefield at Eutaw Springs, but once more Greene was the final victor.

Stuart, like Cornwallis and Rawdon before him, found that he had paid so heavy a price he could not keep the battleground that he had won. He buried his dead, including that stout fighter, Marjoribanks, and took his badly mauled army back to the safety of the Charleston fortifications.

Nathanael Greene followed and drew a tight line around the largest city in the South. In all the Carolinas and Georgia, which at the beginning of the year the British seemed to have won completely, the only places where the British flag still flew were over the ports of Charleston and Savannah, protected by the guns of the British fleet. Nathanael Greene, who never won a battle and never lost a campaign, had saved the South.

From Fred Cook and Bruce Lancaster, *The American Revolution,* (New York: American Heritage, 1959), pp. 163-177

R.E. Dupuy and W.H. Baumer

Wars with the Barbary Pirates, 1801-1816

Blackmail Unlimited

Blue water and hot sands, gleaming minarets and slavery; of such stuff was Mediterranean life to Yankee ships and sailormen from 1785 to 1802. For this was the lair of Blackmail Unlimited--Morocco, Algiers, Tunis, and Tripoli--the four Berber Muslim states bordered a two-thousand-mile stretch of the North African coast. Morocco was a flourishing monarchy, the other three were provinces of the Ottoman Empire, owing at least nominal allegiance to the Supreme Porte. Piracy was their trade, blackmail their price for immunity.

Here the Stars and Stripes meant nothing and the plight of the Boston brig *Polly* and her crew in 1793 was remarkable only because one of her forecastle hands was sufficiently articulate to put down on paper his grim story after they had been ransomed.

The *Polly*, Cadiz-bound, was hailed and boarded by an Algerine brig off Cape St. Vincent.

> About one hundred of the Pirates jumped on board us, all armed, some with Scimetars and Pistols, others with pikes, spears, lances, knives, etc. As soon as they came on board they made signs for us all to go forward, assuring us in several languages that if we did not obey their commands they would immediately massacre us all . . . . They then went below into the cabin, steerage and every place where they could get below deck and broke open the Trunks and Chests there, and plundered all our bedding, clothing, books, Charts, Quadrants and every moveable article. They then came on deck and stripped the clothes off our backs, all except a shirt and a pair of drawers.
>
> When we had been taken into [Algiers] we were conducted to the Dey's palace by a guard. When we were brought before the Dey he said he was determined never to make a peace with the United States, adding, "Now I have got you, you Christian dogs, you shall eat stones." He then picked out four boys to wait upon himself and then ordered the rest of us to be conducted to the prison. . . .

Prison, wrote Foss, was a wretched place, crawling with vermin and filled with Turks, Moors, Arabs, Christians, and "a Jew or two." The Turks, he commented, were "drunken"; why, we do not know. Each prisoner was given a dirty blanket and a small loaf of black, sour bread; then he was loaded down hand and feet with chains weighing from twenty-five to forty pounds, all fastened to the waist.

The overseer's whip and goad, together with the bastinado for the more obdurate, spurred the half-starved captives in their incessant hard labor. Disrespect to the Muslim faith might bring roasting at the stake, or impalement. And the rebellious slave who killed a Muhammadan was simply tossed off the city wall; were he lucky he would be dashed to immediate death below. But more probably he would lodge on one of the iron hooks studding it and hang there in agony for days before he died.

Foss's story, supplementing the numberless other reports of atrocities to American sailormen and American pocketbooks, did much to harden the resolve of both Congress and administration for the excision of this ulcer, festering ever since the United States became a nation.

For centuries the Barbary corsairs had plied their trade, harrying Mediterranean traffic, despoiling the southern European coasts, and even moving north along the Atlantic. Despite their respectively great naval power in the seventeenth and eighteenth centuries, England, France, and Spain, immersed in successive wars with one another, had found it more to their advantage to pay tribute which--to a great extent--left their merchant trade unhampered. And, so far as the North American Colonies were concerned, their commerce, up to the time of the Revolution, was of course under England's protection. The smaller European maritime nations paid tribute also, in varying amounts.

American commerce in the Mediterranean had become very prosperous; the Mediterranean basin actually absorbing one-quarter of the colonial export of dried and pickled fish and one-sixth of its flour, wheat, and rice. Rum, lumber, beeswax, and onions were other fairly important American exports. The Revolution cut this traffic short. But it started again immediately upon the war's conclusion, and by 1790 nearly one hundred American merchantmen annually called at Mediterranean ports.

Unfortunately, being no longer under the wing of English treaties and the guns of the Royal Navy, this rich traffic was now fair game for the corsairs. The United States, a weak confederation, had no Navy and Congress had little desire to build one.

Appeasement, then, by palm-greasing, was the solution; appeasement that grasped at straws insofar as results were concerned, for treaties unsupported by force meant nothing to the blackmailers.

There was one exception--Sidi Mohammed, Sultan of Morocco. With him it was possible to conclude a treaty in 1786 which was respected. It cost the United States some £5,000, as well as a quantity of ordnance, but Mohammed--an enlightened and temperate ruler--freed all American prisoners and respected American ships. His successors, with some variations, followed his policy.

With the other members of Blackmail Unlimited, it was different. To

Algeria, we gave £40,000 for relief of prisoners in 1793, nearly $1,000,000 for a treaty in 1796, and four ships in 1797, 1798, and 1799--the specially built frigate *Crescent*, thirty-six, the brig *Hassam Bashan*, and two schooners, *Hamdullah* and *Lalah Eisha.*

The United States paid $107,000 to Tunis in 1798, along with jewels, small arms, and other presents for the Dey in succeeding years. Tripoli demanded $100,000 yearly in tribute from 1787 forward, but it was never paid. However, we did pay over $80,000 in 1796 and 1799, and in 1802, the sum of $6,500 to ransom the crew of the American brig *Franklin* who had been held in prison. All in all, the United States spent some $2,000,000 in tribute--sufficient to have built an imposing fleet. But we are getting ahead of our story.

It is interesting to note that Thomas Jefferson, who as President would win the reputation of being a pacifist, was one of the few American statesmen of the period who advocated taking a strong stand against the Barbary corsairs. As early as 1786, when Minister to France, he asserted that a fleet in being would arm the President "with the safest of all instruments of coercion."

For several years Portugal had provided some protection for American shipping, by patrolling the Straits of Gibraltar and keeping the pirates from entering the Atlantic. But in 1793 a treaty between Portugal and Algiers, oddly contrived by the British Consul at Algiers, unlocked the gate and Algerian corsairs surged out into the Atlantic. Eleven American merchantmen were captured. When the news reached the now constitutionally organized United States, public opinion forced congressional and administration hands, as maritime insurance rates jumped from ten per cent to a breathtaking thirty per cent. A Navy would be constructed. Six magnificent frigates, product of Joshua Humphreys' and Josiah Fox's drawing boards, were laid down in 1794. But the Congress, impecunious, in appropriating $668,888 for the new ships, stipulated that construction should cease when and if a satisfactory treaty with Algiers be concluded.

Meantime diplomacy was at work. In 1795 Dey Hassan Pasha of Algiers after much dickering accepted an American offer to pay a lump sum of $642,500 for ransom of the prisoners and an additional annual tribute of naval stores equaling $21,600. In addition, presents were to be presented the Dey twice a year equaling $21,600. In addition, presents were to be presented the Dey twice a year equaling similar blackmail imposed on Holland, Sweden, and Denmark. The shameful compact was signed in September and work on the new warships ceased.

For several years American merchantmen plied the Mediterranean in comparative peace under this thralldom, while our trade waxed. In 1799 an approximate $8,800,000 worth of goods moved in American bottoms to Spain and Italy, and by the next year it approximated some $11,000,000. This was too rich a morsel for the corsair states to ignore, so conditions worsened as Tunis and Tripoli screamed for bigger chunks of blackmail and Algiers, whose share of our tribute was the largest, became impatient for more. Meanwhile the quasi war with France in the Caribbean was in full flower, engaging the new United States Navy that had come into being in 1798.

So the United States continued to sign agreements and pay tribute. When tribute was sent in the fall of 1800, near the close of the quasi war with France, the Barbary buccaneers' bellicosity became even greater because of an unfortunate turn of events.

Captain William Bainbridge, in USS *George Washington*, twenty-four, arrived at Algiers in September 1800, carrying the annual tribute. Dey Bobba Mustapha--successor to Hassan--was having difficulties with the Sultan of Turkey, his overlord. So, when Bainbridge, and our Consul, Richard O'Brien, paid their respects to the Dey, they received an amazing proposition.

Bobba Mustapha, whom William Eaton, our Consul at Tunis, later described as a "huge shaggy beast, sitting on his rump upon a low bench with his hind legs gathered up like a tailor or a bear, who extended his forepaw as to receive something to eat," informed Bainbridge that the *George Washington* would carry his presents and his Ambasador to the Sultan of Turkey at Constantinople. Bainbridge, hotly protesting, was answered, "You pay me tribute, by which you become my slaves. I have a right to order my slaves as I please." To a man of the American's temperament there could hardly have been anything more galling, but there was very little he could do about it. His ship lay under some two hundred guns of the Algerian fortifications; if he refused the insolent demand, not only would he lose his ship, but the corsairs would be loosed against American merchantmen.

So, after much haggling, the *George Washington*, Constantinople bound, cleared Algiers harbor on October 19, loaded to the scuppers with the most heterogeneous cargo ever put aboard a United States warship. The frigate, we must remember, was a converted merchantman of 624 tons displacement and 108 feet long. Not only did she have on board her normal armament and stores and a crew of 130 souls, but packed in her steerage were the Algerian Ambassador and his suite--some hundred or more persons, including Negro slaves, half of them women. Stowed in her hold was *backsheesh* to the Sultan of Turkey--$800,000 in specie, plus an immense quantity of jewels and a menagerie of wild life for his zoo: lions, tigers, antelope, ostriches, and parrots. Two Arabian chargers for the Sultan topped the list. The Dey, it seems, was in the bad graces of the Sultan, hence his desire to make amends.

How they all existed in this modern Ark one cannot imagine. But Bainbridge ran a taut ship. His crew, put on a strict half-ration of rum, kept their tempers remarkably as they pushed their way through the crowded decks on their lawful occasions.

It was an extremely unpleasant trans-Mediterranean trip, against headwinds most of the way and in poor company. The Americans derived what amusement they could from tacking the ship frequently while the Muslims were at prayer, so five times daily they had to flop back and forth on the deck like dying fish to keep their faces properly turned toward Mecca.

One can well imagine that Bainbridge, smarting under the humiliation imposed on his nation, his ship, and himself, was in no mood for trifling as the *George Washington*, with a brisk following wind, moved up into the Dardanelles at long last. Abreast of the guardian forts at the entrance to the Sea of Marmora--beyond which no foreign warship could move without personal permission of the Sultan--her eight-gun salute began to boom out as the ship slowed. The swirling cloud of white powder smoke surrounding her doubled in size as a shore battery promptly returned the courtesy. But no expected rattle of anchor chain through hawse-hole came to the ears of the garrison. Instead, *George Washington* emerged from the thinning smoke with topsails sheeted home again and before the Turks realized what was happening she was out of gunshot and bowling into the Sea of Marmora.

So it was that a dawn next day, November 9, 1800, a shocked captain of the harbor of Constantinople (Stamboul), came scurrying in his barge to hail this insolent armed stranger, anchored unbidden in the Golden Horn, and flying a flag whose like he had never seen before. He doubted the actual existence of the United States, until informed that the country was part of the new world discovered by Columbus. Rushing back to report, he later brought back word that the Sultan regarded it as a good omen that the Stars and Stripes, like the Turkish flag, bore a representation of heavenly bodies.

There was till some boggling by Turkish official underlings but, thanks to the good offices of Britain's Ambassador to the Sublime Porte, Thomas Bruce, Earl of Elgin, an *entente cordiale* was arranged with the High Admiral of Turkey, Capudan Pasha Hassan, who took Bainbridge under his personal wing. Hassan, brother-in-law to Sultan Selim III, shared his relative's dislike for the Dey of Algiers. He actually stamped on and spat upon the Dey's letter, while the unfortunate Ambassador was refused acceptance, although his tribute, menagerie and all, was quickly grabbed.

Bainbridge's culture and natural charm stood him in good stead with the Capudan Pasha, who obtained a *firmin* (passport) which placed the American officer under the special protection of the Sultan. There was a series of friendly dinners; there was also some talk of a trade treaty with this nation discovered by Columbus. In such favorable circumstances Bainbridge may be said to have really laid the ground for the trade treaty which would later be negotiated with Turkey.

On December 30, 1800, the *George Washington* departed, honored by special salutes from the Dardanelles forts. This time a chastened Algerine delegation gloomed in her steerage. On January 21 Bainbridge brought her into Algiers, dumped his passengers, and presented the Day with Sultan Selim's arbitrary demand for a high cash tribute, an immediate declaration of war against France, the liberation of all prisoners with English "recommendations," and an agreement to provision such British vessels as might ask for it.

Bobba Mustapha exploded, threatened Bainbridge. But when Bainbridge pulled the Sultan's *firmin* from his pocket and shoved it into the Algerine's face, Bobba, a deflated balloon, became fawningly agreeable. But there was more to come. The Dey, obeying the Sultan's orders, chopped down the French Consulate's flagpole as a declaration of war and ordered the immediate expulsion of the French delegation--some forty-odd men, women, and children. Disobedience would mean slavery; a foregone conclusion it would seem, for transportation was refused.

Once more the Sultan's *firmin* was waved. Bainbridge gathered the unfortunate French citizens on board the *George Washington*, cleared the port January 30, 1801, and deposited them at Alicante, Spain, on February 6. Then the *George Washington* pointed west for the United States, Bainbridge breathing his fervent prayer: "I hope I may never again be sent to Algiers with a tribute except it be from the mouth of a cannon." His prayer, as it turned out, would be answered shortly.

War and Tribute

The fact that Algiers had been able to commandeer an American ship of war was soon common talk along the Barbary Coast. American prestige sunk lower than ever, as did that of other Christian nations such as Denmark and Sweden, who had also been subject to depredations. Particularly obstreperous was the Bashaw of Tripoli, Yusuf Karamanli, a usurper, who for nearly two years had been haggling and bargling with our Consul James L. Cathcart, over his share of American largesse. He demanded ships, he demanded cash, he repudiated treaties. Finally, on May 10, 1801, despite the diplomatic efforts of Cathcart, he declared war on the United States. Following the symbolic cutting down of the flagpole at the consulate, his so-called "navy"--three small vessels under Murad Rais— put to sea to intercept American shipping at the Straits of Gibraltar.

The entire situation, in the opinion of United States Consul William Eaton in Tunis, was ridiculous. He constantly pointed out that the Barbary States were weak and so defenseless that any reasonable naval force could smash them. He could see no justification for permitting them to threaten nations possessing fleets of good ships and competent sailors. In a letter to the Secretary of State, Eaton, sarcastic, remarked: "What would the world say if Rhode Island should arm two old merchantmen, put an Irish renegade in one and a Methodist preacher in the other, and send them to demand a tribute of the Grand Signor?"

What the Tripolitan despot didn't know was that already an American squadron was on its way to the Mediterranean. Thomas Jefferson, just become President, and enraged at the humiliating experience of the *George Washington*, and the demands of Tripoli, had dispatched Commodore Richard Dale with the frigates *President*, forty-four, Captain James Barron; *Philadelphia*, thirty-six, Captain Samuel Barron (James Barron's brother); and *Essex*, thirty-two, under Bainbridge; and the schooner *Enterprise*, twelve, Lieutenant Andrew Sterett. Dale, his flag in the *President*, had orders to visit the Barbary ports on a defensive mission but to open hostilities with any nation that declared war. In such case he was to "cruise off that port so as to effectually prevent anything from coming in or going out"; he was also to "sink, burn or destroy their ships wherever you find them." This latter injunction was Jefferson's own hair-splitting decision: he believed that without formal declaration of war by the Congress no prizes could legally be taken.

At Gibraltar, July 1, Dale learned of Tripoli's war declaration. Murad Rais, with his *Meshouda* and a sixteen-gun brig, was also nestling there, sheltered by English neutrality. Dale, leaving *Philadelphia* to watch the Tripolitans, dispatched *Essex* to collect American merchantmen in neutral ports and convoy them to the Atlantic. With *President* and *Enterprise*, he cruised the Barbary Coast and took up station off the harbor of Tripoli for eighteen days. The Bashaw, understandably disturbed, offered to treat for peace but before negotiations commenced Dale was forced to depart for Malta to get fresh water.

En route, Sterett's *Enterprise* fell in with the lateen-rigged polacca *Tripoli*, fourteen, manned by eighty men. The corsair moved in dangerously close to the *Enterprise* in preparation for boarding, a favorite tactic of the Barbary pirates. But Sterett, as good a seaman as the Navy had, maneuvered sharply, kept up a gunnery fight, and at the end of three hours had the satisfaction of seeing the enemy strike.

As soon as the *Enterprise* tried to take possession, however, the *Tripoli* broke out her colors again and came rushing in with the evident intention of boarding her stationary opponent. Evading her, Sterett's six-pounders were opened. Once more the Tripolitan hauled down his colors, only to resume action again. This time the *Enterprise* literally pounded the polacca into submission, raking her several times. The corsair captain, his ship dismasted, now personally threw his colors into the sea.

Sterett reported that action "commenced immediately at pistol shot which continued three hours with incessant firing. The *Tripoli* then struck her colors. The carnage on board was dreadful, she having twenty men killed and thirty wounded . . ." Not a man was wounded on the *Enterprise* and she sustained no material damage to hull or rigging.

For his brilliant exploit the thanks of Congress and a sword were given to Sterett and an extra month's pay was awarded to the officers and men. The *Tripoli,* her guns and stores dumped overboard, was set free to make her way back to Tripoli as best she could. There the enraged Bashaw had her commander, Mohammed Sous, paraded through the streets mounted backward on a jackass, with the entrails of a sheep hung about his neck.

As for Sterett, his gunnery officer, the ever present David Porter, and the schooner *Enterprise*, they sailed for home in October 1801, since Commodore Dale did not believe it safe to cruise the Mediterranean in the winter.

Dale had ordered *Philadelphia* to base at Syracuse and cruise occasionally off Tripoli, and he assigned *Essex* to remain off Gibraltar and Algeciras to protect American merchantmen at the western end of the Mediterranean.

Before returning under orders to the United States, Dale in the *President* visited Algiers in the hope of persuading the Dey to agree to peace. He and Consul O'Brien made representations to the Dey but procured only airy promises.

On the way out to Algiers harbor on November 30, the *President* struck a rock and damaged her keel. Dale made for Toulon, France, the best place for repairs, but before he was allowed to dock he had to spend fifteen weary days in quarantine. The repair of the damaged keel forced him to stay at Toulon until early February 1802. He was visited there by the Admiral of the Swedish Navy with a proposal for joint operations against Tripoli which Dale's instructions did not permit. However, he did work out a joint plan of blockade and convoy.

Meanwhile the American squadron in the Mediterranean was temporarily reinforced in the early part of 1802 by the arrival at Toulon of the frigate *Boston*, twenty-eight, commanded by Captain Daniel McNeill. She had brought the new American Minister, Robert R. Livingston, to France. Dale decided to maintain *Boston* with the *Essex* on patrol in the Mediterranean; all other vessels of the squadron were ordered home because one-year enlistments of the seamen were about to expire.

For his part, William Eaton, our Consul at Tunis, was very distressed at the passive campaign forced upon the Americans by the inaction of Congress. As yet, war had not been declared against Tripoli, and Jefferson's administration still persisted in the illusion that we were at peace with the world. To his friend Congressman Samuel Lyman of Massachusetts, Eaton wrote describing the negligible effects of Dale's expedition and urging Congress to put more vigor into the campaign.

In the second year of the war against Tripoli, the United States Navy ordered a new squadron to the Mediterranean. Command was first offered to Commodore Thomas Truxtun, the hero of the quasi war with France. Because of a scarcity of captains, no one was appointed to command his flagship, *Constellation*, in which he had won two famous victories. Refusing to act as captain of his own flagship, the testy Truxtun declined the command and resigned from the Navy.

Captain Richard V. Morris succeeded Truxtun. As it turned out, no more unlikely naval commander could have been chosen. He took with him in his flagship *Chesapeake*, by special permission, his wife, baby son, and a Negro maid. He then permitted wives of other officers and men to make the cruise.

Peppery William Eaton would later sum up Morris' Tripolitan saga with the acid remark in his letter-book: "The government might as well station a company of comedians and a seraglio before the enemy's nest."

Morris' instructions were explicit; he was to safeguard American shipping and maintain a strict blockade of Tripoli. Instead, he would scatter his ships throughout the Mediterranean while most of the time he kept far from the scene of action.

The new commodore got away in the *Chesapeake* in early April 1802 but the frigate sprung her mainmast four days out of Hampton Roads, so most of the ships in his squadron reached the Mediterranean before him.

It was an imposing array. First to sail was the little *Enterprise*, still under Sterett's command. Then came *Constellation*, thirty-six, Captain Alexander Murray; *John Adams*, twenty-eight, Captain John Rodgers; and *New York*, thirty-six, Captain James Barron. The *Adams*, twenty-eight, Captain Hugh Campbell, was last to leave the United States.

Captain Murray, old, deaf, and headstrong, was senior officer in the Mediterranean until Morris arrived. Murray's first errand was to deliver a long-awaited present of jewelry to the Bey of Tunis. He was, understandably, received graciously. As a result, in his innocence of Barbary affairs, he reported to the Secretary of the Navy that Algiers and Tunis were now well disposed to the United States, and that Tripoli was ready to come to terms.

Actually, delivery of the jewels only brought a more exorbitant demand from the Bey of Tunis. In his boundless greed, he sent word that now he expected the gift of a brig of war.

Murray's education soon began. Tripolitan pirates had taken the Philadelphia brig *Franklin*, off Cape Palos, Spain; Murray just missed intercepting them as they raced for Tripoli, and had to content himself with a long-range bombardment of the port. One of the *Chesapeake's* cannon balls crashed through the palace walls, to the terror of the Bey's seraglio, and his own rage. Then Murray sailed away.

In late May, Commodore Morris reached Gibraltar, where the *Chesapeake's* mast was repaired. By the time she was again fit for duty, the Sultan of Morocco kicked over the traces, molesting United States merchantmen. This new complication kept Morris in the vicinity of Gibraltar for most of the summer, which delighted the seagoing Mrs. Morris, thus able to become a part of the social scene in the British colony.

Sultan Muley Soliman, son of the amiable Mohammed, came into the picture through one of the many fantastic incidents studding this Mediterranean campaign. In some fashion he had purchased from Tripoli the *Meshouda* (ex-*Polly*), Murad Rais's flagship, long bottled up in Gibraltar by American warships. Murad himself and his crew had long since returned to Tripoli by one means or another.

Muley Soliman wanted to send his new acquisition to Tripoli, loaded with grain and--possibly--contraband of war. When his demand for her free passage was turned down, he went into a tantrum, but actually had done nothing more warlike than make threats and take a few American vessels. Negotiations dragged on until August when our consul at Tangier, James Simpson, annonced that peace with Morocco had been restored. Simpson, as a mark of American good will, now gave the *Meshouda* a passport but with strict proviso that she was not to enter Tripoli.

During the fall of 1802 Sweden made peace with Tripoli, handing over a flat payment of $150,000 and promising an annual tribute of $8,000. In addition, Napoleon sent the Bashaw a fine fourteen-gun sloop of war as a gift. These settlements left the United States not only with the problem of fighting the war alone, but also set a precedent as to the price of peace.

Morris' lackadaisical attitude made matters worse. From Gibraltar he went to Malta, where he found safe haven. Later, after Christmas 1802, he moved to a cozy anchorage at Syracuse in Sicily. So the great expectations in the United States for this naval expedition faded. Actually the nation lost ground, for the blockade of Tripoli was ineffectual, except as an irritant.

Also during the year, William Eaton, whose interest and operations along the Barbary Coast far exceeded his normal duties as United States Consul of Tunis, clashed with Commodore Morris. Morris gave a cold shoulder to Eaton's scheme to unseat the usurping Bashaw Yusuf Karamanli in Tripoli; as a result Eaton left for the United States to lay his scheme before President Jefferson, who approved. We shall hear more of the doings of this bustling American Machiavelli.

Not until the end of January 1803 did Morris make a real move. By the time *Constellation* had gone home. With *Chesapeake*, *New York,* and *John Adams* he put out for Tripoli, while *Enterprise* sailed for Tunis. But gale winds broke up the huffing, puffing commodore's plans. His provisions exhausted, he put back to Gibraltar, making brief visits to Tunis and Algiers, where he received cool receptions.

At Gibraltar, Morris shifted his flag to the *New York*, now under Captain Isaac Chauncey, with daring David Porter as first lieutenant. Isaac Hull took over the ubiquitous little *Enterprise*, Sterett going home in *Chesapeake*. Now Morris made another try for Tripoli, assembling *New York, John Adams,* and *Enterprise* at Malta, where the *Adams*, formerly blockading the *Meshouda,* also joined. But only *John Adams* was ready for a cruise and John Rodgers put out on May 3. Off the port he fell in with the *Meshouda* (ex-*Polly*), making for Tripoli under Moroccan colors, and picked her off.

Morris at long last appeared off Tripoli, to establish the blockade. It was late May; he had been on the station for a year and now for the first time set eyes on his major blockading objective. A fleet of grain feluccas--lateen-rigged galleys--escorted by eleven gunboats, attempted to run into the port. Morris made chase but the gunboats huddled under the shore batteries, while the feluccas were beached beyond the old port. David Porter, reconnoitering, requested permission to make a night attack. Morris authorized a daylight assault. Porter with a detachment of some fifty marines and bluejackets made a landing under shore fire and the feluccas were set ablaze. After some heavy hand-to-hand fighting, in which Porter was wounded, the expedition disengaged, covered by the ships' guns, and under command of Lieutenant James Lawrence. American loss is uncertain; reports range from fifteen killed and wounded to just four men wounded beside Porter--one marine and three bluejackets. All casualties were retrieved. Approximately half the grain--some two hundred tons--was destroyed.

Under flag of truce, Morris now went ashore to dicker with Yusuf. But, like most of Morris' efforts, the gesture was abortive. Yusuf would talk only if money was forthcoming. He actually threatened to keep Morris as hostage, but was dissuaded. So Morris returned to his ship, and, amazingly enough, sailed away June 10 in *New York,* leaving John Rodgers, senior captain, to command the squadron: *John Adams, Adams,* and *Enterprise.*

Forthright John Rodgers craved action, and he got it. The Bashaw, feeling his oats, on the night of June 21, sent his own squadron out--a twenty-two-gun polacca, escorted by nine gunboats. Rodgers, expecting some such move, had stationed *Adams* west of the harbor entrance, *Enterprise* to the east, and in *John Adams* lay in the center. Shortly after dawn *Enterprise* made signal that something was up. Rodgers, standing down, was informed that a large vessel had taken shelter in a cove some twenty miles to the east.

Both American vessels closed in, to find the corsair polacca moored in the bay, with springs on her cables, prepared to fire in any direction, while the gunboats crawling along the coast were assembling in the shoal waters around her. On the shore Rodgers also saw "a vast number" of cavalry and infantry. Rodgers worked his frigate in carefully, chose a good range, and opened fire. The Tripolitans could not match *John Adams'* long twelve-pounders, in range or accuracy. After forty minutes of it they abandoned ship, and Rodgers signaled *Enterprise* in "to amuse the enemy" while he skirted around some dangerous reefs and lowered his boats to take possession. Seeing that they had only the schooner to deal with, the Tripolitans began to come out and climb aboard their ship again, but *Enterprise* was now close in and firing fast the little guns of her broadside. By the time Rodgers retrieved his boats and brought the frigate into action again, smoke and flame were spurting from the polacca's portholes. A few minutes later she blew up.

Rodgers waxed almost poetic in his description of the explosion, which, he wrote, caused "a Huge Column of smoke, with a Pyramid of Fire darting vertically through its Centre interspersed with Masts, Yards, Sails, Rigging, different parts of the Hull &c and the vessel in an instant dashed to Attoms." Tripolitan losses in the explosion and from the naval cannonade of the shore must have been serious. Neither casualties nor damage were suffered on board the American vessels.

It was a nice little victory, badly needed to restore American morale. Unfortunately it was not followed up. By Morris' orders, Rodgers was to raise the blockade five days after the commodore's departure, and the sea was again opened to Tripolitan corsairs.

However, the scenes were shifting. In July 1803 the smart topsail schooner *Nautilus*, twelve, Lieutenant Richard Somers, came winging into Malta with dispatches recalling Morris to the United States. He faded forever from the Mediterranean, September 25, 1803, in *Adams* thirteen days after the arrival of his successor Commodore Edward Preble.

New Broom

Flint-faced Edward Preble, Captain, USN, his commodore's pennant flying in USS *Constitution*, forty-four, passed eastward through the Pillars of Hercules on September 12, 1803, bringing a breath of fresh air to all Americans in the Mediterranean. Both Jefferson and the Congress had decided that something had to be done.

Three small vessels, tailored to fit the needs of a Mediterranean coastal campaign, had been rushed to completion: for fine brigs *Siren* and *Argus*, both sixteen-gun sloops of war; and the schooner *Vixen*, fourteen. The schooner *Nautilus*, just completed, had been purchased and fitted to carry fourteen guns. These handy craft, together with the frigates *Constitution* and *Philadelphia*, made up a task force suited to the situation. The happy choice of Preble, tenth in rank on the captains' list, ensured real leadership.

Preble, as unyielding as the granite of his own Maine rockbound coast, was forty-two years old--actually at least a decade older than any of the officers in his new command, whom he sarcastically lumped at first as "nothing but a pack of boys!" He was hot-tempered but not rash; dyspeptic (his constitution ruined by captivity in the notorious British prison ship *Jersey* during the Revolutionary War); the strictest of disciplinarians; a perfectionist. At the beginning of the campaign he was cordially hated by most of his subordinates; by its end they adored him. Above all, as both friend and foe soon discovered, it could be said of him, as Lincoln would later say of Grant: ". . . He fights!"

He proved that once to the satisfaction of his own officers and crew by threatening to fire on a British frigate off Gibraltar which had arrogantly refused his hail for identification. He proved it again when he learned on arrival that Sultan Muley Soliman of Morocco threatened war on the United States. Preble sailed into Tangier harbor October 5, with *Consti-*

tution and *Nautilus*, followed by the home-going *New York* and *John Adams*, and the little *Enterprise*. The squadron, cleared for action, anchored off the fortress walls at point-blank range, presenting a combined broadside of more than sixty guns. Preble, leaving behind written instructions that should "the least injury" be offered him, bombardment must start "regardless of my personal safety," went ashore in style to beard the Sultan, with Tobias Lear, new Consul General to Algiers, beside him.

He was received courteously and escorted to the palace, where, stony-faced, he refused to surrender his sidearms, or to kneel to Muley Soliman.

"Are you not in fear of being detained?" asked Muley.

"No, sir. If you presume to do it my squadron in your full view will lay your batteries, your castle, and your city in ruins."

This was language a North African despot could understand. The net result was that a placid Muley Soliman re-ratified his father's peace treaty of 1786. No more would tribute be paid; no more would American shipping be molested. Nor did Preble at the time even make a token gesture of *bakshesh*. The aroma of his saluting powder smoke was sufficient.

Preble moved to accomplish his principal mission; *Constitution* and smaller vessels cruising the Mediterranean, while *Philadelphia*, back again with Bainbridge in command, Porter her first lieutenant and Jacob Jones her second, sailed to Tripoli to establish the blockade. With her went newly arrived *Vixen*, Master Commandant John Smith. The commodore felt that this fast frigate-schooner combination could handle both offshore and close-in sweeps.

Bainbridge--unlucky Bainbridge--taking station, received information of two Tripolitan war vessels cruising the Mediterranean. In the belief they were probably going westward toward Gibraltar, he dispatched *Vixen* to look for them off Cape Bon. Toward the end of October *Philadelphia* was driven to sea by one of the storms common at that time, and as she was returning to her station on the morning of October 31, she sighted a Tripolitan vessel making for the harbor.

The *Philadelphia*, thirty-eight, gift of the city for which she was named, was a beautiful ship designed by Josiah Fox, Humphreys' assistant, as a somewhat lighter and less expensive version of one of the famous forty-fours. She carried twenty-two-pounder carronades topside. Underwater she had the famous Humphreys' lines, and aloft a quite unusual spread of sail which made her exceptionally fast.

The frigate now bore up in chase, with the lead line going constantly and getting seven to ten fathoms. It suddenly shoaled to a half six. Bainbridge had the helm put hard down and the yards braced sharp up, but the ship had so much way on that before she could lose it, misfortune once more struck at her captain. She went hard and fast on an uncharted reef. Bainbridge did everything a seaman's ingenuity could suggest, but to no effect. Canted over, unable to fire a gun at the numerous Tripolitan gunboats which presently came out, the frigate had to be surrendered, and for the second time in his career one of the best ship captains in the American Navy found himself a prisoner.

For Bainbridge and his men it was the beginning of an eighteen-month imprisonment. For Preble, who learned of the disaster when he spoke with a British frigate November 10, the news was shocking. He had lost one of his two frigates. Worse yet, it appeared that the Tripolitans had succeeded in floating the ship, repairing the Americans' hasty efforts to scuttle her, and that she was now resting in Tripoli harbor, her guns retrieved and remounted. This was a serious reversal of the balance of naval power, which could not be tolerated.

Establishing a base at Syracuse, Sicily, Preble kept up the blockade of Tripoli through the bitter winter months with his smaller ships. Transferring his flag from *Constitution*--far too valuable now to be risked except for a main effort--Preble cruised in *Enterprise* and *Vixen* when he was not busy working out plans for the *Philadelphia*'s destruction.

Meanwhile, the safety of the men and officers of the *Philadelphia* aroused international interest and brought offers of mediation from many sources. The United States diplomatic representatives abroad were probably less than discreet in their appeals for help from the European powers. The American Ministers to Spain, France, and Russia all attempted to obtain the intercessions of those states. Sweden was asked for help, and Denmark was already assisting in the relief of the prisoners. President Jefferson was annoyed at the undignified tone of our many solicitations, saying, "I've never been so mortified as at the conduct of our foreign functionaries on the loss of the *Philadelphia*."

But Preble was not interested in ransom efforts; his method of bargaining would be by cutlass and fire. The Tripolitan ketch *Mastico*, lately captured by *Enterprise*, would be his vehicle, and twenty-five-year-old Lieutenant Stephen Decatur, Jr., skipper of *Enterprise*, the commander. Decatur had volunteered to take *Enterprise* herself in, daring the Tripolitan guns, but Preble would have none of that; the little schooner was needed with the squadron.

So on the night of February 16, 1804, under a full moon, lateen-rigged *Mastico*, rechristened USS *Intrepid*, slowly crept into Tripoli harbor, with English colors drooping from her masthead; to all outward appearance a slovenly Maltese trader. On her deck, in Moorish costumes, were Decatur, his pilot, a brave Sicilian shipmaster named Salvador Catalano who had volunteered for the job; and a couple of sailors.

Below decks, crouched and huddled amid barrels of gunpowder and pitch, were nine officers, fifty-odd bluejackets, and eight marines--volunteers all for one of the most extraordinary and daring raids ever attempted by the United States Navy. They were to board the *Philadelphia* as she lay under the Berber batteries, destroy her by burning and scuttling, and then--God willing--make their way out of the harbor and join USS *Siren* which was standing by outside the port to cover their retreat.

Among Decatur's nine young officers--nucleus of a United States Navy which would write its name large in the not too distant future--were Lieutenant James Lawrence--whose dying injunction of "Don't give up the ship!" would become a Navy slogan; Midshipman Charles Morris-- known to a later generation as "Statesman of the United States Navy"; and another midshipman who one decade later would throttle a British invasion by his victory on Lake Champlain: Thomas Macdonough.

The *Philadelphia*, both broadsides double-shotted, lay under the guns of the Bashaw's castle, moored so as to sweep the harbor entrance. Her position and condition were known to Decatur, for not only had Bainbridge been in correspondence with Preble--using "sympathetic" ink —but Catalano himself had been in the harbor since her capture.

Intrepid got to within a hundred yards of *Philadelphia* when she was hailed and ordered to stand clear. Catalano, pouring out his troubles in lucid Mediterranean *lingua franca,* told of an anchor lost by storm; he begged permission to moor alongside until daybreak. Permission was granted, lines were passed. Then, as the ketch nosed up, someone on the frigate noted an anchor in plain sight on her bow.

A shriek of alarm was followed by an American cheer as willing hands tailing on the lines brought the vessels together. Then the boarders swarmed over to clear the frigate's deck with cutlass and boarding pike. Some twenty Tripolitans were cut down as they huddled on her forecastle; the remainder of her crew leaped overside into the harbor waters. Rehearsed in their duties, the boarding parties scattered their combustibles in cockpit, steerage, and storerooms, set the torch, then scampered for their ketch, even as flames were licking from *Philadelphia*'s gun ports.

The lines were cast off and *Intrepid*, propelled now by sixteen sweeps and towed by two small boats, moved out toward the mouth of the now illuminated harbor, target for every gun the excited Tripolitans could bring to bear. It was a thirty-minute job well done, with Decatur the last man to leave; he leaped for *Intrepid*'s rigging as she cast loose. Fortunately, the frantic gun crews on shore, strong in sound and fury, were short on expertise. One shot through the ketch's topsail was the net damage, although *Philadelphia*'s loaded broadside guns, discharged by the fire, also sent round shot splashing about in the channel as well as ashore.

Decatur and his little ship made the entrance, met *Siren*'s waiting boats sent by Lieutenant Charles Stewart to support his close friend and crony. Then the two vessels made off. Not a man had been scratched. Inside the harbor *Philadelphia*, her hawsers burned away, drifted crazily across the port, and blew up under the castle, to the shock and consternation of the entire city. There her timbers sizzled throughout the night.

Swift recognition of the amazing exploit followed. On Preble's immediate warm recommendation Decatur would soon be commissioned a full captain--the youngest man in the United States Navy to reach the grade. And from England's Lord Nelson came a terse sailor's acknowledgment of "the most bold and daring act of the age." In all probability Decatur would cherish that accolade even more than he did the sword that Congress presented him.

The question once was, and occasionally still is, debated as to why Decatur did not attempt to bring the frigate out instead of destroying her after he had gained possession. Those who argue that it could have been done seem to have forgotten one thing: Bainbridge had cut away her foremast before surrendering, and it had not been replaced. She, therefore, had no headsail and, as the breeze was onshore, could not have been worked out under canvas. It does not seem likely that seventy-four men in a sixteen-oared ketch could have towed her out by hand with everybody shooting at them and the Tripolitan gunboats certain to intervene.

The burning of the frigate completely restored the strategic situation. It was now no longer necessary to hold the *Constitution* in reserve; there was no longer any enemy heavy ship that could drive off our light cruisers. The big frigate could therefore be used in the direct attacks on the city which Preble had intended; but it was late summer before the elimination of a threatened difficulty with Tunis and the end of the onshore gales gave opportunity.

During this time the Commodore maintained a blockade on Tripoli and kept two or three vessels of his squadron cruising the Mediterranean in search of any Tripolitan ship that might attempt escape from the port. He also arranged with the King of the Two Sicilies--Ferdinand IV--for the loan of six small flat-bottom gunboats, each armed with one long twenty-four-pounder; and two bomb ketches, carrying each a thirteen-inch mortar. With the vessels came also the loan of ninety-six Neapolitan seamen. Junior officers from Preble's squadron commanded each of the vessels, with cadres of bluejackets to stiffen the crews. When these new additions had been shaken down Preble moved.

The walled city of Tripoli, with its castle and shore batteries, bristled with at least 115 heavy cannon. Tripolitan naval forces inside the harbor, which was protected by a screen of reefs, were a ten-gun brig, two armed schooners, two large galleys each mounting several guns, and nineteen gunboats; each of these last carried either an eighteen- or a twenty-four-pounder and two small howitzers. The corsair navy was commanded by our old acquaintance Murad Rais, the renegade. On shore the Bashaw mustered some twenty-five thousand troops.

On July 25, when Preble commenced his bombardment, the American squadron consisted of the *Constitution*, four brigs—*Argus, Siren, Vixen,* and *Scourge*; two schooners, *Nautilus* and *Enterprise*; the six Neapolitan gunboats and two mortar ketches. Its fire power totaled 156 cannon of all calibers.

After several days of boisterous weather, during which the little gunboats and mortar ketches were only saved from foundering by excellent seamanship, the weather cleared. On the morning of August 3 the squadron stood in. *Constitution*, followed by the brigs and schooners, engaged the shore batteries, while the mortar ketches hurled their big projectiles into the town. The gunboats made for the enemy's defensive line of gunboats spread in front of the two gaps in the reefs.

Decatur, commanding the flotilla, led one division of three gunboats against five Tripolitan vessels clustered in front of the eastern pass; Somers led the other three against the hostile boats screening the western pass.

As the shooting against the castle began, the Tripolitan gunboats came straight on toward contact, banging through the powder smoke, for they prided themselves greatly at hand-to-hand fighting, and their equals in their game had not been found in the Mediterranean during three hundred years. They got their bellyful from Decatur, who slammed his bow against one of their boats, boarded against odds of two to one, and in ten minutes had the adversaries all down or overboard except five who hid in the hold.

Lieutenant John Trippe carried another after a desperate battle in which he drove a boarding pike through the Tripolitan skipper after taking eleven scimitar wounds. Joseph Bainbridge's boat of Decatur's division had her lateen yard shot away and could not close; neither could two of Somer's craft, which were unable to beat against a contrary wind fast enough to reach hand-to-hand action. Somers finally found himself alone against five enemy gunboats, "advancing and firing," as he later reported. But with round shot and grape from his one twenty-four-pounder, Somers halted them. They wove ship to escape under the protection of the shore batteries, and the amazing Somers actually chased all five of them back behind the reefline. Meanwhile Lieutenant James Decatur of Somers' division came down to join his brother's battle and delivered into one of the Tripolitans a fire so fierce that she hauled down her flag. He swept alongside to take possession; just as he mounted the rail, the Tripolitan captain produced a pistol and shot him through the head.

The news came to Stephen Decatur as he was towing out his own prize. He shouted to the eleven men who remained unhurt in his own boat and, casting loose his prize, turned back toward the treacherous Moor in a frenzy of rage, slamming into her side and leaping aboard almost in unison. The Tripolitan captain was a giant of a man; Decatur's cutlass snapped off against his boarding pike, and the American took a thrust that tore his arm and chest, but he grappled with the big man, and the two went to the deck, Decatur on top. Another Moor was swinging a deadly blow at Decatur's head when an incredibly courageous seaman named Daniel Frazier, already wounded in both arms, pushed in to take the blow on his own skull. The struggling pair rolled, the Tripolitan captain working one arm free to yank out a dagger; but Decatur managed to hold his wrist with one hand while with the other he fired a pistol through his pocket, bringing down his huge enemy like the carcass of a bear.

That finished it; the rest of the Tripolitans on the gunboat gave up; the other vessels had fled. The wind changing, Preble broke off action and the squadron hauled offshore. The captain's barge was sent for James Decatur, who would die before sunset, and there was a sad, proud evening in the squadron as it prepared for another bout. Another there would be--and more than one--but the Tripolitans would try handgrips no more.

Lieutenant Stephen Decatur boarded the *Constitution* to make his report to Commodore Preble. As young Decatur stepped on the quarterdeck, his uniform torn and bloody, face pale and eyes sad at the loss of his dearly loved brother, he saluted and said, "I have brought you three of the enemy's gunboats, sir."

Preble seized the lieutenant, shaking him, and shouted, "And why did you not bring me more?" Then swinging on his heel he strode into his cabin. Decatur and his fellow officers were dumbfounded. A few minutes later, an orderly came with the message that the commodore wished to see "Captain" Decatur in his cabin.

No sound came from the cabin for a long time while the officers listened. At last, some of them, fearing the worst, rapped on the door and opened it. Preble and Decatur were seated side by side on the narrow bench, and both men were in tears.

Four days later the squadron again bombarded Tripoli, but on this occasion none of the enemy vessels closed in for an attack. During this attack one of the gunboats of the United States force blew up, killing and wounding eighteen of her crew.

That same day the frigate *John Adams*, bringing dispatches and news--both good and bad--from home, joined the squadron. Promotions and encomiums for Decatur and the others engaged in the *Philadelphia* raid were accompanied by the bitter news that Preble would be superseded.

Aroused by the *Philadelphia* disaster, the administration had decided to increase the naval effort. One million dollars had been appropriated. Four fine frigates were on their way to the Mediterranean—*President*, Captain George Cox; *Congress*, Captain John Rodgers; *Essex*, Captain James Barron; and *Constellation*, Captain Hugh A. Campbell. Commanding, with his broad pennant in *President*, would be Commodore Samuel Barron, senior captain in the Navy. So, because of seniority and despite his age, stodginess, and ill health, Barron would displace Preble and the fine edge of leadership be blunted. Navy Secretary Robert Smith wrote Preble his regret that the Department had been "unavoidably constrained" in the matter; "as the Frigates cannot be commanded but by Captains, we of necessity have been obliged to send out two Gentlemen senior to yourself in Commission."

Preble, not unnaturally chafing under the situation, nevertheless pressed his efforts against Tripoli. The *John Adams* was no reinforcement--her gun carriages had been removed so that she could carry supplies to the squadron. So the force in hand must do. On August 24 the squadron anchored off the harbor in the dusk and all through the night pounded the place. Another night attack, August 28-29, showered the town, the Bashaw's castle, and all the shore batteries. At dawn the little gunboats, which had pushed close in, withdrew, having exhausted their ammunition, and *Constitution* stood boldly in to batter the castle and nearby batteries. Tripoli had become an unhealthy place in which to live.

Preble stressed this by bombarding again in broad daylight, September 3. Murad Rais brought this action on by moving his gunboats and galleys out east of the inner harbor. The commodore sent his own gunboats after the enemy, supported by his brigs, while the mortar ketches once more pounded the town. *Constitution* capped the climax by moving so close in shore that she was able to put no less than eleven broadsides into the Bashaw's castle. Then the squadron hauled off once more.

At eight o'clock that night the little *Intrepid*--the ketch in which Decatur and his band had bearded the Bashaw and burned the *Philadel- phia*--moved toward Tripoli's harbor mouth. In her hold she carried one hundred barrels of gunpowder, over which were laid 150 fused shells. The entire combustible mass was linked by a powder train calculated to burn not more than fifteen minutes.

Preble's plan was that *Intrepid*, transformed into what in naval parlance of those days was termed an "infernal," should be brought into the harbor, and under the castle walls, where the Tripolitan light craft nestled at night. There the match was to be ignited. If all went well, Richard Somers--it was Captain Somers now--and his twelve volunteer companions, Lieutenants Henry Wadsworth and Joseph Israel and ten bluejackets, would jump into the two lightest and fastest pulling boats in the squadron and make their getaway before *Intrepid* blew up and devastated castle and shipping. Off the harbor mouth the escorting *Argus, Vixen,* and *Nautilus* waited in the night.

They waited for more than one hour. Then the black of the harbor mouth was split wide in a blinding flash, and the roar of a great explosion rumbled out. What had happened? No one to this day knows. Perhaps the premature explosion was an accident. More probable--and this was the opinion of Preble--*Intrepid* was assailed by Tripolitan guardboats and Somers, as he had declared he would do, simply hurled a lighted lantern into his magazine and blew his ship up.

On September 10, word came of the *President*'s arrival at Malta with Barron. Preble, hauled down his pennant, sailed for Malta in *Constitution*, whose command he had given to Decatur. He took care that the gunboats and personnel loaned by the King of the Two Sicilies be returned to him. On January 10, 1805, in *John Adams*, Preble put the Straits of Gibraltar hull down behind him. He carried with him many comments, and letters of commendation, from old friends and acquaintances on the station--from the governor of Malta to the Pope of Rome. Pius VII had taken care to write to President Jefferson that "The American Commander, with a small force and in a short space of time, has done more for the cause of Christianity than the most powerful nations of Christendom have done for ages."

But greatest treasure of them all to Preble was a document presented by young Captain Decatur just before his departure, in a little scene on quarter deck.

Fifty-three men had signed that scroll, with Stephen Decatur's name leading; fifty-three of that galaxy of Navy folk who would forever be known as "Preble's Boys." They were the youngsters whom he had molded and trained, bullied and praised to become iron men in wooden ships. They had hated him in the beginning. Now they would proudly announce: "We, the undersigned officers of the squadron under your command, cannot in justice suffer you to depart without giving you some small testimony of the very high concern in which we hold you as an officer and a commander."

The stormy Mediterranean winter had set in even before Baron's arrival, causing cessation of naval operations. The new commodore, returning to Malta and then to Syracuse, took with him most of his squadron, and the war against Tripoli drifted to a stalemate, with another token blockade.

But over to the east, a backfire was about to be ignited, far beyond the sands of the Libyan Desert.

General William Eaton

Restless William Eaton had never ceased seeking opportunities to permanently solve the problem of Tripoli. He believed that the only way to deal with the Bashaw was to dethrone him. Now he was back from the United States--a passenger in the *President*--with the nebulous title of Naval Agent, and Jefferson's blessings to prosecute his scheme to restore the rightful Bashaw of Tripoli--Hamet Karamanli--to the throne from which his half brother Yusuf had ousted him.

Hamet, whom Eaton always referred to as the "rightful Pasha of Tripoli," was somewhere in the interior of Egypt, where, after escaping from Yusuf's clutches, he had thrown in his lot with a group of rebellious Mamaluke beys warring with the Turkish viceroy. Eaton's problem was to find his candidate, rally around him an army of dissident Arabs and Tripolitans, and launch him on the path of conquest.

This man Eaton was a fighter. He was also a leader, who had been weaned on the discipline and daring of Anthony Wayne at Fallen Timbers. His pugnaciousness and rigid sense of honor had plunged him into several scrapes with higher authority, so in 1797 he had resigned his captaincy in the 4th Infantry to take up the post of Consul at Tunis.

Eaton had authority to draw upon Commodore Barron for money, men, and munitions. However, Navy Secretary Smith's weasel-worded orders to Barron, combined with the Commodore's own indifference and the diplomatic dabblings of Tobias Lear, choked the supply line. The net result was that Eaton's fantastic scheme became one of the most bizarre adventures in the history of American military action.

Eaton sailed to Cairo in the smart little *Argus*, now commanded by Lieutenant Isaac Hull. While Hull waited, Eaton ferreted out Hamet, far inland, and persuaded him to make the move. Back in Cairo and Alexandria, Eaton, with Hull and First Lieutenant Presley N. O'Bannon, USMC, Hull's marine officer, set about gathering a rare assortment of adventurers, Christian and Muslim. As finally assembled at a rendezvous some thirty miles west of Alexandria, the "army's" backbone consisted of ten Americans--Eaton, O'Bannon with a sergeant and six marine privates, and Midshipman Pascal P. Peck, all of the *Argus*. A shady Levantine who called himself "Colonel" Eugene Leitensdorfer served--when he did serve--as interpreter and "engineer adjutant general." There was also a young Englishman from Malta--George Farquharson. Then there were twenty-five cannoneers, scraped from the streets of Cairo, and thirty-eight Greek Christians who turned out to be stout soldiers indeed. Hamet had arrived with ninety followers and an additional Arab force of cavalry headed by two sheiks lured in with their men on promise of money.

On March 6, 1805, this heterogeneous mob moved out, led by Eaton, now clad in a general's uniform as Hamet's commander in chief. Counting camp followers there were some four hundred people in the mass, with two-hundred odd camels and donkeys. Ahead of them were a good thousand miles of desert. Behind them the *Argus* was on the way back to Malta, with Eaton's report and the not unreasonable request that food-stuffs, two fieldpieces, one hundred additional stands of arms, ammunition, $10,000 in specie, and one hundred marines meet him at Derna, 550 miles away along the coast, and halfway to Tripoli.

On April 15 Eaton and his horde arrived on the shores of Bomba Bay, within two days' march of Derna. For forty days the indomitable Eaton had kept his unruly flock--half-starved, thirsty, and mutinous--together by sheer will power and his own two fists, ably aided by O'Bannon and his tough marines. Even Hamet--reluctant dragon--once refused to go on and had to be coerced. The Arabs mutinied at least five times as they clamored incessantly for money. Desertions there had been; that was unavoidable; but not a single casualty. In fact the strength had been increased to twelve hundred souls, of whom 650 were fighting men, by the addition of a forty-seven-tent nomad Bedouin tribe--150 fighting men and their families.

They were out of the sandstorm and drought of the desert now into fertile country, but anxious eyes could find no sail on the horizon. Not until next day did the *Argus* heave in sight. Hull had kept his rendezvous. He brought words of encouragement from Barron; supplies were coming. And come they did shortly in the sloop *Hornet*, ten, Lieutenant Samuel Evans, a converted merchantman purchased at Malta, and *Nautilus,* now under Master Commandant John H. Dent. The *Hornet* brought welcome beef, pork, bread, and other foodstuffs, also a quantity of water. She also brought a welcome $7,000 (Spanish). But of the ammunition, cannon, muskets, and marines Eaton craved, there were none.

In front of him Eaton had a fortified walled town, garrisoned by eight hundred troops. Somewhere to the west, he knew from the Arab grapevine, another field force from Tripoli was moving to attack him. Hamet and his Arabs were once more in a ferment of indecision. To Eaton there was but one solution: attack!

On April 26, Eaton sent a formal demand for surrender to Mustafa Bey, governor of Derna, saying that he wanted no territory, but that he wanted passage through the city and he wanted the supplies which would be needed. Mustafa bluntly replied, "My head or yours!"

The *Nautilus, Argus,* and *Hornet* stood in the harbor. The time for action had come. *Nautilus* and *Hornet* took up positions opposite a battery on the water's edge, and Hull sent a boat from *Argus* with two fieldpieces to the foot of the precipice which had been occupied by Eaton's cannoneers. The cliff was so steep that but one gun could be hoisted up.

Hull, maneuvering the *Argus* into range, poured twenty-four-pound shot carronade shells into the loophole houses, while the other ships engaged the water battery. Eaton divided his forces and attacked from three sides. With him were Midshipman George Mann from the *Argus*--replacing Peck, who had been retained on board--and Farquharson. He led a group on the right flank nearest the sea, while Lieutenant O'Bannon, with his handful of marines, twenty-four cannoneers, twenty-six Greeks, a few Arabs on foot, came in from the southeast and attacked the breastwork from the center. Hamet's own forces swept around the head of a deep ravine and attacked from the southwest where friendly sheiks had promised they could expect the most help from the populace.

The ships silenced the battery on the sea side by 2 P.M., but the enemy did not abandon that position. O'Bannon was stalled in the center, and Hamet's men were useless as shock troops. Eaton found the pressure on his flank increasing. The battle was hanging in the balance when he decided upon a desperate charge.

"We rushed forward against a host of savages more than ten to our one," he reported later to Commodore Barron. "They fled from their converts irregularly, firing in retreat from every palm tree and partition wall in their way. At this moment I received a ball through my left wrist which deprived me of the use of the hand, and, of course, of my rifle." Eaton, wounded, seized his sword and continued the advance, while O'Bannon, his marines, and Midshipman Mann led the charge of the rest of the Christians and the Arab infantry.

The Americans reached the water battery, drove out its remaining defenders, and planted the American flag on the walls. Tripolitan guns still serviceable were turned against the fleeing enemy. All the while the ships poured a destructive fire into houses which harbored snipers. By four o'clock the city had surrendered.

The capture of the city was fortunate, for Yusuf's forces were only two days' march away. The American losses were relatively heavy. Eaton reported that he lost fourteen killed and wounded, three of whom were Marines--one dead and another dying; the rest being chiefly Greeks. Eaton was full of commendation for his subordinates, praising without stint O'Bannon, Midshipman Mann, and the young Englishman George Farquharson, for whom he recommended a United States Marine commission.

When Eaton sent his report to Commodore Barron on April 29, Derna was firmly in American hands. With the support of the Navy, the conquest of the rest of Tripoli seemed assured. Eaton was in high spirits. For a brief moment he experienced the exultation of a conquering hero. As for Derna, the old town would not see such carnage again for 136 years to come, when Rommel's armor boxed in and captured a brigade of British tankers within its walls.

The force from Tripoli was reported to be but a short distance away, so Eaton worked feverishly to restore the defenses of Derna. True enough on the morning of May 1, this force, some three thousand strong, part foot, part horse, hove in sight, under command of one Hassen Bey. Hassen, it seemed, was in no hurry to attack. Not until May 13 did he move. Eaton kept his small force of "regulars"--the marines, the Greeks, and the Levantine gunners--in the waterfront castle, left it up to Hamet to run his own show. Astoundingly enough, Hamet developed not only ability but fortitude. Most of the operations were cavalry skirmishes, with the town's artillery and Hull's little ships occasionally taking a hand at long bowls. The townspeople, too, were now all for Hamet. After a final fight on June 11, when Hamet's troops--covered by artillery fire from the ships--brilliantly repulsed the best that Hassen could produce, the attackers withdrew, this time for good. Hassen's retreat was doubtless expedited by the sight of a large frigate entering the harbor, flying the Stars and Stripes.

But Captain Hugh G. Campbell, commanding *Constellation*, brought neither reinforcement nor comfort. Instead, he informed Eaton that Tobias Lear had negotiated a treaty with Yusuf, handing him $60,000 cash ransom for the *Philadelphia* prisoners. Commodore Barron washed his hands of Hamet and ordered Eaton to evacuate Derna immediately.

Such was the heartbreaking conclusion to an amazingly successful campaign; such the shameful abandonment of an ally. Eaton and his troops were evacuated by the *Constellation*'s boats that night. With them went Hamet and his suite. Behind were left Hamet's sympathizers, cursing the infidels who had betrayed their trust.

The fact that money had been paid in blackmail at the very time that a powerful squadron lay off the Port of Tripoli, and Eaton's expedition was threatening the Bashaw from the east, seemed inexcusable to many people. Preble summed it up for these dissenters as "a sacrifice of national honor" caused by "an ignominious negotiation." But the war with Tripoli was over and no more tribute was to be paid. Algiers and Tunis still remained as potential further blackmailers. Bey Hamouda Pacha of Tunis, emboldened by the Tripolitan outcome, now demanded the return of one of his vessels, which Captain John Rodgers had captured when she with two Neapolitan prizes attempted to run the blockade into Tripoli.

Rodgers, commodore now, for Barron had returned to the United States sick, paraded five frigates and several brigs under the Bey's nose in Tunis harbor on August 1, 1805, and queried whether Hamouda desired peace or war. When the Bey quibbled and frothed Rodgers demanded--and got-- immediate agreement that the United States would be placed on a "most-favored-nation" basis. And that was that; a welcome breath of fresh salt air after the Lear-Barron devious hocus-pocus.

Meanwhile Eaton went home to wrestle unsuccessfully with Congress for the private money he had spent in government service. Hamet became an exile, finally to be reunited with the wife and children Yusuf had held in prison. O'Bannon received a sword from the State of Virginia, but was refused promotion in the Marine Corps. So he resigned to take an Army commission which was never approved by Congress. Bainbridge, back in the Navy, would redeem himself during the War of 1812 by his victory in the *Constitution* over HMS *Java*. However, most of "Preble's Boys" distinguished themselves in that war so some good came of it all.

From R.E. Dupuy and W.H. Baumer, *The Little Wars of the United States,* (New York: Hawthorn, 1968), pp. 26-60.

Chapter 4

19th Century Colonial Warfare

The European dominance that emerged in the 16th century age of oceanic discovery reached in zenith in the 19th century, when the Concert of Europe kept the peace on the Continent, perhaps allowing pent-up military energy to be released upon so many hapless Asian and African peoples. However, all did not go smoothly. For example, the war in Chechnya that Tolstoy describes is eerily similar to the American counterinsurgency in Vietnam. There is a straightforward search-and-destroy strategy, a largely unseen enemy, and a highly quantified, systems-analysis-oriented measure of success based on reaching a hitherto untouched village. A key element of the Chechens' defense, their signals communication network, based on sentinels with lanterns, compromises the Russians during their approach, and sets them up for ambush during their return to base.

The lesson concerning communications retains its value, for as recently as in its Ranger operations in Somalia, modern U.S. special forces were thwarted by an enemy monitoring their approach, and communicating with his own units, via runners and drums. By way of contrast, the 19th century campaign of the French Foreign Legion in Algeria was one in which the counterinsurgent forces keyed on destroying their adversary's lines of communication, a crucial element in their ultimate success. Of course, one must avoid sole-variable explanations in general, and other factors were at work here, especially the forced relocations of those most likely to harbor or support the insurgents. Even then, the conquest of Algeria took nearly two bloody decades. France would lose this colony much more quickly a century later.

Leo Tolstoy

The Raid

War has always fascinated me. I don't mean the tactical maneuvering of whole armies by famous generals—movements of such magnitude are quite beyond my imagination. I have in mind the real essence of war—the killing. I was less interested in the deployment of the armies at Austerlitz and Borodino than in how a soldier kills and what makes him do it.

The time had long since passed when I used to pace my room alone, waving my arms and fancying myself as the inventor of the best way to slaughter thousands of men in an instant, a feat which would make me a general and earn me eternal glory. Now all that interested me was the state of mind that pushes a man, without apparent advantage to himself, to expose himself to danger and what is even more puzzling, to kill his fellow man. I always wanted to believe that soldiers kill in anger; since I could not imagine them continually angry, I had to fall back on the instinct of self-preservation and a sense of duty.

I wondered too about courage—that quality respected by men throughout history. Why is courage a good thing? Why is it, unlike other virtues, often met in otherwise quite despicable persons? Could it be that the capacity to face danger calmly is a purely physical one, and that people admire it just as they admire physical size and muscular strength?

Is it courage that makes a horse hurl itself off a cliff because it fears the whip? Is it courage that drives a child expecting punishment to run off into the woods and become lost? Is it an act of courage for a woman, fearing shame, to kill her new-born child and risk facing prosecution? And is it a display of courage when a man, out of sheer vanity, risks his own life in order to kill a fellow creature?

Danger always involves a choice. What then determines this choice—a noble feeling or a base one? And shouldn't it be called either courage or cowardice accordingly?

These were the thoughts and doubts that preoccupied me. I decided to resolve them by taking part in combat as soon as the opportunity arose.

In the summer of 1845 I was at a small fortified post in the Caucasus. On July 12, Captain Khlopov appeared at the low entrance of my hut. He was in dress uniform—epaulets, sword and all. Since my arrival I'd never seen him in that attire. He must have seen my surprise for he explained: "I've come straight from the colonel. Our battalion is to march tomorrow."

"I've come straight from the colonel. Our battalion is to march tomorrow."

"Any idea where?"

"To Fort N——. That's the assembly point."

"And from there, will there be a raid, do you think?"

"Probably."

"Which direction?"

"All I can tell you is that last night a mounted Tartar arrived with orders from the general for the battalion to move out and to take along two days' rations. Why, where, for how long—don't ask me. We've been given our orders and that's it."

"But if they've ordered you to take only two days' rations, that must mean the troops aren't expected to be on the march more than two days—"

"It means nothing."

"What do you mean?" I asked, surprised.

"Just what I say. When we went to Dargi, we took along rations for a week, but we were gone almost a whole month."

"May I come along?"

"Surely, but if you want my advice, don't. Why run the risk?"

"If you don't mind, I'll not take your advice. I've been here a whole month just waiting for an opportunity to see action. And now you want me to miss my chance."

"All right, come along, though I'm sure it'd be better if you waited for us here. You could get in some hunting while we do the job—that'd make the most sense."

He said it so convincingly that at first I was almost persuaded. Nevertheless, I finally decided to go.

"But what's there for you to see?" he asked, still trying to dissuade me. "If you want to know what a battle looks like, read Mikhailovsky's *Scenes of War*, or something. It's a good book and it gives the whole story. It notes the position of every army corps, and you'll get a good idea of how battles are fought."

"Look," I said, "those are just the things that *don't* interest me."

"What are you after, then? Simply to watch how people die? If so, I'll tell you. In 1832 there was another civilian here with us—some kind of Spaniard, I believe. He came with us on two raids, and I even remember that he wore some sort of blue cloak. Well, it's not hard to imagine how it all ended. He got killed. You see, anything may happen."

Although I felt shamed at the way he put it, I didn't try to make excuses.

"Would you say he was a brave man?" I asked.

"God knows, though I must say he always rode out in front, and wherever there was firing, he was sure to be there."

"So he was brave, then?"

"Well, it doesn't necessarily follow that a man's brave just because he pokes his nose into other people's business."

"What would you call being brave?"

"Brave. Brave?" the captain repeated, as though the question had never occurred to him before. "A brave man is a man who does what he has to do," he said after some reflection.

I remembered Plato's definition of bravery as the knowledge of what should and what should not be feared. Now, despite the generality and vagueness of the captain's definition, I felt he wasn't so far from Plato and that, if anything, his definition was more accurate than that of the Greek philosopher. Had he been as articulate as Plato, he might have said that brave is the man who fears not what should not be feared and fears what should.

I wanted to explain this thought to the captain.

"I think," I said, "that a man faced by danger must make a choice—and if his decision is determined by a sense of duty, it is courage, but if it's determined by a base motive, it is cowardice. So a man who risks his life out of vanity, curiosity, or greed is not brave, and, conversely, a man who avoids danger out of an honest feeling of family obligation or even simple conviction is no coward."

As I talked, the captain looked at me with an odd expression.

"That," he said, starting to fill his pipe, "I wouldn't want to have to prove. But we have a young second lieutenant here who likes to philosophize. You should talk to him about it. He even writes poetry, you know."

I had heard of Captain Khlopov back home in Russia, though I'd only met him here in the Caucasus. His mother owned a small piece of land within two miles of my estate. Before leaving for the Caucasus, I went to see her, and the old lady was very happy that I was going to see her Petey (that's the way she referred to the gray-haired Captain Peter Khlopov) and that I, a "living letter," would tell him about her and take him a small package. She fed me some excellent smoked goose and pie, then went to her bedroom and returned with a largish icon in a black bag with a black silk ribbon attached to it.

"This is Our Lady of the Burning Bush," she said. She made the sign of the cross over the icon, kissed it, and handed it to me. "Please give it to him. You see, when he left for the Caucasus, I said a prayer for him and promised that if he stayed alive and safe I would have this icon of the Mother of God made. And the Holy Mother and the Saints have looked after him; he has taken part in every imaginable battle without once being wounded. Michael, who spent some time with him, told me things that made my hair stand on end. You see, I only hear about him second hand— my son never writes me about his campaigns. The dear boy doesn't want to frighten me."

(Later in the Caucasus I learned from others that Captain Khlopov had been seriously wounded four times. He clearly had never told his mother about his wounds or about his campaigns.)

"So," Mrs. Khlopov went on, "I want him to wear this holy image, which I send him with my blessing. The Mother of God will intercede for him. I want him to wear the icon, especially in battle. You tell him. Just tell him his mother wanted him to."

I promised to carry out her instructions without fail.

"I'm sure you'll like my Petey very much," she went on. "He's such a nice person! You know, a year never goes by without his sending me and my daughter Annie some money. And, mind you, all he has is his army pay! Yes, I thank God with all my heart for having sent me such a son!" she concluded, tears in her eyes.

"Does he write you often?" I asked.

"Seldom, very seldom. Maybe once a year, and usually only to accompany the money. Even then, he doesn't always write. He says that when he doesn't write it means everything's fine, because if something happens, God forbid, they'd let me know soon enough anyhow."

When I gave the captain his mother's present—he had come to my room on this occasion—he asked me for some paper, carefully wrapped up the icon, and put it away. I spoke to him at length about his mother, and during the whole time he remained silent. He went to the far corner of the room and spent what seemed to me an extraordinarily long time filling his pipe.

"She's a nice old thing," he said in a somewhat muffled voice from his retreat. "I wonder if God will ever let me see her again."

There was love and sadness in those simple words.

"Why must you stay out here?" I asked. "Why not ask to be transferred, so you'd be closer to her?"

"I have to serve in the army anyhow, and here I get double pay—quite a difference to a poor man."

The captain lived carefully. He never gambled, seldom went on sprees, and smoked only the cheapest tobacco.

I liked him. He had a simple, quiet Russian face. It was easy and pleasant to look him straight in the eye. And after our conversation I felt great respect for him.

At four the next morning, the captain came to get me. He wore an old, threadbare tunic without epaulets, wide Caucasian trousers, a sheepskin cap once white but now yellowish and mangy, and a cheap saber. He rode a small, whitish horse, which ambled along in short strides, hanging its head and swishing its thin tail. The captain certainly was not handsome and there was nothing martial about him, but everything in him expressed such calm indifference that somehow he inspired respect.

I didn't keep him waiting. I immediately mounted and we rode together out the fort gate.

The battalion, some six hundred yards ahead of us, looked like a swaying black mass. One could tell only that they were infantry by the bayonets that pointed into the air like needles, by the drums, and by the rhythm of the soldiers' singing that reached us from time to time, led by a magnificent tenor voice from the Sixth Company I'd often admired at the fort. The road led through the middle of a deep, wide ravine, and along a small river now in flood. Flocks of wild doves whirled over it, landing on its rocky banks, taking off, swooping down in circles, vanishing from sight. The sun had not yet come up, although the top of the right slope of the ravine was beginning to brighten. The gray and whitish rocks, the yellow-green moss, the dew-covered bushes of dogberry and dwarf elm stood out very clearly against the transparent-gold background of the morning light. But the opposite side of the ravine, still wrapped in thick mist that floated in smoky, uneven layers, was damp and gloomy and presented a wide range of shades—lilac, black, white, and dark green. Right in front of us, sharp against the dark azure of the horizon, the gleaming white snowy mountains rose with amazing clarity, their shadows uncanny and yet harmonious in every detail. Crickets, grasshoppers, and thousands of other insects woke up in the tall grass and filled the air with their varied and continual noises. It seemed as if thousands of little bells were ringing inside our very ears. The air smelled of water, grass, and fog—the smell of a beautiful summer morning. The captain lit his pipe, and I found the smell of his cheap tobacco mingling with that of the tinder extraordinarily pleasant.

In order to catch up quickly with the infantry, we left the road. The captain appeared absorbed in his thoughts and never once took his short pipe out of his mouth. At every step, he prodded his horse with his heels. Rolling from side to side, it left a hardly perceptible trail in the tall, wet grass. Once, from under its very feet, a pheasant rose letting out a cry and making a noise with its wings that would have set the spine of a hunter tingling; then it began to rise. The captain paid no attention whatsoever.

We had almost caught up with the battalion when we heard behind us a galloping horse, and a young, good-looking officer in a tall, white sheepskin cap overtook us. As he passed, he smiled, made a friendly sign to the captain, and flourished his whip. I only had time to notice his graceful way of sitting his horse and holding the reins, his dark handsome eyes, his fine nose, and thin youthful black mustache. What I liked especially about him was that he was still quite young.

"What's he in such a hurry about?" the captain muttered gruffly, without removing his pipe.

"Who is he?"

"Alanin, one of my second lieutenants. He's just a month out of military school."

"I suppose this will be his first time in action?"

"Yes, that's what he's so pleased about," the captain said, slowly shaking his head. "Ah, that's youth for you!"

"How can he help being pleased? I can imagine how interesting it must be for a young officer."

The captain said nothing for a couple of minutes.

"That's just what I meant—youth," he said in a deep voice. "How else can one be pleased about something one has never experienced? And after you've seen it often, you aren't so happy about it any more. Take today, for instance—about twenty officers will take part in this expedition, and the odds are that at least one of them will be killed or wounded. No doubt about it. Today, it may be my turn, tomorrow his, the next time somebody else's. What's there to be happy about?"

The bright sun rose above the mountains, lighting up the valley we were following. The wavy clouds of mist scattered and it grew hot. The soldiers, loaded down with equipment and rifles, trudged heavily along the dusty road. From time to time laughter and snatches of Ukrainian reached us. Some old-timers in white tunics—most of them non-commissioned officers—walked in a group by the roadside. They smoked their pipes and talked quietly. Heavily laden carts, each drawn by three horses, moved laboriously forward, raising a thick cloud of dust that stayed suspended over the road. The officers, on horseback, rode in front. Some of them were putting their horses through their paces: they made them jump, sprint, and come to a dead stop; others were directing the regimental chorus, which, despite the heat and stuffiness, sang one song after another.

A couple of hundred yards ahead of the infantry rode some Tartar horsemen. With them, riding on a large white horse and dressed in Caucasian costume, was a tall handsome officer. Throughout the regiment he had a reputation for reckless courage and for not hesitating to tell anyone what he thought of him. His soft, black Oriental boots were trimmed with gold braid as was his black tunic under which he wore a yellow silk Circassian shirt. The tall sheepskin hat on his head was pushed back carelessly. A powder flask and a pistol were fastened to silver straps across his chest and back. Another pistol and a silver-mounted dagger hung from his belt next to a saber in a red leather sheath. A rifle in a black holster was slung over his shoulder. From his dress, his style of riding, all his movements, it was obvious that he wanted to look like a Tartar. He was even saying something to the Tartars in a language I couldn't understand. But then, judging by the bewildered, amused looks they exchanged with one another, I guessed they couldn't understand him either.

He was one of those dashing, wild young officers who attempt to model themselves on the heroes of Lermontov and Marlinsky. These officers saw the Caucasus only through such romantic prisms, and in everything they were guided solely by the instincts and tastes of their models.

This lieutenant could surely have enjoyed the company of fashionable women and important men—generals, colonels, aides-de-camp. In fact,

I'm certain he was eager to associate with them, being extremely vain. But somehow he felt he had to show such people his rough side, to be rude to them, although quite mildly so. When some lady appeared at the fort, he felt bound to walk under her windows with his pals, wearing a red shirt and slippers and talking and swearing loudly. But this wasn't done so much to offend as to show her by his supreme casualness how easy it would be to fall madly in love with him were he to display the slightest interest.

He also liked to go into the hills at night accompanied by a couple of friendly Tartars, lie in ambush for hostile hillmen, and take pot shots at them. Although in his heart he felt there was nothing particularly heroic about it, he persuaded himself that he had to inflict pain on hostile Tartars, people who had somehow let him down and whom he pretended to loathe and despise.

There were two things that were always with him: a rather large icon around his neck and a dagger fastened to his shirt, which he retained even when sleeping. He had convinced himself that he had enemies, and the idea that he had to avenge himself against someone, wash off some imaginary insult with blood, was very pleasant to him. He was sure that hatred, revenge, and scorn for men in general were refined, romantic feelings.

However, his Circassian mistress, whom I got to know later, told me that he was really a very kind and gentle man and that every evening, after he'd written saturnine thoughts in his diary, he would carefully draw up his accounts on ruled paper, and then get down on his knees and pray to God. And yet this man went to so much trouble to appear as one of his heroes, if only to himself. As to his brother officers and the soldiers, they never saw him in such a light anyway.

Once, on one of his nighttime sorties, he shot a hostile Tartar in the leg and brought him back a prisoner. He kept the Tartar in his house for seven weeks, nursing him and looking after him as though he were his dearest friend. Then, when the prisoner recovered, he gave him all sorts of presents and set him free. Later, during a raid, he was fighting a rearguard action, firing back at attacking Tartars, when he heard his name called from the enemy ranks and saw his former prisoner ride forward, signaling to him to do the same. The lieutenant complied and they shook hands. The mountaineers remained at a distance and did not fire. But as soon as the lieutenant turned his back, several shots were fired from their side, and a bullet grazed the lower part of his back.

On another occasion when I was present myself, a fire broke out in the fort. Two companies of soldiers were detailed to put it out. Suddenly, lit by the red glow of the flames, there appeared among the crowd a tall man on black horse. Pushing people out of his way, the rider rode right up to the flames, jumped off his horse, and entered the burning house. Five minutes later the lieutenant reappeared. His hair had been singed and his forearm was badly burnt when he emerged carrying two pigeons clutched to his breast.

His name was Rosenkranz. He often spoke of his ancestry, which he traced back to the Varangians—the Scandinavian princes who were invited to rule over the Slavs in the earliest era of Russian history. He wanted it clearly understood that he and his ancestors were pure Russians.

The sun was midway across the sky. Its hot rays, piercing the incandescent air, beat down upon the dry earth. Overhead, the dark blue sky was completely clear, although the base of the snowy mountains was already draped in white and lilac clouds. The air was motionless and seemed to be impregnated with a sort of transparent dust. The heat was becoming unbearable.

When we were about halfway to our destination, we halted by a stream. The soldiers stacked their rifles and rushed toward the gurgling water. The battalion commander picked a shady spot where he sat himself on a drum. His whole bearing showed that he was constantly aware of his rank and importance, as he waited to have something to eat with a number of the officers. Captain Khlopov lay on the grass under his company's cart. Lieutenant Rosenkranz and a few other young officers arranged themselves on their outspread cloaks. To judge from the bottles and flasks placed among them, they intended to have a good time. The regimental singers formed a semicircle around them and sang a song of the Caucasus army.

> Recently Shamil decided
> That against us he could rise
> But, of course, he was misguided
> And quite soon we'll make him wise . . .

Also among these officers was Second Lieutenant Alanin, the youngster who'd overtaken us during the morning. He was very amusing; his eyes sparkled, his words became garbled. He wanted to hug everyone and say how much he liked them. Unfortunately, far from making others like him, his naive warmth provoked nothing but sarcasm. Nor did he realize how touching he looked when at last, hot and exhausted, he threw himself down on his cloak, pushed his thick, black hair out of his eyes, and rested his head on his bent arm.

Two officers sat in the shade of a wagon playing cards.

I listened with interest to the conversations among the men and among the officers; I kept observing their expressions. In none could I discover the slightest trace of anxiety that I myself felt; their jokes, their laughter, the stories they told, all expressed a complete lack of concern for imminent danger. It never seemed to occur to any of them that he might no longer be around when we passed this very spot on our return.

It was past six in the evening when, tired and covered with dust, we gained the entrance to Fort N—. The declining sun cast its slanting reddish rays on the picturesque little cannon, on the poplar groves around the fort, on the yellow fields, and on the white clouds which, huddled together near the snowy mountains, formed another range just as snowy, fantastic, and beautiful. The new moon hung above the horizon like a small transparent cloud. In the Tartar village, the faithful were being summoned to prayer from the rooftop of a hut. Our singing soldiers, filled with renewed enthusiasm and energy, were giving their all.

After a brief rest, I cleaned up and went over to see an aide I knew. I wanted him to obtain the general's consent for my plans. Walking to the fort from the outlying village where I had my quarters, I had time to notice around Fort N— things I never expected to find there. I was passed by a pretty two-seater carriage, within which flashed a fashionable lady's hat, while my ear caught snatches of French. Then, going by under the windows of the commandant's house, I heard the measures of a polka played on a piano that needed tuning. After, in a café, I saw some clerks sitting before glasses of wine and I heard one of them say:

"No, my dear chap, speaking of politics, I must insist that Maria Gregorievna is the first among our ladies. . . ."

Further on, a stooped, threadbare, sickly looking Jew dragged along a screeching, broken-down barrel organ, and the whole street resounded with the finale of *Lucia.* Two ladies in rustling dresses, silk kerchiefs on their heads and bright umbrellas in their hands, floated gracefully past me on the planked sidewalk, while two bareheaded women, one in blue, the other in pink, stood by the porch of a small house giggling loudly, obviously to attract the attention of the officers swaggering up and down the street in new tunics with flashing epaulets and white gloves.

I found my friend the aide on the lower floor of the house occupied by the general. I had just time to tell him what I wanted and to hear that he was sure it could be arranged when the pretty carriage I'd noticed earlier rattled past the window and stopped. A tall, straight-backed infantry major got out and entered the house.

"Excuse me," the aide said, "I must go and report to the general—"

"Who is it?" I asked.

"The countless," he said, buttoning his tunic and hurrying upstairs.

A few moments later, a short, very handsome man in a tunic without epaulets but with a white cross in his buttonhole, appeared on the porch. He was followed by a major, the aide, and two other officers. From the way the general moved and from his voice, one could tell he did not value lightly his exalted position.

"*Bon soir, madame la comtesse,*" he said, thrusting his hand through the carriage window.

A small hand in a kid glove pressed his, and a pretty, smiling face appeared under a yellow hat.

Of their entire conversation, I only heard the smiling general say as I passed:

"You know, Countess, that I have sworn to fight infidels. Do please be careful—I want no infidelity in you. . . ."

Laughter came from the carriage.

"*Adieu donc, cher général.*"

"*Non, au revoir,*" the general said, walking up the steps, "and please don't forget that I've invited myself to your tea party tomorrow."

The carriage rattled away.

"There's a man," I thought on my way home, "who has everything anyone could want—rank, wealth, and fame. And now, on the eve of a battle in which no one knows how many lives may be lost, this man is off flirting and promising to take tea tomorrow."

I thought then of the remark I'd heard a Tartar make: only a poor man can be brave. "When you become rich," he said, "you become a coward." But then, the general had much more to lose than most people, and, even among the Tartars, I'd never seen such elegant indifference in the face of possible doom. This thoroughly confused my theories about courage.

Later, in the house of the same aide, I met a young man who surprised me even more. He was a young lieutenant from another regiment, a man of almost feminine docility and shyness. He had approached the aide to complain indignantly against some people who, he said, had conspired to leave him behind during the coming operation. He said it was disgusting to act that way, that it was poor camaraderie, that he'd always remember it, etc. I watched his face carefully and listened to his voice, and I was fully convinced that he was not putting on an act—he was honestly indignant and depressed because they wouldn't let him fire at Tartars and be exposed in turn to their fire. He felt like a child unjustly spanked. To me, none of it made any sense.

The troops were to move out at ten P.M. At eight-thirty, I mounted and rode over to see the general. But then I decided that both the general and the aide must be busy, so I tied my horse to a fence and sat down on the doorstep where I would catch the general as he was leaving.

The cool of evening replaced the heat. The glaring sun had gone, and in its place the crescent moon formed a pale silvery semicircle in the dark starry sky. It was beginning to set. Lights appeared in the houses and earthen huts and shone through the cracks in the shutters. Beyond the moonlit, whitewashed huts, the tall, slender poplars looked even taller and darker.

The long shadows of the houses, trees, and fences lay in beautiful patterns on the white, dusty road. From the river came the strangely reverberating croaking of the frogs. In the streets, one heard hurried steps, voices, and hoof beats. From the outlying village came the sounds of the barrel organ playing some aria from an opera and then a waltz.

I won't go into my thoughts, mostly because I'm ashamed of the gloom that pervaded me amid the joyful excitement of the others and also because they have nothing to do with this story. Still, I was so deeply immersed that I never noticed the town clock strike eleven and the general and his retinue pass by.

I hastily jumped on my horse and hurried to catch up with the detachment.

The rearguard was still inside the fort, and I had difficulty making my way across the bridge which was cluttered with gun carriages, ammunition wagons, the supply carts of various companies, and, in the midst of it all, officers shouting orders.

Finally, I managed to get past the gates. I had to ride in the darkness past the detachment, which stretched over almost a mile, before I caught up with the general.

As I was passing by the guns drawn out in single file with officers riding between, I was shocked at the discord wrought in the quiet harmony of the night by a harsh voice shouting with a German accent:

"Hey, you—give us a light!"

This was followed by the eager voice of a soldier:

"Shevchenko, the lieutenant wishes a light."

The sky gradually became overcast with long, gray clouds which left but a few scattered gaps for the stars. The moon had disappeared behind the black mountains on the nearby horizon to our right; but the peaks were bathed in its pale, quivering light while the foothills were plunged in deep black shadows. The air was warm and so strangely still that not the smallest cloud, no blade of grass stirred. It was so dark that one could not recognize objects even close at hand. On the sides of the road, I kept seeing crags, animals, strange people, and I realized they were bushes only by their faint rustle and the freshness rising from the dew with which they were sprinkled. In front of me I saw an uninterrupted wall sinking and rising, followed by a few moving shapes—the mounted vanguard and the general with his retinue. Behind me another dark but shorter mass was swaying—the infantry.

The troops were so silent that one could hear clearly all the mysterious sounds of the night: the sad wail of a faraway jackal, now desperate sobs, now mad guffaws; the ringing, monotonous sounds of crickets, frogs, and quail; a curious approaching rumbling for which I could not account; and all the nocturnal, hardly audible sounds of nature which can be neither understood nor explained. All blended into that harmony one refers to as the stillness of night. The dull thudding of hoofs and the rustling of the tall grass given forth by the slowly moving force dissipated into this harmony.

Only now and then could the rumbling of a heavy gun carriage, the clang of bayonets, a few brief words, the snorting of a horse be distinguished.

Nature breathed out peace and strength.

Was it possible that there was no place for men in this beautiful world under this immense starry sky—that hatred, vengeance, and the passion for destruction could lurk in the hearts of men amid such natural beauty? Surely all these evil instincts should vanish in contact with nature—the most direct expression of beauty and goodness.

We had been riding for more than two hours. I was drowsy and shivering. In the darkness I kept seeing the same vague objects: a way off a black wall and moving shapes; near me the crupper of a white horse, its swishing tail and widespread hind legs, and a back in a white Circassian coat, crossed by the black line of a swaying rifle and the white handle of a pistol in an embroidered holster. The glow of a cigarette threw light on a blond mustache, a beaver collar, and a hand in a kid glove.

I'd let my head droop toward the horse's neck, close my eyes, and forget myself for a few moments. Then, I'd be jolted awake by the familiar tramping and rustling; I'd look around and feel that I was standing still while the black wall was moving toward me or that the wall remained fixed and I was about to smash into it. On one of these occasions I was struck by the increase in the rumbling which I'd been unable to account for. And now it dawned on me that it was the sound of water. We were entering a deep gorge and approaching a mountain stream in flood. The rumbling became louder, the damp grass grew thicker, there were more and more bushes, and the horizon narrowed. Now and then bright lights flared up at various points, then vanished immediately.

"Do you know what those lights are?" I whispered to one of our Tartars who was riding next to me.

"You really don't know?"

"I do not."

"The enemy. They tie straw to poles, fire them, and wave them about," he said.

"Why do they do that?"

"To tell everyone Russians are coming. There's a little running around going on in that village over there," the Tartar said and laughed. "Everybody's dragging his belongings and going down into the ravine . . ."

"How do they know, off in the mountains, when a detachment's on the way?"

"How can they not know? They always know. That's the kind of people we Tartars are."

"Then their leader Shamil must be getting ready to fight?" I asked.

"No," he said, shaking his head. "Shamil won't take part in the fighting himself. He'll send his aides to lead the fight while he watches the battle through a spyglass."

"Where's his home, do you know? Far away?"

"No, not far. About eight miles over there to the left."

"How do you know? Have you ever been there?"

"I've been there. All of us have been in the mountains."

"Have you ever seen Shamil?"

"No, one doesn't see Shamil that easily! There are a hundred, three hundred, maybe a thousand guards circling around him and he's always in the center," the Tartar said with obvious admiration.

Above, the sky, now clear, was growing lighter in the east. The Pleiades were sinking below the horizon. But the ravine through which we moved remained damp and dark.

Suddenly, a little way ahead of us, there were several flashes, and a moment later bullets whistled past. The silence was pierced by shots fired close by and shrill cries. The advance patrol of enemy Tartars whooped, fired at random, and scattered.

All became quiet again. The general summoned his interpreter. The white-clad Tartar rode up to him and for a long time whispered and gesticulated. Then the general issued an order.

"Colonel Khasanov, have the men deployed in open order," he said in a quiet but clear drawl.

The detachment reached the river. By daybreak the black mountains and the gorges had been left behind. The sky, strewn with pale stars, looked higher. The east was a glowing red; a cool, penetrating breeze came from the west; and a white mist floated like smoke above the river.

A native guide led us to a ford. The cavalry vanguard started across. The general and his retinue followed. The horses were up to their chests in water, which gushed violently between protruding, whitish rocks, foaming and rushing around the animals' legs. The horses, bewildered by the noise of the water, kept lifting their heads and pricking up their ears, but they made their way smoothly and carefully over the uneven riverbed. The riders pulled up their feet and their weapons. The foot soldiers stripped down to their shirts and tied their clothes in bundles to the end of the rifles. Then, carrying their rifles above their heads, each holding onto the man in front, they entered the river in groups of twenty. The physical effort required to withstand the current could be seen on their faces. The artillery men, shouting loudly, drove their horses into the river at a trot. Water splashed over the guns and the green ammunition cases. Wheels rang against the stony bottom. The heavy horses pulled determinedly, and, with water foaming around their wet tails and manes, finally clambered up onto the opposite bank.

The crossing completed, the general's expression became thoughtful and serious. He turned his horse, and followed by the cavalry, he rode off at a trot through a glade that opened out before us. Cossack patrols were dispatched around the outskirts of the forest.

Suddenly, among the trees, we saw a man on foot wearing a Circassian shirt and a tall sheepskin cap. Another followed, then another. . . . I heard one of the officers say:

"Tartars . . ."

A puff of smoke appeared from behind a tree. . . . Then the sound of a shot, followed by another. The noise of our fire drowned out that of the enemy. But now and then, a bullet would zoom by like a bee, as if to prove that we were not doing all the shooting. The infantry raced to take their positions. The gun carriages moved at a trot to their chosen emplacements. Then came the booming report of the guns, followed by the metallic sound of flying grapeshot, the hissing of rockets, and the crackle of rifle fire. Cavalry, infantry, and artillery scattered all over the vast clearing. The puffs of smoke from the cannon, rifles, and rockets fused with dewy greenness and the mist. Colonel Khasanov arrived at full gallop and stopped his horse abruptly in front of the general. He saluted and said:

"Shall I order the cavalry charge, sir? They're carrying their banners . . ." He pointed with his riding whip at a mounted detachment of enemy Tartars led by two men on white horses. The men had long poles in their hands, with bits of red and blue material tied to them; these the hillmen use as banners, though any chieftain can make himself such an emblem and carry it around.

"All right," the general answered. "Good luck."

The colonel whirled his horse about, drew his saber, and shouted: "Hurrah!"

"Hurrah! Hurrah! Hurrah!" came from the ranks as the cavalry followed.

Everyone watched tensely. There was one banner, then another, another, and yet another. . .

Without waiting for the attack, the enemy fled, disappearing into the forests and then opening fire. Bullets continued to whistle through the air.

"A beautiful sight," the general remarked, bouncing gracefully up and down in the saddle, on his thin-legged black horse.

Striking his horse, a major rode up to the general and said with an affected lisp: "It is indeed beautiful, sir. War in such beautiful surroundings is a delight."

"*Et surtout en bonne compagnie*," the general said with an amiable smile.

The major bowed.

At that moment, the sharp, unpleasant hissing of an enemy cannon ball sounded above our heads. It hit somewhere behind us, and there was a cry. A soldier had been wounded.

This cry affected me in a strange way. The battle scene immediately lost what beauty it may have had for me. But no one else seemed particularly concerned: the major, whose conversation was punctuated with laughter, seemed to laugh even louder; another officer in the middle of explaining something repeated the last few words, fearing his audience might have missed them. The general didn't even glance in the direction from which the cry had come; looking elsewhere, he said something in French.

The officer in charge of the artillery rode up, saluted, and asked: "Shall we give 'em a taste of their own medicine, sir?"

"All right, give 'em a scare," the general said nonchalantly, lighting a cigar.

The battery took up its position and the barrage began. The earth groaned, there were constant flashes of light, and the smoke, which almost completely hid the gun crews, stung our eyes.

The village was being bombarded. Then Colonel Khasanov reported to the general again and was ordered to lead the cavalry to the village. With warlike hurrahs, the cavalry disappeared in its own cloud of dust.

The show may have been really impressive to an initiate. But to me, an outsider, the whole thing was spoiled by the fact that all this commotion, enthusiasm, and shouting seemed rather pointless. It made me think of a man violently swinging an ax and hitting nothing but air.

When the general and his retinue, to which I had attached myself, reached the village, it had already been occupied by our troops, and all its inhabitants had disappeared.

The neat, oblong huts, with their flat, earthen roofs and picturesque chimneys, were scattered over irregular rocky ground. Between hills flowed a small river. On one side of the village were green orchards of large pear and plum trees while, on the other, strange shadows thrown by the perpendicular gravestones of a cemetery and the long poles surmounted by multicolored balls and pennants marked the graves of warriors.

The troops were assembled by the village gate.

"Well," the general said, "what do you say, Colonel, shall we let them do a bit of looting? These fellows here look as though they wouldn't mind at all," he added with a smile, pointing at the Cossacks.

I was struck by the contrast between the flippant tone of the general's words and their grim implication.

A minute later, a stream of Cossacks, dragoons, and foot soldiers was pouring with obvious delight along the winding lanes of the empty village, bringing it to life. Then, a roof collapsed somewhere; an ax resounded against a heavy wooden door; a stack of hay, a fence, a whole hut—went up in flames; a Cossack came running, dragging a bag of flour and a carpet; a soldier, beaming with pleasure, emerged from a hut with a tin basin and some bright piece of material; another, with outstretched arms, tried to corner a couple of chickens which, cackling madly, rushed up and down along a fence in a panic; another soldier found an enormous jug of milk, drank some of it, and, laughing loudly, threw it on the ground.

The battalion with which I had come from Fort N— had also entered the Tartar village. Captain Khlopov had installed himself comfortably on top of a flat roof and was puffing thin whiffs of cheap tobacco smoke from his short pipe with such detached equanimity that the very sight of him made me forget that I was in a conquered village and made me feel completely at home.

"Ah, there you are," he said, seeing me.

Rosenkranz' tall figure kept appearing and disappearing in various parts of the village. He kept issuing orders and looked very busy and preoccupied. At one point I noticed his triumphant air as he emerged from a hut followed by two soldiers leading a tied-up Tartar. The Tartar was very old and wore only a tattered shirt and a pair of patched, threadbare trousers. He was so frail that his arms, tightly bound behind his hunched, bony back, seemed barely attached to his shoulders. He could hardly lift his deformed, bare feet. His face and even a part of his shaven head were covered with deep furrows and his twisted, toothless mouth, set between a cropped mustache and beard, kept opening and closing as though he were trying to chew something. But in his red, lashless eyes, there was a stubborn spark indicating an old man's indifference to life.

Through the interpreter, Rosenkranz inquired why he hadn't left with the rest.

"Where could I go?" the old man asked, calmly looking away.

"Where the others have gone."

"The warriors went to fight the Russians, and I'm an old man."

"Aren't you afraid of the Russians?"

"What can they do to me? I'm an old man," he said tonelessly, looking at the circle of men that had formed around him.

Later, I saw this same old man jolting along tied behind a Cossack's saddle. And he continued to look around with the same detached expression. They needed him to exchange for Russian prisoners.

I climbed onto the roof of the hut where the captain was and sat down next to him.

"There don't seem to be many of the enemy around," I said, in the hope of finding out what he thought about the battle that had taken place.

"Enemy? There aren't any," he said, surprised at my question. "You haven't seen the enemy yet. Wait until evening; there'll be plenty of 'em to see us off over there." He pointed with his pipe toward the woods we had crossed in the morning.

"What's going on?" I interrupted the captain, pointing to a group of Don Cossacks clustered together.

From the center of the group I heard something that sounded like the cry of a child and the words: "Stop it, don't flash your saber that way, they may see you over there. . . Hey, Evstigneich—got a knife?"

"They're up to something, the bastards," the captain said calmly.

At that moment, young Second Lieutenant Alanin, his face flushed and fortified, rushed toward the Cossacks from around a corner.

"Leave him alone! Don't hurt him!" he shouted in a boyish voice.

Seeing the officer, the Cossacks stepped aside, and one of them let loose a little white goat. The second lieutenant stepped in front of the men overcome with embarrassment. Then, seeing the captain and me on the roof, he turned even redder and ran toward us.

"I thought they were killing a child," he said with an awkward smile.

The general and the cavalry left the village first. Our battalion formed the rearguard. Khlopov's and Rosenkranz' companies were to move out together.

Captain Khlopov's prediction proved correct. No sooner had we reached the narrow woods than enemy Tartars, both on horseback and on foot, started popping up all around us, so close that at times I could clearly see some of them darting from one tree to another, their backs bent very low, their rifles clutched in both hands.

The captain removed his cap and crossed himself. Some old soldiers did the same. From among the trees came the high-pitched shouts of the enemy baiting our men. There was a succession of dry, crackling rifle shots; bullets whizzed by from both directions. Our men fired back in silence, except for a few muttered remarks that the enemy had it easy among the trees and what the devil was the artillery waiting for.

And soon the artillery did join in. The cannon spat grapeshot into the forest. This seemed to weaken the enemy. But no sooner had our troops gone a few more yards than the enemy fire again increased, along with the war cries and the baiting.

Before we were even half a mile from the village, enemy cannon balls started screaming over our heads. I saw one of them kill a soldier. . . But why dwell on that horrible scene which I myself would give anything to forget?

Lieutenant Rosenkranz, firing his own rifle, kept galloping from one end of the line to the other, shouting instructions to his men in a hoarse voice. He was somewhat pale, and this pallor seemed to suit his well-formed, manly face.

Second Lieutenant Alanin was in ecstasy: his handsome dark eyes shone with daring, his mouth was slightly twisted into a smile. Several time he rode up to the captain to ask permission to charge.

"We'll stop 'em," he pleaded. "I'm sure, sir, we'll throw 'em back."

"No need for it," the captain answered tersely. "All we're to do is cover our withdrawal."

Khlopov's company was holding a sector at the edge of the forest. The men were lying on the ground, firing at the enemy. The captain, in his threadbare tunic and shabby sheepskin cap, sat on his dirty-white horse, the reins loose in his hands, his knees sharply bent in the short stirrups. He sat there immobile, saying nothing; his soldiers knew their business and there was no need to order them around. Only now and then did he shout sharp reminders to some to keep their heads low.

There was nothing very martial about Captain Khlopov's appearance, but its directness and simplicity struck me. "Here's one who's really brave," I felt instinctively.

He was the same as ever; the same quiet movements, the same even voice, the same lack of affectation on his plain, straightforward face. Possibly, though, his eyes were somewhat more intent as a result of his total concentration; he looked like a man quietly and efficiently going about his business.

Yes, he was just as he always was—whereas in the others I could detect at least some difference from their everyday behavior: some wanted to appear calmer, others more determined, still others more cheerful than they'd have been under ordinary circumstances. But from the captain's face it was obvious that it had never even occurred to him that he might need to disguise his feelings.

The Frenchman during the battle of Waterloo who said, *"La garde meurt mais ne se rend pas,"* and other heroes, often French, who coined such historic phrases were really brave and may have actually made their memorable statements. The main difference, however, between their courage and the captain's is that even if resounding words stirred inside his heart, he'd never have uttered them, because for him they'd have spoiled a great deed. And the captain must have felt that when a man senses within himself the strength to perform a great deed, words become superfluous. This, I believe, is a peculiarity of Russian bravery. And how can a Russian not be offended when he hears Russian officers spouting French clichés in imitation of obsolete concepts of French chivalry?

Suddenly from the platoon under Second Lieutenant Alanin there came a rather uncoordinated and subdued "hurrah." I looked that way and saw a score or so of soldiers, their rifles in their hands and their equipment on their backs, running with difficulty across the plowed field. They stumbled again and again but kept going, shouting as they ran. The young second lieutenant rode at their head, holding his unsheathed saber high in the air.

Then they all vanished into the forest. . .

After a few minutes of whooping and crackling, a frightened horse emerged from the trees. Then I saw some soldiers carrying the dead and wounded. Among the latter was their young officer, Second Lieutenant Alanin. Two soldiers held him under the arms. His pretty-boy face was ashen, and bore only a faint trace of the enthusiasm that had animated it a minute earlier. His head was unnaturally pulled in between his shoulders and hung down on his chest. Under his unbuttoned tunic, a small bloody stain showed on his white shirt.

"Ah! What a shame!" I said, involuntarily turning away from the sight.

"Sure, it's a pity," an old soldier next to me, leaning on his rifle, said gloomily. "That kid wasn't afraid of anything. And it doesn't make sense, does it?" He looked intently at the wounded youngster. "Still, he was stupid, and now he's paid for it."

"And what about you, are you afraid?" I asked him.

"What do you think?" he asked.

Four soldiers were carrying the second lieutenant on a stretcher. Behind them, a medical orderly led a thin, old horse loaded with two green cases containing medical supplies. They waited for the doctor. Officers kept riding up to the stretcher, trying to comfort the wounded youngster.

"Well, Alanin, old man, it'll be a while now before you can dance again," Rosenkranz said to him with a smile.

He must have assumed that these words would cheer up Alanin. But Alanin's cold, sad look showed that they'd not produced the desired effect.

Captain Khlopov rode up. He looked closely at the wounded man, and his usually cold, indifferent face expressed honest sorrow.

"Well, dear boy," he said, with a warmth I hadn't expected of him, "looks like it was God's will that it should happen this way."

The wounded man turned toward him. A sad smile brought his pale features to life.

"Yes. I disobeyed you, sir."

"You'd better say it was God's will," the captain said again.

The doctor arrived. He took bandages, a probe, and some other instrument from the medical orderly, rolled up his sleeves, and, smiling cheerfully, approached the wounded man.

"Looks like they drilled a neat little hole in you," he said in a light, casual tone. "Let me have a look at it."

The young man complied. He looked at the doctor with a reproachful surprise that passed unnoticed. The doctor started to examine the wound, pressing so hard all around it that the young man, at the limit of his endurance, pushed his hand away with a moan:

"Leave me alone," he said in a hardly audible voice. "I'll die anyway."

Then he fell back. Five minutes later, when I passed by him again, I asked a soldier:

"How's the second lieutenant?"

"He's dying," the man said.

It was late when the detachment approached the fort in a wide column. The soldiers were singing.

The general rode in front and, to judge by his satisfied expression, the raid must have been a success. And indeed it had been; for the first time the Russians had succeeded in setting foot in the village of Mukay—and had achieved this at the cost of very few lives.

Rosenkranz silently thought back over the day's action. Captain Khlopov, deep in thought, walked with his company, leading his little whitish horse by its bridle.

The sun sank behind the snowy chain of mountains, casting its last reddish beams on a long thin cloud that hung motionless in the clear, translucent air above the horizon. The snowy mountains began to vanish in the violet mist, and only their upper reaches stood out with uncanny clarity in the crimson glow. The moon had already risen and was beginning to whiten and detach itself from the darkening azure of the sky. The green of the leaves and grass turned slowly to black and became wet with dew. The dark masses of moving soldiers produced rhythmical waves among the rich green meadows. Drums, tambourines and songs resounded over everything. The chorus leader of the Sixth Company sounded forth in full voice, and the notes of his pure, vibrating tenor, filled with feeling and power, floated through the clear evening air.

Leo Tolstoy, The Raid, from *The Cossacks and the Raid,* trans. by. A.R. MacAndrew (New York: Signet, 1961) pp. 183-211.

Wyatt Blassingame

How the Legion Began

History sometimes turns on small and trivial matters.

There are a lot of flies in Algeria, and where there are flies people carry fly swatters. This seemingly unimportant fact had a lot to do with the formation of the French Foreign Legion, and the Legion has influenced the course of world colonial history.

It happened this way.

For hundreds of years modern civilization, even time itself apparently, did not touch northwest Africa. In Tunis, Algeria, Morocco, the deys, as the local sultans were called, ruled over courts where customs had gone unchanged for centuries. There were no roads, just caravan trails over which passed pack trains of camels and horses. Along the coasts men lived by piracy, attacking the passing ships of any nation and making slaves of the men and women captured. Americans, the British and French, people of almost all western nations, were enslaved in this way.

In 1815 Stephen Decatur sailed a squadron of American ships into Algiers and made the dey promise to stop robbing merchant ships that flew the Stars and Stripes. The promise was not too well kept. Other countries also protested, and it was on one of these occasions that the fly swatter came into use.

It was a hot day in 1827 and the flies were bothering Dey Hussein, the ruler of Algeria. The French consul, who continued to argue that French trade should be protected, also bothered him. The Dey was not a man of infinite patience. Already irked by the heat and the flies, he finally lost his temper and smacked the consul in the face with his royal fly swatter.

This was too much for French dignity. And it may be that France, which wanted to control the Mediterranean and expand its territory, was looking for an excuse to invade Algeria. Soon French warships blockaded the harbor of Algiers, French troops went ashore, and in July, 1830, the city surrendered.

But at almost exactly this same time Charles X, the French king who had ordered the attack on Algiers, was losing his own throne in a revolution. He was replaced by King Louis Philippe, who immediately found himself with a foreign war on his hands and one that was not going too well. French troops still held Algiers, but they had not been able to enlarge their bridgehead. Louis Philippe had either to evacuate the city, which would have been a serious blow to his prestige, or send in fresh troops. And there were not too many Frenchmen anxious to go and fight in Africa.

It was then that Louis Philippe got his idea.

It was a time of great upheaval throughout Europe, as so many times have been. In a short hopeless war Poland had attempted to gain its freedom from Russia, and now the Poles who had fought against the czar were fleeing from his armies. In Germany, Austria and Italy there had been uprisings. From all over Europe men were pouring into France seeking sanctuary. Many of them were trained soldiers. Why not give them a chance to enlist under the French flag and go to fight the Moors in Africa?

It was not an altogether new idea. Many countries, from the very beginning of history, have made a practice of hiring foreign soldiers. The Pope had a Swiss guard, and so had a number of earlier French kings. George III of England had hired German soldiers to fight against the Colonies in the American Revolution.

So at first there was nothing particularly unusual about the French Foreign Legion. A Frenchman could join if he wished, and so could anyone else. There were seven battalions, and two of these were made up of Swiss. The Swiss have traditionally served as professional soldiers for France. Once an officer from another country said to a Swiss soldier in the Legion, "You Swiss always fight for money. In my country we fight for honor."

The Swiss soldier merely looked at him, "Yes," he said. "Everyone fights for what he needs most."

It was in the spring of 1832 that the Legion landed in Africa. They were something to see, these men who were to develop into the world's greatest fighting unit. They wore the uniform of the regular French infantry: red trousers and a heavy blue coat with a high collar—a poor uniform for the blistering heat of Africa. Their flag was a French tricolor, and on it was the picture of a rooster standing on top of a globe marked "France." Under this were the words, *The King of the French to the Foreign Legion.*

They came from all over Europe, these men. There were big men and small ones. There were men of royal blood and men who could not write their name. There were criminals and boys who had never yet needed to shave.

But they had one thing in common, one thing that Legionnaires have always had in common and must have: They were brave.

From the beginning the Legion fought well, and fought often. It pushed back the Moors. It built the first of the many roads that Legionnaires would build. And it suffered a crushing defeat in its first major battle.

Under a General Trézel the Fourth and Fifth Battalions were sent out to capture the white-walled city of Constantine to the east of Algiers. It was from here that Ahmed Bey sent warriors to harry the French, so the French generals felt the city must be taken.

The Legion never reached it. In a narrow gap in the mountains they were met by Abd-el-Kader, the leader of all the Arabs, and a force that outnumbered the Legion four to one. With their red trousers and blue coats gleaming in the sun, the Legionnaires attacked but could not break through. Then the Arabian cavalry swooped upon them, a foot soldier riding behind each cavalryman. The Legion retreat was cut off. The carts carrying the wounded were upset and many of the wounded butchered. When finally the battalions fought clear, they had lost more than a quarter of their men.

And shortly afterward something happened that has never happened again in all the Legion's history. The King of France loaned the whole Legion--men, guns and equipment--to the Queen of Spain! And the Legion sailed away to fight for her.

It all came about in an odd way.

Ferdinand VII, King of Spain, had died leaving a baby daughter as his only child. According to the old law only a man could rule, but before his death Ferdinand VII had changed this. He ordered that the throne should go to his child whether it was a boy or a girl. His wife was to rule as regent until the child was old enough to take over. The King's brother, Don Carlos, opposed this. The throne, he said, was rightfully his after his brother's death. So there was civil war between the followers of the Queen

Regent, Maria Cristina, and those of Don Carlos. It was to help Cristina that Louis Philippe loaned her the Foreign Legion in 1835.

And it was now that the Legion began to take shape, to turn into that strange and wonderful body of fighting men it has been ever since.

Until this time the various nationalities within the Legion had been segregated as much as possible. There were two battalions of Swiss, a battalion of Germans, one of Poles, and so on. These units were jealous of one another; they fought almost as much among themselves as they did against the enemy. But when the Legion went into Spain this was changed. Men of all nations were mixed together in the same battalions and much of the old jealousy ended.

But the fighting was just beginning. The Legionnaires moved east and north from Tarragona, fighting battle after battle. Gradually the forces of Don Carlos were pushed back toward the Pyrenees. More than once the main body of the Queen's army got in trouble, and it was the Legion that staved off defeat and carried the day. But the war dragged on with no conclusive victory for either side.

Louis Philippe, having turned the Legion over to the Spanish Queen, apparently forgot it. At least he sent no pay for the soldiers. The Queen did not pay them either. That, she said, was up to Louis Philippe. Even food and equipment were rarely issued. Cholera broke out among the troops and as many died of disease as were killed in battle. When the Legion landed in Spain there had been more than three thousand men, formed in five battalions. Because of losses they had to be re-formed into three battalions, then two, then one.

And still they fought. Hungry, sick, wearing tattered and filthy uniforms in freezing weather, they kept fighting. And it was now, suffering and fighting together, that they began to feel that fierce, powerful *esprit de corps*, the mystery of the Legion, which has survived ever since.

At the Battle of Barrastro on the plain of Aragon an incident occurred that illustrates how the men of the Legion were beginning to feel about it. Don Carlos had hired a foreign legion of his own, and at this battle the two forces took up position so close together that the soldiers could call back and forth to one another. Men in the French Foreign Legion recognized countrymen and friends among the enemy and shouted greetings.

Then one Legionnaire, a German, saw his brother in the ranks of the Carlists and called to him, "Heinrich, what are you doing there?"

"Fighting for Don Carlos," his brother shouted back. "And you?"

For a moment the Legionnaire did not answer. What, he thought, were he and his comrades fighting for? Not France. And certainly not Spain. The Legionnaires had come to hate Spain and the Spanish. They were not even fighting for money, since they were not being paid.

And then he knew. "For the Legion!" he shouted. "I fight for the Legion!"

Later Legionnaires would compose a song to sing as they marched:

My homeland is my regiment!
My mother have I never known.
My father fell in battle, young.
In this world I am alone.
The Legion is my only home!

And it was for the Legion they fought.

When the war in Spain had lasted for a year, Louis Philippe decided to recall his troops to France. But by now there was very little left of the Legion. A year of battle and disease and hunger had almost wiped it out. Of the more than 3,000 men who had landed at Tarragona, there remained only 63 officers and 159 men!

These marched north toward France, carrying their weapons with them. Queen Cristina sent a message after them. She had not paid them during the year they fought for her, but now she offered to give any officer of the Legion a commission in her own army--but only as a second lieutenant, regardless of the officer's rank.

The Legion's reply was brief. It stated that no corporal of the Legion would accept a commission even as major in the Queen's "army of bandits and barbarians."

The Legion Fights in Algeria

Even while the Legion was still in Spain, Louis Philippe realized that he could not complete his conquest of Algeria without it. So he began to recruit new Legionnaires and send them to North Africa. There they were joined by the tattered remnants of the army which had fought for the Spanish Queen. And so the Legion was re-formed.

The French did not want Algeria only because the dey had once slapped their consul in the face with a fly swatter. This country is composed mostly of high, barren mountains and beyond them the Sahara Desert: an ocean of rolling dunes that goes on and on for hundreds of miles. But along the Mediterranean slopes there are good grazing lands for cattle and sheep and horses. In the valleys the rich soil produces excellent crops of wheat and oats and corn, oranges, apricots and grapes. It was for this fertile farming land and for the harbors along the coast, from which their fleet could operate in the Mediterranean, that the French wanted Algeria.

The walled city of Constantine, near which the Legion had suffered defeat in its first major battle, was still an obstacle. So once more--the date was now 1837--the Legion moved to attack it, opposed as before by the

Arabian leader, Abd-el-Kader.

Abd-el-Kader was an unusual man. An excellent general, a poet, a superb horseman, he was said to be a descendant of Mohammed himself. The Arabs followed him with fanatical devotion. They were Moslems, and the Moslem religion taught that any man who died fighting men of another faith was transported instantly to heaven. With such a reward waiting for them, they did not hesitate to fight to the death. They were soldiers whom even the toughest of Legionnaires could respect.

Moving slowly, carrying its supplies with it, the Legion made its way to Constantine. The city was protected on one side by a sheer cliff a thousand feet high. On the other three sides was a great white wall. Against this the Legion turned its artillery. A hole was battered in the wall and with a cry the men rushed forward.

But beyond this wall was another. From behind it rose the houses of the city, and from every window a turbaned Arab fired at the Legion with a long-barreled rifle. In the face of this fire the sappers, the engineers of the Legion, ran forward to blow a hole in the second wall. But as they tried to do so, the Arabs themselves blasted the wall over on top of them.

One of the Legion officers was a young Frenchman named Saint-Arnaud, who would one day be a general under Napoleon III and play a large part in French politics. Now, as the soldiers wavered in the face of the Arabians' fire, he gave the cry that from that time on was to be the rallying cry of the Legion.

"A moi, la Légion!" he shouted, and raced forward into the dust of the collapsing wall.

"La Légion!" the Legionnaires cried, and rushed after him.

After that it was hand-to-hand fighting, French bayonet against Arabian sword, as house by house the Legionnaires pushed through the city.

When it was all over, Saint-Arnaud told his men, "Our Legion has become immortal." But another soldier was, perhaps, more accurate when he said the Legion was a *"troupe de guerre,"* meaning that they were the professionals at fighting.

But Abd-el-Kader was not captured at Constantine. Somehow he escaped, and with his men he still held practically all of Algeria except for a few cities along the coast. When the Legion tried to lure him into a pitched battle, the Arabs would fight for a while, then suddenly disappear into the hills, form again and strike at the Legion's rear. Time and again Abd-el-Kader and his men swept down from the mountains to strike at some isolated party of Legionnaires or at French colonists farming the land. Then, before the Arabs could be forced into battle, they would disappear into the mountains again.

It was a slow and bloody war, much like the Indian wars in the early years of our country. The Arabs were splendid fighters, but they were also savagely cruel. Instead of taking prisoners, they tortured and killed any man they caught. And it was the Arabian women who took the most delight in torture. They followed their men into battle, usually coming so near that they could scream encouragement during the fighting. Then, if the Legion was forced to retreat, they would rush forward to loot and mutilate any bodies left behind.

But the Legion did not leave its wounded to fall into the hands of the enemy. Even the dead were brought in and buried so the Arabs could not find them. This became an unwritten law of the Legion; it was part of its *esprit de corps*. Prince Aage of Denmark, who joined the Legion as an officer, wrote about this.

He was in charge, the Prince said, of a group of Legionnaires who had been sent into the mountains to build a new outpost. The men were carrying heavy rocks and piling them into a parapet behind which they could take shelter if the Arabs attacked. One of the men refused to work. He was a big man with a hard face and a black beard. He looked straight at the Prince and said he was not going to carry any more rocks.

As punishment the Prince gave orders that the man should not be fed until he went back to work. At each meal the cook would carry a plate of food to the man and ask if he was ready to go back to work. The man did not answer but merely shook his head. The food was thrown on the ground. After a few days' starvation the man went back to work, still without speaking. Watching him, the Prince felt certain he would never make a good soldier and decided to have him transferred.

Then one day the Arabs attacked without warning, catching some Legionnaires outside the fort. Several fell, wounded. Inside the fort the Legion opened fire, and the Arabs, hidden behind rocks on the mountain, fired back. On the open ground between them lay the wounded.

Suddenly the Prince saw a man climb over the parapet of the fort and begin to run forward, exposed to the full fire of the Arabs. A bullet struck him and he staggered but kept going. He picked up one of the wounded soldiers and brought him back to the fort. Without pausing he went out again and again until all the wounded were inside. Then he collapsed from his own wound.

It was the man who, a few days before, had refused to work!

Gradually, building roads and forts as they went, the Legion pushed Abd-el-Kader and his men back into the mountains of the Grand Atlas. Here in the snow the Legion fought in the same uniform it wore in the scorching heat of the desert. France furnished it with no other, though the Legion soon learned to make its own adaptations.

For more than fifteen years Abd-el-Kader continued to fight. But the Legion forts cut his lines of communication. It became more and more difficult for him to assemble large bodies of troops and to supply them once he got them together. Some of the tribes deserted him and began to fight on the side of the French. Finally he was forced to flee into Morocco.

But the Moroccans would not have him. They put him back across the border. Most of his army was gone. The dark, bearded, handsome man mounted his horse and rode into the Legion camp, asking for General Lamoricière. "I have come to surrender," he told the General.

The French had learned to respect him as a brave and intelligent man. He was sent with all his wives into exile where he lived comfortably. Years later one of his grandsons served as an officer in the French army in World War I.

But the surrender of Abd-el-Kader brought only a short period of peace for the Legion.

Back in France strange things had been happening. Louis Philippe had never been too popular. There had been at least six attempts to assassinate him, one by a man who had invented what the historians of the day called "an infernal machine," a kind of forerunner of a modern machine gun. One historian says it had twenty-five barrels, another says one hundred. Whatever the exact number, it must have been considerable. When the would-be assassin fired the gun at Louis Philippe, who was riding down a Paris street in the royal carriage, twelve persons were killed and twice that many wounded. The King was not touched.

His luck, however, could not hold forever, and in 1848 a revolution sent him into exile. Louis Napoleon, the nephew of Napoleon Bonaparte, was elected President of the new French republic. But under the law the President could not succeed himself, so Louis Napoleon declared himself Napoleon III, Emperor of France. And soon after this, as Napoleons have a way of doing, he got himself involved in a war.

From North Africa the Legion sailed away to fight it.

From Wyatt Blassingame, *The French Foreign Legion,* (New York: Random House, 1955), pp. 19-41

Chapter 5

The Civil War

It is commonly argued that the Confederacy faced insuperable material odds in its secessionist war; and that, once Grant, Sherman and Sheridan came along, the South's advantages in military effectiveness and leadership disappeared. These views neglect the area of special operations, though, a sphere in which the South had almost all the advantages, throughout the war. First, the Confederacy stood strategically on the defensive, often able to fight on terrain of its own choosing, and with a supportive local population. This latter factor contributed greatly to the success of Mosby, in particular. Second, in Forrest and others, the South had a cadre of gifted commanders adept at raiding, whose skills were never matched on the Union side. Finally, the logistical technology of the time, which keyed on rail transportation of armies and their supplies, proved particularly vulnerable to disruption from raiders. Had the Confederacy stood on the defensive with its regular forces and torn up the Federals with raids behind the lines, it could well have enjoyed a series of Fredericksburg-like victories against a Union army ever more pressed to maintain its combat readiness.

Why, then, did Lee and his lieutenants insist on pursuing the offensive? Perhaps because the American military, of which they had been an integral part, was steeped, then as now, in the ideas of Jomini. This Napoleonic-era staff officer, whose *The Art of War* propounded a series of explicit principles of strategy, enshrined, among other things, the notion of taking the offensive to strike at some ill-defined "decisive point." In pursuit of this chimera, Rebel offensives foundered, again and again, from Antietam and Gettysburg in the Eastern theater, to Chickamauga in the West. This was the path to ruin, one which might have been avoided had the ideas of Clausewitz been made available to the Confederates.

The German philosopher of war held, in *On War,* that the *defensive* was stronger than the offensive, one of his many direct critiques of Jominian thought. However, one cannot judge Lee and others too harshly in this matter, as the first translation of Clausewitz into English didn't appear until 1874, at least a decade too late for the "Lost Cause."

Archer Jones

Military Means, Political Ends

Any estimate of the role of strategy in the outcome of the Civil War would necessarily involve giving strategy a broad definition, one going beyond strictly military concerns to include such important and interrelated topics as diplomacy, economic mobilization, and finance. But to do this would make strategy too broad to provide a focused perspective on the war, one which would clearly illuminate the contribution of military strategy to victory and defeat.

Nevertheless, military strategy has such a close relation to the war's political objectives and concerns that any intelligible treatment must show its links to politics. Further, it is convenient to distinguish between military and political strategy by defining the former as military action designed to deplete the hostile military force and the latter as military action intended to produce a political result directly. Yet military and political strategy rarely have such clear-cut boundaries because most military actions have political effects. Thus northern and southern strategists had to consider the political effect of their military actions on not only the enemy but on the attitudes of foreign powers and the opinions of their own people, including the citizen soldiers. The attitude of the public had great importance in this war, the first large-scale, prolonged conflict between democratically organized countries in the age of mass circulation newspapers and widespread literacy.

The first Union strategic plan, a political strategy offered in the spring of 1861 by General in Chief Winfield Scott, proposed to use the pressure of a blockade and a campaign to control the Mississippi River to induce the seceded states to return to the Union. Though its elements became part of Union military strategy, it failed to promote a compromise. The failure of political strategy meant the North had to rely on military strategy. With a two to one numerical superiority of uniformed men, the Union armies, some foresaw, would gain a quick victory. And this would have happened had the tactical offensive had as much strength as the defensive and pursuit more speed than retreat. Under these circumstances Union armies could have defeated the Confederates in battle and then followed, overtaken, and beaten them over and over until they had depleted Confederate military forces and won the war. But, as had been true in western Europe for centuries, the opposite conditions actually prevailed, with the tactical defensive proving stronger than the offensive and retreat faster than pursuit. Thus generals commanding the weaker forces usually had a choice between fighting and withdrawing, and if they elected to fight, they could do so in a strong position and face to face with their adversaries.

So the traditional ascendancy of the strategic defensive guaranteed that the North would face a long, hard task in trying to deplete an enemy equal in combat quality while invading a hostile country big enough to provide the Rebel armies with ample opportunities for retreat. Moreover, the Federals faced supply difficulties unknown to western Europe because the thinly populated South did not produce enough food to feed the huge northern armies unless they could remain in motion. This meant that, unless on the move and finding new supplies, the invaders had to rely on rations brought by river and railroad to supplement what they could find in the country. With smaller armies, the Confederates had fewer difficulties and, when they retreated, would leave behind for the Yankees a country denuded of supplies and railroads in need of repair.

Most Federal generals understood the dominance of the tactical and strategic defensive and recognized that they had only limited opportunities to deplete Rebel armies through combat. This led them to the tacit decision to seek to conquer the South's territory as the means of weakening its armies. The loss of control of territory would deprive the southern armies not only of their food and other production but of the manpower the lost area would have provided for the armies. Thus implicitly the Union generals rejected a combat strategy for wearing down the Rebels and adopted a logistic strategy of diminishing their armies by reducing their base for supply. Old, like most strategic ideas, this went back beyond ancient times. Julius Caesar, distinguishing between a logistic and a combat strategy, said he preferred "conquering the foe by hunger rather than by steel."

The Confederacy explicitly understood the military menace presented by such a logistic strategy when President Jefferson Davis pointed out that the "general truth that power is increased by the concentration of an army is, under our peculiar circumstance, subject to modification" because the "evacuation of any portion of territory involves not only the loss of supplies, but in every instance has been attended by greater or less loss of troops."

Both governments also recognized the political significance of the gain and loss of territory because these provided a measure of military success and failure. This sign of achievement or discomfiture could affect the attitude of European powers and public opinion in both the North and South. Federal military victory could have played a part in a strategy which aimed at compromise and early reconciliation, and Confederate triumphs could have helped their initial strategy of gaining a quick victory through the intervention of European powers. The South had confidently expected that, when British textile factories stopped when the war cut off the supply of southern cotton, the British government would intercede to aid the South and so ensure its independence.

When "King Cotton" failed to bring intervention, the Rebels increasingly looked to the effect of their military actions on northern public opinion. They believed that a resolute and successful resistance could convince a majority of Yankees that victory would cost more in money, time, hardship, and casualties than saving the Union was worth. Increasingly, Confederate leaders and people, including the soldiers, looked to the Union presidential election of 1864 as the crucial time when the North could have a referendum on whether or not to continue the war. And Confederate leaders were also aware of the effect of military operations on their own people and on their estimation of whether the price of independence seemed too high. But the six-year Confederate presidential term precluded as early a southern referendum on the war.

Acutely aware of the influence of military events on northern public opinion, President Lincoln also found himself caught between the professional soldiers' views of military reality and the civilian perspective, which tended to see war almost exclusively in terms of battles. So the populace demanded battles from generals when most of them realized the ineffectiveness of a combat strategy. By the fall of 1862, Lincoln had come to understand the intrinsic indecisiveness of military operations but knew no way to interpret that to the people or to explain warfare in terms of the logistics and strategy of campaigns instead of succession of battles that rarely did more than produce short retreats by the defeated.

So the military strategy for both sides had to respond to political as well as military considerations. For the Union this created some tension because the slow working of a logistic strategy implemented by territorial conquest would have less appeal and inspire less popular confidence than a combat strategy, which concentrated on winning battles. Yet such a disregard of the primacy of the defensive could well have resulted not only in too many lost battles but in depleting the northern armies at a higher rate than the southern forces.

On the other hand, in defending against the Union's logistic strategy by giving priority to territorial defense, President Davis also pursued the political strategy which would have the best chance of discouraging the North. Moreover, maintaining the Confederacy's territorial integrity had an important effect on southern morale. In fact, it is doubtful that, in spite of its obvious merit, the Confederacy could have adopted a military strategy of employing deep withdrawals—the public would have responded to the retreats by becoming discouraged about the prospect of gaining independence at a reasonable cost.

The kind of military strategy needed to conquer territory can appropriately have the name persisting. This contrasted with the even older raiding strategy, which aims at accomplishing its military or political objective through a transitory presence in the hostile country. To fight to gain and retain control of enemy territory, soldiers used an operational strategy to guide army movements. That employed by northern and southern generals came from the wars of the French Revolution and Napoleon. With their proximity in time to the civil War comparable to that of World War II and the 1990s, these wars had the same popular appeal as that which the World War has in the 1990s. In addition to the history of the campaigns, readers could find military writers who explained the principles underlying Napoleon's success. The most prominent of these, Antoine-Henri Jomini, a general in the French and then the Russian army, provided a foundation for the other authors. His 1838 *Summary of the Art of War*, available in English in 1854, brought together all of his ideas in succinct form, but readers needed a good knowledge of Napoleon's campaigns in order to understand the points he made. There is not much evidence to support the thesis that he had a broad influence on Civil War soldiers and none that the ideas he propounded antedated and were antithetical to Napoleon's practice.

Napoleonic strategy depended on rapid maneuvers with armies dispersing to move quickly or to find, confuse, or engage the enemy; the armies concentrated to fight. Much of this power of maneuver depended on the division, a unit of 3,000 to 8,000 men, able to fight independently because it usually included artillery and cavalry as well as infantry. Army commanders maneuvered divisions whose generals marched and fought with their infantry brigades and artillery and cavalry units.

From dispersal to cover a wide area or to deceive the enemy, Napoleonic strategy used concentration to bring superior force against the enemy. If a general found his adversary divided, he would try to concentrate most of his men against one part. The other basic Napoleonic maneuver occurred when a general succeeded in taking all or part of his army into the enemy's rear. The Civil War soldiers called this a turning movement, using the same term for this strategic maneuver as for the comparable tactical move.

The generals did not start as masters of the Napoleonic art of war but engaged in a course of self-teaching and emulation of good models presented by their fellow generals, enemy as well as friendly. Thus the campaigns of the war displayed an increasing sophistication in operational strategy. Nevertheless, the first campaign of the war showed many of the

elements that would characterize the war's subsequent operations.
In July 1861 the North had political motives in inaugurating the
campaign of the Battle of Manassas—to respond to the popular desire for
military action and to drive back the Rebel army of General G.T.
Beauregard in northern Virginia, almost insolently close to Washington.
So, in July 1861, General in Chief Scott ordered forward General Irvin
McDowell's army of 30,000 green troops stationed in Washington. Well
aware that General J.E. Johnston's Confederate army in the Shenandoah
Valley, less than 100 miles west of Washington, could reinforce Beauregard,
Scott intended the Union army of Scott's opponent, General Robert
Patterson, to keep Johnston occupied. Patterson failed. when McDowell
began his advance and Beauregard telegraphed for aid, President Davis
ordered Johnston to reinforce Beauregard. This he did, moving part of the
way by railroad and arriving in time to give the Rebels a slight numerical
superiority in the battle and help defeat McDowell's well-conceived
attack.

Because the two Confederate armies were closer together than the
Union armies of Patterson and McDowell, they could have won any race
to concentrate on the Manassas battlefield, a situation for the southern
forces which Jomini had called interior lines. In this campaign the
Confederates had used the telegraph and the railroad to apply Napoleon's
strategy of concentrating dispersed forces; this use of the products of the
industrial revolution to expand the application of Napoleonic strategy
would characterize the Civil War and become a particular feature of Rebel
strategy.

By defeating the Union's strategic goal of driving them back, the
Confederates won the campaign. Yet many have criticized them for not
pursuing their beaten foe. But, as disorganized by victory as the Federal
army by defeat, they could do little to overtake their retreating adversary
or take the strategic and tactical offensive, cross the Potomac River, and
capture Washington.

In the form of casualties, campaigns have tactical as well as strategic
results. The casualties, or manpower depletion, of each army are a
byproduct of any combat, even that which implemented a logistic rather
than a combat strategy. The best measure of this bit-by-bit depletion, or
attrition, is to state it as a percentage of the combatants' total forces. In
the battle and campaign of Manassas the defeated Federals lost 9 percent,
the victorious Rebels less than 7 percent, of their army. In the political
domain this campaign heartened the Rebels and discouraged the Yankees;
yet, by showing many in the North that their armies could not win quickly,
doubtless it conferred some benefits.

The essentially political objective of driving back the Rebel army near
Washington, now commanded by J.E. Johnston, remained the Union
strategy in Virginia. Well aware of the superiority of the tactical and
strategic defense, McDowell's successor, General George B. McClellan,

had no desire to attempt to advance directly on Johnston's army. Instead, he planned to use the fine communications provided by the Chesapeake Bay and Virginia's rivers to carry out a strategic turning movement. Since to reach the rear of the Confederate army near Washington required surprising Johnston, something McClellan could not achieve, the Union general settled for a landing at the tip of the Peninsula between the James and York rivers and an advance up the Peninsula to the vicinity of Richmond. This move would draw Johnston's army away from Washington to defend Richmond, thus accomplishing the minimum strategic objective of the campaign.

Moreover, McClellan could advance up the Peninsula without serious frontal combat because Union command of the rivers would enable him to force Johnston back by the threat of landing troops in his rear. The Union general believed that his approach to Richmond would so threaten the Confederates that they would attack to drive him away, giving him the advantage of the tactical defensive.

All went according to McClellan's plan, his army reaching the vicinity of Richmond in May 1862. Johnston then lashed out at him in the Battle of Fair Oaks. McClellan's men repulsed the attacks and inflicted on the Rebels the loss of 6,000 killed, wounded, and missing, suffering 5,000 casualties themselves. This gave them a victory of attrition, McClellan losing 5 percent of his 100,000 men, Johnston 10 percent of his 60,000. An even broader and more pertinent measure made a still more favorable comparison. Since all Union forces outnumbered the Confederates by at least two to one, the southern losses, as a percentage of total troops available, amounted to more than double the Union's.

Thus McClellan's strategy had worked as intended. And, by repulsing the attack, the general had gained the strategic success of maintaining his threatening position. Because the defeated Rebels did not retreat, however, they deprived the Yankee army of this essential symbol of victory and, consequently, of much of its political effect in either the South or North.

When a wound dictated Johnston's replacement, President Davis gave the army to General R.E. Lee. The new commander, who also subscribed to the thesis that McClellan's army could capture Richmond by a siege, saw its presence as a serious political embarrassment and wished to recover the valuable farming areas given up to Union occupation because of McClellan's advance. Moreover, Richmond, as a major industrial center, had great logistic importance. In late June, after concentrating troops at Richmond, Lee attempted to drive McClellan back by turning him. But, since the turning force arrived a day late, the Confederates made only frontal attacks. McClellan responded by withdrawing his army to the James River, an excellent alternate supply line. In pursuing the Union army, the Confederates made more attacks, giving the name Seven Days' Battles to the conflict. In this battle McClellan gained a tactical victory in terms of attrition, suffering fewer than 16,000 casualties to the Rebels' more than 20,000, meaning that the South's percentage loss was again more than double the North's. In pushing the Federal army away from Richmond, the Confederates had attained only their minimum strategic goal, but the victory, signalized by McClellan's retreat, had a positive effect in the South and quite a negative one in the North.

In assessing the Seven Days' Battles, President Lincoln noted the political "importance to us, for its bearing upon Europe, that we should achieve military successes; and the same is true for us at home as well as abroad." He also knew that his army had won a tactical victory because he realized that "in men and material, the enemy suffered more than we," and "is less able to bear it." So he found it frustrating that such a "half-defeat should hurt us so much" in "moral effect." But for the public, which army retreated determined the victory; and to many, battles seemed the essence of warfare.

Before McClellan began his Peninsula campaign in March 1862, General H.W. Halleck, the Union commander in Missouri and West Tennessee, had already made a dramatic advance. With no major political objective, he launched a military operation designed to drive the Rebels from southern Kentucky and the western half of Tennessee and take control of the Mississippi River as far south as Memphis, Tennessee. Halleck could conduct such an ambitious campaign in spite of the tremendous obstacle of the winter mud because he could move in steamers on the western rivers and had the support of a U.S. Navy gunboat flotilla. The Ohio, Mississippi, Tennessee, and Cumberland rivers all interconnected and all but the Ohio served as routes of invasion for Halleck's forces.

Anticipating just such an advance, the Confederates had built forts on the banks of the rivers and armed them with heavy guns to prevent the passage of even armored gunboats. These forts could stop gunboats but could not cope with the troops that Halleck sent with them in steamers. In February 1862, Halleck dispatched 15,000 men under General U.S. Grant up the Tennessee, escorted by Flag Officer Andrew H. Foote's flotilla. Following Halleck's directions, Grant landed near Fort Henry and sent part of his army to turn it. Before the Union force could reach the fort's rear, the Confederate garrison escaped and marched eastward a few miles to join the garrison of Fort Donelson on the Cumberland River.

Grant then marched after them and, coming up behind Fort Donelson, immediately surrounded it while drawing from the river supplies and reinforcements sent by Halleck. Cut off and its huge garrison inadequately supplied, the fort surrendered. Instead of emulating Jefferson Davis's prompt action to concentrate against McDowell in the Manassas campaign, the Rebel commander, A.S. Johnston, had failed to use his rivers and railways to concentrate his forces against Grant. Instead, when Fort Henry fell, he acknowledged defeat by abandoning Kentucky but reinforcing Fort Donelson with enough men to add a tactical disaster to the strategic defeat. Then, seeing Union forces on the Tennessee River turning their positions and those on the Cumberland able to do the same, the Confederates evacuated Nashville and their strongest fort on the Mississippi.

In less than three weeks Halleck, Grant, and Foote had demolished the whole Confederate position, taken thousands of square miles of fertile farming country, and captured the important commercial and industrial center of Nashville—a major triumph for the North's logistic strategy. And they had won an important victory of attrition, for Grant in taking Fort Donelson had suffered 3,800 casualties but had inflicted 16,600 on the enemy, mostly in prisoners. The dramatic advance and the fall of the fort had enhanced northern morale and had a negative effect on southern expectations for an early victory.

Yet the swift and unexpected catastrophe transformed Confederate command behavior. A.S. Johnston and General Beauregard, his new second in command, used the railroad to concentrate most of Johnston's forces at Corinth, a railway junction in northern Mississippi. President Davis made an equally emphatic response in also ordering to Corinth a small force from Charleston, South Carolina, substantial numbers from New Orleans, and General Braxton Bragg and most of his men from the Gulf coast. These forces moved rapidly by railroad and steamer. Relying largely on the telegraph and steam, the Confederate command made a concentration which, by including troops from the Atlantic and Gulf coasts and Arkansas, had a truly national scope, the kind of concentration which Napoleon, depending on human and animal mobility only, had employed only within a single theatre of war. With this concentration they planned a counterattack to recover some of the immense logistic and political losses of February. They aimed to strike Grant, halted on the Mississippi River about 20 miles north of Corinth, before he could receive the reinforcement of General D.C. Buell's army, ordered by Halleck from Nashville to march to his aid.

On April 6, just as McClellan began moving on the Peninsula, A.S. Johnston began the Battle of Shiloh with a surprise assault on Grant's army. But, reinforced by Buell, Grant repelled the attack in a two-day battle in which Johnston died. In failing to recover lost ground, the Confederates suffered another strategic defeat and, in losing 10,600 men to Grant's and Buell's 13,000, suffered another tactical setback of attrition. The northern criticism of Grant for allowing the Rebels to surprise him diluted the victory's positive effect in the North.

Halleck then assumed personal command of the armies of Grant and Buell, took Corinth, ordered Buell eastward to take Chattanooga, and then went to Washington to become Union general in chief. Here he arrived in time to try to cope with a different type of Confederate offensive.

The Seven Days' Battles having caused casualties of more than 20 percent of the large southern army, Davis and Lee had agreed on the need for a less costly form of counterattack. In abandoning the idea of offensive battles, their new approach resembled McClellan's strategy. Lee stated it succinctly as a policy of "not attacking them in their strong and chosen positions. They ought always to be turned." Like McClellan's strategy, Lee's aimed not to reach the enemy's rear so much as to compel his retreat by the threat of doing so. He demonstrated it in his campaign against General John Pope's Federal army covering Washington.

In making the orthodox move of using his interior lines to concentrate against Pope, Lee planned "to avoid a general engagement" and only oblige Pope to retreat "by manoeuvering." In this way he would attain the basic logistical objective of his new style of counterattacking, to recover the "beef, flour, & forage" of the area north of Richmond. To conduct his turning movement Lee sent half of his force under General T. J. Jackson to Pope's rear, where it destroyed the railroad and supply depot at Manassas and then withdrew westward to leave Pope a clear route of retreat to Washington. Thus Lee implemented his concept of the defensive turning movement to force the enemy back without battle.

But Pope made an unsuccessful frontal attack on Jackson on the old battlefield of Manassas. The next day, when the other half of Lee's army arrived on Pope's flank, the Union general had to retreat to Washington. but at 9,000 losses, compared with Pope's 16,000, Lee had avoided a consequential tactical defeat of attrition. Moreover he gained his strategic objective and secured a splendid victory, which encouraged the Rebels and dismayed many Yankees.

Lee immediately adapted his new turning strategy to deal with his always pressing supply problems by deciding to cross the Potomac well to the west of Washington with the idea of spending the fall in Maryland, his army dining on the recent harvest there while his quartermasters and commissaries brought in the Virginia harvest to carry his army through the winter. Unlike his just-completed campaign of the Second Battle of Manassas, an application of persisting strategy, his move into Maryland could not give him permanent occupation of his position there. With only a limited area of control and without rail connections to the Confederacy, he was carrying out a raid, which meant that he could have only a temporary presence, departing in the late fall after a fine period of living at the enemy's expense.

But his ability to do this depended on the enemy, and Lee apparently thought that McClellan's traditional caution and deliberateness in preparation and movements would mean a long time before he advanced. Returned from the Peninsula and commanding his and Pope's armies, McClellan began moving toward Lee with unaccustomed celerity and accelerated when he captured Lee's plans. The campaign had the essentially political objective of driving the Rebels back to Virginia.

In mid-September, ten days after McClellan left Washington, Lee received his attack in the Battle of Antietam. In a costly defensive battle, the Confederates succeeded in fending off the clumsy attacks of the large Federal army. But, concentrated to fight, Lee could not forage to feed his raiding army. McClellan, on the other hand, had access to a railroad which enabled him to supply his men while they remained poised to fight the Rebels again. Thus Lee's success in resisting McClellan's attacks, a tactical victory in battle, did not alter the need to retreat to Virginia, a move Lee made after waiting a day to prove he had won the battle.

Since the political definition of losing is retreat, Lee had lost the battle. Since he would have had too withdraw after any battle, his decision to fight assured a negative political result in the South and a positive one in the North. The battle, and Lee's retreat, provided Lincoln with the opportunity to make his politically significant Preliminary Emancipation Proclamation and may even have forestalled British diplomatic intervention. Had McClellan been unwise enough to retreat when his attacks failed, Lee would still have had to withdraw because he could not disperse to forage in the presence of a large Union army under McClellan, or his successor, who doubtless would have responded to the northern political need by making a renewed advance on Lee. So strategically and politically Lee's Antietam campaign was a fiasco. It was really doomed to fail, but Lee could have mitigated the political damage by ending his raid without a battle. The Confederate capture of a large Federal garrison made the loss ratio in the campaign essentially neutral.

While Lee deliberately combined the raid with the turning movement, General Braxton Bragg conducted a campaign in Kentucky which he converted into a raid when he could not complete the classic turning movement. Assuming command in northern Mississippi, Bragg immediately moved half of his army by rail south to Mobile, Alabama, and then north through Atlanta to Chattanooga. Here, in conjunction with General Edmund Kirby Smith's Confederates in East Tennessee, he advanced northward, passing east of the flank of General Buell, who based his army on Nashville and the railroad, to Louisville. It looked as if he might succeed in turning Buell and recovering Middle Tennessee.

Seeing himself turned, Buell began moving north along the Louisville and Nashville Railroad. But Bragg kept ahead of him and when, in southern Kentucky, he established his army on Buell's railroad and blocked his retreat, Bragg had completely turned Buell. The Confederate general, realizing that his strategic offensive with the turning movement had given him the advantage of the tactical defensive in the coming battle, ordered his army to begin digging entrenchments to strengthen its defense. But Buell declined to fight a battle, and with ample supplies in depots along his railroad he could afford to wait. But Bragg could not tarry in an area of low agricultural productivity while remaining concentrated to block Buell. Thus thwarted by Buell's better supply situation, Bragg converted his invasion into a raid by moving off the railroad and marching northwest to join Kirby Smith in the fertile Blue Grass region of central Kentucky.

Buell promptly marched north of Louisville, incorporated reinforcements into his army, and moved into central Kentucky to drive Bragg out.
After an inconclusive battle at Perryville, Bragg realized that he could not
face Buell who could supply himself by means of the railroads from
Louisville and Cincinnati. So he and Kirby Smith retreated by the route
through eastern Kentucky and eastern Tennessee by which Kirby Smith
had come.

Bragg's spectacular raid raised and then dashed Rebel expectations.
The public did not realize that, as Lee had in the Antietam campaign, Bragg
had made a raiding rather than a persisting advance. Thus they expected
the Confederate troops to hold central Kentucky. It also proved a political
failure in that Kentuckians disappointed the Confederates' expectations
that many would volunteer for the Rebel army. In terms of its minimum
strategic objective, to remove the threat to Chattanooga, Bragg had
succeeded when he established his army only about 30 miles southeast of
Nashville. The campaign suffered no adverse attrition.

Even before the Kentucky and Antietam campaigns, raiders had
already had a decisive influence on operations in the West. In spite of
overwhelming numbers, Buell had failed to take Chattanooga in July and
August of 1862. He owed his defeat to the disabling of his supply lines
largely by raids conducted by Confederate cavalry which broke his
railroad in Kentucky as well as Tennessee. They easily wrecked a railroad
by taking up rails and, especially, by burning the wooden bridges and
trestles which so often carried the tracks.

In this work the regular cavalry had effective assistance from southern
guerrillas, quite active in Middle Tennessee. Here they controlled the
countryside through intimidating the Union supporters in the country by
burning houses and beating or killing people. They proved adept raiders
of vulnerable railways, often moving through familiar country at night to
shift a rail or burn a bridge.

Both guerrillas and regular cavalry could take advantage of the offensive superiority of the raid over the persisting defense that tried to interdict
movements into Union territory, protect hundreds of miles of railroad, and
intercept the raiders. The raid gained its dominance over the defense by
its ability to exploit retreat's advantage over pursuit, and the ambiguity of
the raiders' movements. With the intruders' wide choice of objectives and
routes, defenders did not know where to head off their incursion and, if
successful, would find their adversary retreating rather than fighting. The
raiders' ability to withdraw by a different route than that of their advance
gave the defenders an equally difficult task to intercept retreat. In their
raids, guerrillas could use an additional mode of retreat when they ended
their raid by blending in with the civilian population.

When the effectiveness of the raid and the strength of the guerrillas had
required Buell to use two divisions to guard his communications and

control the occupied areas, he had made a representative Union defensive commitment. As the northern armies moved beyond the river which had provided secure as well as efficient transportation, they had to commit a third of their forces to defending their communications, thus weakening their main armies which were striving to conquer Confederate territory.

In their war against the guerrillas, Federal troops emulated their adversary in using intimidation, often not pausing to try a captive before killing him. They used reprisals, like burning farms and even villages, but their most effective means in Middle Tennessee proved to be a version of the traditional hostage technique. By taking the property of wealthy citizens when a guerrilla raid occurred nearby, they convinced them to use their considerable influence to make the guerrillas desist. Arming local Unionists also had excellent results, one Union officer noting that these local forces, who knew and hated their Rebel enemies, were "killing many of the worst men in this part of the state and will soon drive the guerrillas out." Toward the end of the war a Union officer could report from Middle Tennessee that a "most distinguishing feature in this country . . . is the manner in which these people are cowed by the force of the Govt."

Coping with Rebel raids had fully occupied Halleck's first three months as general in chief. He then turned his attention to implementing for December 1862 simultaneous advances of all the main armies east of the Mississippi. Though operations had usually occurred at the same time in east and west, Halleck's effort amounted to something of an innovation. Simultaneous advances, that is, concentration in time, could counter the Confederate concentration in space, practiced on a national scale in the Shiloh campaign. Thus, by engaging every Rebel army at the same time, concentration in time could nullify concentration in space.

The first move occurred in Virginia, where McClellan's successor, General Ambrose E. Burnside, marched from northern Virginia toward Richmond, drawing Lee after him to halt Burnside and repulse his inept attack at the Battle of Fredericksburg on December 13. Although Burnside's advance recovered some territory, the battle losses contributed nothing to attrition and had a negative effect on the northern perception of the likelihood of a victory at a reasonable cost.

In Mississippi, Grant advanced down the railroad to turn and capture Vicksburg, the most important of the two remaining Confederate strongholds on the Mississippi. But he had not gone far when Rebel cavalry raids broke his railroad and destroyed his depot. Deprived of supplies, he withdrew just as General William T. Sherman led an expedition down the river to the city. After an essentially hopeless attack against fortifications, Sherman also fell back. These defeats, coming about without big battles or consequential attrition, amounted to a significant political defeat, and not merely because of the effect on the morale of the two publics. Vicksburg itself had little military importance, the Confederacy having negligible trade between its two halves and the North losing only a modest transportation advantage from its inability to use the river. But control of the historically important river would be a major symbol for both sides, sustaining the North in its quest for victory and making many more southerners doubtful of the possibility of independence at a reasonable cost.

At the end of December, Buell's successor, General William S. Rosecrans, marched against Bragg to destroy him in battle. Predictably, he failed but, with equal losses, gained a victory of attrition and, by Bragg's 20-mile retreat, brought the northern public very welcome relief from the gloom of the successive defeats in December.

By early 1863, Halleck and Lincoln had completed their formulation of Union strategy. Not abandoning concentration in time but assigning priority to objectives, they placed their main emphasis on opening the Mississippi, adding an advance up river to Grant's augmented downstream effort. Second, to complete the conquest of Tennessee and open the way to Georgia, they strengthened the forces operating against Tennessee with an army corps from Virginia. In Virginia they accepted the stalemate which the year's operations had shown existed there. Moreover, Halleck was certain that a siege of Richmond would not only fail to take the city but would enable the fortified Confederates so to economize on men as to transfer troops to other theatres. Since the Rebels at Fredericksburg were 50 miles from Washington, keeping Lee at this barely acceptable political distance from the northern capital became the main objective for the army in Virginia. Lincoln also insisted on trying to hurt Lee's army by catching him in a mistake or conducting a campaign aimed at harming him.

In the spring of 1863 the Confederate secretary of war asked Lee whether he could spare some men to reinforce Tennessee. Lee, faced with the conflict between his knowledge of strategy and his desire not to lose any men, responded with a variety of arguments against giving up any troops. He also included the suggestion that he could help Tennessee more by making another raid like his Antietam campaign. This exchange with the Secretary has helped some to see Lee as attempting to win the war with his army in Virginia, or, overlooking the defensive character of his strategy and the three defensive battles since the Seven Days' Battles, as pursuing the unrealistic strategy of trying to annihilate the enemy in battle.

Happily for an understanding of his strategy at this time, he gave his wife a clear statement of the basic Confederate political strategy and his means of implementing it. Of the strategy for dealing with the Yankees, he wrote: "If we can baffle them in their various designs this year & our people are true to our cause . . ., I think our success will be certain." Trusting soon to have his "supplies on a firm basis," he continued: "On every other point we are strong. If successful this year, next fall there will be a great change in public opinion at the North. The Republicans will be destroyed & I think the friends of peace will become so strong as that the next administration will go in on that basis. We have only therefore to resist manfully." Clearly he had so far succeeded in baffling the enemy, and resisting manfully did not include an attempt to destroy the enemy in battle or try to win the war with offensive action.

After an initial effort by Burnside had bogged down in the winter mud, at the end of April, Burnsides' successor, General Joseph Hooker, attempted to hurt Lee with a good plan to turn him. But Hooker did not act with sufficient vigor at the Battle of Chancellorsville and Lee turned his turning movement; ultimately the Union general withdrew. Though he had heavy losses, he achieved some favorable attrition, but the battle and the retreat affected the publics in the usual way.

At the same time, the navy ferried Grant's army east across the Mississippi, enabling him to avoid vulnerable railroad communications and to turn Vicksburg from below. He then marched to the city's rear and bottled it up. Moreover, he captured an army of nearly 30,000 in the city, making it a victory in terms of casualties as well as a major political triumph. This opening of the Mississippi had a profound effect by spreading hope in the North for an early victory and in the South widespread pessimism.

Meanwhile, Lee had repeated his Antietam campaign on a more ambitious scale, advancing into southern Pennsylvania. Neither he nor President Davis intended this campaign to have any effect on the siege of Vicksburg. In addition to having a logistical motive, as earlier, Lee also wished to avoid again defending near Fredericksburg and having to fight a costly battle to protect his valuable supply area north of Richmond. If, on the other hand, he fought a battle in Pennsylvania, he could choose his position and compel the Union army to fight another battle of Fredericksburg. But again Lee overlooked the political effect of fighting. Even a victorious defensive battle would look like a defeat because of the inevitable retreat of a raiding army forced to concentrate and unable to forage.

The campaign followed its predictable course, giving the Confederacy the strategic success of living at the enemy's expense while crops matured in Virginia. But, instead of a Battle of Fredericksburg, Lee, attempting to exploit what he mistakenly believed was a serious Union dispersal, attacked the army of Hooker's successor, General George G. Meade, and suffered a costly defeat in a three-day battle at Gettysburg. In losing perhaps as many as 28,000 men to the North's 23,000, the battle became a disaster of depletion for the Confederate army, and his inevitable retreat to Virginia, seemingly the result of the battle rather than his inability to forage, made it a serious political defeat also.

One could reasonably expect the South to have abandoned the war when confronted with the loss of the Mississippi, the consequent symbolic separation of the country, and Lee's failure in Pennsylvania in a campaign which to many people seemed a bid to win the war by invading the North. But the South continued its burdensome struggle for independence.

Increasingly southerners looked to the 1864 elections in the North when they hoped that their steadfast resistance would have convinced the voters that restoring the Union was not worth the cost of the apparently endless war.

While Grant awaited Vicksburg's surrender and Lee marched to Gettysburg, Rosecrans, a convert to the turning movement, displayed an exceptional mastery when he turned Bragg back to the Tennessee at a cost of only 600 casualties. In August he moved again and gained another bloodless strategic victory, this time crossing the Tennessee River and turning Bragg out of Chattanooga and back into north Georgia.

But this victory triggered a long-contemplated Confederate concentration against Rosecrans's army. Essentially reenacting the Shiloh concentration, the Confederate command brought troops to northern Georgia from East Tennessee and Mississippi and sent two divisions from Lee's army. With these forces Bragg counterattacked at the Battle of Chickamauga, driving the Federal army into Chattanooga and besieging it there. This counteroffensive had the strategic merit of driving Union forces out of northern Georgia. The victory had the expected political impact of inspiriting the Confederates and discouraging the North. But losing over 18,000 to the Union's 16,000 men made it a serious tactical defeat of attrition. The casualties suffered in this counterattack illustrate a cost of the Confederacy's logistically important and politically essential strategy of defending its territorial integrity.

It had taken the Union armies 19 months from the capture of Nashville in February 1862 to the fall of Chattanooga to advance along the 100 miles of railroad between the cities, a line surrounded by guerrillas and vulnerable to cavalry raiders. Grant and his friend and collaborator William T. Sherman knew the difficulties of implementing Union strategy, because, in taking Vicksburg they had faced a Confederate general who had equal numbers. Although Grant had twice as many men as the Confederates, he had committed half to holding West Tennessee and northern Mississippi and protecting their railroads from guerrilla and cavalry raids.

During the early winter of 1863-64, Grant completed the formulation of a new strategy, one in which the Union would give up its reliance on the persisting strategy of territorial conquest but still pursue its logistic strategy of crippling the Rebel armies by depriving them of their supply base. Instead of a persisting strategy he would use raids to break the southern railroads and thus isolate the armies from the farms, factories, foundries, and ports that sustained them. Rather than using cavalry, he planned to rely primarily on infantry armies which had the manpower to do a thorough job of destruction. The armies would also live at Rebel expense and destroy agricultural and industrial resources as well as railroads.

By changing to raids, the Union would shift to a strategy in which the offensive dominated the defensive. Exploiting the ambiguity of the raiders' objectives and routes of advance and withdrawal, large armies could penetrate the South and do great damage as they moved through. Grant planned three such raids: one for the winter from southeastern Virginia through North Carolina would break the two railroads to Virginia and end with the capture of the port of Wilmington; anther, for the spring and using troops from west of the Mississippi, would land to capture the port of Mobile, Alabama, and march inland to destroy the railroads and threaten Atlanta; and the third raid, originating in northern Georgia, would begin after the capture of Atlanta and go to the Atlantic or Gulf coast, breaking Georgia's railroads on the way to the coast.

In February, Sherman demonstrated the new strategy when he led 21,000 men, mostly infantry, on a 300-mile round trip march from Vicksburg to Meridian, Mississippi, to destroy the railroads, warehouses, and works. In wrecking 115 miles of track and destroying 61 bridges, he exhibited the raid's effectiveness in implementing a logistic strategy.

Even though Grant became general in chief in March 1864, no raid opened the spring campaign of 1864. Lincoln and Halleck had refused to order the winter North Carolina raid, and Sherman, commanding the army in northern Georgia, had to take Atlanta first, a more difficult task because the troops were not ready for the Mobile raid. So the 1864 campaign followed the usual pattern of simultaneous Union advances in east and west, with Grant directing Meade in Virginia and Sherman moving on Atlanta. Grant aimed to keep Lee so occupied that he could not emulate the Chickamauga campaign by sending men to help oppose Sherman. Although Grant had hopes of capturing Richmond by cutting its communications from the rear or reaching them after he had turned Lee back to the city, the essence of his strategy lay in Sherman's taking Atlanta and beginning his raid.

But the people in the North and South had their attention focused not on Sherman but on Virginia, where Grant would face Lee. This put great pressure on Grant to win battles to meet popular expectations, especially in the year of such a crucial election. In his campaign he usually fought Lee prior to turning him, and he had made a very serious effort to defeat him at Spotsylvania. Secretary of War Stanton gave publicity to these battles and to the subsequent turning movements as pursuits of the vanquished. But the conflicts occurred so close together and each cost so many casualties that many people, confronted by appalling losses in a short time, did not see the battles as victories, nor believe that the Rebels had lost more men, nor accept that Grant needed to amass such casualties just to push Lee back. When the campaign ended in June, the army had begun to besiege Petersburg, 25 miles south of Richmond and a key to its communications but neither an impressive ending for the campaign nor a fair recompense for the loss of 70,000 men. Grant's campaign thus constituted an encouragement for the South and a political liability for Lincoln, whose re-election chances it hurt, especially as the likely Democratic nominee was

General McClellan, whose 1862 campaign had reached a comparable strategic position with negligible casualties. Actually Lee had suffered about half of Grant's losses, thus giving the Union only a slight victory of attrition.

Meanwhile, using the minimum of combat, Sherman methodically turned his adversary back toward Atlanta, moving slowly as he repaired, fortified, and garrisoned the railroad in his rear. Sherman did not complete his last turning movement into Atlanta's rear and take the city until September 1. Though a major victory for and the last application of the old persisting logistic strategy, the fall of Atlanta, a manufacturing and railroad center, had far more political than military importance. The northern public celebrated it as a sign that the Union could win the war in a reasonable time. It thus aided the election of Lincoln, though continuation of the conflict seemed not to depend on him because General McClellan, as the Democratic nominee, had declared that he would accept no peace without reunion. Yet the re-election of Lincoln gave much emphasis to the North's determination and so dashed southern hopes more than McClellan's declaration. The brother of Confederate Vice President A.H. Stephens thus estimated the effect of the defeat of northern peace advocates on southerners' confidence in victory at a bearable cost: "It has been sustained, and the collapse prevented even up to this time, only by the hopes which our people had from the peace party in the North." When the peace party lost, confidence among southern citizens and soldiers dropped markedly. The significantly increased rate of desertion from the Rebel armies illustrated this.

So the war showed signs of drawing to a close before Grant could apply his innovative strategy. Sherman had delayed beginning his raid, because, after the fall of Atlanta, his opponent, General John B. Hood, first turned him back nearly to Tennessee and then marched away to menace Middle Tennessee and suffer defeat at Nashville. After reinforcing the Federal forces in Tennessee, Sherman abandoned Atlanta and began his raid in mid-November, taking a month to reach the Atlantic, where he captured Savannah and established a base. He had destroyed 200 miles of railroads and many cotton mills, took 7,000 horses, and, he reported, "consumed stores and provisions that were essential to Lee's and Hood's armies." Sherman had always been aware of the political significance of his raid and had viewed it not only as intimidation but as an evidence of Union victory, which would symbolize defeat for the Rebels. He expressed this idea when he wrote that "if the North can march an army right through the South, it is proof positive that the North can prevail in this contest." Since Sherman's raid did persuade some southerners and strengthen the conviction of others that independence was costing more than its value, it constituted a significant political triumph as well as a major victory for the logistic strategy.

Sherman received Grant's authorization for a new raid into the

Carolinas in the winter of 1865. At last able to carry out his full scheme of raid, Grant directed 40,000 men to Mobile for a raid into Alabama. Cavalry had a role too, when a large force from Tennessee struck the Alabama industrial center of Selma. The other major cavalry raid, which occurred in Virginia, northwest of Richmond, wrecked the canal along the James River as well as the railroads. Grant believed that this panoply of raids would "leave nothing for the Rebellion to stand upon." Yet already, in the fall and early winter of 1864-65, some 40 percent of the Confederate soldiers east of the Mississippi deserted. So, before Grant's logistic raiding strategy of destruction of transportation, industrial, and agricultural resources could deplete the Confederate armies, they already were dwindling away because soldiers, like civilians, found the price of independence too high.

So, unlike the defeat of Germany in World War II, the Civil War did not end almost entirely as a result of military victory. The Confederate armies melted away not because men lacked supplies but because they and their families no longer had the political motivation to continue. Understood in these terms, what contribution did the military strategy make to victory and defeat?

The blockade, which, because it did not deny the South essential imports, failed to have a major military effect but did make a significant political contribution. It did this through accentuating the hardships of the war by reducing the southern standard of living and denying consumers enough of many of the imports, such as coffee, which they valued. This was a cost of war which northerners did not have to bear.

The strategy of the war on land had conscious political objectives and had the same harmony the blockade showed between military means and political needs. Choosing a logistic strategy because of the impracticality of the combat alternative, the Union had a strategy which, by conquering places, could give continual evidences of success to its soldiers and public.

Assuming that the Confederates were correct that the morale of their people required maintaining their territorial integrity and that discouraging the northern public needed this also, then the South pursued a politically as well as militarily wise strategy when it sought to protect its resources from conquest by Union armies. But this strategy involved much combat and, consequently, the wear on morale of heavier casualties than the alternative military strategy of less combat and of deep withdrawals. These would have exposed the Federal armies to profound logistical problems and the exhaustion of constant harassment by guerrillas. Yet, in addition to the political objection to sacrificing so much territory, this strategy could hardly have left slavery unaffected.

As far as acting to conciliate or intimidate the enemy, the Union armies generally kept themselves in harmony with political strategy, seeking to propitiate southerners, as well as such a destructive organization as an army could, and thus keeping in step with Lincoln's conciliatory reconstruction plan. It largely reserved intimidation for guerrillas, applied it effectively, and so cowed enemies that it could not conciliate.

The South made effective use of a cavalry raid against the invaders' railroads, thus exploiting the particular vulnerability of railroads and of armies dependent on bases. This, like guerrilla warfare, proved very effective and had no particular political impact. The defensive turning movement, best exemplified in Lee's Second Manassas campaign, was a valuable military innovation and fully in harmony with Confederate political goals. When combined with the raid and used once by Bragg and twice by Lee, it had the raid's traditional merit of living at the enemy's expense but, as used, had a negative political effect when combined with a battle prior to withdrawal. We cannot know whether, without the battles, people would still have seen such raids as defeated invasions. But clearly the battles presented a rare instance of such dissonance between military action and political goals.

Grant's raiding strategy, like the Confederate cavalry and guerrilla raids, aimed to exploit the vulnerability of railroads and of armies which depended on bases. When conducted like Sherman's to Meridian, in Georgia, and in the Carolinas, they had a favorable political impact because in the North they looked like victories and in the South, defeats. One can only wonder what would have happened if the Union had used them a year or more earlier. It is easy to speculate that their military and political effectiveness would have ended the war sooner and with fewer casualties.

Thus, for the most part, military strategy harmonized, and was made to harmonize, with political needs. In that neither belligerent outshone the other in its strategy, military strategy had a neutral effect in the war. But the similarity in strategy only occurred because enough soldiers on each side understood Napoleonic strategy and many displayed adaptability and innovativeness. Resemblance also stemmed from the role of public opinion, crucial for both belligerents, which meant that military campaigns often had to meet a double criteria for victory, the popular as well as the strategic. This interrelation of military events and strategy with public opinion reached a peak in the campaigns which preceded the crucial Union election of 1864. The attention both sides gave these campaigns shows how fully both military and civilian leaders understood the important connections between military means and political ends and shaped strategy accordingly.

From Gabor Boritt, ed., *Why the Conferderacy Lost,* (London: Oxford University Press, 1992), pp.45-77.

Bruce Catton

Total War and an Election

In the presidential campaign of 1864, what men said made very little difference. It was what the men in uniform did that mattered. Everything depended on them. If they should start to win, Lincoln would win. If they could not win, Lincoln could not win.

No one understood this better than General Joe Johnston. Lincoln needed a smashing victory, such as the capture of Atlanta. Otherwise, McClellan would be elected President--and his party was ready to make peace.

Johnston believed that the South's only hope was to hold out until the election. As long as he was in command of the Confederate forces at Atlanta, he would give the Union no chance for a victory. He refused to allow Sherman to lure him into a battle. He played a waiting game, delaying, stalling for time. But Jefferson Davis did not see things this way, and Davis had the final say. He believed the war had to be won on the battlefield, and to do that the Confederates must fight. And so he had removed Johnston, putting General John Bell Hood in his place.

A brave and dashing fighter, Hood had been wounded in the arm at Gettysburg. He had recovered in time to fight at Chickamauga, where he lost a leg. Patched up, and riding strapped to his saddle, he was then given corps command under Johnston. Now he was in full charge of Johnston's army. The trouble was that he was not suited for the top job.

Hood realized that he was expected to fight and he lost no time in getting to it. Rather less than half of the Union army was moving on Atlanta from the east, tearing up the Georgia Railroad as it advanced. The rest of the army, under General Thomas, was crossing Peachtree Creek, north of the city. Hood spotted a gap of several miles between the two Union forces and set out to destroy Thomas.

The Rebel attack, on July 20, was not quite fast enough to catch the Yankees crossing the creek. Even so, it was a hard and sudden blow, and the Union line sagged. But there never was a better defensive fighter than Thomas, who was known as the "Rock of Chickamauga." He brought up his artillery, and the Rebels were driven off with heavy losses.

Hood withdrew into Atlanta, and two days later he struck again. This time he swung east, against General James B. McPherson's Army of the Tennessee. McPherson had left one of his flanks exposed, and Hood hoped to hit it the way Jackson had hit Hooker at Chancellorsville. He almost succeeded, in a desperate fight that became known as the Battle of

Atlanta.

Hood's troops went into action yelling "like demons," and slowly the Union line began to retreat. A Confederate corps punched a hole in the Union center, forcing the Yankees to fight on two fronts. At one point in the battle, McPherson's horse was seen, bleeding and riderless. McPherson was found dead, riddled by rifle bullets, and Sherman wept when the body was brought to him.

In spite of McPherson's death, the Yankees held on. Sometimes they rolled from one side of their earthworks to the other, fighting off consecutive charges from front to rear. At dark, Hood broke off the action, his flank attack a failure. He pulled his battered troops back inside the fortified lines of Atlanta. The two battles had cost him more than 13,000 men, and now he was pinned in his earthworks.

Sherman had already cut the railroads that came to Atlanta from the north and east. Now he had the Army of Tennessee march behind his lines and sweep in on Atlanta from the west. He hoped to reach the Macon and Western Railroad, which ran southwest from the city. On July 28, Hood came out to attack him. There was a hard fight at Ezra Church, west of the city, and once again the Confederates were forced back. Sherman was a long step nearer the capture of Atlanta. Hemmed in on three sides, it was bound to fall in time.

As the siege of Atlanta began, Sherman's chief worry was his own railroad connections. The line went back to Chattanooga, down the Tennessee Valley to Bridgeport, and up through Nashville to Kentucky. His supplies came in on this line; if they were cut off he would have to retreat. And roaming the area was the rough slave trader who had become a genius of cavalry--General Nathan Bedford Forrest.

"Forrest is the very devil," Sherman had written. It was necessary to hound Forrest "to the death, if it cost 10,000 lives and break the Treasury. There never will be peace in Tennessee till Forrest is dead." Early in June, Sherman had sent a cavalry column under General Samuel D. Sturgis into Mississippi to stop Forrest. The two met at Brice's Crossroads, where Forrest's 3,300 troopers threw back Sturgis' 8,000 men. A soldier who took part in the day-long fight said it was "so close that guns once fired were not reloaded, but used as clubs . . . while the two lines struggled with the ferocity of wild beasts." Sturgis was badly beaten, and Forrest was free to go almost where he pleased.

Sherman tried to stop him again in July, ordering a strong expedition under General A.J. Smith to move down from Memphis into Mississippi. Near Tupelo, Smith ran into a force made up of Forrest's troopers and Rebel infantry. Forrest was wounded and the Confederates were driven off. It was clearly a Union victory, but Smith failed to follow it up. Instead, he retreated to Memphis.

In August, Smith made another try. Forrest slipped past him and entered Memphis itself. He was riding a buggy, his wounded foot propped up on a special rack. Although his stay was brief and did no harm, it got Smith's troops recalled to Memphis. Forrest was till free to go where he pleased. At the same time, the Federal moves accomplished one thing. They kept Forrest so busy he could not strike at Sherman's supply line, and the Yankees stepped up the pressure on Atlanta. Hood pulled his troops out, retreating to the south, and on September 2 the Union army occupied the city. Sherman wired Lincoln, "Atlanta is ours, and fairly won."

Here was the victory Lincoln needed. It followed another, on August 5, when tough old Admiral Farragut had closed the port at Mobile. He had steamed in through a mine field, and mines were called "torpedoes" in those days. His battle cry of "Damn the torpedoes—full speed ahead!" stirred the entire North.

Still a third Union victory was in the making, farther north, in the Shenandoah Valley. The valley was of great importance to the Confederacy. Immensely fertile, it supplied Lee's army with meat and grain. Besides, any Rebel army moving through the valley could threaten Washington and such cities as Philadelphia and Baltimore. Grant's master plan called for laying waste the rich farmlands of the valley so that it could no longer support a Confederate army.

Franz Sigel, the first general assigned to the job, failed completely. David Hunter, who replaced him, did not do much better. After defeating a small Confederate force, he turned east to Staunton, burning and destroying as he went. Near Lynchburg he found Jubal Early, ready as usual to make a stand. Although the Union force outnumbered Early's 15,000 men, Hunter cautiously fled to the mountains of West Virginia.

Early was chased back into Virginia after threatening Washington, but his pursuers could not catch him. Using tactics much like "Stonewall" Jackson's, he dodged and outmaneuvered 45,000 Federals. Grant realized he had to stop Early, and he picked Phil Sheridan to do it.

The thirty-three-year-old Sheridan was young for such an important command. Bowlegged, short, and slight, he did not look impressive, but he turned out to be a brilliant leader and a tough fighting man. His orders from Grant were to destroy both Early and the valley. He was to lay waste the farmlands, so that even a crow flying over them would have to carry its own rations.

On August 7, 1864, Sheridan took command of the newly named Army of the Shenandoah. He began cautiously, for Early was a hard hitter and his men were rugged veterans. On September 19, Sheridan attacked near Winchester. The attack was bungled, and the Federals were soon in trouble. Riding his big black horse Rienzi, Sheridan galloped to the front. He waved his hat and shouted to his officers, "Give 'em hell. . . . Press them, General, they'll run!" The Union army surged forward, breaking the Confederate lines. Early retreated, after losing 4,000 men. Three days later he tried to make a stand at Fisher's Hill, and again he was badly beaten.

As the Rebels retreated south, Sheridan followed them, burning and destroying. Crops ready for harvest went up in smoke and flame. Two thousand barns were burned, mills and storehouses were destroyed, cattle were either slaughtered or driven off. Never again would the Confederate army feed off this once-fertile garden. Nothing would be planted in the burned-over land until after the war. As the Federals finally withdrew, a Rebel saw "great columns of smoke which almost shut out the sun by day, and . . . the red glare of bonfires which . . . crackled mockingly in the night air."

By early October Sheridan was able to report to Grant that "the Valley, from Winchester to Staunton, ninety-two miles, will have but little in it for man or beast." The middle of the same month found Sheridan's men encamped at Cedar Creek, twenty miles south of Winchester. Sheridan left them there while he traveled to Washington to attend a conference.

Early was not far from the Union force. His supplies were dangerously low, and it was impossible for him to live off the valley. He had to either get out or fight. He decided to fight, and at dawn on October 19 he attacked.

That morning Sheridan was at Winchester, where he had stopped overnight on his way back from Washington. He was awakened by the sound of gunfire, and at first he thought it was his own artillery feeling out the enemy. Still, he was uneasy. After a quick breakfast, he started riding his horse Rienzi toward Cedar Creek.

Sheridan later wrote that at the crest of a hill "there burst upon our view the appalling spectacle of a panic-stricken army . . . all pressing to the rear in hopeless confusion." He soon learned from the soldiers what had happened. Early had smashed the Union's left flank, and with it an entire army corps. Taken by surprise, the Yankees had been shoved back four miles, and many of them had fled.

Sheridan rose in the saddle and said, "We will go back and recover our camp." Spurring his horse, he waved his hat and rallied his troops. "Turn back! Turn back! Face the other way!" he shouted. Groups of stragglers turned to follow him. Soldiers who had been making coffee by the roadside kicked over their coffee cans and swung into line. Sheridan rode furiously, pushing on to the battlefront.

Late that afternoon, the re-formed Union army charged the Rebels. The Confederate line crumbled, and by sundown Early had been driven off. The Confederacy's hold on the Shenandoah Valley was broken for good.

Sheridan's ride became a legend; a song about it went all across the North. His victory in the valley, together with those of Sherman at Atlanta and Farragut at Mobile Bay, made the people forget their war weariness. No longer could the Democrats say that the war was a failure. Not that they gave up their campaign against Lincoln. They still called him an ape, a gorilla, a buffoon, and whispered all sorts of stories about him.

The Republicans also played rough. In control of the government, they used every political trick they could to win the election. They forced government employees to contribute money to the party treasury. They passed laws allowing soldiers to vote in camp, and whole regiments were furloughed so that the men could go home and vote.

Election day, November 8, 1864, was cold and wet in Washington. Few people visited Lincoln in the White House that day. At seven o'clock in the evening he splashed through the rain to the War Department telegraph office to get the election returns. As the Republican votes began to pile up, Lincoln relaxed and began telling funny stories. At two in the morning, when he left the telegraph office, his re-election seemed certain.

Complete election returns gave Lincoln 2,203,831 votes to McClellan's 1,797,019, with an electoral vote of 212 to 21. In some states, such as New York, Lincoln barely managed to win. McClellan got forty-five per cent of the national vote, which showed that a surprisingly large number of Northerners were dissatisfied. However, they were still a minority. A substantial majority of the people had told Lincoln that they wanted him to carry on the war to a victorious end.

What had happened on the battlefield was only part of the reason Lincoln was re-elected. He had made many mistakes, especially in the way he handled military matters during the first two years of the war. He had been criticized both for going too far on the slavery question and not going far enough. At times he had seemed more of a politician than a leader. But, in spite of everything, he had kept on waging war. The people re-elected him because they believed in him and in what he was doing.

While Sherman and Sheridan and Farragut had been winning their victories, Grant was still dug in at Petersburg. His Army of the Potomac had had a fearful campaign. For more than five months it had been in almost daily contact with the enemy. It had fought the hardest, longest, costliest battles ever seen on the American continent.

The Army of the Potomac had won no glory. Its casualties had been extremely heavy, and yet it had no really clear-cut victory to its credit. It had done just one thing--the one thing that was needed for the final Union victory. It had forced Lee to stay near Richmond and fight a defensive war he could not win.

Lee's army of Northern Virginia and Grant's Army of the Potomac had worn each other out. The campaigns that would decide the war would therefore be made far to the south and west, where the Confederates were at a disadvantage. Lee's army no longer had the room and strength to maneuver as it did in the past. Grant had seen to that. Lee could do no more than protect the capital, while Federal armies crushed all the life out of the Confederacy.

Lincoln's re-election was the clincher. It meant that Lincoln would support Grant, who would never let up in his pressure on the South. After the election in November, victory for the Union could only be a question of time.

Even so, the fighting went on, and there was hate in the land. During all of his campaign in the Shenandoah Valley, Sheridan was troubled by Confederate guerrillas. They were bands of irregular fighters who raided outposts, burned Yankee wagon trains, and shot sentries and couriers. Because of them, Sheridan had to use a sizable number of men for guard duty. The Union soldiers considered the guerrillas to be criminals, and usually hanged any they captured. The guerrillas hanged Yankees in return, and the hate grew more bitter.

Many of the guerrillas were no better than organized outlaws. They often raided civilians, and they did the Confederacy more harm than good. A Rebel cavalryman complained that "they roam broadcast over the country, a band of thieves, pillaging, plundering . . . an injury to the cause." The Confederate commanders discouraged guerrilla warfare, and Lee said, "I regard the whole system as an unmixed evil."

The most successful of the guerrillas was Colonel John S. Mosby. He controlled the area north of the Rappahannock in Virginia, and it was called Mosby's Confederacy. Sheridan gradually cleared the Shenandoah Valley of guerrillas, but there seemed to be no way of stopping Mosby's bands. Late in November, Union cavalry rode across the Blue Ridge Mountains, into Mosby's Confederacy. Their search failed to turn up Mosby and his men. Hoping to starve the guerrillas out, the troopers set the area aflame, and the once-lovely valley was left a blackened ruin.

West of the Mississippi, in Kansas, Missouri, and Arkansas, guerrilla warfare was especially violent. Fighting between Union and pro-slavery men had begun in the 1850's, and during most of the Civil War the area lived under a rule of terror. In the Ozark Mountains, Southern sympathizers hanged men "with no charge against them except that they had been feeding Union men." James H. Lane, a Senator from Kansas, led Unionist troops in sacking and burning pro-Confederate settlements. Sometimes neighborhood feuds got all mixed in with the business of fighting the enemy, and old grudges were settled in blood.

The most murderous of all the guerrillas was William C. Quantrill, who led a pro-Southern band in Kansas. Among his followers was Bill Anderson, who tied the scalps of his victims to his horse's bridle. Jesse James and Cole Younger learned their trade as outlaws under Quantrill.

Quantrill made his worst raid on August 21, 1863, when with 450 men he attacked the town of Lawrence in Kansas. About 150 unarmed citizens were butchered. An eyewitness wrote, "The whole business part of the town, except two stores, was in ashes. The bodies of dead men . . . were laying in all directions." Another eyewitness said, "It is doubtful whether the world has ever witnessed such a scene of horror. . . ." In October Quantrill staged another massacre at Baxter Springs. Union troops hunted him for months, but he was not caught until after the war. In May, 1865, he was shot while trying to escape capture in Kentucky.

Guerrilla warfare went on even after the fighting between the regular troops had stopped. In the fall of 1864, the Confederates made their last offensive west of the Mississippi. Sterling Price and 12,000 troopers rode into Missouri, threatening St. Louis, Jefferson City, and Kansas City. On October 23, a Union force under Samuel Curtis met Price near the town of Westport. Curtis had won the battle at Pea Ridge in 1862, and once again he was successful. Aided by cavalry, he whipped the Rebels, driving them into Arkansas. The war in that part of the West was practically over.

From Bruce Catton, *The Civil War,* (New York: American Heritage, 1961), pp. 168-179.

Chapter 6

World War I

How does one measure the effectiveness of special operations? In the case of a single *coup de main,* the answer seems obvious, as the action will have a clear military result (e.g., rescue of hostages, destruction of a given target, etc.). In protracted special operations, however, the process grows more subtle, a point raised implicitly by the Q-ship phenomenon. These decoys, whose crews must have been very "special" indeed, sank few U-boats, but forced them to alter their operational doctrine radically, reducing their effectiveness on patrol. Fear of Q-ships fostered sinkings without warning, which had the unintended effect of angering neutrals, the United States in particular, with dire effects for the German cause.

With regard to such "externalities," one must also conclude that Lawrence's insurgency nurtured modern Arab nationalism, having profound unintended consequences whose effects are still being felt. As to measures of effectiveness, the Arab revolt affords ample room for analysis as well. Though limited in its attritional effects upon the Turkish army, Lawrence's campaign did, with scant resources, tie down large numbers of the enemy, and did physically conquer a great deal of territory in support of Allenby's regular maneuvers. All this, it should be noted, was achieved against an opponent capable of tremendous doggedness on the battlefield, as the Allies found out to their horror at Gallipoli.

Interestingly, the effort to curtail the depredations of the U-boats sparked another special operation, the commando raid on the German submarine base at Zeebrügge, which featured some of the most savage hand-to-hand fighting of the war. With regard to insurgent warfare, it should also be noted that Lawrence didn't stand entirely alone in this war, as German General von Lettow-Vorbeck's campaign in East Africa rivals the revolt in the desert, at least in terms of operational complexity and effectiveness. In terms of the political consequences of special operations, though, both the Q-ships and Lawrence's campaign had powerful effects, sometimes unintended, that make them more analytically valuable than either of these other two cases.

Lowell Thomas

Trapped by a Q-Ship . . .

At sunset I was sitting at supper in our little officers' mess room. From near by came loud, gay talk in English. Our prisoners, the five captains, were having their evening meal. We were running awash.

"Sailing ship ahoy!" the call came.

I hurried to the conning tower and, telescope at eye, scrutinized a little three-mast schooner to our starboard.

A warning shell at a distance of four thousand yards, and the schooner lowered her topsails. The crew took to the lifeboats. Everything looked all right, but I was suspicious. I had heard of sailing ships with British submarines in tow--neat trap. Then when a U-boat drew to fire a few shells at the water line, it was saluted with a torpedo.

"Keep on firing," I called to our gun crew, and then sent the order through the speaking rube: "Half speed ahead."

I wanted to investigate, and we might as well be certain that the ship was abandoned before we drew too near. The sun was sinking below the horizon and dusk was gathering.

We drew up slowly, our shells popping on the deserted deck. "Good shooting," I remarked to my two companions, Lieutenants Ziegner and Usedom. The schooner's deck was a mass of wreckage. The *U-93* circled around the craft while we all scanned it through our powerful binoculars. No, it had no submarine in tow, and was surely deserted. Nobody would stay aboard and take that amount of shelling. We were only eighty yards away, lying parallel with it, when I gave the order.

"Hit her at the water line and sink her."

As our first shell hit just at the water line, there was a loud whistle aboard the schooner. The white war ensign of Great Britain ran up the mast. A movable gun platform slid into view. A roar and a rattling, and 7.5 cm. guns opened at us, and machine guns, too. We offered a fair, broadside target. One shell put our fore gun out of commission and wounded several of the gun crew. Another crashed into our hull.

"Both engines full speed!" I yelled; "helm hard aport!"

The *U-93* leaped forward and swung around quickly, so that it was stern on to the enemy. More shells hit us while she turned the quarter circle.

"*Was zum Teufel!*" (What the devil!) I felt the vibration of our engines stop. Yes, the engines were cut off. I had given no such command. The only explanation was that the shell fire had damaged them. We were now only five hundred yards away from the muzzles of those large, fire-spurting guns, and were drifting slowly around. Engines stopped and one gun disabled--that was uncomfortable. Shells were striking the boat and exploding with savage pow-pows.

"Man the after gun!" I shouted.

We had one piece of ordnance left, could still put up a fight. Three men responded to the command. I leaped aft with them, and we four worked the gun. A shell burst in our faces. The petty officer of the gun crew fell back with his head blown off. Then I felt a cold sensation about my legs. We were up to our knees in water.

A moment later we were swimming in the Atlantic. The *U-93* had sunk beneath us. I could see her black shadow vanish in the depths of the ocean. A dreadful pang of anguish shot through me at the thought of my fine new boat and my crew going down to their last port on the cold, silent bottom of the sea, and a touch of ironic pity for those five captains who, skippers of prosaic freighters, had never signed any papers with articles about making a last voyage in an iron coffin. "Friday the 13th!" That damned idea flashed into my mind. No time for thinking; I myself was drowning. My heavy leather jacket encumbered me so that I could scarcely move my arms. I tried to work it off, but could not. My thick, warm clothes beneath it were absorbing water and becoming like a suit of leaden armour. My fur-lined boots with thick wooden soles were sodden. They pulled me down as if they were iron weights attached to my feet.

I was sinking when I heard shouts and saw a black shadow in the dusk. I yelled in return and struggled with renewed courage.

"Hello--keep going--we'll be there in a minute," the calls came cheerily. I replied with shouts between gulps of water.

The last thing I remember is seeing a small boat only five yards away. When I recovered my senses I was on the deck of the schooner. They told me I was going down when the boat reached me. The British officer who happened to be at the wheel had to jump into the ocean after me. The boat had also picked up the other two men who were at the gun with me when the *U-93* sank.

The little schooner, which hadn't seemed worth bothering about--I wish, we hadn't--was the *Prize*, the British *Q-21*. Those Britishers played that Q-Ship game with skill and nerve. The *Prize* was little more than a tin shell filled with wood. She was stuffed with lumber, the idea being to keep her afloat as long as possible as little more than a camouflaged gun platform. Any other species of craft would have sunk a couple of times from the damage our shells did. We had shot her pretty nearly to pieces. The deck was knocked into kindling wood, and below every wall was smashed. You could see through partition after partition into ten rooms. I marveled at the bravery of these Britishers who in their hiding place could take a shelling like that and then run their gun platform out and start to fight. Some of them had been wounded during the encounter.

An officer took me to his cabin and himself pulled off my sodden clothes and heavy boots. He rubbed me dry with a towel and then gave me some of his own clothes to put on. I was still shaking with cold. He thought it was fright and pointed to a motto on the wall which read: "We are all brothers in Christianity." Those Britishers lived up to the motto in the way they took care of their prisoners. While I was being made comfortable in the cabin the sailors were taking care of my two men.

A little while later I was in the officers' mess, where they gave me cocoa and cigarettes. Suddenly a petty officer reported;

"We are sinking, sir."

"Eh," I said to myself, "evidently I have been saved only to be lost again! Blast this Friday the 13th!"

The *Prize* was in a sinking condition. Our shells had bored some pretty holes at the water line. Men were working frantically, trying to plug them. Others laboured at the furiously rattling pumps. The boat promised to sink at any minute.

"Fire!" the shout rang out.

"Friday the 13th," I groaned.

Our shell fire had destroyed one of the *Prizes* auxiliary motors, and when they started the other one it took fire for some reason or other. I saw an officer go streaking by with a fire extinguisher. He put out the blaze. That was my first glimpse of Lieutenant W.E. Sanders, the skipper of the *Prize*.

A bit later he came into the officers' mess, a tall, slender chap in his twenties with a good-looking English face, fine brown eyes, and blond hair which sprawled all over his head.

"Where is the U-boat captain?" he demanded.

I stood up, and he came to me with a good, friendly smile and grasped my hand.

"My dear fellow," he said, "I am sorry for you. Please feel that you are my guest. But," he exclaimed ruefully, "I'm sorry I can't give you better quarters, especially as we are about ready to sink."

He was a New Zealander, a soldier, a sailor, and a gentleman. I felt it was not so bad to have been defeated by such a fine chap and his nervy crew.

They tried to cheer me, for I looked pretty glum. It was of no use. I couldn't forget my crew, my friends going down out there, drowned like rats in a trap, with some perhaps left to die of slow suffocation. I could imagine how some might even now be alive in the strong torpedo compartments, lying in the darkness, hopeless, waiting for the air to thicken and finally smother them. No, they were not rapping on the iron hull. They knew no help could ever reach them. Aboard the *U-93* we had been like a gang of brothers. Most of my men had been with me from the beginning of the war. In summer the whole crowd had often visited my country place. There was not room in the house for them all, and some of the men slept in the haystacks. At times I took them on pleasure jaunts, and always we laughed and joked together. And then the prisoners--the British sailors of the gun crews--well, they had enlisted for warfare; but the unfortunate five merchant captains--those skippers certainly had been caught in the toils of evil destiny. That night I could not sleep. I was haunted by the vision of my boat going down, of that vanishing dark shadow I had seen while I lay struggling in the water.

The *Prize* was in a bad way. The pumps struggled their hardest against the water that poured in. All possible weight was shifted from the side where the shell holes were, so that the gaping rents might be kept above water. Luckily the ocean was perfectly calm. If any kind of sea began to run at all she would sink in a few minutes. Nor could the boat get under way. The wireless had been shot away and she could not call for help. There was no wind for the sails and the motor would not start. The English machinist had no experience with Diesel engines and was helpless. Sanders came to me in desperation.

"Captain," he asked, "do your men know anything about Diesels?"

"Why, one of them is an expert," I responded.

Among the two that had been saved along with me was Deppe, who knew Diesel engines as a parson knows his Bible. I ordered him to the motor. A few minutes later I heard the engine start. Deppe came back strutting.

"They know nothing about motors," he observed loftily.

The *Prize* was under way now, with the motor whirring. If she had had to lie there motionless much longer she would probably have encountered weather that would have sent her down. We had been able to lend our captors a lively hand at a time when it counted, a small return for the handsome way we had been treated.

The sea remained calm, and for three days and a half we headed toward the English coast at a rate of two and a half miles an hour. Then a British cruiser hove in sight and took the *Prize* in tow to Kinsale harbour in the south of Ireland. In port I immediately had a bath and washed my clothes. I found three handkerchiefs in my pockets and was happy. With such trifles can a tragedy of the sea be forgotten for a while.

A steamer took the *Prize* in tow next day and we started across the Bristol Channel to Milford Haven. I sat on the deck of the shell-blasted hulk watching the dim coast of Ireland through a glass.

"Hey, what's this?" I said to myself.

In the distance I saw the conning tower of a submarine. I could recognize the craft as one of those built at the Germania yards at Kiel.

The officer of the deck was near me, scanning the sea with his glass.

"Sailboat over there," he said to me offhand.

From afar the conning tower of a submarine often looks like the sail of a ship.

"Yes, sailboat," I responded in a musing voice.

The U-boat was coming our way. I wondered what its commander, some comrade of mine, thought of the steamer towing this stack of lumber which they called the *Prize*.

"Submarine ahoy!" the alarm went around.

All hands scurried about, preparing for a fight.

"And now," said I to myself, "I will learn what it is like on this side of the fence."

The U-boat submerged. Of course, my brother in arms down there was not going to walk right up to anything so strange and possibly suspicious as this steamer towing a battered hulk. Generally speaking, it looked as if somebody might get torpedoed. No, it wasn't amusing on this side of the fence.

It seemed as if the bad luck of that ill-omened departure was still on our trail and determined to have a finishing go at us. Our steamer with the *Prize* in tow could do nothing to elude a torpedo shot. I expected an explosion at any moment.

A cloud of smoke, and a flotilla of destroyers came rushing along. That eased the situation a lot. The U-boat would attempt no attack with that school of fishes around. The surmise was correct. We saw no further sign of the submarine. I afterward learned that it was commanded by my friend, Commander Ernst Hashagen, and when I saw him again I cussed him out roundly for having given me such a fright.

We arrived at Milford Haven in the morning.

Lieutenant Sanders shook hands with me and wished me godspeed, at the same time asking the officers who were taking me away to treat me well. That was the last I ever saw of the gallant young officer. He was given the Victoria Cross for his brave fight against the *U-93*. Later he carried on in the *Prize*, which had been repaired for further Q-ship duty. One day the *Prize* encountered a U-boat, but this time it was an unlucky day for Sanders and his men. The *Prize* was sunk, and her captain and crew went down with her.

The officers in whose charge I was took me to breakfast, a real British breakfast and not the continental rolls and coffee. We had kippers and eggs and marmalade. They were spick-and-span in their smart uniforms. I felt like a tramp. My uniform was stained with grease and salt water, the gold braid was green, and one trouser leg was a dreadful sight to look at. A deflected machine-gun bullet had ripped it and I had sewed it up with white thread--what sewing!

One of them began to question me. I made it clear that I was disinclined to talk about my boat, but told him of the five captains who were aboard the *U-93* when she disappeared and gave him the names of their boats, so that their relatives might be informed of their loss. The officer understood my reticence and said:

"I have only one more question. Do you know who sank the *Horsa*?"

What the deuce was the matter now, I wondered. Certainly we of the *U-93* had behaved ourselves well and magnanimously in the case of the *Horsa*.

"I sank the *Horsa,*" I replied.

I was scarcely prepared for the effect this statement made. My questioner jumped to his feet and grasped my hand.

"I have wanted to meet the man," he exclaimed, "who rescued and took care of a crew as you and your men did."

The survivors of the *Horsa*, upon getting to shore, had talked to the high heavens of the way we of the *U-93* had used them, especially of our fishing the men from under the boat.

"Strange how destiny works." I mused. I had been in the U-boat warfare for two years and a half--and a cruel iron warfare it was. I had sunk many ships and drowned many men, and never once had I or my command found an opportunity to do anything exceptional in the way of a good, human deed--save in the case of the *Horsa*. And now that one good deed, which had taken place just before I was captured, had come back to me with a swift blessing. I had already been treated well by my captors, and from now on, I knew, would be treated better.

Donnington Hall, I was told, was the best prison camp in England, and if there were any better they must have been deluxe places indeed. It was one of the most beautiful country seats in England, a great gray castle in a perfect setting on green lawns and oak trees. Sheep were grazing on the meadows and birds singing in the trees. The only things to mar the general aspect of sylvan delight was a barbed wire fence, high and formidable around the prison enclosure, and a line of armed guards. There I met a number of U-boat officers, a zeppelin commander, and various military officers. They were a jolly company in a lovely place. The only trouble was that it was a prison.

[In a wartime issue of a British newspaper I ran across an account of a dispute in the House of Commons over the excessive expenditures incurred in fitting up Donnington Hall for a German officers' prison camp. Donnington Hall has long been the most famous country seat in Leicestershire, its history going back to the Tudor period. It was once the seat of the Hastings family. The remodeling of the house for the German òfficers, and the putting in of bathrooms and billiard tables, brought forth much ironic comment in the House of Commons. "Great idea," one Britisher remarked; "make it so comfortable they won't ever want to go back to Germany!"]

The Commander was a hook-nosed Britisher with a big, fearful mustache. Lieutenant Piquot he was, a formidable name that I shall never forget. He had fierce ways and a gruff, fierce voice. When he talked at you, you thought he was going to eat you. I was afraid of him at first, but presently I found that Piquot always growled. Growling was his natural language. He growled the most when he was the most pleasantly disposed toward me.

"The Admiralty," he said with his gruffest voice and most forbidding expression, "has sent instructions that we are to see that you are comfortable."

"You will make me comfortable if you will smile--just once," I felt like saying, but prudence persuaded me to confine my remarks to a mere "thank you."

We prisoners were not allowed by the regulations to write more than two letters home each week, but I was given permission to send any number. I wrote first to my wife and then to the families of each member of my crew. It was a mournful task. I did my best to cheer the ones bereft by telling them that their loved ones had died heroically in the performance of their duty and for their Fatherland. I did not have to invent one particle when I spoke of the affection I had for each man.

Three weeks after my entrance into the prison camp I heard an astonishing report. The *U-93* had got back to Germany. It was impossible! Why, I had seen that boat ripped and smashed by shell fire. And then she had gone down beneath my very feet. So I scarcely dared believe the report until I talked to the tigerish Piquot.

"It's true," quoth he in his most tigerish. "It has come from the captains you had as prisoners."

Later on I was to learn the story of what had happened, and that story, I think you will agree with me when you hear it, is indeed one of the epic tales of the World War.

From Lowell Thomas, *Raiders of the Deep,* (New York: Doubleday, 1928), pp. 181-191.

T.E. Lawrence

The Raid Upon the Bridges

October, accordingly, was a month of anticipation for us, in the knowledge that Allenby, with Bols and Dawnay, was planning to attack the Gaza-Beersheba line; while the Turks, a quite small army strongly entrenched, with excellent lateral communications, had been puffed up by successive victories to imagine that all British generals were incompetent to keep what their troops had won for them by dint of sheer hard fighting.

They deceived themselves. Allenby's coming had re-made the English. His breadth of personality swept away the mist of private or departmental jealousies behind which Murray and his men had worked. General Lynden Bell made way for General Bols, Allenby's chief of staff in France, a little, quick, brave, pleasant man; a tactical soldier perhaps, but principally an admirable and effaced foil to Allenby, who used to relax himself on Bols. Unfortunately, neither of them had the power of choosing men; but Chetwode's judgement completed with the Guy Dawnay as third member of the staff.

Bols had never an opinion, nor any knowledge. Dawnay was mainly intellect. He lacked the eagerness of Bols, and the calm drive and human understanding of Allenby, who was the man the men worked for, the image we worshipped. Dawnay's cold, shy mind gazed upon our efforts with bleak eye, always thinking, thinking. Beneath this mathematical surface he hid passionate many-sided convictions, a reasoned scholarship in higher warfare, and the brilliant bitterness of a judgement disappointed with us, and with life.

He was the least professional of soldiers, a banker who read Greek history, a strategist unashamed, and a burning poet with strength over daily things. During the war he had had the grief of planning the attack at Suvla (spoiled by incompetent tacticians) and the battle for Gaza. As each work of his was ruined he withdrew further into the hardnesses of frosted pride, for he was of the stuff of fanatics.

Allenby, by not seeing his dissatisfaction, broke into him; and Dawnay replied by giving for the Jerusalem advance all the talent which he abundantly possessed. A cordial union of two such men made the Turks' position hopeless from the outset.

Their divergent characters were mirrored in the intricate plan. Gaza had been entrenched on a European scale with line after line of defences in reserve. It was so obviously the enemy's strongest point, that the British higher command had twice chosen it for frontal attack. Allenby, fresh from France, insisted that any further assault must be delivered by overwhelming numbers of men and guns, and their thrust maintained by enormous quantities of all kinds of transport. Bols nodded his assent.

Dawnay was not the man to fight a straight battle. He sought to destroy the enemy's strength with the least fuss. Like a master politician, he used the bluff Chief as a cloak for the last depth of justifiable slimness. He advised a drive at the far end of the Turkish line, near Beersheba. To make his victory cheap he wanted the enemy main force behind Gaza, which would be best secured if the British concentration was hidden so that the Turks would believe the flank attack to be a shallow feint. Bols nodded his assent.

Consequently the movements were made in great secrecy; but Dawnay found an ally in his intelligence staff who advised him to go beyond negative precautions, and to give the enemy specific (and speciously wrong) information of the plans he matured.

This ally was Meinertzhagen, a student of migrating birds drifted into soldiering, whose hot immoral hatred of the enemy expressed itself as readily in trickery as in violence. He persuaded Dawnay: Allenby reluctantly agreed: Bols assented, and the work began.

Meinertzhagen knew no half measures. He was logical, an idealist of the deepest, and so possessed by his convictions that he was willing to harness evil to the chariot of good. He was a strategist, a geographer, and a silent laughing masterful man; who took as blithe a pleasure in deceiving his enemy (or his friend) by some unscrupulous jest, as in spattering the brains of a cornered mob of Germans one by one with his African knob-kerri. His instincts were abetted by an immensely powerful body and a savage brain, which chose the best way to its purpose, unhampered by doubt or habit. Meiner thought out false Army papers, elaborate and confidential, which to a trained staff officer would indicate wrong positions for Allenby's main formation, a wrong direction of the coming attack, and a date some days too late. This information was led up to by careful hints given in code wireless messages. When he knew the enemy had picked these up, Meinertzhagen rode out with his note books, on reconnaissance. He pushed forward until the enemy saw him. In the ensuing gallop he lost all his loose equipment and very nearly himself, but was rewarded by seeing the enemy reserves held behind Gaza and their whole preparations swung towards the coast and made less urgent. Simultaneously, an Army order by Ali Fuad Pasha cautioned his staff against carrying documents into the line.

We on the Arab front were very intimate with the enemy. Our Arab officers had been Turkish Officers, and knew every leader on the other side personally. They had suffered the same training, thought the same, took the same point of view. By practising modes of approach upon the Arabs we could explore the Turks: understand, almost get inside, their minds.

Relation between us and them was universal, for the civil population of the enemy area was wholly ours without pay or persuasion. In consequence our intelligence service was the widest, fullest and most certain imaginable.

We knew, better than Allenby, the enemy hollowness, and the magnitude of the British resources. We under-estimated the crippling effect of Allenby's too plentiful artillery, and the cumbrous intricacy of his infantry and cavalry, which moved only with rheumatic slowness. We hoped Allenby would be given a month's fine weather; and, in that case, expected to see him take, not merely Jerusalem, but Haifa too, sweeping the Turks in ruin through the hills.

Such would be our moment, and we needed to be ready for it in the spot where our weight and tactics would be least expected and most damaging. For my eyes, the centre of attraction was Deraa, the junction of the Jerusalem-Haifa-Damascus-Medina railways, the navel of the Turkish Armies in Syria, the common point of all their fronts; and, by chance, an area in which lay great untouched reserves of Arab fighting men, educated and armed by Feisal from Akaba. We could there use Rualla, Serahin, Serdiyeh, Khoreisha; and, far stronger than tribes, the settled peoples of Hauran and Jebel Druse.

I pondered for a while whether we should not call up all these adherents and tackle the Turkish communications in force. We were certain, with any management, of twelve thousand men: enough to rush Deraa, to smash all the railway lines, even to take Damascus by surprise. Any one of these things would make the position of the Beersheba army critical: and my temptation to stake our capital instantly upon the issue was very sore.

Not for the first or last time service to two masters irked me. I was one of Allenby's officers, and in his confidence: in return, he expected me to do the best I could for him. I was Feisal's adviser, and Feisal relied upon the honesty and competence of my advice so far as often to take it without argument. Yet I could not explain to Allenby the whole Arab situation, nor disclose the full British plan to Feisal.

The local people were imploring us to come. Sheikh Talal el Hareidhin, leader of the hollow country about Deraa, sent in repeated messages that, with a few of our riders as proof of Arab support, he would give us Deraa. Such an exploit would have done the Allenby business, but was not one which Feisal could scrupulously afford unless he had a fair hope of then establishing himself there. Deraa's sudden capture, followed by a retreat, would have involved the massacre, or the ruin of all the splendid peasantry of the district.

They could only rise once, and their effort on that occasion must be decisive. To call them out now was to risk the best asset Feisal held for eventual success, on the speculation that Allenby's first attack would sweep the enemy before it, and that the month of November would be rainless, favourable to a rapid advance.

I weighed the English army in my mind, and could not honestly assure myself of them. The men were often gallant fighters, but their generals as often gave away in stupidity what they had gained in ignorance. Allenby was quite untried, sent to us with a not-blameless record from France, and his troops had broken down in and been broken by the Murray period. Of course, we were fighting for an Allied victory, and since the English were the leading partners, the Arabs would have, in the last resort, to be sacrificed for them. But was it the last resort? The war generally was going neither well nor very ill, and it seemed as though there might be time for another try next year. So I decided to postpone the hazard for the Arabs' sake.

However, the Arab Movement lived on Allenby's good pleasure, so it was needful to undertake some operation, less than a general revolt, in the enemy rear: an operation which could be achieved by a raiding party without involving the settled peoples; and yet one which would please him by being of material help to the British pursuit of the enemy. These conditions and qualifications pointed, upon consideration, to an attempted cutting of one of the great bridges in the Yarmuk Valley.

It was by the narrow and precipitous gorge of the River Yarmuk that the railway from Palestine climbed to Hauran, on its way to Damascus. The depth of the Jordan depression, and the abruptness of the eastern plateau-face made this section of the line most difficult to build. The engineers had to lay it in the very course of the winding river-valley: and to gain its development the line had to cross and recross the stream continually by a series of bridges, the farthest west and the farthest east of which were hardest to replace.

To cut either of these bridges would isolate the Turkish army in Palestine, for one fortnight, from its base in Damascus, and destroy its power of escaping from Allenby's advance. To reach the Yarmuk we should need to ride from Akaba, by way of Azrak, some four hundred and twenty miles. The Turks thought the danger from us so remote that they guarded the bridges insufficiently.

Accordingly we suggested the scheme to Allenby, who asked that it be done on November the fifth, or one of the three following days. If it succeeded, and the weather held up afterwards for a fortnight, the odds were that no coherent unit of von Kress's army would survive its retreat to Damascus. The Arabs would then have their opportunity to carry their wave forward into the great capital, taking up at the half-way point from the British, whose original impulse would then be nearly exhausted, with the exhaustion of their transport.

For such an eventuality we needed at Azrak an authority to lead the potential local adherents. Nasir, our usual pioneer, was absent: but out with the Beni Sakhr was Ali ibn el Hussein, the youthful and attractive Harith Sherif, who had distinguished himself in Feisel's early desperate days about Medina, and later had outnewcombed Newcombe about el Ula.

Ali, having been Jemal's guest in Damascus, had learned something of Syria: so I begged a loan of him from Feisal. His courage, his resource, and his energy were proven. There had never been any adventure, since our beginning, too dangerous for Ali to attempt, nor a disaster too deep for him to face with his high yell of a laugh.

He was physically splendid: not tall nor heavy, but so strong that he would kneel down, resting his forearms palm-up on the ground, and rise to his feet with a man on each hand. In addition, Ali could outstrip a trotting camel on his bare feet, keep his speed over half a mile and then leap into the saddle. He was impertinent, headstrong, conceited; as reckless in word as in deed; impressive (if he pleased) on public occasions, and fairly educated for a person whose native ambition was to excel the nomads of the desert in war and sport.

Ali would bring us the Beni Sakhr. We had good hopes of the Serahin, the tribe at Azrak. I was in touch with the Beni Hassan. The Rualla, of course, at this season were away at their winter quarters, so that our greatest card in the Hauran could not be played. Faiz el Ghusein had gone into the Lejah to prepare for action against the Hauran Railway if the signal came. Explosives were stored in desirable places. Our friends in Damascus were warned; and Ali Riza Pasha Rikabi, the city's military governor for the innocent Turks, and at the same time chief agent and conspirator for the Sherif, took quiet steps to retain control if the emergency arose.

My detailed plan was to rush from Azrak, under guidance of Rafa (that most gallant sheikh who had convoyed me in June), to Um Keis, in one or two huge marches with a handful of, perhaps, fifty men. Um Keis was Gadara, very precious with its memories of Menippus and of Meleager, the immoral Greek-Syrian whose self-expression marked the highest point of Syrian letters. It stood just over the westernmost of the Yarmuk bridges, a steel masterpiece whose destruction would fairly enroll me in the Gadarene school. Only half a dozen sentries were stationed actually on the girders and abutments. Reliefs for them were supplied from a garrison of sixty, in the station buildings of Hemme, where the hot springs of Gadara yet gushed out to the advantage of local sick. My hope was to persuade some of the Abu Tayi under Zaal to come with me. These men-wolves would make certain the actual storming of the bridge. To prevent enemy reinforcements coming up we would sweep the approaches with machine-guns, handled by Captain Bray's Indian volunteers from cavalry division in France, under Jemadar Hassan Shah, a firm and experienced man. They had been months up country, rail-cutting, from Wejh, and might fairly be assumed to have become experts on camel-back, fit for the forced marches in prospect.

The demolition of great underslung girders with limited weights of explosive was a precise operation, and demanded a necklace of blasting gelatine, fired electrically. The *Humber* made us canvas straps and buckles, to simplify the fixing. None the less, the job remained a difficult one to do under fire. For fear of a casualty, Wood, the base engineer at Akaba, the only sapper available, was invited to come along and double me. He immediately agreed, though knowing he had been condemned medically for active service as the result of a bullet through the head in France. George Lloyd, who was spending a last few days in Akaba before going to Versailles on a regretted inter-allied Commission, said that he would ride up with us to Jefer: as he was one of the best fellows and least obtrusive travelers alive, his coming added greatly to our forlorn anticipation.

We were making our last preparations when an unexpected ally arrived in Emir Abd el Kader el Jezairi, grandson of the chivalrous defender of Algiers against the French. The exiled family had lived in Damascus for a generation. One of them, Omar, had been hanged by Jemal for treason disclosed in the Picot papers. The others had been deported, and Abd el Kader told us a long story of his escape from Brusa, and his journey, with a thousand adventures, across Anatolia to Damascus. In reality, he had been enlarged by the Turks upon request of the Khedive Abbas Hilmi, and sent down by him on private business to Mecca. He went there, saw King Hussein, and came back with a crimson banner, and noble gifts, his crazy mind half-persuaded of our right, and glowing jerkily with excitement.

To Feisal he offered the bodies and souls of his villagers, sturdy, hardsmiting Algerian exiles living compact along the north bank of the Yarmuk. We seized at the chance this would give us to control for a little time the middle section of the Valley railway, including two or three main bridges, without the disability of raising the country-side; since the Algerians were hated strangers and the Arab peasantry would not join them. Accordingly, we put off calling Rafa to meet us at Azrak, and said not a word to Zaal, concentrating our thoughts instead of Wadi Khalid and its bridges.

While we were in this train of mind arrived a telegram from Colonel Bremond, warning us that Abd el Kader was a spy in pay of the Turks. It was disconcerting. We watched him narrowly, but found no proof of the charge, which was not to be accepted blindly, as from Bremond, who was more a liability than our colleague; his military temper might have carried away his judgement when he heard Abd el Kader's outspoken public and private denunciations of France. The French conception of their country as a fair woman lent to them a national spitefulness against those who scorned her charms.

Feisal told Abd el Kader to ride with Ali and myself, and said to me, "I know he is mad. I think he is honest. Guard your heads and use him"' We carried on, showing him our complete confidence, on the principle that a crook would not credit our honesty, and that an honest man was made a crook soonest by suspicion. As a matter of fact, he was an Islamic fanatic, half-insane with religious enthusiasm and a most violent belief in himself.

His bullet-headed stupidity broke down Ali's self-control twice or thrice into painful scenes: while his final effort was to leave us in the lurch at a desperate moment, after hindering our march and upsetting ourselves and our plans as far as he could.

Starting was as difficult as ever. For my bodyguard I took six recruits. Of these Mahmud was a native of the Yarmuk. He was an alert and hot-tempered lad of nineteen, with the petulance often accompanying curly hair. Another, Aziz, of Tafas, an older fellow had spent three years with the Beduin in avoidance of military service. Though capable with camels, he was a shallow spirit, almost rabbit-mouthed, but proud. A third was Mustafa, a gentle boy from Deraa, very honest, who went about sadly by himself because he was deaf, and ashamed of his infirmity. One day on the beach, in a short word he had begged admittance to my bodyguard. So evidently did he expect to be refused that I took him; and it was a good choice for the others, since he was a mild peasant, whom they could bully into all the menial tasks. Yet he, too, was happy, for he was among desperate fellows, and the world would think him desperate. To balance his inefficiency on the march I enrolled Showak and Salem, two Sherari camel-herds, and Abd el Rahman, a runaway slave from Riyadh.

Of the old bodyguard I gave Mohammed and Ali a rest. They were tired after train-wrecking adventures; and, like their camels, needed to pasture quietly awhile. This left Ahmed the inevitable head man. His ruthless energy deserved promotion, but the obvious choice as ever failed. He misused his power and became oppressive; so it was his last march with me. I took Kreim for the camels; and Rahail, the lusty, conceited Haurani lad, for whom overwork was the grace which kept him continent. Matar, a parasite fellow of the Beni Hassan, attached himself to us. His fat peasant's buttocks filled his camel-saddle, and took nearly as large a share in the lewd or lurid jokes which, on march, helped pass my guards' leisure. We might enter Beni Hassan territory, where he had some influence. His unblushing greed made us sure of him, till his expectations failed.

My service was now profitable, for I knew my worth to the movement, and spent freely to keep myself safe. Rumour, for once in a helpful mood, gilded my open hand. Farraj and Daud, with Khidr and Mijbil, two Biasha, completed the party.

Farraj and Daud were capable and merry on the road, which they loved as all the lithe Ageyl loved it; but in camp their excess of spirit led them continually into dear affairs. This time they surpassed themselves by disappearing on the morning of our departure. At noon came a message from Sheikh Yusuf that they were in his prison, and would I talk to him about it? I went up to the house and found his bulk shaking between laughter and rage. He had just bought a cream-coloured riding-camel of purest blood. The beast had strayed in the evening into the palm-garden where my Ageyl were camped. They never suspected she belonged to the

Governor, but laboured till dawn dyeing her head bright red with henna, and her legs blue with indigo, before turning her loose.

Akaba bubbled immediately in an uproar about this circus beast. Yusuf recognized her with difficulty and hurled all his police abroad to find the criminals. The two friends were dragged before the judgement seat, stained to the elbows with dye, and loudly protesting their entire innocence. Circumstances, however, were too strong; and Yusuf after doing his best with a palm-rib to hurt their feelings, put them in irons for a slow week's meditation. My concern made good his damage by the loan of a camel till his own should be respectable. Then I explained our instant need of the sinners, and promised another dose of his treatment for them when their skins were fit: so he ordered their release. They were delighted to escape the verminous prison on any terms, and rejoined us singing.

This business had delayed us. So we had an immense final meal in the luxury of camp, and started in the evening. For four hours we marched slowly: a first march was always slow, and both camels and men hated the setting out on a new hazard. Loads slipped, saddles had to be re-girthed, and riders changed. In addition to my own camels (Ghazala, the old grandmother, now far gone in foal, and Rima, a full-pointed Sherari camel which the Sukhur had stolen from the Rualla) and those of the bodyguard, I had mounted the Indians, and lent one to Wood (who was delicate in the saddle and rode a fresh animal nearly every day), and one to Torne, Lloyd's yeomanry trooper, who sat his saddle like an Arab and looked workman-like in a head-cloth, with a striped cloak over his khaki. Lloyd himself was on a thoroughbred Dheraiyeh which Feisul had lent him: a fine, fast-looking animal, but clipped after mange and thin.

Our party straggled. Wood fell behind, and my men, being fresh, and having much work to keep the Indians together, lost touch with him. So he found himself alone with Thorne, and missed our turn to the east, in the blackness which always filled the depths of the Itm gorge by night, except when the moon was directly overhead. They went on up the main track towards Guweira, riding for hours; but at last decided to wait for day in a side valley. Both were new to the country, and not sure of the Arabs, so they took turns to keep watch. We guessed what had happened when they failed to appear at our midnight halt, and before dawn Ahmed, Aziz and Abd el Rahman went back, with orders to scatter up the three or four practicable roads and bring the missing pair to Rumm.

I stayed with Lloyd and the main body as their guide across the curved slopes of pink sandstone and tamarisk-green valleys to Rumm. Air and light were so wonderful that we wandered without thinking in the least of to-morrow. Indeed, had I not Lloyd to talk to? The world became very good. A faint shower last evening had brought earth and sky together in the mellow day. The colours in cliffs and trees and soil were so pure, so vivid, that we ached for real contact with them, and at our tethered inability to carry anything of them away. We were full of leisure. The Indians proved bad camel-masters, while Farraj and Daud pleaded a new form of saddle-soreness, called 'Yusufiyeh', which made them walk mile after mile.

We entered Rumm at last, while the crimson sunset burned on its stupendous cliffs and slanted ladders of hazy fire down the walled avenue. Wood and Thorne were there already, in the sandstone amphitheatre of the springs. Wood was ill, and lying on the platform of my old camp. Abd el Rahman had caught them before noon, and persuaded them to follow him after a good deal of misunderstanding, for their few words of Egyptian did not help much with his clipped Aridh dialect or the Howeiti slang with which he asked it out. He had cut across the hills by a difficult path to their great discomfort.

Wood had been hungry and hot and worried, angry to the point of refusing the native mess which Abd el Rahman contrived them in a way-side tent. He had begun to believe that he would never see us again, and was ungrateful when we proved too overcome with the awe that Rumm compelled on her visitors to sympathize deeply with his sufferings. In fact, we stared and said 'Yes,' and left him lying there while we wandered whispering about the wonder of the place. Fortunately Ahmed and Thorne thought more of food: and with supper friendly relations were restored.

Next day, while we were saddling, Ali and Abd el Kader appeared. Lloyd and I had a second lunch with them, for they were quarrelling, and to have guests held them in check. Lloyd was the rare sort of traveler who could eat anything with anybody, anyhow and at any time. Then, making pace, we pushed after our party down the giant valley, whose hills fell short of architecture only in design.

At the bottom we crossed the flat Gaa, matching our camels in a burst over its velvet surface, until we overtook the main body, and scattered them with the excitement of our gallop. The Indians' soberly laden camels danced like ironmongery till they had shed their burdens. Then we calmed ourselves, and plodded together gently up Wadi Hafira, a gash like a sword-cut into the plateau. At its head lay a stiff pass to the height of Batra; but to-day we fell short of this, and out of laziness and craving for comfort stopped in the sheltered bottom of the valley. We lit great fires, which were cheerful in the cool evening. Farraj prepared rice in his manner for me as usual. Lloyd and Wood and Thorne had brought with them bully beef in tins and British army biscuits. So we joined ranks and feasted.

Next day we climbed the zigzag broken pass, the grassy street of Hafira below us framing a cone-hill in its centre, with, as background, the fantastic grey domes and glowing pyramids of the mountains of Rumm, prolonged to-day into wider fantasies by the cloud-masses brooding over them. We watched our long train wind upwards, till before noon the camels, Arabs, Indians and baggage had reached the top without accident. Contentedly we plumped ourselves down in the first green valley over the crest, sheltered from the wind, and warmed by the faint sunshine which

tempered the autumn chill of this high tableland. Someone began to talk
again about food.[1]

Food was going to be our next preoccupation, and we held a council in
the cold driving rain to consider what we might do. For lightness' sake we
had carried from Azrak three days rations, which made us complete until
to-night; but we could not go back empty-handed. The Beni Sakhr wanted
honour, and the Serahin were too lately disgraced not to clamour for more
adventure. We had still a reserve bag of thirty pounds of gelatin, and Ali
ibn el Hussein who had heard of the performances below Maan, and was
as Arab as any Arab, said, "Let's blow up a train." The word was hailed
with universal joy, and they looked at me: but I was not able to share their
hopes, all at once.

Blowing up trains was an exact science when done deliberately, by a
sufficient party, with machine-guns in position. If scrambled at it might
become dangerous. The difficulty this time was that the available gunners
were Indians; who, though good men fed, were only half-men in cold and
hunger. I did not propose to drag them off without rations on an adventure
which might take a week. There was no cruelty in starving Arabs; they
would not die of a few days' fasting, and would fight as well as ever on
empty stomachs; while, if things got too difficult, there were the riding-
camels to kill and eat: but the Indians, though Moslems, refused camel-
flesh on principle.

I explained these delicacies of diet. Ali at once said that it would be
enough for me to blow up the train, leaving him and the Arabs with him to
do their best to carry its wreck without machine-gun support. As, in this
unsuspecting district, we might well happen on a supply train, with
civilians or only a small guard of reservists aboard, I agreed to risk it. The
decision having been applauded, we sat down in a cloaked circle, to finish
our remaining food in a very late and cold supper (the rain had sodden the
fuel and made fire not possible) our hearts somewhat comforted by chance
of another effort.

At dawn, with the unfit of the Arabs, the Indians moved away for Azrak,
miserably. They had started up country with me in hope of a really military
enterprise, and first had seen the muddled bridge, and now were losing this
prospective train. It was hard on them; and to soften the blow with honour
I asked Wood to accompany them. He agreed, after argument, for their
sakes; but it proved a wise move for himself, as a sickness which had been
troubling him began to show the early signs of pneumonia.

The balance of us, some sixty men, turned back towards the railway.
None of them knew the country, so I led them to Minifir, where, with Zaal,
we had made havoc in the spring. The re-curved hill-top was an excellent
observation post, camp, grazing ground and way of retreat, and we sat there
in our old place till sunset, shivering and staring out over the immense plain
which stretched map-like to the clouded peaks of Jebel Druse, with Um el

Jemal and her sister-villages like ink-smudges on it through the rain.

In the first dusk we walked down to lay the mine. The rebuilt culvert of kilometre 172 seemed still the fittest place. While we stood by it there came a rumbling, and through the gathering darkness and mist a train suddenly appeared round the northern curve, only two hundred yards away. We scurried under the long arch and heard it roll overhead. This was annoying; but when the course was clear again, we fell to burying the charge. The evening was bitterly cold, with drifts of rain blowing down the valley.

The arch was solid masonry, of four metres span, and stood over a shingle water-bed which took its rise on our hill-top. The winter rains had cut this into a channel four feet deep, narrow and winding, which served us as an admirable approach till within three hundred yards of the line. There the gully widened out and ran straight towards the culvert, open to the sight of anyone upon the rails.

We hid the explosive carefully on the crown of the arch, deeper than usual, beneath a tie, so that the patrols would not feel its jelly softness under their feet. The wires were taken down the bank into the shingle bed of the watercourse, where concealment was quick; and up it as far as they would reach. Unfortunately, this was only sixty yards, for there had been difficulty in Egypt over insulated cable and no more had been available when our expedition started. Sixty yards was plenty for the bridge, but little for a train: however, the ends happened to coincide with a little bush about ten inches high, on the edge of the watercourse, and we buried them beside this very convenient mark. It was impossible to leave them joined up to the exploder in the proper way, since the spot was evident to the permanent-way patrols as they made their rounds.

Owing to the mud the job took longer than usual, and it was very nearly dawn before we finished. I waited under the draughty arch till day broke, wet and dismal, and then I went over the whole area of disturbance, spending another half-hour in effacing its every mark, scattering leaves and dead grass over it, and watering down the broken mud from a shallow rain-pool near. Then they waved to me that the first patrol was coming, and I went up to join the others.

Before I had reached them they came tearing down into their prear-ranged places, lining the watercourse and spurs each side. A train was coming from the north. Hamud, Feisal's long slave, had the exploder; but before he reached me a short train of closed box-wagons rushed by at speed. The rainstorms on the plain and the thick morning had hidden it from the eyes of our watchman until too late. This second failure saddened us further and Ali began to say that nothing would come right this trip. Such a statement held risk as prelude of the discovery of an evil eye present; so, to divert attention, I suggested new watching posts be sent far out, one to the ruins on the north, one to the great cairn of the southern crest.

The rest, having no breakfast, were to pretend not to be hungry. They all enjoyed doing this, and for a while we sat cheerfully in the rain, huddling against one another for warmth behind a breast-work of our streaming camels. The moisture made the animals' hair curl up like a fleece, so that they looked queerly disheveled. When the rain paused, which it did frequently, a cold moaning wind searched out the unprotected parts of us very thoroughly. After a time we found our wetted shirts clammy and comfortless things. We had nothing to eat, nothing to do and nowhere to sit except on wet rock, wet grass or mud. However, this persistent weather kept reminding me that it would delay Allenby's advance on Jerusalem, and rob him of his great possibility. So large a misfortune to our lion was a half-encouragement for the mice. We would be partners into next year.

In the best circumstances, waiting for action was hard. To-day it was beastly. Even enemy patrols stumbled along without care, perfunctorily, against the rain. At last, near noon, in a snatch of fine weather, the watchmen on the south peak flagged their cloaks wildly in signal of a train. We reached our positions in an instant, for we had squatted the late hours on our heels in a streaming ditch near the line, so as not to miss another chance. The Arabs took cover properly. I looked back at their ambush from my firing point, and saw nothing but the gray hill-sides.

I could not hear the train coming, but trusted, and knelt ready for perhaps half an hour, when the suspense became intolerable, and I signaled to know what was up. They sent down to say it was coming very slowly, and was an enormously long train. Our appetites stiffened. The longer it was the more would be the loot. Then came word that it had stopped. It moved again.

Finally, near one o'clock, I heard it panting. The locomotive was evidently defective (all these wood-fired trains were bad), and the heavy load on the up-gradient was proving too much for its capacity. I crouched behind my bush, while it crawled slowly into view past the south cutting, and along the bank above my head towards the culvert. The first ten trucks were open trucks, crowded with troops. However, once again it was too late to choose, so when the engine was squarely over the mine I pushed down the handle of the exploder. Nothing happened. I sawed it up and down four times.

Still nothing happened; and I realized that it had gone out of order, and that I was kneeling on a naked bank, with a Turkish troop train crawling past fifty yards away. The bush, which had seemed a foot high, shrank smaller than a fig-leaf; and I felt myself the most distinct object in the country-side. Behind me was an open valley for two hundred yards to the cover where my Arabs were waiting and wondering what I was at. It was impossible to make a bolt for it, or the Turks would step off the train and finish us. If I sat still, there might be just a hope of my being ignored as a casual Bedouin.

So there I sat, counting for sheer life, while eighteen open trucks, three box-wagons, and three officers' coaches dragged by. The engine panted slower and slower, and I thought every moment that it would break down. The troops took no great notice of me, but the officers were interested, and came out to the little platforms at the ends of their carriages, pointing and staring. I waved back at them, grinning nervously, and feeling an improbable shepherd in my Meccan dress, with its twisted golden circlet about my head. Perhaps the mud-stains, the wet and their ignorance made me accepted. The end of the brake van slowly disappeared into the cutting on the north.

As it went, I jumped up, buried my wires, snatched hold of the wretched exploder, and went like a rabbit uphill into safety. There I took breath and looked back to see that the train had finally stuck. It waited, about five hundred yards beyond the mine, for nearly an hour to get up a head of steam, while an officers' patrol came back and searched, very carefully, the ground where I had been seen sitting. However the wires were probably hidden: they found nothing: the engine plucked up heart again, and away they went.

Mifleh was past tears, thinking I had intentionally let the train through; and when the Serahin had been told the real cause they said, "Bad luck is with us." Historically they were right; but they meant it for a prophecy, so I made sarcastic reference to their courage at the bridge the week before, hinting that it might be a tribal preference to sit on camel-guard. At once there was uproar, the Serahin attacking me furiously, the Beni Sakhr defending. Ali heard the trouble, and came running.

When we had made it up the original despondency was half forgotten. Ali backed me nobly, though the wretched boy was blue with cold and shivering in an attack of fever. He gasped that their ancestor the Prophet had given to Sherifs the faculty of "sight," and by it he knew that our luck was turning. This was comfort for them: my first installment of good fortune came when in the wet, without other tool than my dagger, I got the box of the exploder open and persuaded its electrical gear to work properly once more.

We returned to our vigil by the wires, but nothing happened, and evening drew down with more squalls and beastliness, everybody full of grumbles. There was no train; it was too wet to light a cooking fire; our only potential food was camel. Raw meat did not tempt anyone that night; and so our beasts survived to the morrow.

Ali lay down on his belly, which position lessened the hunger ache, trying to sleep off his fever. Khazen, Ali's servant, lent him his cloak for extra covering. For a spell I took Khazen under mine, but soon found it becoming crowded. So I left it to him and went downhill to connect up the exploder. Afterwards I spent the night there alone by the singing telegraph wires, hardly wishing to sleep, so painful was the cold. Nothing came all the long hours, and dawn, which broke wet, looked even uglier than usual.

We were sick to death of Minifir, of railways, of train watching and wrecking, by now. I climbed up to the main body while the early patrol searched the railway. Then the day cleared a little. Ali awoke, much refreshed, and his new spirit cheered us. Hamud, the slave, produced some sticks which he had kept under his clothes by his skin all night. They were nearly dry. We shaved down some blasting gelatin, and with its hot flame got a fire going, while the Sukhur hurriedly killed a mangy camel, the best spared of our riding-beasts, and began with entrenching tools to hack it into handy joints.

Just at that moment the watchman on the north cried a train. We left the fire and made a breathless race of the six hundred yards downhill to our old position. Round the bend, whistling its loudest, came the train, a splendid two-engined thing of twelve passenger coaches, traveling at top speed on the favouring grade. I touched off under the first driving wheel of the first locomotive, and the explosion was terrific. The ground spouted blackly into my face, and I was sent spinning, to sit up with the shirt torn to my shoulder and the blood dripping from long, ragged scratches on my left arm. Between my knees lay the exploder, crushed under a twisted sheet of sooty iron. In front of me was the scalded and smoking upper half of a man. When I peered through the dust and steam of the explosion the whole boiler of the first engine seemed to be missing.

I dully felt that it was time to get away to support; but when I moved, learnt that there was a great pain in my right foot, because of which I could only limp along, with my head swinging from the shock. Movement began to clear away this confusion, as I hobbled towards the upper valley, whence the Arabs were now shooting fast into the crowded coaches. Dizzily I cheered myself by repeating aloud in English "Oh, I wish this hadn't happened."

When the enemy began to return our fire, I found myself much between the two. Ali saw me fall, and thinking that I was hard hit, ran out, with Turki and about twenty men of his servants and the Beni Sakhr, to help me. The Turks found their range and got seven of them in a few seconds. The others, in a rush, were about me--fit models, after their activity, for a sculptor. Their full white cotton drawers drawn in, bell-like, round their slender waists and ankles; their hairless brown bodies; and the love-locks plaited tightly over each temple in long horns, made them look like Russian dancers.

We scrambled back into cover together, and there, secretly, I felt myself over, to find I had not once been really hurt; though besides the bruises and cuts of the boiler-plate and a broken toe, I had five different bullet-grazes on me (some of them uncomfortably deep) and my clothes ripped to pieces.

From the watercourse we could look about. The explosion had destroyed the arched head of the culvert, and the frame of the first engine was lying across the ruined tender of the first. Its bed was twisted. I judged them both beyond repair. The second tender had disappeared over the further side; and the first three wagons had telescoped and were smashed in pieces.

The rest of the train was badly derailed, with the listing coaches butted end to end at all angles, zigzagged along the track. One of them was a saloon, decorated with flags. In it had been Mehmed Jemal Pasha, commanding the Eighth Army Corps, hurrying down to defend Jerusalem against Allenby. His chargers had been in the first wagon; his motor-car was on the end of the train, and we shot it up. Of his staff we noticed a fat ecclesiastic, whom we thought to be Assad Shukair, Imam to Ahmed Jemal Pasha, and a notorious pro-Turk pimp. So we blazed at him till he dropped.

It was all long bowls. We could see that our chances of carrying the wreck were slight. There had been some four hundred men on board, and the survivors, now recovered from the shock, were under shelter and shooting hard at us. At the first moment our party on the north spur had closed, and nearly won the game. Mifleh on his mare chased the officers from the saloon into the lower ditch. He was too excited to stop and shoot, and so they got away scathless. The Arabs following him had turned to pick up some of the rifles and medals littering the ground, and then to drag bags and boxes from the train. If we had had a machine-gun posted to cover the far side, according to my mining practice, not a Turk would have escaped.

Mifleh and Adhub rejoined us on the hill, and asked after Fahad. One of the Serahin told how he had led the first rush, while I lay knocked out beside the exploder, and had been killed near it. They showed his belt and rifle as proof that he was dead and that they had tried to save him. Adhub said not a word, but leaped out of the gully, and raced downhill. We caught our breaths till our lungs hurt us, watching him; but the Turks seemed not to see. A minute later he was dragging a body behind the left-hand bank.

Mifleh went back to his mare, mounted, and took her down behind a spur. Together they lifted the inert figure on to the pommel, and returned. A bullet had passed through Fahads face, knocking out four teeth, and gashing the tongue. He had fallen unconscious, but had revived just before Adhub reached him, and was trying on hands and knees, blinded with blood, to crawl away. He now recovered poise enough to cling to a saddle. So they changed him to the first camel they found, and led him off at once.

The Turks, seeing us so quiet, began to advance up the slope. We let them come half-way, and then poured in volleys which killed some twenty and drove the others back. The ground about the train was strewn with dead, and the broken coaches had been crowded: but they were fighting under eye of their Corps Commander and undaunted began to work round the spurs to outflank us.

We were now only about forty left, and obviously could do no good against them. So we ran in batches up the little stream-bed, turning at each sheltered angle to delay them by pot-shots. Little Turki much distinguished himself by quick coolness, though his straight-stocked Turkish cavalry carbine made him so expose his head that he got four bullets through his head-cloth. Ali was angry with me for retiring slowly. In reality my raw hurts crippled me, but to hide from him this real reason I pretended to be easy, interested in and studying the Turks. Such successive rests while I gained courage for a new run kept him and Turki far behind the rest.

At last we reached the hill-top. Each man there jumped on the nearest camel, and made away at full speed eastward into the desert, for an hour. Then in safety we sorted our animals. The excellent Rahail, despite the ruling excitement, had brought off with him, tied to his saddle-girth, a huge haunch of the camel slaughtered just as the train arrived. He gave us the motive for a proper halt, five miles farther on, as a little party of four camels appeared marching in the same direction. It was our companion, Matar, coming back from his home village to Azrak with loads of raisins and peasant delicacies.

So we stopped at once, under a large rock in Wadi Dhuleil, where was a barren fig-tree, and cooked our first meal for three days. There, also, we bandaged up Fahad, who was sleepy with the lassitude of his severe hurt. Adhub, seeing this, took one of Matar's new carpets, and, doubling it across the camel-saddle, stitched the ends into great pockets. In one they laid Fahad, while Adhub crawled into the other as make-weight: and the camel was led off southward towards their tribal tents.

The other wounded men were seen to at the same time. Mifleh brought up the youngest lads of the party, and had them spray the wounds with their piss, as a rude antiseptic. Meanwhile we whole ones refreshed ourselves. I bought another mangy camel for extra meat, paid rewards, compensated the relatives of the killed, and gave prize-money, for the sixty or seventy rifles we had taken. It was small booty, but not to be despised. Some Serahin, who had gone into the action without rifles, able only to throw unavailing stones, had now two guns apiece. Next day we moved into Azrak, having a great welcome, and boasting--God forgive us--that we were victors.

1. At this point, Lawrence's narrative lingers on the lengthy march to the railroad bridges, the loss of surprise, due both to a traitor and a too-noisy approach, and the decision to seek an alternate target.

From T.E. Lawrence, *Seven Pillars of Wisdom,* (New York: Doubleday, 1926), pp. 343-354; 382-390.

Chapter 7

World War II in Western Europe and North Africa

Special operations formed a continuing, vital aspect of this war from beginning to end, and some brief mention must be made of at least some of those cases *not* chosen for inclusion. On the allied side, the Special Operations Executive and the OSS kept quite busy trying to obey Winston Churchill's order to "set Europe ablaze." They succeeded in this, through a variety of actions, not least in the efforts of the Jedburghs and the Maquis to cripple German rail connections in France prior to the Normandy invasion. This irregular campaign helped enormously to keep the German Seventh Army isolated during the period immediately after D-Day.

Another area of special operations was Norway, which featured two crucially important actions. One aimed at shifting the naval balance of forces along the route of the Arctic convoys, which brought the Soviets the materials so vital to their war effort. This operation featured an attack by mini-submarines, or "X-craft," against the battleship *Tirpitz,* which succeeded in crippling it sufficiently to allow bombers eventually to finish it off. Another key raid occurred against the German heavy water plant at Vemörk, a central element of the Nazi nuclear weapons production effort. This first "counterproliferation" action, though unsuccessful, did prompt the Germans to try to move production out of Norway, allowing a further commando effort to be made during shipping, which was successful this time.

On the Axis side, mention must be made of the exploits of Otto Skorzeny, whose rescue of Mussolini from a mountaintop prison must rank close to Entebbe as an archetypal example of this type of operation.

Here, also, one may see profound political consequences, as the rescue of *Il Duce* allowed for the establishment of a puppet Italian state in Northern Italy that contributed, for two years, to the German ability to hold back the allied advance. On the Italian side, the efforts of their frogmen to sink or disable British battleships, from Alexandria to Gibraltar, is nothing short of astonishing, and had a powerful, direct impact on the naval balance of forces in the Mediterranean.

Of the other special operations included in the following excerpts, several observations should be made. First, with regard to airborne assault, one can see that the temptation to "regularize" these forces, to place them into conventional campaign situations, was too great to resist. The German attack on Crete exemplifies this problem, though the Allies exhibited this same tendency at Arnhem later in the war. Think, for a moment, of alternative uses of these very special forces. Had the Germans engaged in some introspection on this point, they might have used them to greater effect against "softer" targets. For example, a paratroop operation to take over virtually undefended Vichy Syria, pre-empting the British, could have turned the North African campaign decisively in favor of the Axis. Certainly this would have proven a better use than a direct assault on a heavily defended target.

The other readings, which all revolve around the North African and Mediterranean campaigns, make a variety of important points of their own. Lodwick's recounting of the activities of the Special Boat Service illustrates the manner in which even very small numbers of commandos can tie down, and force the dispersed deployment, of much greater numbers of the enemy. The failed British commando raids, first to kidnap or kill Rommel, later to cripple Tobruk as a logistical base for the *Afrika Korps,* demonstrate, respectively, the crucial impact of chance factors and the need to keep planning as simple as possible. The raid on Tobruk is one of the best examples of seeing a simple, good idea hijacked by bureaucratic political interests. Finally, in the activities of the German Brandenburgers, one sees the clever uses to which commandos may be put in support of conventional forces that have been thrown on the strategic defensive.

Cajus Bekker
Coup de Main at Eben Emael

The take-off signal flashed in the darkness and the sound of aero-engines rose to a roar as the first three Ju 52s began to move across the airfield. They did so more sluggishly than usual, for each dragged a heavy burden--a second aircraft without engines: a glider!

As the tow-rope grew taut the latter jerked forward and jolted faster and faster down the runway. Then, as the towing craft left the ground, the glider pilot drew the stick carefully towards him, and the rumbling of his undercarriage grew suddenly silent. Seconds later the glider was sweeping noiselessly over hedges and fences and gaining height behind its Ju 52. The difficult towed take-off had been accomplished.

The time was 04.30 on May 10, 1940. From Cologne's two airfields, Ostheim on the right bank of the Rhine, Butzweilerhof on the left, sections of three Ju 52s were taking off at thirty second intervals, each towing a glider. Becoming airborne, they steered for a point above the green belt to the south of the city, there to thread themselves to a string of lights that stretched towards Aachen. Within a few minutes forty-one Ju 52s and forty-one gliders were on their way.

The die had been cast for one of the most audacious enterprises in the annals of war: the assault on the Belgian frontier fortress of Eben Emael, and the three bridges to the north-west leading over the deep Albert Canal--the key-points of the Belgian defence system to the east.

In each of the forty-one gliders a team of parachutists sat astride the central beam. According to their appointed task their number varied between eight and twelve, equipped with weapons and explosives. Every soldier knew exactly what his job was once the target was reached. They had been rehearsing the operation, initially with boxes of sand and models, since November 1939.

They belonged to "Assault Detachment Koch". Ever since this unit had reached its training base at Hildesheim, it had been hermetically sealed off from the outside world. No leave or exeats had been granted, their mail was strictly censored, speech with members of other units forbidden.

Each soldier had signed a declaration: "I am aware that I shall risk sentence of death should I, by intent or carelessness, make know to another person by spoken word, text or illustration anything concerning the base at which I am serving."

Two men were, in fact, sentenced to death for quite trifling lapses, and only reprieved after the operation had succeeded. Obviously its success, and thereby the lives of the paratroops, depended on the adversary having no inkling of its imminence. Secrecy was carried so far that while the men knew the details of each other's roles by heart, they only discovered each other's names when all was over.

Theory was succeeded by practical exercises by day, by night, and in every kind of weather. Around Christmas time the operation was re-hearsed against the Czech fortified emplacements in the Altvater district of the Sudentenland.

"We developed a healthy respect for what lay ahead of us," reported First-Lieutenant Rudolf Witzig, leader of the parachute sapper platoon which was due to take on the Eben Emael fortifications single-handed. "But after a while our confidence reached the stage where we, the attackers, believed our position outside on the breastworks safer than that of the defenders inside."

Outside on the breastworks. . . but now did they propose to get that far?

The construction of the fortress, like that of the Albert Canal itself, dated from the early 'thirties. Forming the northern bastion of the Lüttich (Liège) defences, it was situated just three miles south of Maastricht, in a salient hard by the Belgian-Dutch frontier. In that position it dominated the Canal, the strategic importance of which was plain: any aggressor advancing along the line Aachen-Maastricht-Brussels would have to cross it. The defence had made preparations so that all its bridges could be blown at a moment's notice.

The fortifications themselves were embedded in a hilly plateau, and extended for 900 yards north and south, 700 yards east and west. The individual emplacements were scattered, seemingly at random, over a five-cornered area. In fact, with their artillery casemates, armoured rotating cupolas carrying 75-mm and 120-mm guns, plus anti-aircraft, anti-tank and heavy machine-gun positions, they constituted a shrewdly planned defence system. The different sectors of the complex were connected by underground tunnels totaling nearly three miles in length.

The fortress seemed all but impregnable. On its long north-eastern flank was an almost sheer drop of 120 feet down to the Canal. The same applied to the north-west, with a similar drop to a canal cut. To the south it was protected artificially--by wide anti-tank ditches and a twenty-foot-high wall. On all sides it was additionally protected by concrete pillboxes let into the side of the walls or cuttings, which bristled with searchlights, 60-mm anti-tank guns and heavy machine-guns. Any enemy attempt to get into the place seemed doomed to failure.

The Belgians had foreseen every possibility but one: that the enemy might drop out of the sky right amongst the casemates and gun turrets. Now this enemy was already on his way. By 04.35 all the forty-one Ju 52s were air-borne. Despite the darkness and the heavily laden gliders behind them there had not been a single hitch.

Captain Koch had divided his assault force into four detachments, as follows:

1. "Granite" under First-Lieutenant Witzig, eighty-five men with small arms and two and a half tons of explosives embarked in eleven gliders. Target: Eben Emael fortifications. Mission: to put outer elements out of action and hold till relieved by Army Sapper Battalion 51.

2. "Concrete" under Lieutenant Schacht. Ninety-six men and command staff embarked in eleven gliders. Target: high concrete bridge over Albert Canal at Vroenhoven. Mission: to prevent bridge being blown, form and secure bridgeheads pending arrival of army troops.

3. "Steel" under First-Lieutenant Altmann. Ninety-two men embarked in nine gliders. Target: steel bridge of Veldwezelt, 3 3/4 miles NW of Eben Emael. Mission: as for "Concrete."

4. "Iron" under Lieutenant Schächter. Ninety men embarked in ten gliders. Target: bridge at Kanne. Mission: again as for "Concrete."

Rendezvous was duly made between the two groups of aircraft, and all set course for the west, following the line of beacons. The first was a fire kindled at a crossroads near Efferen, the second a searchlight three miles further on at Frechen. As the aircraft approached one beacon, the next, and often the next but one, became visible ahead. Navigation, despite the dark night, was therefore no problem at least as far as the pre-ordained unhitching point at Aachen. Yet for one aircraft--the one towing the last glider of the "Granite" detachment--things went wrong while still south of Cologne.

Just ahead and to starboard its pilot suddenly noticed the blue exhaust flames of another machine on a collision course. There was only one thing to do: push his Ju 52 into a dive. But he had, of course, a glider in tow! The latter's pilot, Corporal Pilz, tried frantically to equalize the strain, but within seconds his cockpit was lashed as with a whip as the towing cable parted. As Pilz pulled out of the dive the sound of their mother aircraft died rapidly away and suddenly all was strangely silent.

The seven occupants then glided back to Cologne—one of them the very man who was supposed to lead the assault on the Eben Emael fortress, First-Lieutenant Witzig. Pilz just managed to clear the Rhine, then set the glider softly down in a meadow. What now?

Climbing out, Witzig at once ordered his men to convert the meadow into an airstrip by clearing all fences and other obstacles. "I will try to get hold of another towing plane," he said.

Running to the nearest road he stopped a car and within twenty minutes was once again at Cologne-Ostheim airfield. But not a single Ju 52 was left. He had to get on the phone and ask for one from Gütersloh. It would take time. Looking at his watch he saw it was 05.05. In twenty minutes his detachment was due to land on the fortress plateau.

Meanwhile the Ju 52 squadrons, with their gliders behind them, droned westwards, climbing steadily. Every detail of their flight had been worked out in advance. The line of beacons to the German frontier at Aachen was forty-five miles long. By then the aircraft were scheduled to reach a height of 8,500 feet: a flight of thirty-one minutes, assuming the wind had been correctly estimated.

Squatting in their gliders, the men of detachment "Granite" had no idea that their leader had already dropped out of the procession. For the moment it was not all that important. Each section had its own special job to do, and each glider pilot knew at exactly which point of the elongated plateau he had to land: behind which emplacement, beside which gun turret, within a margin of ten to twenty yards.

It would moreover have been bad planning if the loss of individual gliders had not been provided for. As it was, each section leader's orders included directions as to what additional tasks his team would have to perform in the event of neighbouring sections failing to land.

Nor was Witzig's glider the only one to drop out. Some twenty minutes later that carrying No. 2 Section had just passed the beacon at Luchenberg when the Ju 52 in front waggled its wings. The glider pilot, Corporal Brendenbeck, thought he was "seeing things," especially when the plane also blinked its position lights. It was the signal to unhitch! Seconds later the glider had done so--all thanks to a stupid misunderstanding. It was only half way to its target, and with an altitude of less than 5,000 feet there was no longer a hope of reaching the frontier.

The glider put down in a field near Düren. Springing out, its men requisitioned cars and in the first light of day sped towards the frontier, which the Army at this time was due to cross.

That left "Granite" with only nine gliders still flying. Sooner than expected the searchlight marked the end of the line of beacons came into view ahead. Situated on the Vetschauer Berg north-west of Aachen-Laurensberg, it also marked the point at which the gliders were to unhitch. After that they would reach the Maastricht salient in a glide, their approach unbetrayed by the noise of the towing aircraft's engines.

But in fact they were ten minutes too early. The following wind had proved stronger than the met. men had predicted, and for this reason they had also not reached the pre-ordained height of 8,500 feet, which would enable them to fly direct to their target at a gliding angle of one in twelve. Now they were some 1,500 feet too low. Lieutenant Schacht, leader of "Concrete" detachment, wrote in his operations report: "For some undisclosed reason the towing squadron brought us further on over Dutch territory. Only when we were some way between the frontier and Maastricht did we unhitch."

Obviously the idea was to bring the gliders up to something like the decreed altitude. But if this move contributed to the security of the force in one way, it certainly hazarded it in another. For now the droning of the Junkers engines alerted the Dutch and Belgian defence.

The time was shortly after 05.00 hours--nearly half an hour still before Hitler's main offensive against the West was due to open. Though eight to ten minutes ahead of time owing to the wind, the gliders needed, in fact, another twelve to fourteen to bring them over the target. At five minutes before zero hour these silent birds of prey were to swoop down amongst the pillboxes of the Canal bridges and the fortress . . . before any other shot was fired. But now the element of surprise seemed to have been lost.

At last the gliders were set free, and the noise of their mother aircraft died away in the distance. But the Dutch flak was now on its toes, and opened fire on the gliders before they reached Maastricht. The little red balls came up like toys, amongst which the pilots dodged about in avoiding action, happy that they had sufficient height to do so. None was hit, but the long and carefully guarded secret of their existence was now irrevocably exposed.

As long ago as 1932 the Rhön-Rossitten-Gesellschaft had constructed a wide wing-span glider designed for making meteorological measurements at high altitude. The following year, taken over by the newly established German Institute for Gliding Research (DFS) at Darmstadt-Griesheim, this flying observatory--known as "Obs"--was used for the first gliding courses under Peter Riedel, Will Hubert, and Heini Dittmar. It was tested for the first time in tow by Hanna Reitsch, later to become one of the world's best known women pilots, behind a Ju 52.

Ernst Udet soon got wind of the project and went to inspect the "Obs" at Darmstadt. He at once recognised a possible military application. Could not large gliders like this be used for bringing up supplies to the front line, or in support of a unit that had become surrounded? Perhaps it could even operate as a kind of modern Trojan horse by landing soldiers unnoticed behind the enemy's back.

Udet, in 1933, was still a civilian, and not yet a member of the new camouflaged Luftwaffe. But he informed his comrade of World War I, Ritter von Greim, about the "Obs," and shortly afterwards the Institute received a contract to build a military version. The prototype, under the designation DFS 230, duly emerged under the direction of engineer Hans Jacobs. The "assault glider" of World War II fame was thus already born.

Series production started in 1937 at the Gothaer vehicle factory. Its wings were high-set and braced, its box-shaped fuselage was of steel covered with canvas, and its undercarriage jettisonable: the landing was made on a stout central skid. This was another mark of Udet's influence: as early as the twenties he had made some venturesome landings on Alpine glaciers with a ski-undercarriage.

The unladen weight of the assault glider was only 16 cwt, and nearly 18 cwt could be loaded--equivalent of ten men plus their weapons.

By autumn 1938 Major-General Student's top-secret airborne force included a small glider-assault commando under Lieutenant Kiess. Tests had shown that such a method of surprise attack on a well-defended point had a better chance of success than parachute troops. In the latter case not only was surprise betrayed by the noise of the transport aircraft's engines, but even if the troops jumped from the minimum height of three hundred feet they still swayed defencelessly in the air for fifteen seconds. Further, even the minimum time of seven seconds to get clear of the aircraft spread them out on the ground over a distance of about 300 yards. Precious minutes were then lost freeing themselves of their parachutes, reassembling, and finding their weapon containers.

With gliders, on the other hand, surprise was complete thanks to their uncannily silent approach. Well-trained pilots could put them down within twenty yards of any point. The men were out in no time through the broad hatch at the side, complete with weapons, and formed a compact combat group from the start. The only restrictions were that the landing had to await first light, and the area had to be know in advance.

It was this dictate of time that nearly caused the whole Albert Canal and Eben Emael operations to miscarry. For the Army supreme commander proposed to launch the opening attack of the western campaign at 03.00 hours, in darkness. Against this Koch argued that his detachment must make its own assault at least simultaneously with the main one, and preferably a few minutes earlier. And before dawn this was impossible.

At that point Hitler himself intervened and fixed zero hour at "sunrise minus 30 minutes." Numerous test flights had shown that to be the earliest moment at which the glider pilots would have enough visibility.

So it was that the whole German Army had to take its time from a handful of "adventurers" who had the presumption to suppose that they could subdue one of the world's most impregnable fortresses from the air.

At 03.10 hours on May 10th the field telephone jangled at the command post of Major Jottrand, who was in charge of the Eben Emael fortifications. The 7th Belgian Infantry Division, holding the Albert Canal sector, imposed an increased state of alert. Jottrand ordered his 1,200-strong garrison to action stations. Sourly, for the umpteenth time, men stared out from the gun turrets into the night, watching once again for the German advance.

For two hours all remained still. But then, as the new day dawned, there came from the direction of Maastricht in Holland the sound of concentrated anti-aircraft fire. On Position No. 29, on the south-east boundary of the fortress, the Belgian bombardiers raised their own anti-aircraft weapons. Were the German bombers on the way? Was the fortress their objective? Listen as they might, the men could hear no sound of engines.

Suddenly from the east great silent phantoms were swooping down. Low already, they seemed to be about to land: three, six, nine of them. Lowering the barrels of their guns, the Belgians let fly. But next moment one of the "great bats" was immediately over them--no, right amongst them!

Corporal Lange set his glider down right on the enemy position, severing a machine-gun with one wing and dragging it along. With a tearing crunch the glider came to rest. As the door flew open, Sergeant Haug, in command of Section 5, loosed off a burst from his machine-pistol, and hand-grenades pelted into the position. The Belgians held up their hands.

Three men of Haug's section scampered across the intervening hundred yards towards Position 23, an armoured gun turret. Within one minute all the remaining nine gliders had landed at their appointed spots in the face of machine-gun fire from every quarter, and the men had sprung out to fulfill their appointed duties.

Section 4's glider struck the ground hard about 100 yards from Position 19, an anti-tank and machine-gun emplacement with embrasures facing north and south. Noting that the latter were closed, Sergeant Wenzel ran directly up to them and flung a 2-lb. charge through the periscope aperture in the turret. The Belgian machine-guns chattered blindly into the void. Thereupon Wenzel's men fixed their secret weapon, a 100-lb. hollow charge, on the observation turret and ignited it. But the armour was too thick for the charge to penetrate: the turret merely became seamed with small cracks, as in dry earth. Finally they blew an entry through the embrasures, finding all weapons destroyed and the gunners dead.

Eighty yards farther to the north Sections 6 and 7 under Corporals Harlos and Heinemann had been "sold a dummy." Positions 15 and 16--especially strong ones according to the air pictures--just did not exist. Their "15-foot armoured cupolas" were made of tin. These sections would have been much more useful further south. There all hell had broken loose at Position 25, which was merely an old tool shed used as quarters. The Belgians within it rose to the occasion better than those behind armour, spraying the Germans all round with machine-gun fire. One casualty was Corporal Unger, leader of Section 8, which had already blown up the twin-gun cupola of Position 31.

Sections 1 and 3, under N.C.O.s Niedermeier and Arent, put out of action the six guns of artillery casements 12 and 18. Within ten minutes of "Granite" detachment's landing ten positions had been destroyed or badly crippled. But though the fortress had lost most of its artillery, it had not yet fallen. The pillboxes set deep in the boundary walls and cuttings could not be got at from above. Observing correctly that there were only some seventy Germans on the whole plateau, the Belgian commander, Major Jottrand, ordered adjoining artillery batteries to open fire on his own fort.

As a result the Germans had themselves to seek cover in the positions they had already subdued. Going over to defence, they had to hold on till the German Army arrived. At 08.30 there was an unexpected occurrence when an additional glider swooped down and landed hard by Position 19, in which Sergeant Wenzel had set up the detachment command post. Out sprang First-Lieutenant Witzig. the replacement Ju 52 he had ordered had succeeded in towing his glider off the meadow near Cologne, and now he could belatedly take charge.

There was still plenty to do. Recouping their supplies of explosives from containers now dropped by Heinkel 111s, the men turned again to the gun positions which had not previously been fully dealt with. 2-lb. charges now tore the barrels apart. Sappers penetrated deep inside the positions and blew up the connecting tunnels. Others tried to reach the vital Position 17, set in the 120-foot wall commanding the canal, by suspending charges on cords.

Meanwhile hours passed, as the detachment waited in vain for the Army relief force, Engineer Battalion 51. Witzig was in radio contact both with its leader, Lieutenant-Colonel Mikosch, and with his own chief, Captain Koch at the Vroenhoven bridgehead. Mikosch could only make slow progress. The enemy had successfully blown the Maastricht bridges and indeed the one over the Albert Canal at Kanne--the direct connection between Maastricht and Eben Emael. It had collapsed at the very moment "Iron" detachment's gliders approached to land.

On the other hand the landings at Vroenhoven and Veldwezelt had succeeded, and both bridges were intact in the hands of the "Concrete" and "Steel" detachments. Throughout the day all three bridgeheads were under heavy Belgian fire. But they held--not least thanks to the covering fire provided by the 88-mm batteries of Flak Battalion "Aldinger" and constant attacks by the old Henschel Hs 123s of II/LG 2 and Ju 87s of StG 2.

In the course of the afternoon these three detachments were at last relieved by forward elements of the German Army. Only "Granite" at Eben Emael had still to hang on right through the night. By 07.00 the following morning an assault party of the engineer battalion had fought its way through and was greeted with loud rejoicing. At noon the remaining fortified positions were assaulted, then at 13.15 the notes of a trumpet rose above the din. It came from Position 3 at the entrance gate to the west. An officer with a flag of truce appeared, intimating that the commander, Major Jottrand, now wished to surrender.

Eben Emael had fallen. 1,200 Belgian soldiers emerged into the light of day from the underground passages and gave themselves up. In the surface positions they had lost twenty men. The casualties of "Granite" detachment numbered six dead and twenty wounded.

One story remains to be told. The Ju 52s, having shed the gliders of "Assault Detachment Koch", returned to Germany and dropped their towing cables at a prearranged collection point. Then they turned once more westwards to carry out their second mission. Passing high over the battlefield of Eben Emael they flew on deep into Belgium. Then, twenty-five miles west of the Albert Canal they descended. Their doors opened and 200 white mushrooms went sailing down from the sky. As soon as they reached the ground, the sound of battle could be heard. For better or worse the Belgians had turned to confront the new enemy in their rear.

But for once the Germans did not attack. On reaching them the Belgians discovered the reason: the "paratroops" lay still entangled in their 'chutes. They were not men at all, but straw dummies in German uniform armed with self-igniting charges of explosive to imitate the sound of firing. As a decoy raid, it certainly contributed to the enemy's confusion.

The Blood-Bath of Crete

The plan of campaign for spring, 1941, had been fixed in autumn, 1940. As soon as weather conditions permitted, in May, the offensive against the Soviet Union was to be launched.

But Hitler underestimated the ambition of his Italian brother-in-arms, Mussolini. German measures in the Balkans--especially the dispatch of a "military mission" to Rumania to guard that country against Russian enterprises and at the same time provide a spring-board for a German advance to the east--had severely vexed the Italian leader.

"Hitler keeps confronting me with accomplished facts!" he burst out to his foreign minister, Count Ciano. "This time I shall pay him back in his own coin: when I have marched against Greece he will only learn about it from the newspapers!"

He began his venture on October 29, 1940, and just one day later the British occupied Crete--the key position in the eastern Mediterranean. For Hitler it was bad news. On November 20th he wrote to Mussolini and "with the warm heart of a friend" loaded him with reproaches. British bases in Greece would represent a threat to his southern flank. Above all he feared for the Rumanian oil fields of Ploesti, so indispensable for Germany, and now within range of British bombers. He hardly dared, he added, to think about the consequences.

He would, he complained, have asked the Duce "not to take this action without a previous, lightning occupation of Crete, and to this end I wanted to bring you practical proposals--namely, to employ a German paratroop division, and in airborne division."

Thus the possibility of capturing Crete from the air was already under consideration in November 1940. Six months later the thought was put into action. For the Italian offensive was halted almost as soon as it began. In March 1941 British army and air force units gained a foothold on the Greek mainland, but on April 6th Germany attacked Jugoslavia and Greece, and within a few weeks had overrun both countries. By the beginning of May German troops had everywhere reached the Aegean and Mediterranean coasts.

Only Crete still lay ahead, walling in the lesser Greek islands and barring the way to the outer Mediterranean. To this island bastion, 150 miles long and about twenty broad, the British had withdrawn from the mainland. They were resolved to hold on to it.

Let us turn back to April 15th, when the Balkan campaign was at its height. As twice before, in Poland and in France, the *Stukas* and other close-support formations of VIII Air Corps under General Freiherr von Richthofen were hammering breaches in the enemy's defence lines.

On this particular day the chief of *Luftflotte* 4, Air General Alexander Löhr, responsible for operations in the south-east, had an audience with his supreme commander. Goering had set up his headquarters at Semmering in Austria, and listened attentively as Löhr put forward the suggestion of concluding the Balkan campaign with a large-scale operation against Crete by the parachute and airborne units of XI Air Corps.

Five days later, on April 20th, Lieutenant-General Kurt Student, the creator of the airborne forces himself went to see Goering and filled in the details of the plan. For Student, badly wounded at Rotterdam, had after his convalescence at once taken over the newly formed XI Air Corps, which embraced the whole airborne organisation, including the transport units.

Goering's reaction was to send Student, with the Luftwaffe's chief of general staff, Jeschonnek, to the Führer's HQ at Mönichkirchen. That was on April 21st, the day on which the Greeks capitulated to Field-Marshal List's 12th Army. Hitler merely drew attention to the fact that he himself had considered an airborne landing on Crete the previous autumn.

Since then the situation had changed for the worse, and time was now pressing. Apart from the fact that the Balkan campaign had itself postponed the attack on Russia by four weeks--from May to June--every incidental theatre of war had the effect of dissipating German military strength. Not only had the Germans been obliged to go to the help of the Italians in North Africa, but they had also sent X Air Corps to Sicily to support them against the British Mediterranean fleet and Malta.

However, despite the fact that the chief of the armed forces, Field-Marshal Keitel, and his staff recommended that the paratroops would be better occupied in the conquest of Malta--a British base which they considered more important and dangerous--Hitler still gave priority to Crete. He viewed its subjugation as the "crowning glory" of the Balkan campaign. It would be a spring-board against North Africa, the Suez Canal and the whole of the eastern Mediterranean, all of which the Luftwaffe would be able to control. He made just two conditions:

1. The forces of XI Air Corps--one paratroop and one airborne division--must suffice for the operation.

2. Despite the short time in which to prepare, the operation must be launched by the middle of May.

General Student wasted little time considering the matter. He was convinced that his formations could achieve their objective; and Hitler thought so too. After four days Mussolini also agreed, and finally on April 25th Hitler issued his Directive No. 28 for "Operation Mercury"--the capture of Crete.

At their home bases in Germany the paratroop regiments were suddenly alerted. They had just twenty days to get ready for the biggest airborne operation in history. Would they make it?

Difficulties mounted, first in the matter of transport. Major-General Eugen Meindl's Assault Regiment had 220 lorries too few, so the majority had to go by train. After several days they reached Arad and Craiova in Rumania, from where they journeyed another 1,000 miles by road to their base of operations near Athens. For three whole days the "Flying Dutchman"--the cover name for XI Air Corps' column of 4,000 vehicles--was brought to a standstill in the Macedonian mountains. The reason was that 2 *Panzer* Division, returning from Greece, had priority at the narrow passes of Verria and Kosani. For Hitler had expressly ordered that troop concentrations for "Operation Barbarossa" (against Russia) were not to be delayed by the transports for "Mercury" proceeding in the other direction.

The inadequate road system also brought 22 (Airborne) Division--which, with the paratroop force, had a year earlier been committed against Holland--to a halt in Rumania. The Army declared itself in no position to help the division get south. In its place the supreme command put Lieutenant-General Ringel's 5 Mountain Division, already in Greece, under Student's command. Although this was an *élite* force, which had just broken through the Metaxas Line, it had hardly been trained for an air landing in the midst of enemy defences.

On May 14th the last of the paratroops finally reached their appointed base near Athens. These were 1 and 2 Companies of the Assault Regiment, which in the course of organising rail transit for the rest of it, had been temporarily forgotten about. They themselves had had to push all the way from Hildesheim in north Germany by road.

The aircraft units likewise had a struggle to get ready in time for the event. For "Operation Mercury" the air commander, Major-General Gerhard, had ten "*Kampfgruppen* zbV", comprising some 500 Ju 52s, at his disposal. But most of them had during the Balkan campaign been daily engaged in lifting ammunition and supplies, and now both airframes and engines urgently required overhaul.

On May 1st the whole fleet flew off to the north. Dozens of maintenance centres--from Brunswick, Fürstenwalde and Cottbus in Germany to Prague and Brno in Czechoslovakia and Aspern and Zwölfaxing in Austria--dropped all other work to devote themselves to the "good old aunts" of the Luftwaffe, the Ju 52s. By the 15th 493 of them, completely overhauled and many with new engines, had re-landed at bases in the Athens area. It was a masterpiece of organisation and technical achievement.

A second problem, however, was the airfields. The few that had metalled runways, like Eleusis near Athens, were already occupied by the bomber units of VIII Air Corps. There remained only small and neglected fields of sand.

"They are nothing but deserts!" the commander of KG zbV 2, Colonel Rüdiger von Heyking, bitterly reported. "Heavy-laden aircraft will sink up to their axles."

Heyking had the misfortune to be based with his 150-odd Ju 52s of *Gruppen* 60, 101 and 102, at Topolia, on an airfield which an overenthusiastic Army officer had had ploughed up after its occupation "to make it more level." The consequence was that every take-off and landing produced a quite frightful cloud of dust, which rose to 3,000 feet and blotted out the sun. In the course of a rehearsal, von Heyking worked out that after a squadron take-off it took seventeen minutes before one could again see one's own hand and a second squadron could follow.

Conditions were hardly better at the neighbouring airfield of Tanagra, where zbV *Gruppen* 40 and 105 and I *Gruppe* of Air-Landing *Geschwader* 1, under Colonel Buchholz, were based. The remaining four transport *Gruppen* lay at Dadion, Megara and Corinth--their airfields likewise of sand.

But the worst bottle-neck was fuel. To transport the chief combatants to Crete would require three successive flights by the 493 aircraft, and that meant some 650,000 gallons of petrol. Brought by tanker to Piraeus, the port of Athens, it then had to be transferred to forty-five gallon barrels, and finally transported by lorries to the remote airfields. For nothing like a regular ground organisation existed on them.

By May 17th not a single barrel had arrived--because the tanker, on its way from Italy, was blocked in the Corinth Canal. On April 26th parachuted sappers and two battalions of infantry had captured the bridge over this canal intact. But then a British anti-aircraft shell happened to strike the demolition charge after it had been removed, and the resulting explosion flung the bridge to the canal bottom, thus blocking the tanker's passage. XI Air Corps' quarter-master, Lieutenant-Colonel Seibt, had divers flown out from Kiel, and finally on May 17th the waterway was cleared. Next day at Piraeus, the time-consuming process of transferring the fuel into barrels began in feverish haste.

Thus the attack, already postponed till May 18th, was delayed another two days. Even at midnight on the 19th/20th, five hours before take-off, a few Ju 52 squadrons were still unfuelled, and the paratroops--who should have been sleeping--had themselves to lend a hand to roll the barrels to the planes. The tanks of each one had then to be filled painstakingly by hand-pump.

During the night water wagons sprayed the airfields in a vain attempt to lay the dust. The wind direction changed to 180 degrees, and in the darkness the aircraft had to be regrouped at the opposite ends. Finally, at 04.30, the first heavily laden machines rolled over the sand and disappeared into the darkness. With the airfields choking in dust, it took over an hour for the *Gruppen* to assemble overhead and fly off southwards.

The first attacking wave--1 Battalion of the Assault Regiment--was carried in 53 gliders, as at Eben Emael and the Albert Canal. All the rest, some 5,000 men, had to jump--from 400 feet--right amongst the alerted enemy. They could expect no reinforcements until the afternoon. As for the plane crews, they would not know till they got back whether they would find enough fuel at their airfields to transport the second wave.

May 20 1941, 07.05 hours. The bombardment had been in progress for an hour. Squadron after squadron of the Luftwaffe had been going down on a single point of western Crete: the village of Malemes, with its small coastal airfield and Hill107, which commanded the approaches.

First it was bombers: Do 17s of KG 2 and He 111s of II/KG 26. *Stukas* of StG 2 followed with howling dive-bomber attacks. Then fighters of JG 77 and ZG 26 came streaking low over the hills and down along the beach, shooting up the known anti-aircraft and infantry positions.

The men entrenched against them were New Zealanders of 5 Brigade's 22nd Battalion, with other battalions close behind the village--altogether 11,859 men under Brigadier Puttick. They knew just what their enemy was up to. An airborne landing had been expected, with Malemes as one of the three target areas. Never before had British Intelligence been so well informed about a German military plan. Surprise was out of the question.

As the air bombardment ended there was a sudden silence, broken only by a relatively peaceful sound of soughing and crackling, like trees being felled. Great fat birds dropped from the sky, gliding in almost noiselessly, then splintering on hitting the ground. They came dipping into the Tavronitis valley behind Hill 107. One banked steeply down, nearly hit an enemy position, struck the ground with a crack, bounced and went jolting over the rocky terrain. Then ten men inside were thrown forward by the impact. Then, after a final thud that tore open the side of the fuselage, the glider lay still in a cloud of dust, and the occupants rushed for cover to a near-by patch of stunted bush.

That was how, at 07.15, Major Walter Koch landed beside Hill 107 with the battalion staff of 1 Airborne Assault Regiment. Other gliders sailed over their heads, most of them too high. Since unhitching over the sea seven minutes earlier, their pilots had been obliged to steer into the rising sun. Wrapped in early mist, the island dissolved before their eyes and visibility was impaired still more by the smoke of the immediately preceding bombardment. Suddenly they saw Malemes airfield already below them, with their objective, the dry river bed, just beyond. They were

300 or even 600 feet too high, and had to drop steeply down, banking to avoid being carried too far south. Some turned earlier, some later, with the result that they landed far apart instead of together, and many were dashed to pieces on the rocky ground.

Major Koch looked around him in surprise. The terrain was far more hilly than he had supposed--a feature indeterminable from the aerial photographs. The gliders vanished over the summits and landed in a whole series of depressions. Individual sections of troops were thus out of visual touch with each other. To present an effective fighting force they had to unite, but were held down by the enemy's well-directed fire. Each section was thrown on its own resources.

Nevertheless a handful of men, with the battalion staff, stormed the New Zealanders' tented camp on either side of Hill 107. It was studded with bomb craters made by the *Stukas*. According to the German operations plan the enemy was to be "surprised in his tents and prevented from interfering with the airborne landing." But there was no surprise: the camp had been evacuated. They moved on to the Hill, the ultimate target. From there the Germans, instead of the New Zealanders, would command the airfield.

Seconds later they were met by a concentration of fire from close at hand. Major Koch was shot in the head. Officers and men fell, killed or badly wounded. The survivors clawed into the ground, unable to advance another step. The whole terrace-like slope was sown with well-camouflaged defence posts, not a hint of which had been revealed by air reconnaissance.

The Assault Regiment's 3 Company was more successful. Its gliders landed right on the stony, dried up river bed, and within seconds the anti-aircraft positions on either side of its mouth were under fire from many directions. The company commander, First-Lieutenant von Plessen, stormed the western position with one party, while another went for the guns to the east. The surviving New Zealanders put up their hands.

Immediately afterwards dozens of Ju 52 transporters came droning over the coast. At hardly 400 feet, and with engines throttled back, they were as easy to hit as hay-stacks. But the guns were silent, and after the air crews had returned to their Greek bases there was rejoicing at the small losses the first invasion wave had suffered. They owed a debt to the assault units, who had captured the guns so swiftly.

Meanwhile 3 Company had proceeded to the airfield itself. Here the enemy again put up stiff resistance, and the Germans were forced to take cover. Von Plessen tried to make contact with Major Koch, but was halted by a burst of machine-gun fire.

But all the time paratroops were dropping from the transport machines. In a few minutes hundreds of them had reached the ground to the west and east of Malemes. They comprised the rest of Major-General Meindl's Assault Regiment, whose 3 and 4 Companies had landed fifteen minutes ahead in the gliders. Their objective was the airfield, for until one of Crete's three airfields was in German hands, the transports would be unable to land reinforcements--reinforcements that the paratroops would be urgently needing at latest by the second day of the battle.

All this was known to the defenders. Major-General Sir Bernard Freyberg, New Zealand's gallant veteran soldier, who since the withdrawal from Greece had been the Allied commander in Crete, had a force of some 42,000 men--British, Greeks, Australians and New Zealanders-- for the most part in the fortified hill positions adjoining the airfields of Malemes, Rethymnon and Herakleion. At Malemes, especially, the New Zealanders had been practicing defence against airborne landings for weeks. For since the paratroop *coup* at Corinth on April 26th, and the feverish preparations on the Greek airfields--reported in detail to British Intelligence--there was no longer any doubt at General Wavell's Headquarters at Cairo that Crete was the next target for German airborne attack.

Though the heavy bomber and dive-bomber raids of the last few days- -and above all the bombardment that immediately preceded the landings- -had caused losses and pinned the defenders down, most of the positions had escaped simply because they remained quite undetected from the air. The strength of the New Zealanders was virtually unimpaired, as the German paratroops were to discover to their cost.

At 07.20 III Battalion, under Major Scherber, was dropped east of Malemes. From there, after assembling they were to advance against the village and airfield. Their fifty-three transporters, however, steered somewhat further inland so that the men, whose point of landing was the beach, would not be blown out to sea on their parachutes. As a result their descent was made over hilly terrain, supposedly free of the enemy. But it turned out that these hills too were dotted with gun-posts.

The consequences were frightful. Many of the parachutists were mortally hit while still swinging helplessly in the air. Others were left hanging in trees or were injured on striking rocks. The survivors, pinned down by the furious curtain of fire, were unable to reach their weapon containers, parachuted separately. Most of these fell into enemy hands.

Within an hour all III Battalion's officers were either dead or badly wounded. Only individual sections, led mainly by N.C.O.s, managed to hold out in favourable terrain. The whole day long they crouched in scorching heat, wearing the same heavy battle-dress they had used amongst the snow and ice of Narvik. Without water, and with only a few rounds of ammunition apiece, they hung on, hopefully awaiting the night.

When it came, the residue of 9 Company fought their way westwards right through the enemy lines till they reached the Tavronitis valley. Other groups held out for two and three days, until at last they were relieved.

"The bulk of III Battalion," read the Assault Regiment's operations report, "was wiped out after brave resistance. Out of 600 paratroops nearly 400, including their commander, Major Scherber, were killed."

The envelopment of Malemes from the east had failed. Its vital airfield could now only be taken by an attack from the west. There, west of the Tavronitis, II and IV Battalions were dropped, together with the regimental staff. They had more luck, because here the enemy's prepared positions were not occupied. Perhaps the unexpected arrival of the gliders had discouraged the New Zealanders from doing so.

At 07.30 hours nine further gliders sailed down to the bed of the valley and landed close to the only bridge by which the east-west coast road spanned the Tavronitis. Although most of them cracked up on impact, their occupants leapt out and rushed the bridge. Machine-guns hammered forth from the adjacent slopes and the detachment's leader, Major Braun, fell dead. But others reached their objective, and tearing out the demolition charges, secured the crossing.

From now on Major-General Meindl was in a position to direct his forces as they closed up from the west. Captain Walter Gericke, with a hastily gathered task force, advanced against the airfield. But under the searing machine-fun fire from Hill 107, progress was only possible in short rushes.

Somewhere on the slopes of the Hill Major Koch's force, which had landed first by glider, must lie entrenched. But where? To make contact General Meindl raised himself from cover and held aloft a signal flag. He hoped for an answer from the tented camp, where he supposed Koch to be. But it was the enemy that answered: Meindl's hand was hit by a New Zealand sharpshooter, and immediately afterwards he collapsed wounded from a burst of machine-gun fire. Nevertheless, he still kept command, and while Gericke's force attacked the crucial airfield frontally, he instructed Major Stentzler, with elements of II Battalion, to do so from the south.

Yard by yard, and with heavy losses, the Germans won ground. But on the airfield's western boundary, with their target in full view, they could go no further. The enemy was too strong.

Apart from "Force West" at Malemes, the invasion's first wave early on May 20th also included "Force Centre", whose objective was the Cretan administrative capital, Canea. This was to be led by Lieutenant-General Wilhelm Süssmann, commander of 7 Air Division. But the general never arrived in Crete. Twenty minutes after taking off from Eleusis, near Athens, the five towed gliders containing the divisional staff were overtaken by a Heinkel 111. The bomber passed so close to the general's glider that the towing cable parted from the force of its slip-stream. the lightly -built craft, which since the Corinth operation had stood unprotected from the torrid heat, reared upwards and its over-strained wings came off. The fuselage spiraled down and crashed to pieces on the rocky island of Aegina, not far from Athens. So perished the divisional leader and several staff officers before the Cretan operation had even started.

As at Malemes, the first two companies to land at Canea did so by glider, with the mission of capturing the known anti-aircraft positions. But 2 Company, under Captain Gustav Altmann, was met by heavy fire of every calibre even on the approach to its objective, the peninsula of Akroterion. Three or four gliders crashed and the rest landed far apart. So dispersed, the company failed to carry out its mission.

Five other gliders carrying 1 Company, under First-Lieutenant Alfred Genz, reached the ground close to a battery south of Canea. After some bitter close combat the fifty paratroops overcame 180 British and rushed the guns. But they failed to take the Allied command radio station, only a few hundred yards farther on.

Yet another three gliders, under First-Lieutenant Rudolf Toschka, landed in the middle of Canea, and fought their way to the anti-aircraft position there. Then they went to ground, keeping in touch by means of a portable radio with Paratroop Regiment 3, dropped some two miles west of them, and hoping hourly for relief. In answer to their appeals the regiment's I Battalion, under Captain Friedrich-August von der Heydte, managed to get to within 1,000 yards of their surrounded colleagues, then had to withdraw in the face of overwhelming fire-power. From their commanding position at Galtos New Zealanders bloodily repulsed all German attacks directed towards the capital, and British tanks came up in support. Soon I Battalion was fighting for its life.

Major Derpa's II Battalion was likewise repulsed with heavy loss while the companies of III Battalion under Major Heilmann were broken up almost to the point of extinction. The situation compelled the regimental commander, Colonel Richard Heidrich, to radio Genz's little force in Canea: "Try to get through to us under cover of darkness."

There was no longer any question of taking the capital or the neighbouring Suda Bay.

At Athens the staff of XI Air Corps waited in vain for information, and was quite ignorant about the failures both at Malemes and Canea. General Student could only suppose that "Operation Mercury" had fulfilled expectations. The sole reports to hand were those of the returning transport units, and these sounded favourable: "Paratroops dropped according to plan."

Only seven of the 493 Ju 52s carrying the first wave of invasion troops had failed to return, Many of the rest, however, had been compelled to circle their home airfields for up to two hours before they could get down. They had to do so individually through the impenetrable clouds of dust, and the whole thing became a shambles. Planes repeatedly collided on the ground, blocking the way for others. The dust took a greater toll than all the anti-aircraft guns of Crete.

Corps HQ repeated the call-signs of the regiment in Crete again and again, without response. At noon, nevertheless, an airfield servicing team set off for Malemes, where Major Snowatzki was to take over the organisation. As his Ju 52 circled around, the major spotted a swastika flag on the western perimeter, marking the furthest advance of the German forces. He thought, however, that it indicated Malemes had been taken, and ordered his pilot to land. As the machine came in, it became the target for concentrated enemy fire. Its pilot immediately gave full throttle, veered off and managed to get clear. With his aircraft riddled by shots he then flew Snowatzki back to Athens, where for the first time General Student learnt something of the true situation.

At almost the same moment a feeble radio message came through from "Force Central" to the effect that the attack on Canea had been repulsed with heavy loss. But it was 16.15 before the regimental staff at Malemes reported. There the 200- and 80-watt transmitters, brought over by glider, had been destroyed by the crash landings in the Tavronitis river bed. Laboriously the signals officer, First-Lieutenant Göttsche, had created a new one out of undamaged parts.

XI Air Corps' satisfaction at being at last in radio contact with Malemes was soon dissipated by the news that it brought. The first message informed HQ that General Meindl was badly wounded, and the second one read: "Waves of enemy armour from Malemes attacking over airfield and river bed." It seemed the crisis had reached its height. But worse was to come.

According to the plan of operations Rethymnon and Herakleion were to be taken in the afternoon of May 20th by the second invasion wave consisting of Parachute Regiments 1 and 2 under Colonels Alfred Sturm and Bruno Brauer. But now Student delayed their start. After such unfavourable reports from the first wave in the west of the island, it seemed better to throw in reinforcements there. But it was too late. Such a sudden change of objective was bound to have catastrophic consequences.

At the Greek bases there was enough confusion already. The second wave was due to take off at 13.00, but most of the transport units were still not ready. The impenetrable dust, the searing heat, the manifold damage and the laborious refueling from barrels, had all been very time-consuming. Colonel von Heyking, commander of the transport *Geschwader* at Topolia, saw disaster looming, and tried to get the start delayed by two hours. But he failed to get through: the telephone lines were out of order. The over-taxed staff at Corps HQ had the same idea, but was simply unable to pass the new take-off times to all the affected units.

So it happened that bombers, *Stukas* and long-range fighters set about the bombardment of Rethymnon and Herakleion at the original zero hour before many of the transport units had even taken off from their Greek airfields. Moreover the latter failed to follow in ordered sequence. Squadrons and even sections flew singly, bringing in the paratroops piecemeal and without cohesion. The intention of dropping them *en masse* directly after the bombardment was thus thwarted.

"Once more we found ourselves flying south over the sea," reported Major Reinhard Wenning, commander of zbV *Gruppe* 105, one of the few transport units that had left at the original time. "According to plan we should have been meeting preceding planes as they returned. But there was no sign of them."

Reaching Herakleion, Wenning's transport *Gruppe* flew parallel with the coast, and the "dropping" officer put out his yellow flag, the signal to jump, and down went the paratroops. Wenning continued: "Our battalion was supposed to act as a reserve behind other units already dropped. But on the ground we could see no trace of these. All alone, our men encountered savage enemy fire."

Only on its return flight did his *Gruppe* meet other Ju 52 formations, and the last of them arrived no less than three-and-a-half hours after the first. The second "wave" had broken up into a series of ripples. As a result, the paratroops suffered heavy losses. Just west of Herakleion airfield British tanks advanced firing at the Germans as they floated down. Within twenty minutes three whole companies of II Battalion/FJR 1, under Captain Dunz, were wiped out. Neither Herakleion nor Retimo was captured, and their two airfields remained in British hands.

But though the Allied C.-in-C., General Freyberg, had some cause to rejoice, his report betrayed anxiety: "Today has been a hard one. We have been hard pressed. So far, I believe, we hold aerodromes at Rethymnon, Herakleion, and Malemes, and the two harbours. The margin by which we hold them is a bare one, and it would be wrong of me to paint an optimistic picture. . . ."

Freyberg's pessimism was soon to be justified.

In the evening the German paratroops, despite all their losses, won their first, and decisive, success. Two detachments of the Assault Regiment-- one led by First-Lieutenant Horst Trebes, the other by the regimental physician, *Oberstabsarzt* Dr. Heinrich Neumann--resumed the assault on the dominant Hill 107 at Malemes, and fought their way with pistols and hand-grenades to its summit.

"Fortunately for us," Dr. Neumann reported, "the New Zealanders did not counter-attack. We were so short of ammunition that, had they done so, we should have had to fight them off with stones and sheath-knives."

General Freyberg in fact missed his chance that night of turning the tables at Malemes. Next morning it was too late, for by then VIII Air Corps' *Stukas* and fighters, in full command of the air over Crete, were pinning down the New Zealand troops in low-level attacks. The vital Hill 107 remained in German hands.

That morning, May 21st, a section of Ju 52s came in west of Malemes to make a landing. On board was "Special Detail Captain Kleye", with fresh ammunition for the Assault Regiment, whose original supply was fully spent. With the airfield swept by enemy artillery fire, the aircraft had to land on the beach. At the controls of the leading plane sat Sergeant Grünert. He looked down: the beach was studded with rocks. Then, spotting a gap, he dropped his plane into it, put down hard, and with the sand helping to brake, came to rest just short of the rocks. The ammunition, without which the assault on Malemes was doomed to failure, had been saved.

General Student was now resolved to pit all remaining reinforcements against Malemes. This same day the landing of the Mountain Division must begin--cost what it might.

At about 16.00 the first transport squadrons started to land under fire on the narrow runway. Shells from the enemy artillery burst amongst the aircraft. One Ju 52 immediately went up in flames, other sagged with broken undercarriages. But more and more came swooping down, landed and discharged their troops. By the evening Buchholz's transport *Geschwader* had brought in the whole of Mountain Regiment 100, under Colonel Utz--shells providing their baptism of fire even as they landed.

"Malemes was like the gate of hell," reported the divisional commander, Lieutenant-General Ringel. Of every three transporters the enemy succeeded in hitting one, either setting it on fire, or shearing off a wing. Major Snowatzki had the wrecks cleared from the single runway by means of a captured British tank. Soon the sides of the airfield had become a giant aircraft cemetery, containing the remains of eighty Ju 52s.

What had once been considered impossible had come to pass; the airborne landings had turned the scale. Crete was not yet conquered, but the dice were now loaded in favour of the Germans.

From Cajus Bekker, *The Luftwaffe War Diaries,* (New York: Doubleday, 1967), pp. 93-100; 184-202.

Paul Carell

A British Commando Attempt to Capture Rommel

Rommel's men considered him to be invulnerable. "No bullet has ever been forged for the Old Man," they used to say in amazement, or with a shake of the head, when he had once more sensed the danger and moved off in his armoured car just before a shell had burst. They lay in the desert muck under a hail of enemy machine-gun fire--could not even put their noses out of their slit trenches without the risk of having their heads blown off. The attack was halted, Rommel came rushing up and stood upright in the trench, shielding his eyes with his hands against the sun. "What the hell's the matter with you fellows? When things get a bit hot over there you don't have to do a belly-flop every time!" Hardly had he gone than there were casualties once more. It was always the same story. Many of the old desert foxes have told me similar stories--men who returned home with the Iron Cross and the Knight's Cross and who certainly were not scared of a bombardment. Yes, no bullet had ever been forged for Erwin Rommel.

Naturally the legend of Rommel's invulnerability ran the rounds of the front lines; prisoners carried it across to No Man's Land and the German general was soon considered invincible by the Tommies, also. Bewildered British officers took note of this mystique and reported: "Rommel's very name and legend are in the process of becoming a psychological danger to the British Army."

On the 18th June, 1941, among the routed members of the 7th Armoured Division, were our friends, Clark and Miller. How confident of victory they had been when they set out on the 15th in their Mark II. Now it was all over. In the nick of time they had slipped out of Rommel's great "bag" between Sidi Omar, Halfaya Pass and Capuzzo. It was a dispiriting retreat.

Were these Germans really invincible? Could nothing be done to defeat them? These were the thoughts that ran through the heads of the two men. And many others thought the same. Our morale is bad, was the verdict of the Staffs.

Winston Churchill reluctantly relieved Sir Archibald Wavell of his desert command. He was appointed Commander-in-Chief in India. A new man took the helm in Africa, a man with a reputation for drive and stubbornness--Sir Claude Auchinleck. Would he defeat Rommel?

That damned Rommel!

Bold strokes were at that time the order of the day. It was not surprising, therefore, that the thought of taking Rommel prisoner should have blossomed in high places.

Erwin Rommel had no idea of the dark thought harboured by his adversaries. At this particular time he was neither as invulnerable nor as self-assured as legend maintained. He was worried. How would the Africa campaign develop? On the 18th June, the day after his victory, he knew that the German attack on Russia was imminent and that this banished all hopes of his receiving generous reinforcements of armour, aircraft and fighting men.

He knew only too well that Hitler and the German General Staff persisted in thinking on European lines and had little sympathy for the African theatre of war with its great strategical possibilities. The Chief of General Staff, General Halder, held the view that it was impossible to defeat the British in North Africa. For him the North African war was merely a diversionary measure to gain time.

It has often been maintained that Rommel was a magnificent tactician, a brilliant leader of men, but no far-seeing strategist. History, however, has shown that Rommel's strategic plans were by no means fantastic--in fact they were more realistic than those of the Führer who, in the summer of 1941 in the Wolf's Lair at Rastenburg, East Prussia, directed the battles in far-off Russia like some woodland ghost.

Rommel had conceived a bold idea which he duly proposed to Hitler and the General Staff--to take Tobruk and to press on to the Suez Canal. But this was not his final objective. He would continue his advance beyond Basra to the Persian Gulf, using Syria as an occupied base and a main supply centre. Was this fantasy? Was it any more fantastic than Hitler's plan to cross the Caucasus and capture the oil fields of Baku? His plan came to grief; Rommel's plan had a much sounder basis. One need only read General Auchinleck's report, No. 38177, on the African position between November 1941 and August 1942. In this one learns the interesting fact that the British C-in-C in the Middle East actually feared the plan which was in Rommel's mind. There were no strong British forces available to defend Syria. In Iraq and Persia, on the route to the Persian Gulf, he had very weak forces at his disposal. According to Auchinleck, Cyprus could easily be taken by German paratroops. Auchinleck feared for his north flank and prayed that the German leaders would not embark upon the undertaking that Rommel desired.

But in the summer of 1941 Rommel was not only faced with the problem of grand strategy; he also had tactical difficulties. What would happen if the British attacked again? It was obvious that they would try to force a decision. They brought up everything that their ships could carry and British superiority increased day by day.

Tobruk must fall whether Hitler and the German High Command wished it or not. This was Rommel's obsession.

At this moment he received support from an unexpected quarter. It came from the Head of the German Secret Service, the Abwehr: Admiral Canaris, the man who vacillated between "resistance" and duty. Although found guilty of acts of sabotage he rendered great service to the German war leaders.

In Jerusalem Canaris had a very brilliant agent in the person of a British hospital nurse. She learned all manner of important information from wounded British soldiers. She was struck by the remarks of a trusting Englishman who was holding forth about an approaching offensive in North Africa. The sister encouraged other soldiers to discuss the matter and found reasonable confirmation of this information. Her report so impressed the Admiral that he forwarded it to Hitler and Jodl.

Rommel was also informed. His view was as follows: it was most important to take Tobruk with the greatest possible speed. After urgent telephone messages and a long telephone conversation from Rome with General Jodl, he overcame the opposition of the German High Command. As soon as permission had been given Rommel made preparations for the attack. It was to take place, if possible, at the end of October.

Thus a hospital nurse--a German agent in Jerusalem--for a brief moment directed the course of the war.

The British were actually feverishly preparing their offensive. They were dominated by the thought that Rommel must be put out of action. The brain of the German campaign in North Africa must be paralysed and Rommel must be killed or taken prisoner.

The Long Range Desert Group was a special unit created for acts of sabotage and intelligence in the desert. Its counterpart was the Brandenburgers, the German organisation to fight behind the enemy lines.

This Long Range Desert Group was composed of Commando volunteers. Its headquarters were in the caves of the Siwa Oasis and later at Kufra. From there they carried out audacious raids, several hundred miles behind the enemy lines. Outstanding actions were the attacks on German airfields which lay 350 miles behind the front. The Commandos were away for weeks on end in a few trucks, as in canoes on the high seas. They reached their objectives and destroyed nearly every bomber and fighter on the field. They blew up the petrol dumps, caused heavy casualties among the airfield staff and even took half a dozen prisoners on their long journey back to the caves of Siwa.

Suppose such fellows were used against Rommel! They could perhaps shoot the much-feared opponent in his headquarters or take him prisoner; it was merely a question of discovering Rommel's habits.

This was done in due course.

That the British Secret Service made a terrible blunder led to one of the greatest cloak-and-dagger episodes of the African war.

The Quartermaster-General of Panzer Gruppe Afrika, Major Schleusener, had made his headquarters during the German offensive preparations far behind the front in the Cyrene area. It was a historical zone. In antiquity magnificent buildings stood here, for Cyrene was once a charming Grecian settlement. Columns and temples survived until a disastrous earthquake on the Cyrenaican coast destroyed everything. In 1913, after a cloudburst, Italian soldiers found one of the most beautiful works of art in the world in a wadi--the Venus of Cyrene.

Cloudbursts gave no particular cause for surprise, for sudden heavy rainstorms are quite frequent in this region. The ruins of Cyrene stretch almost to the little Italian settlement, Beda Littoria. On a slope stood a gloomy cypress grove with a two-storied house which had served as a prefecture. Round it copses, ravines, caves and rocks . . . The Quartermaster General took up his quarters here in late August 1941.

On the 17th November an autumn gale, which had been raging for several days in the Beda Littoria area, brought a heavy downpour of rain.

The Quartermaster-General Schleusener was not at his headquarters at the time. Like his able deputy, Captain Otto, he lay in hospital at Apollonia. Schleusener had gone down with dysentery and Otto with inflammation of the lungs. Otto's adjutant, Litchwald, was also in hospital with dysentery. Acting Quartermaster-General was therefore Captain G. Weitz. Major Poeschel was acting second-in-command. A couple of dozen officers, orderlies, runners, drivers and the usual personnel to be found on a Quartermaster's staff were sitting in the gloomy building of the old prefecture listening to the rain pouring down.

Shortly before midnight they retired to the various rooms on the ground and first floors where they slept on camp beds.

There were no sentries. What was the use of posting sentries so far behind the front? An M.P. kept watch in the corridor below. His sole weapon was a bayonet. He was less a guard than a distributor of late-arriving mail. A private soldier, Matthe Boxhammer, of the Quartermaster's motorised section was on late duty in the guard tent, where he was allowed to lie down on his camp bed after midnight.

Beda Littoria, situated well behind the lines, was asleep. But in the undergrowth on the heights ghostly figures lurked. They had black-painted faces and wore British battledress. From time to time a shadow moved in the harsh light of a lightning flash. And then it was gone. The thunder growled dully and the last light of Beda Littoria went out. It was ten minutes to midnight.

The ghosts in the cypress grove had come a long journey. Two British submarines, *Torbay* and *Talisman*, had landed them on the night of 15th November in a small deserted creek on the Cyrenaican coast. These were the men who were to kill or capture Erwin Rommel twelve hours before the great British offensive was launched.

To quote Winston Churchill: "In order to strike at the brain and nerve-centre of the enemy's army at the critical moment, fifty men of the Scottish Commando, under Colonel Laycock, were carried by submarine to a point on the coast two hundred miles behind the enemy's line. The thirty who could be landed in the rough sea were formed into two parties, one to cut telephone and telegraph communications, and the other, under Lieutenant-Colonel Keyes, son of Admiral Keyes, to attack Rommel's house."

Everything had been planned in the office of Admiral of the Fleet Sir Roger Keyes. The Admiral was head of all Special Commandos and raiding parties on the British side. He was the man who in 1918 had led the bold attack by a British naval flotilla against the German U-Boat base at Ostend. In those days he blocked the entrance to the harbour with cement ships and inflicted a grievous blow on the German navy. He was eager to repeat his success in 1941.

Of the hundred officers and men who had undergone several weeks' intensive training in London, fifty-three were finally chosen. Geoffrey Keyes, Sir Roger's elder son, at that time a Major, had chosen the toughest youths he could find. His second-in-command was Captain Campbell who spoke fluent German and Arabic.

On the 15th November they landed in a storm on the coast of Cyrenaica. Huge breakers foamed over the *Torbay,* and the submarine was flung about like a box of matches. The rubber dinghy capsized several times, and each time the crew had to be fished out of the sea. Keyes then ordered the men to hold fast to the dinghy line and fight their way ashore. The maneuver was successful. Keyes, Campbell and twenty-two men at last had firm ground underfoot. Things went worse for Colonel Laycock's Commando in the submarine *Talisman.* Two men were drowned. A greater part of the contingent had to abandon their struggle with the waves from exhaustion and be taken on board again. Only seven men reached the shore, thus reducing the strength of the Commando by half. Keyes then decided to concentrate solely on the main action against Rommel.

Colonel Laycock remained behind at the landing place with three men to cover the re-embarkment after the action. The remaining three officers and twenty-five men, shivering with cold, marched for a quarter of an hour inland where a mysterious Arab awaited them. This was Lieutenant-Colonel John Haselden, a senior officer of the Long Range Desert Group, who had lived behind the German lines for some time disguised as an Arab and was one of the key figures of the British Secret Service behind Rommel's front. Haselden acted as a guide. He explained the exact position, which Keyes recorded in his handbook, and gave the latter three Arab guides. The mysterious agent had now completed his job. M15 did not wish to endanger Haselden's life by letting him take part in the action. He disappeared as silently as he had come. Keyes and his men went on their way.

On the night of 17th November, 1941, then, Keyes stood with his Commandos on a sand dune close to Beda Littoria. They took their bearings. Ahead lay the huts, and a little farther away the cypress grove. in the centre were the huge stone buildings. That was the objective. It was where Rommel slept or worked--according to the British Secret Service, and this information had been confirmed by John Haselden from Arab agents' reports. Keyes and his men fully believed this, but all of them were victims of a grotesque error. The reason is not too difficult to discover. At the end of July 1941 General Rommel had been given command of the newly formed Panzer Gruppe Afrika. GHQ was stationed in Beda Littoria. Chief of Staff was Major-General Gause, while General Westphal was G.S.O.1 (Operations). The offices were in the prefecture building and several houses in the neighbourhood had been requisitioned. The offices were in individual buildings and could be recognised by the plates on the doors—Adjutant, C-in-C, G.S.O.1, 2, 3, etc.

These interesting plates were known to the British Secret Service. Presumably agents had photographed both the layout and the nameplates.

At the end of August, however, Rommel left Cyrenaica with his staff for Cantoniera Ain El Gazala, 40 miles west of Tobruk, and later moved to the Cantoniera Gambut between Tobruk and Barbia. The Q.M.G. and his staff took up their quarters at Beda Littoria.

This the British Secret Service did not discover. Did the Arab agents deliberately deceive the British? Was greed on the part of the spies the cause? Whatever the reason, in September, both in Cairo and London, it was believed that Rommel's headquarters were in the prefecture at Beda Littoria. A grave error! But Major Keyes was blissfully unaware of this error and thought he had now reached his goal.

In his farewell letter to his father before leaving he had written: "If the raid succeeds, England will have advanced a step further and that is worth a great deal, even if I fall into the bag." Keyes was not entirely wrong. Even if Beda Littoria was not Rommel's headquarters it was the headquarters of the Q.M.G., the nodal point of all reinforcements and supplies. It was the nerve centre of the German-Italian Panzer Gruppe. Great havoc could have been wrought there.

The rain poured down. Thunder and lighting--as though ordered--were the accompanying music to this adventure. It was 23.59 hours when Keyes gave his men the final details of the plan. He himself, Campbell, Sergeant Terry and six men crept towards the entrance of the prefecture. Three others made their way round to the back door. The German sentry stood in the open front door. Sergeant Terry was to kill him with a dagger. Who knows? Possibly the soldier made an unexpected movement. The blade missed its mark and in a flash there was a tussle in the corridor.

The German called loudly for help, but the thunder and the noise of the storm drowned his cries. The storm also drowned the sound of the demolition of an electricity power house thirty paces from the house; it was blown sky high by men of the Commando.

During the struggle in the dark corridor the raiders could not use their tommy guns. They tried to grab the sentry and silence him. But the German soldier was a strong man and defended himself bravely. Finally he fell against the first door of the corridor. This proved fatal for Geoffrey

Keyes.

There are several British versions of what ensued at Beda Littoria. Churchill writes rather vaguely of it in his Memoirs.

Desmond Young, Rommel's British biographer, gives a detailed description in his book of the raid on the German General's Headquarters. But accurate information about the raid is missing and he does not mention why Rommel was not there. So far the most detailed account of this raid is to be found in the January 1957 issue of the magazine *Men Only*. According to this the German-speaking Campbell called te sentry out of the entrance and Keyes shot him. Then Keyes, Campbell and Terry jumped over the dead man and wrenched open the door of the first room.

"They were faced by a blinding light. The German officers seated round the table, stared motionless at the intruders. Without a word, Keyes mowed down the best men of the German Supply Corps with his tommy gun."

Then, according to *Men Only*. "They went into the next room and once more tore open the door. But here the light had already been switched off and they were met by concentrated revolver fire. Keyes was hit by five bullets but Terry jumped forward and fired a few bursts into the room."

Outside on the dunes Campbell, according to the British official account, realised that Keyes was mortally wounded and that he himself had been hit in the leg. He handed over to Lieutenant Cook who was to take the party back to the beach. Nothing is mentioned about the absence of the Commando troop. To make the account more dramatic four General Staff Officers were presumed to have been killed, but unfortunately Rommel had not been caught, for he had left his headquarters at 20.30 hours to attend the marriage of a sheikh and had only returned at 00.40 hours. In other words, thirty minutes after the raid. Pure bad luck!

There are many similar versions and they are all very dramatic. The British are always depicted as bold and contemptuous of death and the German officers as paralysed with terror. . . .

What is the true story?

I think I have found the true answer. I have questioned all the surviving German eye-witnesses and their reports give an unequivocal picture.

The Assistant Quartermaster, Major Poeschel, remembers the turbulent events of that night extremely well and has given me an impressive account of his experiences and the results of his inquiries. I have been able to augment them with the original report which Sergeant Alfons Hirsch and Corporal Otto Barth compiled the day after the raid. Sergeant-Major Lentzen, the M.O., Doctor Junge, the driver Friedrich Honold and the Wireless Operator Erwin Schauer have furnished important details which throw some light on the event. It seems to me that there is no possible doubt that the raid progressed after the attack on the sentry in the corridor in the following manner:

When the powerfully built sentry fell to the ground with the British soldier in their wrestling match, he hit against the door of the munitions office. Sergeant-Major Lentzen and Sergeant Kovacic, who were sleeping in the room, woke up, jumped from their beds and grabbed their .08s. Lentzen leaped to the door and pulled it open. He sought for a target, raised his revolver and fired. At the same moment Major Keyes hurled two hand grenades which flew past Lentzen's head and exploded in the middle of the room. The blast knocked the Sergeant-Major over but he was unhurt. Kovacic, who was on his way to the door, received the full benefit of the blast and lay dead on the tiles. A third N.C.O., Sergeant Bartel, who was about to jump out of bed, was able to fall back and remained unscathed. Things went at lightning speed. The sequence of the account cannot disturb the unity of the event. Had Sergeant-Major Lentzen's bullets found their mark? We shall see this at once for at that moment the fate of the carefully organised raid was decided. Upstairs on the first floor the Orderly Officer, Lieutenant Kaufholz, had not yet fallen asleep when the cries of the sentry rang out. He was the first person in the house to hear them. He leapt out of bed but had to fetch his revolver from a chest. Then he ran into the corridor and down the stairs. At this moment the hand grenades exploded in the munitions office. By the light of the explosion Kaufholz caught sight of the British soldiers. But Captain Campbell had also spotted the German Lieutenant. Kaufholz was the first to fire and the British Commando leader, Major Keyes, slumped to the ground with a little cry of pain. At the same moment Campbell's tommy-gun barked. The banisters were splintered but the burst had hit Kaufholz. While the Lieutenant writhed in his death agony and fell to the ground, he fired and hit Campbell in the shin. The British officer collapsed.

Thus the two leaders of the raid were out of action. In the dark corridor remained only Sergeant Terry and two privates. Voices rang out from the first floor and the German officers rushed from their rooms. The surprise is now over, thought Terry. But where are the others who should have entered the house by the back door? Yes, where on earth are the others?

At this moment there was wild machine-gun fire outside. Are the Germans counter-attacking, Terry wondered. Once more it was one of those tragic errors, for there was no question of any German counter-attack. Something rather eerie had happened. Lieutenant Jaeger, in the next room to the munitions office, had been virtually flung out of bed by the explosion of the hand grenades. His room was separated from this office by a partition of three-ply wood. It was smashed to pieces. Jaeger in his pyjamas jumped out of the window—which had been blown in by the explosion. This was his undoing. Outside, in his light pyjamas, in the pouring rain and lit up by a lightning flash he ran straight into a British sentry's tommy-gun. The Tommy did not hesitate or call for surrender. What could they have done with prisoners? Firing from the hip he shot the unfortunate Lieutenant to pieces from a distance of ten feet. He was riddled with bullets.

But these shots were soon avenged. These were the shots which Sergeant Terry and his men in the dark corridor had heard and had caused the Sergeant to surmise that fighting had broken out outside. Deprived of their leader, they rushed into the open air.

The shots which had killed Lieutenant Jaeger had the same effect on the second Commando which was still outside the back door, unable to enter the house. Actually these men had the best prospect, if not of capturing Rommel, of putting the Q.M.G.'s headquarters completely out of action five hours before the British offensive. A can of water was the fly in the ointment and Major Keyes could not possibly have taken this can of water into account.

The back door led into a small office that had formerly served as a kitchen. It was crammed full of files and office tables. A small hatch at the back of the room led via a spiral staircase to a cellar. Here Sergeant-Major Alfons Hirsch and Corporal Barth had their sleeping quarters. The corporal was an elderly man who hated to have open doors at night. Since the back door had no lock he placed a full can of water before the door every evening and barricaded it from behind with a filing cabinet. This was a lock that no skeleton key could open. Although the raiders tried to force it the door refused to yield. They remained outside and held a conference while their leaders, Campbell and Terry, had already been discovered in the house corridor and the fighting had started. When the tommy-gun fire which mowed down Lieutenant Jaeger was heard coming from the garden the troops at the back door suspected a trap, and took to their heels.

"Lower your torches," Major Poeschel shouted to the German officers as they rushed out of their rooms on the first floor. But the nightmare was over. From outside came one more burst of machine-gun fire. A long scream rent the night, then everything was silent.

On the stairs they found the dead Lieutenant Kaufholz and in the corridor lay a British officer with a blackened face: the courageous Major Keyes. He had been killed by a shot through the chest which broke his sternum and had entered his heart and lungs. He had a second light wound in the thigh. This shot had obviously been fired by Sergeant-Major Lentzen. The shot that killed him must have been fired by Kaufholz, for Keyes, according to Campbell's later report, after throwing his grenade and after Lentzen's firing had cried to Campbell: "Damn it, I've been hit!" At the same moment in the glare of the grenade explosion he had seen Kaufholz on the stairs and called to Campbell: "Look out! Let him have it!" Then he collapsed after Kaufholz had fired. Almost simultaneously Campbell's machine-gun rang out and in the exchange of shots that followed Kaufholz's gun spat and smashed Campbell's shin bone. The Captain crawled as far as the door. There he stumbled over the legs of the sentry who lay with the upper part of his body in the office, his back riddled with hand grenade splinters, but by some miracle, not mortally wounded.

The whole operation came to grief because of this sentry. He is the only man whose name, despite all my efforts, I have been unable to discover. This is because he belonged to an M.P. unit, and the Q.M.G.'s staff kept no record of the personnel of this unit. An unknown soldier.

Outside after a search the German patrols came across the body of Lieutenant Jaeger. But towards the end a tommy-gun had spoken again and a man had uttered his death cry. They sought for a long while and then in the light of their torches they discovered the fourth dead German. This was Gunner Boxhammer of the Q.M.G.'s Motorised Detachment. Matthe Boxhammer, a 20-year-old youth from Malling in Bavaria, had been on duty to receive later incoming mail and to show the couriers to their quarters which lay some way off on the Via Balbo. Boxhammer in his small tent had obviously heard the sentry's cries for help, had jumped up without a thought and run to the prefecture entrance to help his comrade. He ran straight into the retreating Sergeant Terry and his men who mowed him down with a burst of tommy-gun fire in his belly. Matthe Boxhammer's death notice was worded quite correctly: "The fatal bullet hit him as he was trying to come to the aid of a stricken comrade."

The nightmare was over. The great adventure had failed. It failed as a result of a few unforeseen circumstances and the work of a few men. It is unthinkable what would have happened had they managed to enter the prefecture without making a sound and destroyed the whole of the Q.M.G.'s apparatus five hours before the British offensive started, or for a few hours had been in a position to give confusing orders to the Panzer Gruppe.

There remains only to add a little human story told to me by the surgeon, Doctor Werner Junge:

Captain Campbell had received a shot from a tommy-gun or a revolver at close quarters which had completely smashed his shinbone in the centre. He had no other wounds. By rights the leg should have been amputated, since the prospect of healing was very small and the danger of infection very great. At his request, Doctor Junge did not amputate and tried to save the leg. Since Junge spoke fluent English he was given orders to question Campbell. The latter did not betray the fact that he knew German. Junge could discover nothing of any importance. On the contrary, Campbell saw at once through the Doctor's game and said at last in German: "You needn't bother--you won't get anything out of me."

Doctor Junge kept Campbell in plaster for fourteen days in hospital until Derna had to be evacuated and the patient was sent by air to an Italian hospital. "Campbell was a charming man," said Junge. "As a doctor I should be very interested to learn whether I had saved his leg. I wore his 'sand-creepers,' as we called the British crêpe-soled shoes in the desert, for the rest of the war. They brought me more luck than they brought him, but I didn't get up to such escapades as he did."

And what was the fate of the rest of the members of the Commando? The fleeing soldiers had not dared to return immediately to the waiting submarine. Fearing that a large search party would be sent out they hid with the Arabs. Not until next morning was a thorough combined German-Italian search made! For days on end the countryside was combed, Arab huts were ransacked and the Military Police searched every corner. They looked intently at the Arabs, but nothing could be got out of these alternately passive or wildly gesticulating fellows. Not a British soldier, not a piece of uniform.

Then an Italian Carabiniere arrived who had lived for many years in the region and knew it like the palm of his hand. "I'll show you how you should act," he said proudly. He fetched an Arab girl from the village and had a long gesticulating palaver with her. The sense of it was as follows:

"You and your family will be given eighty pounds of corn and twenty pounds of sugar for each Britisher that you betray to us."

Eighty pounds of flour and twenty pounds of sugar--they represented a real treasure for the Arabs at that period. Their greed for this treasure was stronger than the British pound notes or the Senussi Chief's talisman which each one carried representing a kind of passport. The lady left and soon the first British were taken from the very huts which the German Military Police had searched so thoroughly. They were clothed in Arab rags. Eventually the entire Commando fell into German hands. Only the crafty Sergeant Terry managed to escape with two men and found his way through to the British lines. The prisoners were not treated according to Hitler's orders as partisans, which would have meant that they would have been shot: Rommel ordered them to be treated as prisoners-of-war. The fallen British leader of the raid was buried in the cemetery of Beda Littoria with full military honours next to the four dead Germans.

The British Raid on Tobruk

"Egypt is the most beautiful country in the world, and it is at its most beautiful from the terrace of the Royal Yacht Club in Alexandria," is a saying among the inhabitants of that city. Those who visited it during the war found it a fairy-tale city. They sat in the shade with a view of the turquoise blue sea and the white sails of the yachts. The guests were officers, wealthy people and smart women.

Off shore at the beginning of September, 1942, the 10th and 15th M.T.B. Flotillas carried out manoeuvres. They had small landing craft in tow. They practised disembarkation and re-embarking. It was a great success. The Egyptian ladies who took tea every afternoon on the yacht club terrace brought their opera glasses so as not to miss a single phase of this regatta. The British Naval Staff frowned but their faces brightened when they heard one of the women say: "What nationality are those naval officers' uniforms?"

"Greek, my dear, Greek. I heard it from my husband," supplied her friend.

"Greek?"

"Yes, Greek instructors."

Her friend was a trifle obtuse. "Where have the Greeks come from?"

"From Greece."

"Oh, of course."

The Greek instructors taking part in the M.T.B. exercises off Alexandria had been a good idea on the part of the British Secret Service. The Axis troops in the Mediterranean were soon instructed to be on the alert. "Beware of an attempted invasion of Greece."

The exercises at Alexandria had nothing to do with Greece.

The affair had started at the beginning of July, 1942, when Colonel John Haselden, chief of the Long Range Desert Group, conceived the idea of dealing a heavy blow to Rommel's fuel supplies. He proposed to blow up the large oil storage tanks in Tobruk. Since the staff in Cairo that summer seized upon anything which gave them a glimmer of hope, Haselden's plan found many supporters.

The original plan was soon enlarged. Not only were the oil storage tanks to be blown up, but also the important German repair workshops in Tobruk. The legendary 548th Recovery Regiment, which repaired Rommel's tanks and vehicles, had to be destroyed. These capable fellows ran the finest German tank factory on African soil. This was the opinion of the R.E.M.E. chief in Cairo. At the same time the ammunition dumps and the harbour installations were to be destroyed. Then they must liberate the British prisoners, and . . . and . . . thus Haselden's sabotage plan developed into a G.H.Q. affair, a combined land-sea-air operation with its goal three hundred miles behind Rommel's line.

On the 21st August the heads of the three British services, air, land and sea, sanctioned the plan. It was the middle of September. The danger to the British front was actually past, for the battle of Alam Halfa had destroyed Rommel's striking power. But the operation was not abandoned.

On the 13th September the Medical Service Corporal, Albert Goldman, who had been transferred from Crete to the 2/220th Company, North Africa, was marching with five of his men into Tobruk. They had just landed on the airfield and were looking for quarters. A few captured 3-tonners drove past them. The men were about to stop these trucks but saw that they were full of ragged British P.O.W.s who had obviously come from the desert--in actual fact from El Alamein. In the cabins the German sentries sat close together.

Goldman waved to the Tommies and one of them waved back. "Poor bastards!" thought the N.C.O.

They saw the German sentries lift the barrier for the trucks at the advanced post. A Fieseler Storch hovered over the road and accompanied the convoy for a time. Then everything was swallowed up. Albert Goldmann and his men marched past the old barbed wire entanglement and the debris of the war. The sea gleamed ahead of them and there was no gunfire. The war and the front line were far away. Night fell swiftly. Goldmann and his squad stumbled into an abandoned flak emplacement. "We'll stay here," said the corporal," make yourselves comfortable."

In the meantime the trucks with the British prisoners had driven down the main street towards the harbour. They turned to the right. "Halt!" Two M.P.s stood there with torches. "Your papers, please," they cried to the German officer in command. "Coming!" was the reply. He dismounted, accompanied by a tall grenadier. The British in the truck suddenly fell silent. It was almost sinister. Then two torches fell to the ground: there was a faint moan and a stifled scream.

"Press on," ordered the man in the German officer's uniform, replacing a long knife in the pocket of his trousers.

An Italian officer at his sentry box stopped the column. In the middle of the conversation three flak shots were fired, the signal for an air alert. A scream was suppressed and an Italian oath was drowned in the noise of the anti-aircraft fire. The huge German grenadier handed an Italian sub-machine gun to one of the British prisoners in the truck. "He won't need this where he's gone."

The sky suddenly sprang to life. The R.A.F. were there--punctual to the minute. But today there were many more bombers than usual.

As on every evening about 20.00 hours the men of the Heavy Flak Unit 114 on the Tobruk promontory waited for the routine attacks by the British. The aircraft arrived on time. First the normal formations. They were fired on and turned away. But then the radar recorded further formations flying in. Wave after wave appeared. The flak had no idea that it would use up all its ammunition that night; 3,500 rounds were fired by the first battery alone.

"Operation Agreement" was supported by nearly two hundred aircraft. For four hours Wellingtons bombed the city. They destroyed the telephone lines, attacked flak positions, kept officers and men in the bunkers and thus prepared the way for Haselden's commando raid. The commando which had driven through Tobruk in the guise of a convoy of P.O.W.s was trying to form a bridgehead on the Umm-Esc-Sciause Bay. The orders of Special Commando Y1 were as follows:

Colonel Haselden was to drive the ninety men, disguised as British prisoners-of-war, in three trucks to Tobruk. German-speaking members of the commando in German uniforms played the part of guards. Under cover of the air attack Haselden was to occupy a bridgehead to the south of the harbour bay. The coastal artillery and flak located there had to be captured. If this succeeded, the naval forced off Tobruk would be given the signal to land by flares. Marines were to be landed on the north beach of Tobruk from destroyers, and storm troops from M.T.B.s south of Haselden's occupied bridgehead. About six hundred and fifty men were to be landed and together with Haselden's group were to capture the city, held by German supply units, flak and Italian coastal artillery. All important installations were to be destroyed. The return journey was to be made in M.T.B.s and destroyers. A special unit under Captain Lloyd-Owen, which had driven with Haselden through the desert to Tobruk, was to wait outside the city and penetrate the fortress during the air attack. Owen's task was to seal off the entrance road, capture the German radio and radar stations, carry off the most important material, put the staff headquarters out of action and cut all communications. That was the plan.

It was not lacking in audacity. Haselden's Long Rangers travelled fifteen hundred miles from Cairo through the desert. It was by the same route, though in the opposite direction, which Captain Count Almaszy had taken four months earlier with his Brandenburgers to drop Rommel's agents, Eppler and Sandstede at Assiut.

Offshore, units of the British Mediterranean Fleet waited. The two destroyers *Sikh* and *Zulu,* eighteen M.T.B.s, eight Hunt class destroyers and the cruiser *Coventry*. The maps which Colonel Haselden carried were accurate, and the aerial photographs correct in every detail.

They found the wadi which split the proposed bridgehead in two. Major Campbell took thirty men to the east and Haselden the remainder of the men to the west. Campbell disappeared into the darkness. Haselden's men opened the door of the first Italian hut where the staff of an Italian coastal battery sat by candlelight with blacked-out windows drinking Chianti. The Italians looked up in surprise. Before they could understand why men in German officers' uniforms stood in the doorway revolvers in hand, it was already too late. Hand grenades burst and machine-guns rattled. There were screams and groans. They were drowned by the din of the air attack as the bombs rained down on Tobruk. The Tommies carried the corpses outside and settled in their new headquarters. The signalers rigged up their sets and Colonel Haselden had his staff headquarters.

The next hut was a quarter of a mile away. In spite of the air raid alert the Italians were asleep. David Sillito kicked open the door, flashed his torch and gave orders to fire.

The commando leader, Macdonald, spotted the subterranean gun emplacements. He heard the Italian gunners snoring. He gave his order in a whisper. Hand grenades were thrown down the ventilators. Screams and explosions. His men went on throwing their grenades until there was silence.

Things proceeded in this manner on the west side of Umm-Eac-Sciause Bay. Only on one occasion did a few Italians offer resistance in a guardhouse. Lieutenant Graham Taylor was wounded in the arm and chest. His bodyguard, Mackay and Allardyce, threw so many hand grenades into the small building that there were no survivors.

Everything had gone according to plan. The personnel of an entire Italian unit lay dead in their huts or at their guns.

"Fire the green flares," ordered Colonel Haselden. This was the signal that the west side of the bay was in British hands. Lieutenant Scott was posted at the end of the promontory. He saw the signals, turned to the east and waited for Campbell's flares. As soon as these were fired he had to inform Haselden's headquarters by flare so that a signal could be sent to the fleet. This signal meant: "The bridgehead is ours." Scott would then fire his flares out to sea and the waiting M.T.B.s could sail in under cover of darkness. Campbell's flares were never fired.

At 01.30 hours waves of Wellingtons were still arriving over Tobruk. For half an hour they had dropped no more Christmas trees over the northern part of the harbour because the destroyer invasion fleet needed the darkness.

Colonel Hartmann's heavy battery on the point had, by this time, fired 6,500 shells. Twenty-three bombers were brought down. The first telephone calls sounding the alarm came through: "The Tommies have landed."

The G.H.Q. staff had foregathered in the Director of Military Intelligence's headquarters in Cairo. They kept looking at the clock. The landing had been timed for 01.00 hours. Now it was nearly an hour later. If by 02.00 hours the code word had not been given the Naval commando was to return from the mission.

Ten minutes before zero hour . . . five minutes . . .

The duty aide brought in the order to cancel the operation. Without a word he laid it on the table. The buzzer went . . . The message was decoded. It was the long awaited message. The staff officers left at once.

Major Campbell had finally given the signal that he had captured the Italian batteries on the eastern side of the bridgehead. Things had not gone as smoothly for him as for Haselden. Campbell could not hold the captured battery positions and had been forced to blow up the guns. Nevertheless, the bridgehead was firmly in commando hands, although they were a little behind schedule. The Navy could begin. But now fate took a hand. Campbell's signaller, Tom Langton, who like Scott in the Haselden contingent was to light up the eastern corner of the bay, had lost his portable searchlight. The M.T.B.s missed the little bay. Only two of the eighteen found it. The others circled out to sea or round the harbour entrance.

What had happened to the destroyer flotilla? The Tribal destroyers *Sikh* and *Zulu*, camouflaged as Italian warships, had been cruising close inshore off Tobruk. After receiving the code word they sailed with a delay of one hour to the coastal sector north of the harbour entrance to land the marines before entering the harbour and attacking the shipping and coastal targets.

The first trouble started with the lowering of the clumsy landing-craft. In spite of this, the first wave went ashore, though half an hour late. The destroyers retired offshore; forty minutes later they were still waiting to lower the second wave into the returning landing-craft. But the landing-craft did not return. A signal was received that the leader of the first wave had been driven ashore with engine trouble. The other craft had no leader and lay beached waiting for orders.

The destroyers now went close inshore to speed up the action. But suddenly the 60 cm. searchlight of No. 1 Battery 1/46th Flak Regiment, under Lieutenant Muller-Frank, turned its beams on the water. It picked up the destroyer *Sikh*.

The destroyer began to fire its pom-poms. Italian coastal artillery returned the fire and the ship's gun replied.

In the meantime the signals sergeant of the Vieweg Battery had mobilised his Lieutenant with the report: "Our set registers three warships at six thousand yards."

Now, for the first time, at 04.00 hours the Tobruk staffs were alerted and the German commandant received his report. Now they believed the first excited reports of the fugitive Italian gunners from Umm-Esc-Sciause Bay that British forces had landed. They had laughed then. Now their laughter was silenced. They could see that a British flotilla lay off Tobruk.

But where was the Owen special unit--the Group Y2? Was it not yet in Tobruk? To Haselden's chagrin it was not. Owen and his men had been in the city. They, too, had been allowed to pass the German and Italian posts. Wherever they encountered difficulties the dagger and the wire noose proved effective. Owen, however, waited in vain for radio communication with Haselden, for the code word indicating that the first blow had succeeded. He felt that the time-table of the plan was irreparably delayed. At 01.00 hours, when the British landing-craft had not come ashore, he turned about and left Tobruk. He was the only man to save his commando. But the vitally important 88 mm. batteries on the point and the airfield were not captured. The radio and telephone centres remained intact. As a result Haselden and the fleet had already lost half the battle.

At 05.10 hours Lieutenant Vieweg opened fire on the destroyer *Sikh* with his gun Dora. The first shot was beyond the target but the second was a direct hit.

Firing orders for all guns with open sights! This was the best target practice they could possibly hope for, although the flak gunners were slightly out of practice.

Vieweg controlled the whole battery by radio, and lobbed flak shells to burst a few feet above the deck of the *Sikh*. The British warship returned this fire but Captain Ruhau's No. 3 Battery alone received direct hits.

The *Sikh*, on fire with a slight list, sheered off. *Zulu*, although damaged, tried to take the *Sikh* in tow, but a lucky hit from an 88 mm. shell broke the tow-line.

The crew of the *Sikh* abandoned ship. Their commander and part of the ship's company were picked up later. The *Zulu* was also sunk by flak and an Italian battery firing a captured 75 mm. gun. Only the small Hunt destroyers got away in this action, although some of them were very heavily damaged.

At 07.00 hours three British M.T.B.s entered the harbour at full speed. Before the flak could fire an Italian fighter arrived, and, in a low level attack, sank the British craft. It was a nightmare.

At the southern end of Tobruk and in the wadi of the little bay Haselden's men lay under withering machine-gun fire and a hail of hand grenades. And here at last died Colonel Haselden, the guiding spirit of the Long Range Desert Group, his head resting on a Tommy gun. It was the end of a great adventurer. Major Campbell also lay dying on the beach of the little bay, weapon in hand.

By the afternoon of the 14th September it was all over. Commandos of the German recovery and supplies units combed the neighbourhood and took prisoners. The German High Command issued the following communique:

"Last night in the Tobruk sector the enemy attempted to land in several places with land and naval forces. The attempt failed as a result of immediate action taken by Italian and German troops."

Half a dozen of Haselden's men and a handful of Marines took to the desert.

Five weeks later, almost dead with thirst, filthy dirty, thin as skeletons, seven men fell into the arms of a British reconnaissance unit. Exactly two months after the action another British patrol found Lieutenant David Lanark wandering, like a half-crazed ghost, through the desert. The last man from Haselden's Tobruk raid had reported back.

Brandenburgers in Action Behind the Front

The hand grenades were still bursting in the Christmas battle for Longstop Hill when in the Beurat position, one hundred and twenty miles from Tripoli, a young captain stood with Colonel Bayerlein poring over the map of the southern Tunisian sector. Three points had been marked with blue crosses behind the enemy's lines--three bridges over rivers and wadis on the Oran—Algiers railway line in the Tebessa, Gafsa, and Tozeur sector. The railway could become an important lifeline for the Allied supplies. Along the track also ran telephone and telegraph wires: supply and intelligence leads. They must be put out of action.

In his general report of the battles waged by his 90th Army Korps in Tunisia, General Nehring mentioned the various operational and tactical actions. "Additional precautions: sabotage and fighting commandos were sent far to the west. Unfortunately no records of their successes against railway bridges and supply dumps are available."

No records. This was a good thing, for the Allied Information Services made a lengthy search for them at the end of the war. These dashing commandos were to be put under lock and key.

Today, at last, some of the details can be given of these bold mission.

Captain Fritz von Koenen was a farmer's son from South-West Africa, and spoke English as well as his mother tongue. He led the 13th Company of the Brandenburg Regiment. The first half company arrived with Koenen in Tunisia at the same time as the first paratroops. The second half company was flown over from Naples on the 5th December. They were quartered in idyllic Hammamet by the sea, in a villa among the orange and lemon groves. But they had no opportunity for relaxation. When things got hot during those first few weeks of the Tunisian campaign, the Koenen Special Commando could be seen in action although, as a rule, the Brandenburgers were not used in the fighting line. Their business was quite different. Brandenburgers sat behind the enemy lines and acted as observers for their own artillery. They cut communications, altered signposts, rendered tracks impassable and achieved a great deal more besides.

About midnight on Boxing Day, 1942, the Brandenburgers set off once more. From Bizerta airfield three Ju 52s took off for the south, each with a glider in tow.

Towed gliders were not particularly comfortable contraptions. The passengers sat one behind the other on a board with hand grips. For the feet there was a wooden thwart.

From time to time Captain von Koenen, who sat behind the glider pilot, looked round and took stock of his men. There was Sapper Sergeant Hans Neumann who had been on many missions. Behind him sat the interpreter, Reginald Dade. Then came Sergeant Sloka and five other men. The glider could not take any more. There was no conversation. Everyone knew the plan and his own particular role. Each of them knew that under their seats were crates full of weapons, tools and four hundred pounds of explosive.

The tow line twinkled in the moonlight; deep below them gleamed the Mediterranean. In a wide sweep the three parent machines made for the land at seven thousand five hundred feet. It had been agreed that the gliders were to be released thirty-five miles before the objective. The light signals flashed from the leading plane. The pilots released the hawsers; the sound of engines died away and Koenen's gliders continued noiselessly on their way. Below in the moonlight lay the railway line and the bridge which crossed the Wadi el Kebir in a wide arc.

The pilot continued to glide for a while then put his nose down. The wind whistled as they dived at breakneck speed for the ground. The men clung on like grim death. Every man's thought was: Well, let's hope we get away with it. They could not forget that they were sitting on four hundred pounds of explosive. The pilot flattened out at the right moment. The perspex cockpit was opened and the skids scrunched on the gravel. They were bound with barbed wire, which made a good brake.

A little way off the second glider had landed. He, too, had landed without breakage. The third was nowhere to be seen. Not until their return did they discover that the Ju towing this glider had joined up with another formation. The pilot noticed his error too late.

Captain von Koenen, Sergeant Neumann and the runner, bent double, ran over to the three-hundred-yard long bridge. "A fine piece of engineering," said Koenen. Cautiously they crawled closer. They suspected enemy sentries, but the French were sitting on the far side in the small station building, drinking Algerian wine. Perhaps they were asleep. Koenen peered through his night field-glasses. He could read the black letters of the station's name: Sidi bou Baker.

"The coast's clear."

The runner hurried back. Sergeant Sloka came up with the others, panting heavily. They were carrying the explosive. Koenen removed the safety devices.

Neumann directed the setting of the charges. Two charges of eight pounds on the bridge upperworks. Six pounds at each end of the bridge on the track. Two huge charges of one hundred and sixty pounds lashed to the broadside of the centre pile. In the meantime a man climbed up a telegraph pole to cut the wires. Since he had no pliers he smashed the wires with a mattock. The copper hummed, and as the last wire broke the mast toppled to one side and nearly took the man with it. Now for the fuse!

"Where are the fuses?"

They were in the third glider which had disappeared.

Neumann had spares with him. These infernal machines with their ripcord had the disadvantage of burning for only sixty seconds. That gave very little time. They must be careful. Neumann blew his whistle as a signal to pull the cord for both the main charges.

The moon was bright. The whistle rang out, the three men on the upper works pulled their cords and ran. Neumann listened. No. 1 burning. A hiss from the next. Okay. Twenty seconds had gone. Now he must get going. At that moment his foot caught in the telegraph wires. He fell. Sergeant Sloka jumped fifteen feet from the bridge into the wadi to rescue Neumann, but sprained his ankle in the attempt. Fortunately Neumann had struggled to his feet and could now rescue his helper. He picked Sloka up and dragged him to the edge of the wadi. They flung themselves on the ground. At that moment the first charge exploded on the rails. But what had happened to the other two? They should all have exploded at the same time. Neumann stood up and looked over towards the bridge. Then fresh columns of flame rose in the air. The blast tore his legs from under him and flung him to the ground. Fragments whistled overhead but the men felt no fear, only triumph. They had succeeded.

When the dust cloud had subsided, the bridge stood in the moonlight like a jagged tooth.

Originally, the assembly place after the action was to have been in a little depression to the south. But this turned out to be too near to the station building from which the French were now firing wildly with their machine-guns. Koenen ordered them to assemble at the gliders.

"Everyone here?"

"No."

Two men were missing. Sergeant Sloka volunteered to go and look for them. The others made for the hills. Charges had previously been secured to the gliders. Seconds later they blew up as the shadowy figures moved away.

By daybreak the Arab guides had found a little wadi in the Jebel bou Ramli. The men flung themselves down on the ground to sleep. They could only continue their journey at night.

Towards midday there was an alert. Arabs entered the little wadi. The interpreter was sent forward. He was seen to gesticulate. Then they all came running. One threw off his burnous. It was Berger, one of the two missing men. As a Palestinian German he had been able to make himself understood by the Arabs in a near-by village, and with unerring instinct they had led him to the right hiding-place. Proudly they palavered with Reginald Dade, Koenen's interpreter, and offered to bring the column safely out of the danger zone. As soon as darkness fell they broke camp. The Arabs led the men through the Jebel on a long trek of forty miles past the city of Gafsa, and then by shepherds' tracks through the Jebel Orbata. On the sixth day after their action, Koenen entered Maknassy. Twelve hours later an Arab troop brought in the second missing man, the Bavarian Hannes Feldmann. He was riding on a donkey and looking the picture of health. It must not be forgotten that the Arabs risked the death penalty for helping a German. Sergeant Sloka never returned. Agents reported that a French patrol had found and shot him.

On the night Captain von Koenen flew with his twenty men to Wadi el Kebir, ten other men of his company, led by Lieutenant Hagenauer and the sapper Sergeant, Poldi, flew in a glider to blow up the bridge of Kasserine. But this expedition was ill-fated. They crashed on landing. Finally the whole group was captured by a French armoured reconnaissance patrol. Only two men, Corporal Franz Wodjerek and Sergeant Willi Clormann, escaped and reached the German lines after an eleven-day march. All they had between them were sixty-seven cigarettes, a bottle of Coca Cola and two revolvers, each with seven bullets. They, too, were helped by Tunisian peasants.

A fortnight later, on the 10th January, another commando was despatched to blow up a bridge in the Tozeur sector in Southern Tunisia, the third blue cross on the map. Captain Bisping in charge of the commando and Sergeant-Major Klima decided to do the job in a truck from Kibili, since their objective lay north of the Schott Jerid salt pan and there was an advanced Italian strongpoint in the Jebel Morra. But the approach of the commando was spotted by French security forces. Only with great difficulty could the Brandenburgers save themselves by flight. Shrewdly they made a second attempt the following night and this time they succeeded. Sergeant-Major Klima calmly secured the explosives to the central pile. A charge was laid on the girders and the rest between the rails. Klima lit his ten-minute fuses and the commando set off at full speed in the truck. After ten minutes they halted at the edge of the Jebel. Night fieldglasses out! The bridge looked majestic in the moonlight. Fifteen minutes went by.

Klima grew nervous.

Twenty minutes.

"Something wrong—I must go and have a look."

Captain Bisping restrained him. At this moment they heard a train in the distance. The locomotive's whistle blew as it approached the bridge. They all stared intently and then came the explosion. The men jumped into their truck and drove off at top speed.

The aerial photographs taken the following evening showed a locomotive and the smashed coaches of a train between the debris of the blown-up bridge.

The British attempted a reprisal action. A British submarine landed a commando at Hammemet with the object of blowing up Koenen's headquarters. But Koenen's second half company were on the alert. Hermann

Müller, who was on guard on the beach, heard the sound of a grinding boat and then the click of barbed wire being cut. He fired three white flares. By their light they saw shapes moving. A wild chase ensued. The commando made off, but within the next forty-eight hours the eight men who had been landed by the submarine, including a British captain, were tracked down and caught by Colonel von Hippel's newly formed Arab Legion. A lieutenant of the Long Range Desert Group who had tried to swim back to the submarine was washed up dead on the shore.

From Paul Carell, *The Foxes of the Desert*, (New York: Bantam, 1962), pp. 44-56; 256-263; and 326-331.

John Lodwick

Raiders From the Sea

One of the most exasperating features of raiding in the Aegan at that time was the frequent restriction in our choice of targets. There existed, in fact, another organisation which in view of its tradition of anonymity we will call Force X. This Force X was doing splendid work collecting and collating Intelligence, landing agents and distributing supplies to members of the Greek resistance on the mainland. Secrecy, however, was an essential of their trade, and secrecy could not very well be maintained if a S.B.S. raid brought a swarm of Gestapo men to some island where an agent was employed, say, in a study of the German gun positions.

Somebody had therefore to yield precedence, and the victims were more often than not S.B.S. This may seem a small matter, but pushed to its logical conclusions, the results were sometimes quite extraordinary. At one time, every single island in the Aegean, with the uninteresting exception of Pserimo, was out of bounds to S.B.S. for any purpose other than that of reconnaissance. Let us see how this could occur. . .

Well . . . a brigadier in Force X would announce to his immediate subordinate, a colonel, that an agent was to be landed, on, say, Syros, in the Cylcades on such and such a date.

"You might see that Jellicoe's bandits keep quiet during that time," he would add. "This fellow is valuable. I want him given time to settle in."

The colonel would go away, brooding over the grave words of his chief. Presently, an edict would be issued that Syros was out of bounds to S.B.S. for a period of two weeks. In due course this edict would pass to another department. This department would have no idea of the reason for the order, but it would be slow in noting that Syros lay in the centre of the Cyclades.

"Well, if they can't go there," someone would say, "it stands to reason that we can't have them mucking about in the neighbouring islands." The entire group of twenty-three Cyclades would then be placed out of bounds to S.B.S. for a period of a fortnight. Two or three further pieces of hanky-panky of this nature and S.B.S. would be left with a couple of barren rocks, a dismantled lighthouse at one end and a disused goat-pen at the other.

On the famous occasion when David Sutherland's choice of targets was down to Pserimo, he sent an expedition there in desperation, captured a caique and an Italian, and then complained in restrained but measured terms. The bans were lifted . . . or when not lifted (dare I say it?) were circumvented:

("It's no use cursing me," officers would say, "I only went to the bloody island to reconnoitre. How could I help it if the German got in my way . . . I mean, what would *you* do in my place?")

Such protestations of innocence, if insincere, were not infrequent.

Lassen was now back. The wound sustained in Calchi had turned septic. Lassen had spent two months in hospital in Alexandria with a disgusting little dog lurking under his bed. This dog, Lassen claimed, against all evidence, to be a Maltese terrier. Its habits, which Lassen encouraged, were lubricious and obscene. He arrived with it now in time for the raids on the Cyclades.

On all the outlying members of that group, the Germans maintained small garrisons, who consisted for the most part of young naval ratings, entrusted with a shipping watch. They also possessed radio transmitters with which to report the movement of hostile air and surface craft. Brigadier Turnbull's plan, which was approved in early April 1944, was no less than the liquidation of these posts on a single night.

Sutherland's squadron was mobilized for this task. My patrol was given Mikonos, in may ways the easiest of the group to attack.

Lassen, with his own patrol, and Keigh Balsillie's under his command, was to attack Santorin. Nobby Clarke was to visit first Ios and then Amorgos, where the enemy had recently reestablished themselves.

These raids were successful, the various garrisons either being taken alive or liquidated, their radio sets destroyed, and the German information service paralysed for a long period to come.

Before the war, Mikinos was a tourist resort, deriving considerable prosperity from the Delphic ruins on near-by Delos. Its buildings were in consequence more modern and their sanitation more advanced than in those encountered throughout the Dodecanese. Mikinos is well populated. We landed on a dark night in conditions of secrecy, but not many hours had elapsed before the news of our arrival had spread. That day chanced to be a Sunday, the eve of the Greek National Festival of St. George. By ten o'clock in the morning I was receiving deputations who had come considerable distances in order to welcome us. The men, stiff in their festive clothes, with starched collars, saluted with dim memories of military service . . . the women, perched primly on mule back, gazed at us solemnly and threw flowers. It was all very touching. We were the first allied troops to visit Mikinos since the declaration of war.

It goes without saying that everybody knew of the arrival of the *Inglesi* with the exception of the Germans. There were nine Germans on Mikinos. Seven lived in the best villa in the town. Two were stationed in a lighthouse some distance away. Throughout the day their movements were reported to us. The Germans, it seemed, were getting drunk.

Next morning, at first light, we attacked the villa. Simultaneously, three young Greeks, who had volunteered to work for us, were sent up to the lighthouse to dispose of the two men there.

The German sentry at the villa was shot at once by Rifleman Lynch. The villa was then rushed, but the occupants had had time to collect their wits. They barricaded themselves in a single room, whilst one of their number threw grenades down the stairs at us. We now sent for the mayor of the town. This man spoke German and had a German wife. He was brought to the garden wall and told to order the garrison to surrender. The Germans made no reply. Although unable to stand up in their room without drawing a volley of shots, they could hear aircraft overhead and shrewdly guessed them to be friendly. They began to fire Very lights in the hope of attracting attention. The aircraft, which were in fact Junkers, escorting a convoy, did not see the Very lights.

The young Greeks now arrived with the two prisoners from the lighthouse. I took one of these prisoners to the garden wall and ordered him to tell his comrades that unless they surrendered immediately we would burn the house down with the aid of a dump of petrol in its grounds. This was a bluff, for it would have taken us the entire day to place that petrol in position. The Germans, however, had no means of knowing this. They surrendered immediately. The villa was delivered over to the exultant civilian population, who looted it efficiently. British and Germans adjourned to a local hotel for lunch.

On the first floor of the Bank of Athens, in Santorin town, was a billet containing forty-eight Italians and twenty Germans. There were other targets on Santorin but Lassen reserved this one for himself. He took with him Stefan Casulli and twelve men. Despite many sentries and police dogs, surprise was achieved. The billet, from which exit was impossible, became a death-trap for its occupants. "There was," wrote Lassen, "a grand mix-up in the dark."

He is too modest. In point of fact, Lassen, accompanied by Sergeant Nicholson, walked from room to room. They paid the greatest attention to detail. First, Nicholson would kick the door open . . . then Lassen would throw two grenades inside . . . then Nicholson, firing his Bren from the hip, would spray the walls and corners . . . finally, Lassen, with his pistol, would deal with any remaining signs of life.

Next day, of all the enemy in this billet, only four Germans and six Italians were seen by the townspeople.

Unhappily, this massacre, although almost complete, was not achieved without loss. Stefan Casulli . . . standing *in* a doorway instead of to one side of it . . . was shot through the chest. He died immediately. His companion, Sergeant Kingston, a medical orderly, received a bullet in the stomach, from which wound he succumbed on the following day. Marine Trafford and Guardsman Harris--the latter Bill Blyth's batman--were slightly wounded by the sentries outside the billet. They forgot their pain in the pleasure of watching four fear-crazed Italians jumping through the windows from a height of forty feet.

Two other attacks were taking place in Santorin at the same time as Lassen's. Sergeant B. Henderson, a physical training instructor, familiarly known as 'The Brown Body' in consequence of his nudist tendencies, was sent to investigate the house occupied by the German Commander and his orderly. Not unnaturally, Henderson now heard what he described as "the murmur of voices issuing from the rear of the house."

He dashed round just in time to find the German officer making an undignified escape through the back streets.

Keith Balsillie was fulfilling his mission thoroughly. Keith was fortunate in having with him on this job Corporal Karl Kahane, a fluent German speaker. Led by Kahane, the party entered the first German billet. They found a man asleep in bed.

"For you, my friend," said Kahane, "the war is over. Now be a good fellow . . . get dressed and lead us to your comrades."

The German was persuaded by the logic of Kahane's remarks--which admittedly were supported by considerable fire-power--that he immediately conducted Balsillie to a second house. Here, three more Germans were found asleep in bed. These Germans also allowed themselves to be convinced and the procession, now swollen in numbers, moved on to a third house, where yet another trio of Germans were found asleep in bed. Here, at least, there was a little variety, for two of the Germans were in bed together. Only one German now remained in the area and he, hearing of the fate of his comrades, tamely presented himself of his own accord. Balsillie prepared the radio station for demolition and withdrew to contact Lassen.

Next day, as might be expected, there was considerable air activity over the island. Santorin is crescent-shaped, the spawn of that extinct volcano which affords its deep harbour moderate shelter. There is very little cover in Santorin and had the defending ground forces not been virtually exterminated, things might have gone badly for Lassen. Fortunately the enemy command in the larger island of Melos seem to have thought that the island had been captured. They did not appear with reinforcements for over forty-eight hours. Lassen was able to collect his scattered forces and to evacuate in comfort.

Subsequent events in Santorin throw interesting sidelights on the mentality of both Germans and Greeks. The Germans gave Stefan Casulli and Kingston a funeral with full military honours. On the same day they issued a proclamation demanding the names of those who had helped the British. Six Greeks, including the mayor of a village, presented themselves voluntarily. They were shot.

We must now turn to the third leg of this most successful experiment in concerted attack. Nobby Clarke and his patrol, had landed in Ios on 25th April. As on the other two islands, the Germans here were careless in the extreme . . . a state of affairs which must be attributed to the enemy's practice of censoring all news of our raids, with the result that all who had not actually suffered were unaware of the disasters that might come with the night.

Corporal Holmes, sent with a small party to collect three of the garrison, was unable to make the capture. The Germans, when approached, seized a number of children and held these unfortunate little creatures in front of them to cover their withdrawal.

Nobby Clarke, with Pomford and McClelland, was more fortunate. Forcing their way into a house, they surprised two Germans who were undressing. These men were more courageous than their comrades. Refusing to surrender, they attacked the invaders with bare hands and were killed. A third German, who was visiting his mistress in another part of the town, was captured as he was about to get into bed with her. This man was most disconsolate. Had he know that his mistress, herself, had supplied the information concerning his whereabouts, he might have been more disconsolate still.

Nobby Clarke marched his captives along the quay. Presently, footsteps were heard. Two men were seen approaching. When challenged they opened fire. The British replied with grenades but the intruders succeeded in getting behind a house. Covered by the house they escaped to the hills.

Unperturbed by this setback, Clarke proceeded with the business of the evening. He blew up the telegraph and cable stations and detonated a dump of 75 mm. shells. In the harbour he sank one caique and unloaded the food from a second, for distribution to the civilian population. On the following day he requested the mayor to send a messenger to the surviving Germans with orders that they report to him immediately, under pain of being hunted down without mercy. The credulous Germans, who might easily have remained hidden, surrendered half an hour later.

Clarke then sailed for Amorgos, where he was joined by Flying Officer Macris and five men of the Greek Sacred Squadron. There were ten Germans now on Amorgos, all living in a house in the chief town. That night the house was surrounded and fire opened upon it by two Bren guns. Macris and another Greek climbed up some trellis work and tossed grenades into various rooms. At a blast from Clarke's whistle, firing ceased and the Germans were invited to surrender. Instead of capitulating they made a sortie with arms in their hands. Eight of them were killed as they reached the open; the remaining pair escaped to the hills.

Thus concluded forty-eight hours of British intervention in the Cyclades. Casualties suffered by the enemy were forty-one killed, twenty-seven wounded and nineteen made prisoner. S.B.S. losses in the three operations were two killed and three slightly wounded, of a total expeditionary strength of thirty-nine men.

The list of stores and equipment of all kinds lost by the enemy I need not enumerate.

The immediate result of these raids was the distribution of large garrisons of German mountain troops throughout the Cyclades. Sutherland, however, remained sceptical as to the ability of the enemy to defend even his own living-quarters against determined infiltration. To prove his point, he dispatched Lassen and thirteen men to Paros, a large island lying only seventy miles from Athens. An air landing-strip had recently been completed on Paros. Workmen of the Todt organisation still slept in tents along its fringe.

Lassen, as was his custom, divided his party into small groups, each with a separate target. The main attack failed--the alarm being given almost at once by some unusually alert sentries--but the subsidiary expeditions were in each case successful. Private Perkins, accompanied by a Greek officer penetrated into one house to discover a German officer standing uncertainly in pyjamas and holding a Lüger.

"Hands up," said Perkins, who spoke good German, "everything is finished for you."

The German officer does not appear to have believed this. He replied with an incredulous "Was?" and a shot. The Greek killed him. In the next room the pair found and killed three private soldiers.

Sergeant Nicholson and Marine Williams, detailed to capture a second German officer, discovered their quarry hiding behind a door, clad in a flowered dressing-gown. He accompanied them without fuss. Several other German occupants of the house hid beneath beds and inside cupboards. They hoped to avoid capture. Nicholson and Williams who were perfectly well aware of the number of people in the house made no attempt to search it. Withdrawing, they threw phosphorus and fragmentation grenades through all the windows. Three of the men hidden were killed.

So, incidentally, was Nicholson's prisoner, hit first in the neck by one of his own snipers and subsequently in the chest by a grenade explosion. Nicholson, who had wasted several perfectly good field-dressings and mouthfuls of brandy in an endeavour to save the man, returned sadly to the rendezvous.

A strange, plump, freckled, kilted figure now enters the story. It is that of Captain Douglas Stobie, a very early member of Special Air Service, who had had the misfortune to break a leg in Tunisia; in consequence of which disaster he had been invalided home. He arrived back now, bringing with him a tommy-gun, the largest biceps and calf measurements in the Middle East, and a huge file of papers, apparently the result of some disagreement with the Army Pay Office. Stobie, it seemed, had not received his servant allowance or some such emolument for the period of his convalescence in the United Kingdom. He was determined that justice should be done to him. Briefed to accompany Nobby Clarke on a raid in Naxos, he took his file with him. During the intervals of planning and fighting, Stobie composed letters of complaint.

The Naxos operation was most successful. This was the first island in which guerrillas were encountered and their assistance was invaluable. Clarke and Stobie found Naxos well guarded and in a state of considerable alertness following the raid on Paros. They decided to devote their attention to a single German garrison of one officer and seventeen men. The three houses in which this group lived were surrounded and progressively demolished by large explosive charges. All the Germans became casualties, though Clarke was obliged to leave the wounded behind, owing to the approach of an enemy relief column.

The final operations of Sutherland's squadron, prior to handing over to Lapraik, are of minor importance. Sutherland himself, who had been chafing at base for weeks, was now finally able to get out and, with a motley force, penetrated deep into the Cyclades, sinking a caique in Siphnos and capturing a stray German in the same island.

Harold Chevalier, also with a scratch force, accompanied a naval patrol traveling north. Caiques of all sizes were stopped and searched in the waters between Samos and Chios. Eventually patience was rewarded by the appearance of a ship which could be commandeered with a clear conscience. The four Germans on board her were made prisoners.

Throughout this whole period, the naval liaison work, under Commander John Campbell, R.N.R., was a very high order. Motor launches carrying S.B.S. parties never hesitated to go close inshore, lay-off--sometimes for hours--within shouting distance of enemy observation posts and, in more than one case, re-embarked personnel under the immediate threat of air attack.

The legacy awaiting Lapraik when he left Alexandria to take over the conduct of operations was unenviable. Patterson had stirred up the

Dodecanese to such an extent that every garrison was now wide awake. Sutherland had intensified Patterson's policy and, with the additional advantage of fine weather, had caused nearly 4,000 German reinforcements to be transferred from the mainland to the Cyclades. In these two groups, no island remained which had not been visited at least once. Tactical surprise could still be achieved by the switching of patrols from one area to another, by simultaneous attacks in islands widely separated, by feints and carefully spread rumours. Gone for ever though, were the days when the German defenders would be found in bed. The German defenders now slept increasingly in slit trenches with barbed wire for their eiderdown.

Lapraik in person did not appear immediately. Like Mark Antony before him, he remained brooding upon certain splendours to come in Alexandria. In his absence, Stewart Macbeth assumed command of the squadron. Two or three abortive attacks in the Dodecanese quickly convinced Macbeth that here was a field rather more than well ploughed. He decided to try the Sporades, a small group lying close to the mainland and never before raided.

Macbeth's plan was an interesting and novel one. A squadron of motor torpedo-boats was about to be sent to these waters to prey upon enemy shipping. S.B.S. personnel would act as the eyes and ears of the navy, ascertaining what anchorages were safe for them when they wished to lie up--providing shore guards and boarding-parties and, finally, attacking such opportunist targets as presented themselves.

Unfortunately, as far as the motor torpedo-boats were concerned, the plan miscarried owing to technical difficulties--but not before Captain James Lees, with three men, and Lieutenant Bob Bury, with Corporal Denham and two others, had sailed and were beyond recall. These two parties, working in different area, were for the next fortnight to have the varied and exciting time enjoyed by all troops who have the good fortune to be out of radio communication with their base.

Jimmy Lees landed on the small island of Strati on 22nd June 1944. He found no Germans, and was immediately caught up in the whirlpool of local politics. Strati was, in fact, under the control of E.A.M., the political movement later to prove so intransigent on the mainland. Emissaries of E.A.M. who were, at this epoch, friendly enough, presented themselves at Jimmy Lee's hide-out, a cave, and invited him to choose a less modest residence. Jimmy Lees installed his party in an empty villa. He was enjoying a well-earned sleep there when the chief of the local gendarmes called, soliciting an interview.

Would His Excellency the English officer be staying long? he inquired.

His Excellency the English officer replied vaguely that he liked the place and might possibly remain a few days.

In that case, said the gendarme, would His Excellency object very much if he and his men searched the villa? A pure formality, of course, but sooner or later the Germans would hear that His Excellency had been on the island. They would than inquire why the leader of the gendarmes had not chased the invaders? Further, if His Excellency could see his way to leaving a few cartridges and . . . say . . . a webbing belt about, matters would be greatly facilitated, for these objects could later be produced as evidence of thoroughness and zeal in respect of the search.

Jimmy Lees politely turned out of his billet and allowed it to be inspected.

Next day, the mayor and all the gendarmes returned and were even more exigent. They now demanded to be arrested and placed in "custody." Nothing less than this, they insisted, would ever satisfy the Germans. Without waiting for an answer they began to bind themselves with rope and chains which they had thoughtfully provided for this purpose. Finally, trussed and powerless, they lay at Jimmy's feet, groaning with all the fervour of men about to be hurried to summary execution. The large number of islanders who had gathered to watch this curious exhibition had not had so much fun for years.

Jimmy Lees, however, was now beginning to weary of farce. He had commandeered two caiques and he informed the officials that if their intentions were really above suspicion, they would accompany him to Turkey and there place themselves at the disposal of the British authorities. The officials agreed, but insisted upon bringing their wives, their families, and their more remote relatives. Jimmy Lees' fleet then sailed, leaving Strati seriously depopulated.

Bob Bury, meanwhile, was laboriously canvassing the northern islands of the Sporades in search of Germans. He drew a blank in Skopelos, the largest of them, and another blank in Yioura. Finally, towing a number of captured caiques, and bored and irritated by the Greeks who perpetually mistook him for the enemy, he was informed that a small German garrison existed on Pelagos. Bury decided to attack it.

The Germans, Bury was told, kept no watch at night; a statement which he received with scepticism. He approached the building, a monastery, with care. Outside it a figure was standing, whom Bury's guide declared reverently to be a monk. Doubts were resolved when the "monk" threw a grenade at the advancing party with most unecclesiastical precision. The grenade failed to explode and the sentry was killed before he could gain cover. Bury now retreated to a safe distance and sent up a prearranged Very light to his armed caique in the bay below. The multiple Browning machine-guns on the caique poured a stream of incendiary bullets on to the monastery and the gorse-covered area around it. The whole headland was soon ablaze, the Germans completely silenced, and those who were not roasted inside the house, dealt with by Bury's party as they emerged.

Captain Charles Bimrose, with Sergeant Waite and ten attempting to embark for Cythera, was less successful than his famous precursors. Unable, owing to bad weather, to land in Cythera, the party finally made port in the Peloponnese, where they were attended by one misfortune after another. First, the accidental explosion of a grenade put three men out of action . . . then the partisan authorities, unable to believe, or unwilling to believe that they were British, held them under arrest for a week . . . finally, when their identity was at last established, they were chased all down the coast by one of the periodical drives by which the enemy maintained his tottering New European order. Bimrose did succeed in taking two prisoners, but these he was forced to hand over to the partisans, who first tortured them and then shot them.

The results of these raids not having been altogether satisfactory, Macbeth decided to make a reconnaissance of Calino, which was reported to have been heavily reinforced following the raid by my patrol in April. Jimmy Lees was selected for the job and took with him ten, under Sergeant Horsfield. The reconnaissance established that no less than sixty Germans were now stationed in the Vathi Bay area, previously unoccupied, and Horsfield, pursuing his investigations too closely, ran into trouble.

"I was looking down at the enemy positions," he said, "when I saw a boy approaching, followed by two Germans. The latter said something to the boy, who pointed towards our hiding-place. When the Germans came within ten yard of us, we stood up and fired . . ."

One German was killed outright: the other, in his attempts to escape, fell over a cliff.

Macbeth now determined that Calino should be attacked in force, and for the first time in S.B.S. history command was given to a Greek officer, Major Kasakopoulos, who with fourteen of his own compatriots from the Sacred Squadron and ten of our men under Sergeant Dryden, landed at the end of June. Major Richard Lea traveled with the party as liaison officer.

Calino was a Pyrrhic victory. "The approach and attack," wrote Lapraik, who seldom minced his words, "were reasonably sound. The withdrawal, however, I do not consider to have been in any way satisfactory." These strictures must not be taken as a condemnation of either Majors Kasakopoulos or Lea. Both these officers behaved with exemplary valour during the action, but they were confronted throughout it by language difficulties and the task of co-ordinating two very differently trained sets of men.

The attack on the Vathi Bay area had been designed for three patrols. By 2200 hours on 1st July these were in position and all telephone lines leading from the area had been cut. At 2247 hours the first shot was fired, killed a German sentry who patrolled a key position. S.B.S., with hand grenades and tommy-guns, forced entrance into the enclosure between the main German billets, and deadly scuffling, in which friends were not easy to distinguish from enemy, took place in the dark. A Greek patrol, attacking from another direction, came within grenade-throwing distance of the houses but was held up by wire and accurate small-arms fire. A second Greek patrol, operating at Piat gun, sent several projectiles into the target which began to blaze.

The German reaction was immediate. The whole valley was lit and remained illuminated by Very lights while from a point some distance away, heavy mortar fire was directed on the battle area in the form of a box barrage round the besieged houses. The defenders of these, however, to the number of eighteen, were now beyond all mortal help.

Much had been achieved, but in the face of German reinforcements arriving from all sides, Major Kasakopoulos gave the order to withdraw. While this delicate manoeuvre was being executed, Sergeant Dryden and Privates Fishwick and Jackson were wounded by a mortar burst. Jackson managed to make his way to safety but Dryden, who might have done so, was given a morphia injection which left him in so comatose a condition that he could barely move. Private Doughty, a medical orderly, very gallantly decided to remain with his patrol leader and the more gravely wounded Fishwick. The trio were conducted to a Greek house and there concealed for the night. Next morning, since neither wounded man was fit to march, the local population decided, after much heart-searching, to reveal their presence to the enemy.

Throughout that night the enemy remained in a state of great tension. Long after all patrols had withdrawn they continued to mortar the valley, destroying some dozens of their own reinforcements in the process. Searchlights swept the eastern shore, and at dawn, fighter planes made their appearance as if in expectation of a major landing.

What became of the three prisoners? Of Doughty, nothing was known until he suddenly turned up again, having released himself in Greece.

Dryden, I saw myself in the Averoff prison at Athens, some two months later. Although very weak from loss of blood, the Germans had forced him to lose more in a transfusion to Fishwick, who died while the pair were under interrogation in Leros. Every conceivable threat and form of intimidation, short of physical violence, were used in an effort to make Dryden give information. When we met in Athens--doubling up and down a prison courtyard--his morale was low, but his determination to remain silent quite unimpaired. Dryden had then been for nine weeks in solitary confinement, on short rations, with the threat of execution hanging over him. Later, he too escaped.

Meanwhile, Lapraik had arrived at Yedi Atala and the reason for his delay became apparent. The greatest operation ever attempted by S.B.S. was to be mounted; an operation revolutionary in conception, involving not only the liquidation of an enemy garrison or an island, but also its capture.

The island--as everyone acquainted with Lapraik could have guessed--was Simi . . .

The Simi operation had been considered for some time, but as long as the enemy possessed destroyers in the Aegean, it had never looked practicable. Destroyers can interfere with landing operations, even at long range and at short notice. At the beginning of the year, there had been four destroyers in the Eastern Mediterranean. Only very gradually were they eliminated.

The German navy in those waters seldom put to sea.

In March, one of these ships was damaged by a British submarine. Later, a second received a bomb amidships from a Beaufighter. Two remained lurking in Leros. In this emergency, Brigadier Turnbull requested London to send him out a small party of Royal Marine Boom Commando troops. A wise move, for though there were still many men in S.B.S. to whom folboating was second nature, the art of infiltration by canoe had undoubtedly declined since the days of 'Tug' Wilson. Folboats, when used at all, were now used to land personnel, their role being no more aggressive than that of a gondola.

When Turnbull's marines first arrived in Middle East experts were inclined to scoff. Their attitude of condescension was abandoned when it was seen with what precision the newcomers handled their craft. In mid-June they went into Portolago harbour, Leros, crossed two booms, sank the surviving destroyers with limpet charges and emerged without loss.

The way was now clear for Simi.

On 6th July Stewart Macbeth returned to base. He had made a personal reconnaissance of the island and pinpointed the enemy dispositions. Two days later the striking force, under Brigadier Turnbull himself, comprising ten motor launches, two schooners, eighty-one members of S.B.S. and one hundred and thirty-nine from the Greek Sacred Squadron were concentrated in Penzik Bay, Turkey, under camouflage. Three parties were constituted: Main Force, under the Brigadier with Lapraik deputizing; West Force, under Captain Charles Clynes; and South Force, under Macbeth. On the night of 13th July the landings were made, and despite great enemy vigilance, passed everywhere unobserved. The only casualties suffered consisted of two Greek officers who fell into the water with heavy packs. They were drowned.

The approach marches were difficult but all three forces were lying up and overlooking their targets before dawn. At first light a barrage was opened upon Simi Castle--the main enemy stronghold--by mortars and multiple machine-guns. Two Germans 'Ems' barges which had left harbour a few minutes before zero hour now came scuttling back. They had sighted the force of five British launches which was coming in to bombard the castle. Both motor launches and S.B.S. opened fire on these ships. Presently, large white flags could be seen waving from their bridges before they ran ashore and were captured in good working order.

"Stud" Stellin was clearing Molo Point. He had taken his first objective without opposition. Ahead of him, Germans were running up the hill to man their machine-gun posts.

"I took a shot with my carbine," said "Stud," "but misfired. I therefore

called upon Private Whalen to give them the works. We strolled in with
grenades, and I think that everybody went a little mad. Soon, all the enemy
were either down and dead, or up and waving their hands."

Stellin locked these prisoners in a church, left a sentry outside it and
moved on to his next objective.

Clynes, scheduled to attack gun positions, gave them three minutes
softening from his Brens and then ordered his Greeks to charge. "All I can
remember, then," he said, "is a general surge up the slope and two small
and pathetic white handkerchiefs waving at the top of it. I ordered a 'Cease
fire' all round, and began to count my prisoners."

By 0900 hours, Main Force Headquarters and the Vickers machine-gun
and mortar troops had advanced to within 800 yards of the castle. Fire was
intensified upon this target from all sides, mortar projectiles crashing on
the battlements and nine-millimeter tracer searching every embrasure.
The enemy reaction was spirited and indicated that they had by no means
abandoned hope. Stellin, moving his patrol to clear some caique yards,
received most of the attention.

"The stuff started to whiz about. We had to cross a bridge. Somebody
in the castle had a very accurate bead on that bridge. We doubled, but
Lance-Corporal Roberts, Private Majury, and Marine Kinghorn became
pinned down under a low parapet, the slightest movement causing fire to
be brought upon them. I told them to stay there . . ."

They did. They were not able to get up until the castle surrendered three
hours later. Roberts, who attempted to while away the time by lighting a
cigarette, raised his head an inch or two. He received a bullet graze from
the temple to the neck.

Clynes had also been sent down to the caique yard with orders to clear
it. On the way he met Lieutenant Betts-Gray, who throughout the action
did excellent liaison work. Betts-Gray was hugging the rocks, pursued by
a hail of fire. Clynes and his patrol were presently pinned down in their
turn. Private Bromley was hit in the arm, and Betts-Gray, who had had
miraculous escapes all day, in the buttocks once, and in the back twice, was
assisted into a house and put to bed.

To the south, Macbeth and Bury, with their forces, had assaulted a
monastery position after considerable mortar preparation. The surviving
enemy were driven down a promontory towards the extremity of the
island, where Macbeth called upon them to surrender. The first demand
written by Bob Bury, was rejected haughtily by the defenders as illegible.
It was rewritten with the aid of a young Greek girl, who volunteered to
carry it through the lines. This civilian armistice commission was
successful and thirty-three more of the enemy laid down their arms.

Around the castle, the situation had developed into a stalemate, with
mortar fire causing the garrison casualties and discomfort, but not sufficient in itself to bring about their surrender. Neither Brigadier Turnbull nor
Lapraik considered that the position could be taken by direct assault. They

decided to consolidate, make the maximum display of force at their disposal and institute surrender parleys.

Accordingly, Brigadier Turnbull sent a German petty-officer, commanding one of the 'Ems' barges, up under escort, with instructions to inform the enemy that they were completely surrounded, that the rest of the island was in British hands, and that further resistance on their part was as senseless as it was likely to prove costly.

The petty-officer returned an hour later. It appeared that the enemy were prepared to talk business. Lieutenant Kenneth Fox, a German speaker, now returned to the castle with the same man. A further hour elapsed during which the only incident was the emergence of a party of Italian *carabinieri* from the stronghold, weeping, and waving a Red Cross flag.

"I thought I recognized one of these fellows," said Lapraik, "and sure enough it was the old rascal who had given us so much trouble during our previous occupation of Simi. He grew very pale when he saw me . . ."

Lieutenant-Commander Ramsayer, the naval liaison officer, was then sent up to expedite matters. He found Fox and the German Commander in agitated conference and himself in imminent danger from our mortar fire. At last, the capitulation was arranged and the garrison marched out. They had barely been collected and counted when three Messerschmitts flew over the port and dropped anti-personnel bombs.

"Too bad," the German Commander is reported to have said, shaking his head. "You see, that's what comes of being late. I thought they had forgotten about us. I radioed for them five hours ago."

Prisoners taken in this action totaled 151, of whom seventeen were wounded. Twenty-one Germans and Italians had been killed. S.B.S. and Sacred Squadron losses were as usual microscopic, and, apart from the two Greek officers drowned, not a single man was killed. Six were wounded.

As soon as the Messerschmitts had disappeared, tea was taken by both armies in the caique yards. Sausages were fried and an ox, provided by the delighted population, roasted on a bowsprit. As for the prisoners, they were so delighted to find themselves treated deferentially instead of being shot out of hand, that they revealed the existence of many a cache of wine in their living-quarters. Bottles were transferred to S.B.S. packs, to be drunk at base.

Meanwhile, Lapraik, Macbeth, and Stellin, well known on the island, were borne to the town hall, where many speeches were made. The town jail was thrown open to the accompaniment of a furore which would have done credit to the storming of the Bastille. Unfortunately, only one prisoner was found inside and he, a Fascist, refused to be liberated.

"I admired these islanders," said Lapraik, "intensely; for they well knew that we could not remain and were rightly apprehensive of reprisals. But this did not diminish in any way their enthusiasm, though they were aware that hostile eyes were watching them, recording every incident. In the end, we caused them immense relief by taking the fifteen foremost quislings away with us."

General demolitions were begun by Bill Crumper and installations as varied as 75-mm. gun emplacements, diesel fuel pumps and cable-heads, received generous charges. Ammunition and explosive dumps provided fireworks to suit the occasion. In the harbour, nineteen German caiques, some displacing as much as 150 tons, were sunk. At midnight the whole force sailed, the prisoners being crowded into the two "Ems" barges. Stellin, with his patrol and Captain Pyke, Civil Affairs Officer, remained behind as rear party, with instructions to report subsequent events on Simi, and to distribute nearly thirty tons of food which had been brought in for the relief of the civilian population.

The German reaction was as expected, and followed the traditional pattern of attempted intimidation preceding assault. On the following morning the town was heavily bombed. Stellin and his men sat tight in their slit trenches. When it was all over they emerged to find, as they had hoped, that two enemy motor launches were attempting to enter the harbour. Such accurate fire was opened on these ships that they withdrew, blazing. So did Stellin, whose keen ear had detected the approach of more bombers, and who knew that this was the prelude to reoccupation of the island.

At three o'clock, from one of the more remote mountains, he watched the German flag hoisted over the citadel. But Stellins's adventures were not yet over; that night the launch re-embarking his party, encountered an "E" boat on the return journey. So many and so various were Stellin's store of captured weapons that every man in his patrol was able to take a personal hand in the battle with a machine-gun. The "E" boat was left in a sinking condition.

The great raid on Simi marked the end of S.B.S. intervention in the Aegean. It had always been intended that the Sacred Squadron should take over this, their natural theatre of operations, as soon as they were fully trained and in a position to assume the heavy commitments involved. That happy state of affairs had now been achieved and Lapraik, instructed by Brigadier Turnbull, was able to write to the Greek Commander: "Your group will operate in the Aegean until further notice. For the present, you will confine yourself to reconnaissance, but in September, raiding activities will be resumed upon a much larger scale. Sergeant Dale, S.B.S., will remain attached to you for Intelligence purposes."

Lapraik, with his men, his prisoners, and his booty, withdrew to Castelrosso, and from Castelrosso to Beirut for a well-deserved holiday. Here they were met by the news that S.B.S. had been asked for in Italy for the purpose of attacking targets in Jugoslavia and Albania. Turkish waters would see them no more.

But it is not possible to leave those waters without some description of extraordinary life led by all ranks there when not on operations.

Picture the deep, indented Gulf of Cos, with uninhabited shores and sullen, fir-covered mountains rising abruptly from the water's edge. In this two hundred miles of coastline it would not be easy for you to find S.B.S., but if you were wise, you would consult your map in search of one of the few streams from which drinkable water might be drawn.

Entering this bay, you would at first judge it to be empty. Closer inspection would show you a large, squat, ugly schooner lying close to one shore, with her gang-plank down and a horde of dories, folboats, rubber dinghies, and rafts nuzzling one flank like kittens about the teats of her mother. Farther off, a full mile away, lie five or six motor launches and an M.T.B. under camouflage, and within gun-and-lime distance of them a sleeker, trimmer, cleaner caique, which is obviously naval property. In this area, too, are other subsidiary caiques. The intervening water is dotted with small boats from which men are fishing . . . mostly with grenades.

Let us approach the large and ugly schooner. She is the *Tewfik* of Port Said, S.B.S. depot ship. In her vast stern a naked figure is crouching, and whittling at something with a knife. It is Lassen, and he is making a bow with which to shoot pigs. Down below, in the murky cabin at the foot of the steep companionway, David Sutherland, pipe in mouth, is writing an operational order. Beside him are rum bottles, magnums of champagne from Nisiros reserved for special occasions, and a neat list showing the casualties inflicted on the enemy during the current month . . . and our own.

"Blyth, Captain H.W., plus 4--OUT--4.4.44. Due in 12.4.44. Overdue. Target, CALCHI."

Presently, Sutherland reaches a difficult point in his work. He takes the pipe from his mouth and shouts:

"Corporal Morris."

A tall, angular, serious, and bespectacled figure comes bowling down the companionway with a file in his hand. Curiously enough, it is the file which Sutherland wants, for Morris possesses second sight. Morris retires. His typewriter, seldom silent, begins clicking again in the distance.

Just forward of the poop, Sergeant Jenkins, known colloquially as 'The Soldier's Friend' by reason of his claims to satisfy everyone, is trying to do three things at once. Sergeant Jenkins is accusing one S.B.S. man of pinching a tin of sausage meat, endeavouring to prevent another from doing the same thing under his very nose, and issuing orders to the Greek cooks concerning dinner.

"Not octopus again," he begs them. "Not octopus, *please.*"

On the hatch beside him, Nobby Clarke, his magnificent moustache stained by indelible pencil marks, is endeavouring to write an operational report under difficult conditions. Two American war correspondents recline on the same hatch in deck-chairs. They are polishing recently acquired Lügers.

Farther forward, Guardsmen O'Reilly, Conby, and D'Arcy, mugs of rum and tea in their hands, are discussing the good old days in Libya. In the black hole behind them which is the main men's quarters, the severe and well-cropped head of Staff-Sergeant-Major John Riley can be seen. Riley, oblivious of the noisy and vulgar game of pontoon going on in his immediate neighbourhood, is playing bridge.

In the forepeak, German prisoners, poking their heads up inquisitively, are being given cigarettes by almsgivers.

Towards dusk, the scene becomes more animated, and the immense capacity of the British soldier for slumber less noticeable. The headquarter signalers are pursued, for they alone have news of what is going on in the latest raids. Perhaps a motor launch returns with the personnel from one of these raids . . . another is almost certainly setting out to continue them. Men who have been bathing, fishing, bartering with the local Turks, return, demanding supper loudly. Aft, Paddy Errett, Cumper's deputy, is cursing and producing perfectly packed explosive charges at two minutes' notice.

A motor boat chugs alongside, and Sutherland is whisked away to Levant Schooner 9, where Lieutenant-Commander Campbell, sherry glass in hand, is entertaining a couple of M.T.B. skippers with the details of their coming patrol, which, to-night, will be north of Cos. "E" boats are expected.

Sutherland and Campbell confer, confide, plot, send signals . . .

Keith Balsillie is zero-ing a German Sniper's rifle found in Piscopi.

Marine Hughes is eating a tin of peaches . . .

'Brown Body' Henderson is unable to find any volunteers for P.T.

South of Samos, Harold Chevalier, two days out from base, has just ordered a German caique to heave-to.

From John Lodwick, *Raiders from the Sea*, (Annapolis, Maryland: U.S. Naval Institute), pp. 137-161.

Chapter 8

The Pacific War

Because the Allies chose a strategy of attacking "Germany first," constraints were imposed on the allocation of resources for campaigns against the Japanese. This meant that the correlation of forces remained in Japan's favor for quite some time. Indeed, even after the debacle at Midway in June 1942, the Imperial Navy continued to enjoy material superiority. Only after the long, attritional struggle for the Solomons did the balance shift decisively; and during this campaign, the Coastwatchers played a vital role as a force multiplier. Their function as an early warning system allowed the outnumbered Marine "Cactus Air Force" and the U.S. Navy to concentrate against larger Japanese naval and air components, dealing them one stinging blow after another. Indeeed, the Coastwatchers formed something of a low technology version of the radar network that the RAF used to fight the greater forces of the *Luftwaffe* during the Battle of Britain, with similar beneficial effect.

While the naval balance turned against Japan in early 1943, its army continued to enjoy a superior position on the Asian mainland virtually throughout the war, at least prior to the Soviet intervention in 1945. In this theater, two fascinating, protracted special operations emerged. First, Milton Miles, a naval officer, took a small mission to China and organized his own insurgency, incorporating bandits, pirates and some Chinese regulars. His exploits rival, in their own way, anything Lawrence had achieved against the Turks during World War I. Further, Miles's experiences gave him a deep respect for the emerging concept of "people's war," leading him to suggest that the Kuomintang's position would deteriorate sharply after the defeat of the Japanese.

The other special operations campaign was waged by Merrill who, under General Joseph Stilwell's command, found his small force being employed, again and again, in regular battle against much larger Japanese formations. His forces thus suffered fatally from the inevitable attrition that accompanies "regularization," much as Orde Wingate's Chindits had. Stilwell, of course, had his reasons, political and otherwise, for using the Marauders in this fashion. Nevertheless, one must blanch at such use of commandos, and look instead to the powerful vision of deep-striking, independent operations suggested by the special operations commanders in the Burma theater of this war. Indeed, military campaigns in the post-Cold War era may rely, one day, upon principles developed on the "road to Myitkyina."

Walter Lord

A Very Private War

Donald Kennedy knew all about Ferdinand the Bull--and he fully appreciated why this most docile of animals was the Coastwatchers' symbol-- but his base at Segi on the southeastern tip of New Georgia was just too valuable to lose, even if it meant fighting back. The location was superb. Protected by uncharted reefs, it offered equally good access either to the north and the waters of the Slot, or to the south and Blanche Channel, busy with Japanese traffic moving in and out of Munda. Other Coastwatchers could pick up and move if hard-pressed--one hill was as good as another--but Segi was unique.

Yet at the start he had so little to defend the place. Just a handful of native scouts and a few rifles. Thanks to the compliant Bogese, the Japanese knew roughly where he was; if they also knew how weak he was, Segi would be doomed. They mustn't be allowed to find out.

His solution was what he called the "forbidden zone." As long as the Japanese kept a safe distance from Segi, the principles of Ferdinand applied, and he left them strictly alone. But if any patrol or scouting force came within the area he deemed essential to the base's security, then it was in the "forbidden zone" and must be attacked at once. It didn't matter whether the Japanese were actually looking for him at the time--or even whether they knew they were near the base--it was enough that they *might* discover him.

Total annihilation was the rule. Every man in the enemy party must be killed or captured. No one must escape to tell the tale. In this way he would still keep the low profile that was so much a part of the Ferdinand idea. He would just be doing it a different way. Instead of dodging the Japanese, he would swallow them up.

At first some minor successes . . . then a big one. About 10 A.M. one bright morning in November 1942 a native scout burst into camp with the news that two Japanese barges were holed up in Marovo Lagoon only five miles north of camp. They were heading east with supplies--certainly weren't looking for Segi--but they *might* discover the base, and Kennedy wasn't about to risk the chance. They were in the "forbidden zone."

Gathering a force of 23 men, including two American flyers awaiting evacuation, he hurried to the scene . . . first by boat, then on foot. Urging the men on was his second-in-command, a burly, good-humored half-caste who had been somewhat redundantly christened William Billy Bennett. An experienced sailor and competent mechanic, he had also been a medical dresser, cook boy, and school teacher at various times in his 22 years. He was loafing at Munda when Kennedy recruited him in 1941, and he quickly proved an invaluable aide. He was not only versatile, but highly articulate. Before every engagement he would "psyche up" the scouts, like a coach giving a locker room pep talk before the big game.

There's no record what he said this time, but it certainly worked. Kennedy's little force struck at 7 P.M., pouring a devastating fire into the two barges which were moored right against the shore. A Japanese machine gun opened up briefly but was soon knocked out, and all was silent.

Billy Bennett boarded one of the barges, only to be greeted by Japanese sailor who jumped him with the handle for lowering the landing ramp. Bennett bayoneted him, and there was no more resistance.

He now threw a lighted dry-leaf torch into the second barge and scrambled aboard. In the glow of the flames he saw a Japanese lying on his stomach a few feet away, aiming a rifle at a scout on the shore. Bennett fired at him point-blank, taking off the top of the man's head. Hearing some sounds below, he next tossed a grenade down the engine hatch, slammed the lid, and rashly sat on it. He somehow escaped injury in the blast that followed, and the battle was over. Every Japanese was killed; their weapons carried off, their barges towed into deep water and sunk. No trace of them remained whatsoever. To the enemy command at Munda it was one more mysterious incident where their personnel simply vanished.

To Kennedy it was a bonanza. He not only built up his arsenal, but he vastly strengthened his standing with the local natives. Ferdinand was too sophisticated a concept to stir much enthusiasm, but a devastating ambush was something else. New recruits began drifting in from the nearby islands and villages. Seni, chief of the Mindi-Mindi Islands just east of Segi, signed on as a scout and received a rifle. He then ambushed a patrol of six Japanese, killed one, and got a second rifle. Recruiting one of his tribesmen, he ambushed five more Japanese--and got five more rifles. He repeated the process until he ended up with 32 armed men, all at Kennedy's service.

Shortly afterwards another local chief, Ngato, asked Kennedy's permission to attack a reconnaissance party of five Japanese on an island 30 miles up the Marovo Lagoon. At the moment Kennedy had only one rifle to spare, but Ngato assured him guns wouldn't be necessary. And so it proved. Taking six of his natives in a canoe, the old chief paddled up to the island and made friends with the Japanese. Then, while they lay sleeping that night, he crawled into their hut and stole all their weapons.

Next morning when the Japanese discovered what had happened, a general scuffle broke out, and at this point Ngato's plan hit an unexpected snag. Two of the enemy happened to be jiujitsu experts, and they gave the natives a hard time indeed. Finally the local villagers rushed to the rescue and, with the ratio "about 20 to 1," the patrol was subdued. Trussed up, the Japanese were brought back to Segi in triumph and thrown into Kennedy's POW pen.

More recruits drifted in, until Kennedy ultimately had what amounted to a private army of 70 men--half of them armed--not counting Seni and Ngato's tribesmen. He drilled them relentlessly, even teaching them a certain amount of spit and polish. They could go through the manual of arms like a Guards Regiment, and at Segi the day began with a bugler blowing reveille.

Discipline was always tough. In this kind of warfare the lives of all could depend on one man's performance, and Kennedy demanded unswerving obedience. The disobedient were likely to end up "across the drum"--which meant a good lashing while lying across a 44-gallon drum, feet on one side, hands touching the ground on the other. But Kennedy himself never administered the beating--it was done by other natives--in an effort to avoid racial implications. These harsh punishments did spawn a certain amount of grumbling, but it was not so much resentment as the griping of tough troops who will put up with almost anything for a commander they believe in.

As Kennedy's army grew, so did its arsenal. Each skirmish added more Japanese weapons to the collection. Ultimately the stockpile at Segi included one 20-mm. cannon, 8 machine guns, 2 submachine guns, 12 pistols, and 60 rifles.

Along with his army Kennedy was also accumulating a private navy. On one occasion his men stole a 57-foot diesel barge while the crew was ashore foraging for food. Another time U.S. fighter planes shot up two barges nosed against the shore, causing leaks that flooded their batteries. Unable to start the engines, both crews headed home on foot. Once they were out of sight, Kennedy's scouts plugged the leaks, pumped out the water, and towed the barges back to Segi. Two days later another Japanese barge appeared with a spare engine for one of the damaged craft. While the crew was off searching for it, the scouts stole the spare engine too.

The Kennedy fleet eventually boasted six barges altogether, one of which he armed with machine guns from a downed B-24.

But the flagship of his navy was no barge. It was then ten-ton schooner *Dundavata*, a marvelously picturesque two-master with wheezing engine that formerly belonged to the Seventh Day Adventist Mission on Choiseul. With Billy Bennett coaxing her along she could make seven knots in a following sea.

The *Dundavata's* big chance came in April 1943. Two of Kennedy's scouts arrived one evening to report that a whaleboat loaded with Japanese was coming up the Marovo Lagoon from Wickham Anchorage. It was methodically probing every isle and inlet along the way, obviously trying to locate the Coastwatching base.

There was no time to lose. The information was already late. The scouts had been delayed by a native missionary named Punda, who did not believe in the war and tried to argue them out of reporting back. He failed, but they did listen--and lost some valuable time.

Kennedy hurriedly rounded up a dozen men, and the *Dundavata* shoved off from Segi that night. Turning east down the Marovo Lagoon, the little schooner looked about as warlike as she ever could. Her upper works were camouflaged with leaves and branches, and a .50-calibre Browning machine gun was mounted on the bow. She also carried two lighter machine guns salvaged from a couple of downed Zeros, and nearly all the crew had rifles. Kennedy, Billy Bennett, and most of the men were on the *Dundavata* herself, but a few were towed in canoes trailing behind.

At daybreak one of Kennedy's outlying scouts paddled up to report that the Japanese were ashore on an island just ahead. This was far closer to Segi than Kennedy expected to meet them, and he had to scrap his previous plan for interception. Improvising on the spur of the moment, he anchored behind another island nearby. Assuming the Japanese had sighted him approaching, the *Dundavata* was now screened from their guns. He next posted a lookout in a palm tree with orders to report any enemy move. He was in a good position to intercept, whichever way they went.

Everything taken care of, he settled down with a bottle of whiskey and waited for the Japanese to make the next move. He figured they would stay put until dark--their usual practice--and he decided to take a nap. It was night when one of his chief scouts, John Mamambonima, woke him up, explaining excitedly in pidgin: "Him along. It's time to get up."

Kennedy waited long enough to be sure the Japanese were definitely on their way, then started his engines and slipped out from behind his own island. It was a bright moonlit night, and he soon spotted the whaleboat coming toward him. The Japanese apparently saw him too, for they turned around and began rowing hard for home.

Picking up speed, the *Dundavata* raced in pursuit. Bill Bennett took over the wheel, while Kennedy went forward and personally manned the .50-calibre machine gun. At 500 yards he began firing. A Japanese machine gun opened up in reply, and two bullets clipped Kennedy's thigh. He looked a bloody mess, but he kept blazing away as the distance narrowed between the two vessels.

After three and a half belts, the Browning jammed. Kennedy limped aft, took one of the Zero machine guns, and continued shooting. The Japanese fire fell off, and he sensed he was getting results. Soon the whaleboat lay almost dead in the water, oars smashed or lost, wounded oarsmen slumped in their seats. The *Dundavata* was now only a hundred yards away.

Kennedy shouted orders to ram. Billy Bennett was so excited he turned the wheel the wrong way, and there was an instant of total confusion as Kennedy cuffed him on the head and twisted the wheel the other way, shouting, "This way, you bloody fool, port not starboard!"

The bow wavered a second--not long, but enough for some quick-thinking Japanese to hurl a hand grenade onto the *Dundavata*. It exploded with a roar, scattering everyone and knocking Kennedy to the deck

Next instant the *Dundavata* crashed into the whaleboat, bow rising over the gunwale, capsizing it and dumping the Japanese into the water. The canoes towed by the schooner now cast off and made the rounds, finishing off any swimming Japanese. Kennedy took no prisoners this night.

Some 20 Japanese were wiped out altogether, and as usual the rule was to leave no trace of the engagement. In the morning Kennedy's men buried the ten bodies they found, salvaged some useful gear from the bottom of the lagoon, and sank the hulk of the whaleboat in deep water. His own casualties were miraculously light--thirteen men nicked by grenade fragments, the regular helmsman slightly wounded, and himself with his bleeding thigh. The wound was painful but not serious, and for the present he refused to leave Segi for treatment. He simply "shoved in" some sulfanilamide and carried on.

Such exploits made certain that Donald Kennedy's base at Segi would play an important role as the Allies moved over to the offensive in the South Pacific. The ultimate objective was the great Japanese base at Rabaul. This meant, among other things, clearing the Central Solomons; and this in turn meant seizing the enemy airstrip at Munda near the western end of New Georgia. Admiral Halsey's SOPAC command would be responsible, and the operation was called TOENAILS--a code name that turned out to be uncomfortably prophetic.

Once more the Allies faced landing on shores that were virtually unknown. How to go about it depended on the answers to a number of highly technical questions. Which beaches were long enough for the number of landing craft involved? What were the gradients? Where was the soil of the best consistency for a supporting fighter strip? What size drains would be required? How much Marsden matting would be needed for the airfield?

Not even Kennedy's network could answer questions like these. But there were men who could, and Segi had the guides, interpreters, weapons and canoes to help them.

Lieutenant William P. Coultas was a naval intelligence officer on Halsey's staff who had been to the Solomons on a scientific expedition before the war, knew the jungle, understood the natives, and even spoke pidgin. He was a natural to lead the first of several tactical reconnaissance teams inserted into Segi to survey the area. With him went Captain Clay Boyd of the 1st Marine Raiders, who was an officer with long jungle experience, and three enlisted Raiders carefully handpicked by Boyd.

"Would you like to go north and fight?" Boyd asked Sergeant Frank Guidone one day late in February. At the moment Guidone was stuck on New Caledonia, feeling very much at loose ends. He was a boxer, had been in a good many interservice bouts, and thought Boyd wanted him to go north for some tournament.

"Sure," he said, and then learned he had just volunteered to go behind enemy lines in New Georgia. Marine Gunner Jim James and Corporal Robert C. Laverty presumably understood the question better, but all three were very, very good at adjusting to even the most unexpected developments.

On March 3 they flew to Segi by PBY, landing in the lagoon as fifteen fighters circled protectively above. Kennedy was waiting at the dock to greet them.

To the new arrivals, the organization of the place was simply amazing. They were deep in enemy territory and had expected to find a small hideout manned by a few furtive jungle fighters. Instead they found a teeming secret base. The beaches on either side of the dock were covered by machine guns stolen from the Japanese or salvaged from wrecked planes. More guns were planted up the hill around the old Markham plantation house, which served as Kennedy's quarters. Native lookouts were posted on platforms in the trees, while sentries patrolled the shore in every direction. A chain of signal fires warned of any approaching vessel. The teleradio was in a shack about a half mile into the bush, and even friends were discouraged from learning its exact whereabouts.

Kennedy's organization extended far beyond the base itself. He never expected to hold Segi against a major attack, so "getaway roads" (as he called them) laced the jungle in every direction. He built reserve radio huts as much as ten miles into the bush. Caches of food were stored in secret places. An amazing system of hidden canoes allowed his people to move in any direction at any time.

The new arrivals found Kennedy himself quiet and rather aloof.

Perhaps from months of enforced caution, he did not warm easily to strangers. But professionally they could find no fault. All day he helped them plan schedules and routes. Then as dusk fell, he invited them to join him on his verandah, where they sipped some excellent Scotch.

It was dark now, and a houseboy appeared carrying a lighted Coleman lamp. With the Japanese only a few miles away at Viru harbor to the west and Wickham Anchorage to the east, Clay Boyd was astonished. It struck him as a most reckless thing to do. Kennedy, however, seemed to regard it as a normal amenity, a touch of civilized living he wasn't about to give up simply because he happened to be behind enemy lines.

They dined at 8:00, seated around a table set with silver, china and immaculate linen. Houseboys in jackets served a dinner of chicken and fish with fruit salad. It was all so eye-goggling that it seemed perfectly natural when the party was later joined by a lovely-looking Polynesian girl, who smiled a lot but said little.

Next morning there was more cause for wonder as one of Kennedy's gun crews went through a drill with a .50-calibre machine gun. They simulated firing, then took the gun apart, reassembled it in a speed drill, and continued their simulated firing. It was, Sergeant Guidone felt, a performance that would have put any Marine gun crew to shame. Later in the day he decided to show the natives that he too could do a few fancy stunts with a gun. It was a long time since Quantico, however, and he accidentally fired a shot through the dining room ceiling. Kennedy, Coultas and Boyd were fortunately off somewhere, but the Polynesian girl saw it and dissolved into giggles.

The Marines spent most of the day with Kennedy, poring over a large map of New Georgia. Then at 4:00 p.m. they boarded two large canoes, and with 20 native paddlers and carriers they set out for a first-hand survey of the terrain. All that night they paddled up the Marovo Lagoon. Daybreak, they landed at Revete Inlet and crossed the island on foot . . . then continued up the southern coast by a trail that roughly paralleled the Roviana Lagoon. On the 6th they finally reached a leaf hut known as Horton's No. 2 Camp a few miles short of Munda.

It was hard going all the way, and the natives didn't hide their exasperation. It seemed one more example of the white man's inability to get around. If they had gone by canoe up the Roviana Lagoon, they could have made the trip in twelve hours, as against three days by land. The visitors, of course, weren't interested in speed. They wanted to find out how easily a large body of men could move through the interior . . . how long it would take . . . whether troops could live off the land or must depend on rations. They backed their findings with copious notes and photographs.

Horton's No.2 camp proved a disappointment. Even from the tallest tree they couldn't get a good view of the Munda airstrip (Horton could have told them), and they finally split up for other projects. James, Guidone and

Laverty headed back to survey the Japanese camp at Viru Harbor nine miles west of Segi, while Coultas and Boyd visited Horton's station PWD on Rendova, hoping for a better view of Munda.

They were not disappointed. Ferried across by Willie Paia, one of Kennedy's chief scouts in the Roviana area, they found Dick Horton on his ridge, still enjoying his spectacular view. Nothing escaped his scrutiny--whether a staff car tooling down the Munda runway . . . or barge traffic on Blanche Channel . . . or merely some bored Japanese soldier fishing in Rendova Harbor directly below. Natives stationed in the two treetop lookouts shouted down every movement in the local dialect to the camp cook, who translated it for Horton, who whiled away his idle time practicing yoga. If sufficiently important, it was easy enough to switch to the teleradio.

Some fifteen minutes farther up the mountain was another excellent lookout, where it was possible to sit back in an easy chair and watch the Japanese through a mounted telescope. This was Coastwatching at its most comfortable. Horton was, on the whole very secure in his eyrie, but to be on the safe side, he had a couple of fall-back positions deeper in the interior, where he could always retreat if hard pressed.

Two days of sketching, photographing, gathering data; then on March 13 Coultas and Boyd headed back to Segi, arriving there on the 16th. The others in the party were already waiting after a most successful survey of Viru. They had worked their way to a point only 1200 feet across the harbor from the enemy camp--so close that Frank Guidone amused himself by lining up his carbine sights on a Japanese soldier who was squatting in the water to relieve his bowels.

By March 20 the party was back in Noumea. Their finding, together with data gathered by four Marine teams sent in on the 21st, greatly altered the planning for TOENAILS. Originally the idea was to land in division strength at Segi and push up the coast to Munda. Now this was out. The beach at Segi was too small, and the coastal terrain impassable for any large body of marching troops. But it was also clear that landings could be safely made much closer to Munda . . . that a 200-yard beach at Zanana, five miles east of the airstrip, was a good spot . . . that the reefs around there were tricky but passable . . . that there was a good harbor and few Japanese on nearby Rendova . . . that a separate landing north of Munda would be easier than cutting through the jungle from the east in order to flank the field.

Out of all this grew the final plan for TOENAILS. As hammered out by Admiral Kelly Turner's staff, there would be a two-pronged assault. A Western Group would seize Rendova . . . soften Munda with artillery . . . then cross Blanche Channel and advance on the airstrip; they would be supported by troops landed at Rice Anchorage on the coast north of the field. At the same time, a smaller Eastern Group would take Wickham Anchorage, Viru Harbor, and Segi. As soon as Segi was secure, a fighter strip would be built there to support the advance.

June 13, and Clay Boyd was back at Segi with a team of seven Marine Raiders, including most of the original team in March. With Kennedy providing the guides and carriers as usual, they quickly headed for the interior. By now TOENAILS was set for June 30, and their assignments were very specific--preparing the landing beaches, collecting canoes, cutting paths from Rice Anchorage toward the nearest Japanese stronghold at Enogai.

Operating from a base camp a few miles east of Munda, the group also fanned out on two- and three-man patrols, checking any late changes in enemy dispositions. Toward dusk on one of these patrols Guidone and Sergeant Joe Sciarra were making their way up a mild slope when they suddenly heard a great clatter of pots and pans, along with the sound of Japanese voices. An enemy outpost lay on the other side of the slope, just 50 feet away.

They froze in their tracks. They couldn't go forward, and it was too dark to go back, for fear of the noise they'd make. So for the rest of the night they just sat there, assaulted by a million mosquitoes, listening to Japanese songs, jokes, and laughter. At first light they quietly stole out of range, realizing that only those noisy pots and pans had kept them from walking right into the enemy camp. "If they had been washing the dishes," Guidone later philosophized, "we'd have been caught."

Joe Sciarra did not escape scot-free. He came down with a bad case of malaria and had to be evacuated when Clay Boyd was ordered back to New Caledonia to give Admiral Halsey a personal, last minute briefing before TOENAILS. The rest of Boyd's party continued hacking trails and preparing the landing beaches on New Georgia's north coast.

The Japanese at Munda were not asleep. The navy commander, Rear Admiral Minoru Ota, and his army counterpart, Major General Noboru Sasaki, were both very much aware of the U.S. reconnaissance teams prowling about New Georgia. Scraps of American food had been discovered in a nearby hut, and Ota's young intelligence officer, Lieutenant Satoru Yunoki, pieced together a torn letter to a U.S. Marine from his girl, found on a jungle path only half a mile from the Japanese camp. Along with the constant air attacks now hammering the landing strip, the presence of these visitors suggested an early Allied offensive.

Countermeasures must be increased. The Segi area seemed to be the source of the mischief, but exactly what the Allies had there was still a mystery. Every patrol sent to investigate had simply vanished. The answer, the commanders decided, was stronger patrols and better leadership.

On May 13 new outposts were established on Ramada, Mongo, and several other islands in the Marovo Lagoon north of Segi. Kennedy countered on the 16th by annihilating an eight-man scouting party that came within the forbidden zone. Captured papers indicated that the enemy still didn't know the exact position of his camp.

Meanwhile the Japanese also strengthened their garrison at Viru harbor, on the Blanche Channel side of Segi. The present post commander had shown little energy, and it was hoped that the reinforcements under Major Masao Hara would add some real muscle.

Hara's first attempt was by barge--down Blanche Channel and up toward Segi from the south. As usual, Kennedy's sentries were on the job, and the chain of signal fires blazed their warnings. At Segi Kennedy's army manned their machine guns, ready to give the enemy a lively reception.

But the Japanese still didn't know exactly where the base was located and piled ashore near Nono, a village some five miles short of Segi. There was, of course, nothing there. The troops--bewildered and with no other instructions--went back to Viru through the bush. Kennedy let them go; he had deployed his men for a last-ditch defense and was unable to invoke the forbidden zone rule.

The next party came by land, chopping a trail through the bush from Viru. Reaching the shore again near Nono, they camped for the night, planning to push on in the morning. Sentries were carefully positioned, covering any approach to their camp by land, but the side facing the sea was left unguarded. The shore was a tangle of mangrove roots, and these seemed protection enough against a surprise attack.

Kennedy and his men came in five canoes. Laying to offshore, the scouts disembarked and began wading in. The mangrove roots were indeed good protection against a sudden charge, but not against the tactics used tonight. On signal from Billy Bennett, the scouts began lobbing grenades into the enemy camp. In the darkness the Japanese had no idea where the missiles were coming from. They huddled together in frightened confusion.

Eventually the grenades were all thrown, and the scouts began using their rifles. But by now the Japanese had taken such fearful casualties, the direction of the attack no longer mattered. The survivors straggled back to Viru along the trail they had carved, dragging their wounded with them. They never fired a shot in return.

Nevertheless, Kennedy was under fire that day. As his men opened up with their rifles, bullets began whining around his ears and he suddenly realized that somebody in one of his own canoes was shooting at *him*.

He could never prove who did it, but he had his suspicions. Some time earlier he had fired the native in charge of the POW pen at Segi for failing to lock the gate one night. The man denied any blame, but he was relieved of the key and sent to work in the gardens of Chief Ngato--a humiliating demotion. Tonight, without Kennedy's knowledge, the old chief brought him along on the attack because he seemed so handy with guns.

The Japanese at Viru had now been foiled twice in quick succession, but Kennedy sensed the change in command. No doubt about it, the "new bloke" (as he referred to Major Hara) was far more vigorous than his predecessor. It was a development that made Kennedy more receptive than he should have been to a scheme suggested by another shadowy figure at Segi. Belshazzar Gina had been a native missionary at Simba before the war but was now under a cloud, charged with theft and extortion. While locked up at Segi, he volunteered to spy on the Japanese at Viru, presumably in return for his freedom. His latest report indicated that nine barges were moored across the harbor from the Japanese camp, that they were unguarded and there for the taking.

It looked like a golden opportunity to deprive the new bloke of his transportation. Ordering Gina to stay on the scene, Kennedy quickly assembled an armada of 20 canoes and set off for Viru Harbor. They were well on their way when intercepted by a native swimming out from the shore. It was one of Chief Ngato's men, and he urged the party to turn back. He too had been spying at Viru and he warned that Gina was making things up. In fact, Gina wasn't even at Viru--he was enjoying himself at another village--and the "unguarded" barges were really loaded with armed Japanese.

It was a narrow escape. Only a lucky interception by that daring swimmer had saved the day. Gina was recalled, and the natives urged that he be executed on the spot. Not completely sure whether the man was a traitor or simply irresponsible, Kennedy was unwilling to go that far. Instead he ordered 100 lashes over the drum. This was later reduced to 25, but Gina was never again allowed to leave the camp.

As the threat to Segi continued to grow, on June 11 Lieutenant Commander Don Gumz, skipper of the PBY detachment stationed at Tulagi, got some unusual orders direct from Rear Admiral Marc A. Mitscher, who commanded all the planes in the Solomons. COMAIRSOLS ordered Gumz to fly a "Dumbo" mission to Segi the following morning, stopping at Rennell Island on the way back. The squadron had never before flown a mission to Rennell, isolated as it was some 250 miles south of Guadalcanal. Gumz knew nothing about conditions there, or even where he was expected to land.

A mildly worded plea to COMAIRSOLS for more dope brought only a laconic reply that there wasn't any more. Nor was any explanation offered on the purpose of the mission. Gumz assumed that some hot-shot fighter pilot had gotten himself lost and was on Rennell waiting for a ride home.

Early next morning he took off, and one hour and 48 minutes later set the PBY down in the lagoon off Segi Point. So far the trip had been just another milk run. Now he supposed Kennedy would be bringing out some downed flyers and maybe give him a little info on the Rennell part of the mission.

But there were no downed flyers this morning. Instead, Kennedy had in his canoe the Polynesian girl others had noticed at Segi. In her lap she held a baby, while an older amah-type woman hovered close by. Two young Polynesian men completed the party.

Coming alongside, Kennedy sang out to stand by for passengers. The PBY crew gaped in silent astonishment. It had been far too long since they had seen any girl, much less one as pretty as this. But no one had any comment. Among the grateful American airmen in the Solomons it was well understood that what Kennedy wanted Kennedy got, and Gumz saw no reason to quote him Navy regulations about civilian female passengers on a man-of-war.

The two women were helped aboard and settled on bunks in the cabin, while Kennedy went forward to the cockpit. He asked if Gumz knew Rennell Island, and the Commander said no, but he could probably find it if it was anywhere near the position shown on his chart. Kennedy glanced at it, said it was "good enough" and explained the location of Lake Tungano, where the PBY was to land. Once on the water the two Polynesian boys would guide him to the spot where the passengers would disembark--it was their home. A few more navigating tips; then he scrambled back into his canoe and cast off.

Kennedy now lay to, watching as Gumz taxied into position for takeoff. He was still watching as the PBY circled back overhead before turning south. Gumz had made other trips to Segi, but he had never seen Kennedy watch a departing plane so long and hard before.

The flight to safety was just in time. Four days later, on June 16, Kennedy's scouts ambushed an enemy patrol of 25 men advancing overland from Viru Harbor. The Japanese got away in the darkness, but left behind an assortment of diaries and sketches. From these it was clear that Major Hara now knew exactly where Kennedy's headquarters lay.

On the 17th Hara launched his biggest drive yet. Half a battalion moved out from Viru and headed cautiously for Segi Point. Kennedy didn't know the details, but he knew he was threatened from three directions, and that he couldn't possibly hold Segi against the attack that was taking shape. On June 20 he radioed KEN that he'd have to take to the hills unless he got help.

Admiral Kelly Turner, the Amphibious Force commander for TOE-NAILS, reacted immediately. Segi must not be allowed to fall. It was needed for the fighter strip that would support the attack on Munda. He had planned to land there June 30; now that would obviously be too late. Instead, they must go at once--tonight!

At 8:30 p.m. the old four-pipers *Dent* and *Waters* left Guadalcanal with two companies of Colonel Michael Currin's 4th Marine Raiders. Racing west, they veered into Panga Bay and headed for Segi Point. They reduced speed now--these waters were still uncharted and no one knew whether the channel was deep enough for ships of this size. Twice they scraped bottom, wriggled free, and ploughed on. Soon Kennedy's signal fires began blazing--but this time as beacons rather than warnings.

At 5:00 a.m. they were there. The 400 Marines piled into Higgins boats and chugged toward the beach. As Colonel Currin splashed ashore, he was greeted by a big man in singlet and khaki shorts, with weapon slung casually over his shoulder. He seemed quiet and cultivated, and Currin wondered what such a man was doing in a place like this. It was Donald Kennedy.

Two Japanese parties were approaching too, but the nearest was still at a village called Regi, busily burning the place down. In the race for Segi, Mickey Currin had beaten Major Hara by a good three miles.

Next morning, the 22nd, two companies of U.S. infantry arrived to bolster the position. With them came a Navy survey party led by Commander Wilfred L. Painter. He was in charge of building the fighter strip that would turn Segi into an "unsinkable aircraft carrier."

Bill Painter was a brash, boastful officer, tolerated at headquarters only because he had a knack of living up to his boasts. This time it looked as though he had bitten off more than he could chew. He would be starting completely from scratch, yet he promised he'd have his strip ready ten days after the main landings on June 30. To many people 30 days seemed more likely.

Painter tore into the job as soon as he was off the ship. He had been to Segi twice before--once in February, again in May--to examine the lay of the land. Now he knew exactly what he wanted. Under his crisp directions, the surveyors got out their instruments, began taking sights, driving stakes and unwinding reels of line. His basic idea was to lay out the strip completely in pegs and cord. Then, when the bulldozers and graders arrived on the 30th, he would start building immediately. In this crisscross of string, he could already see taxi loops, drains, gasoline tanks, ammunition dumps, repair shops.

Rendova had visitors too. Around June 20 Kennedy forwarded a team of nine U.S. infantry and artillery officers by canoe. Led by Navy Lieutenant "Red" Redden, they made their way to Dick Horton's camp overlooking Munda. Their job was to explore the shore around Rendova Harbor, where the troops would land on the 30th, and also to find positions for the big 155-mm. guns that would be used to soften up the Japanese. After several days of poking around, most of the party left with the data they needed. Redden and two other officers remained to help guide in the landing craft on D-Day.

About this time RAAF Flight Lieutenant R.A. Robinson led still another party to Horton's camp. "Robbie" Robinson--never to be confused with "Wobbie" on Bougainville--was a free spirited, beer-drinking old-timer who had been a Burns Philp plantation manager on New Britain before the war. Stationed at KEN, he was sent up via Kennedy with two radio operators and a coder to give Horton some extra strength.

At Rendova Harbor and Ugele village the Japanese garrisons warily watched all this activity. Lieutenant (j.g.) Naoto Niyake, a young naval doctor, noted that U.S. planes were constantly overhead, with no Japanese fighters to oppose them. In his diary he compared himself to "a lonely candle standing in the midst of a fierce wind."

And well he might. There were only about 200 Japanese on Rendova altogether. Lieutenant Suzuki, normally in charge of the infantry unit on the island, was down with malaria at Munda, and there was a feeling of futility about the whole defense effort.

Lieutenant Niyake thought about his mother and his girl a good deal, and for solace dipped into his "comfort bag." All he seemed to find was an article entitled "Worry Comes with Birth." Small comfort. By June 25 he was resigned to the end: "I know I shall really feel helpless when the enemy lands. Our reactions now are slow, just like that."

On the night of the 29th Dick Horton put Robinson in charge of the camp and went down to the west coast with Redden and the other two officers. Canoes were waiting, and they paddled to Bau, a tiny islet north of Rendova Harbor. Landing, Horton led Redden to a tree he had picked out on the northeastern tip of the island. From here Redden was to flash a light between 5:00 and 5:15 a.m., guiding in the first troops, a specially trained group of jungle fighters styled "Barracudas." Their leader, on his first mission since the dark days of Guadalcanal, was that tough old Island Snowy Rhoades.

A fierce rain squall and gusts of wind buffeted Horton and Redden as they waited by the tree. Peering into the night, they could see nothing, but at 5 o'clock Redden began flashing his light as directed. Five, ten, fifteen minutes passed. No answering flash . . . no indication that their signal had been seen . . . no sign that any one was coming. . . .

Steaming up Blanche Channel, Snowy Rhoades peered into the mist and could see nothing. He had been chosen to guide in the Barracudas because he had once been manager of the Lever Brothers plantation at Rendova Harbor and knew every inch of the place. But that didn't help tonight. He couldn't pick out the barrier islands that screened the harbor, nor was there any sign of the white light that was meant to mark Renard Entrance, where the landing craft would go in.

The *Dent* and *Waters*, the pair of destroyer-transports bringing the Barracudas, groped along the coast, finally stopping several miles west of where they were meant to be. The Barracudas piled into the Higgins boats, started for the shore, then were recalled at daybreak, when it became clear they were in the wrong place. The other ships in the invasion armada could now be seen gathering off the harbor entrance. Belatedly the *Dent* and *Waters* hurried into position, and once again the Barracudas embarked in the Higgins boats.

They were an odd spearhead. Instead of landing first and wiping out any resistance, they arrived ten minutes behind the troops they were meant to be leading. Making the best of it, Snowy Rhoades led his group through the men already on the beach and advanced into the plantation. Almost at once he walked right into two Japanese soldiers with raised rifles. They seemed undecided whether to fire or run, and before they could make up their minds, he shot them both.

Despite all their forebodings, the Japanese were unprepared when the blow finally fell. At Rabaul, Admiral Kusaka had noted the increase in Allied radio traffic and concentrated his planes for a counterblow, but when the traffic fell off after June 26, he dispersed them again. At Munda, General Sasaki positioned his guns to cover a frontal assault, apparently discounting a landing anywhere else. On Rendova the garrison had gone on the alert during the night, but when nothing happened immediately, they relaxed and were literally caught napping. One outpost managed to fire off four blue flares, trying to warn Munda as the transports arrived.

The garrison at Rendova Harbor opened up briefly with a machine gun, but seeing the size of the U.S. force, the men soon scattered into the bush. Lieutenant Niyake, the pessimistic young doctor, found himself with an isolated group of 22 men. Driven from the plantation, they headed up a trail that led into the mountains.

Holding down Horton's camp PWD at the 2000-foot level, Robbie Robinson had his first hint of trouble early on July 1, the morning after the landings, when a stray Japanese soldier was sighted wandering nearby. Robbie got his Owens submachine gun, sprayed the bush without results.

Around 11:30 scout Pelope Lomae was sitting by a fire cooking tara with several other natives, when they sighted advancing troops advancing up the trail toward the camp. It must be the Americans, they agreed, and delegated Lomae to meet them as the only one of the group who spoke English. He was greeted by a burst of gunfire. Lieutenant Niyake's contingent, retreating up the mountain, had stumbled across the Coastwatchers' hideout.

Robinson and his men began firing back, but the Japanese opened up with a light machine gun, and that proved decisive. No time to do more than grab the codes and maps, remove the crystals from the teleradio, burned the rifles, took the rice supply, and shot the camp dog "Spring." One enemy soldier also had the time and curiosity to disassemble Robinson's Rolls razor, then couldn't get it back together again.

On the run and buffeted by a torrential rain, Robbie's party slipped and slid down the trail that led to the east coast. They were almost at the beach when they met another party coming up. A group of natives was bringing Lieutenant (j.g.) Arthur B. Wells, a downed Navy fighter pilot, to what they thought was the safety of PWD.

Robinson had no time to find this out. Taking one look at Wells, he simply blurted, "I don't know who you are, but fall in line--they're right behind me!"

The combined group now headed downhill, stopping just short of the beach. There were several enemy outposts nearby, and they didn't dare take to the water in daylight. Dusk, and two big canoes appeared. They all got in and started north up the coast. Then a close call with a Japanese barge . . . a wet night on a barrier island . . . and finally on the morning of the 2nd they reached the American perimeter and comparative safety.

Safety--and chaos. The landing craft piled cargo on the beaches far faster than things could be sorted and stored. Soon rations, medical supplies, fuel and ammunition were mixed in a hopeless jumble. To make matters worse, the rain continued. The few plantation roads turned into ribbons of muck--one bulldozer almost sank out of sight.

It looked like a golden opportunity for the Japanese, but at Rabaul Admiral Kusaka was still trying to reassemble his planes. He mounted small strikes on June 30 and July 1, and did manage to torpedo Kelly Turner's flagship *McCawley*. But the *coup de grâce* was supplied by a PT-boat which inadvertently sank the "Whacky Mac," thinking she was Japanese.

On the 2nd Kusaka finally put together a full-scale attack, and it was devastating. Sneaking in from behind the mountains, 68 bombers and fighters caught the Americans by surprise. Fuel dumps exploded in flames, and over 200 men were killed and wounded.

Dick Horton was lucky. He missed the full brunt of the strike. Escaping the confusion on the beaches, he had established himself on a small offshore islet, and it was here that Robinson's party caught up with him. Learning the details of the attack on PWD, Horton now sent a reconnaissance team up the mountain to learn what was left of the camp. Luckily the Japanese missed the hiding place of the spare teleradio. It was brought down to the beachhead, and PWD was soon on the air again.

Beyond the perimeter, Snowy Rhoades took charge of mopping up the scattered Japanese. Learning that a small party was hiding up a river near the southeast coast, he loaded a barge with eighteen U.S. infantry and ten armed natives and went after them. They sneaked to the spot undetected and found the Japanese cooking rice in a small depression near the river bank.

Rhoades asked the lieutenant commanding the infantry to plaster them with a few rifle grenades. The lieutenant pointed out that half his men had taken a wrong turn, and he didn't want to attack until he was at full strength. He then went off to look for the strays, while Rhoades and one of the natives crept closer to watch the Japanese.

Suddenly an officer, wearing a Samurai sword, left the group, strolled to a bush ten yards from Rhoades, and began taking a leak. Snowy froze, hoping the Japanese wouldn't see him and spoil the element of surprise. The officer finished, glanced casually around, and his eyes fell on Rhoades, standing right there in his jungle fatigues.

He let out a startled yell, and Rhoades fired a burst, killing him instantly. As the rest of the Japanese grabbed their guns, Snowy ran for better cover by the river bank. Here he and the native crouched down, listening to the enemy search the bush a few yards away. The native rose up, hoping to get off a shot, but was almost cut in two by a Japanese machine gun. Fighting on alone, Rhoades kept firing at every sound he heard, hoping to give the impression that there was more of him than one.

Finally the U.S. infantry unit moved up and began firing rocket grenades at the roots of a banyan tree where the Japanese machine gun seemed to be located. They silenced the gun, killed a warrant officer manning it, and routed the rest of the enemy party.

By the time Rhoades checked the body of the officer he shot, some American souvenir hunter had already beaten him to the Samurai sword. But he learned the officer's name from his diary. It was Naoto Niyake, the moody young naval doctor. Despite the sword, Niyake met something less than a Samurai's end. He was not filled with martial zeal; he was filled with gloom and self-doubt. He did not die gloriously; he died taking a leak.

Meanwhile the drive on Munda was moving ahead. Early June 30--even before the Rendova landings began--two companies of the 169th Infantry seized the barrier islands guarding the entrance to Zanana beach. They were guided by Clay Boyd, back for another patrol behind enemy lines. July 1, the big 155-mm. guns were landed on Rendova and commenced bombarding the airstrip. On the 2nd Major General John H. Hester began ferrying his troops across Blanche Channel to the Zanana beachhead. Early on the 5th Marine Lieutenant Colonel Harry Liversedge's mixed force of Raiders and Infantry began landing at Rice Anchorage to block off Munda from the north.

Frank Guidone was offshore in a native canoe, marking one flank of the landing beach with a flashlight. A few miles to the west Rear Admiral W.L. Ainsworth's cruisers and destroyers were pounding the Japanese posts at Bairoko and Enogai to cover the landings. As the salvos thundered louder and nearer, Guidone's two native paddlers decided they had had enough. They dived overboard, leaving him teetering alone in the canoe, trying to keep his balance and the light steady at the same time.

Both here and at Zanana the Americans found the going far tougher than expected. Initially taken back, General Sasaki quickly beefed up his defenses with 3000 men brought over from the island of Kolombangara. At Rabaul on July 4, General Imamura promised another 4000 from the northern Solomons, as Admiral Kusaka reactivated the Tokyo Express.

The terrain too proved worse than anticipated, and General Hester's troops were less than prepared to cope with it. Mired down in the swamps and jungle, beset by spirited defenders, the men's morale began to suffer. The advance fell behind schedule. The situation called for a number of remedies--one of them closer fighter support.

At Segi Commander Bill Painter watched the bulldozers clear coconut palms from the area where he planned his runway. The Eastern Force of TOENAILS had arrived on schedule, bringing the heavy equipment

Painter needed to translate his layout of pegs and string into a real fighter strip.

Work began while the ships were still unloading on June 30, and it didn't stop even at night. Correctly gambling that the Japanese were too busy at Munda to bother with Segi, Painter rigged floodlights, and his Seabees worked all night, clearing trees and grading the site. July 1, his trucks began hauling coral from a nearby pit and spreading it on the runway. By noon on the 2nd his rollers were busy smoothing it out.

Then the deluge. On the night of July 3 a blinding tropical storm swept in, stopping work, drenching everything, dissolving the freshly laid coral paving. In a few rain-soaked hours Bill Painter was almost back where he started. He had guessed wrong in using "dead" coral from the pit. Now his only hope was "live" coral from the reef offshore. That wouldn't dissolve, but it was hell to dig.

Dynamite did the trick, cracking the reef, producing great chunks that the Seabees crushed and spread on the runway. Painter urged them on, trying to make up for lost time. He seemed everywhere at once, rarely stopping to eat or sleep. By July 7 he figured he was back on schedule.

Then "Washing Machine Charlie." On the night of the 7th a lone Japanese float plane--probably from Rekata Bay--droned over Segi, disturbing the peace with occasional bombs. They did little damage but stopped all work, as the lights were doused and the men took to their foxholes. It was the same story on the 8th and 9th.

Once again Painter desperately tried to make up for lost time. During the daylight hours practically everyone in the outfit was put to work spreading coral. Clerks and carpenters found themselves wielding shovels.

As the night fell on the 10th, Bill Painter's ten days were up, but he needed another twelve hours. The rollers were still working one end of the runway. But they could finish during the night--and complete the job on schedule--if Washing Machine Charlie didn't turn up. Painter and Captain C.S. Alexander, who would be in charge of the strip, examined the evening sky. Clouds were rolling in, and it looked like no night for Charlie. They radioed that the field would be ready for 30 fighters at daylight.

But Charlie came. The clouds drifted away, and the familiar sound of his engine droned over Segi. When dawn broke, the rollers were still at work. Painter wondered whether to call off the fighters, but Alexander, an old flyer himself, was sure the planes could get in anyhow. The tower would simply warn them to land long. An hour later they began coming in--every landing perfect--and Bill Painter had made good his boast.

Donald Kennedy watched it all a little ruefully. It was his organization and leadership that had held Segi for the day when the Americans needed it. Yet now that they were here, he was almost a misfit. He really didn't belong in this teeming world of bulldozers, supply dumps and repair shops, supported by the hordes of GIs now swarming in. He belonged to a far smaller world built around personal loyalty, personal authority, personal initiative, personal contact.

Now no one even knew who his scouts were. And after some trigger-happy sentry almost shot Kennedy himself one night, he finally moved his headquarters across the channel to Vangunu Island. Here he still serviced KEN with intelligence, but the private war of Donald Kennedy was over.

From Walter Lord, *Lonely Vigil,* (New York: Viking, 1977), pp. 168-191.

Ronald Spector

The Road to Myitkyina

No sooner had the Casablanca Conference adjourned than the ANAKIM plan began to unravel. In Delhi to confer on the project, General Arnold found Wavell's operational plan not so much a plan as "several pages of well-written paragraphs telling why the mission could not be accomplished."

Moving on to Chungking, Arnold received the generalissimo's reluctant assent to the Burma operation; but what Chiang really wanted was an independent army air force for China under General Chennault, a vast increase in supplies flown over the Hump, and five hundred more planes by November. In a letter to President Roosevelt, carried to the U.S. by Arnold, the generalissimo spent one paragraph on the Burma campaign and the remainder on his demands for more air power.

In Washington the generalissimo's demands found a sympathetic audience in the president and his closest adviser, Harry Hopkins. Perhaps a shift of emphasis to air operations might be more rewarding than a slow and costly ground campaign. That view appeared to be confirmed by the outcome of the limited British ground offensive in Burma, launched at the end of 1942.

To boost morale and to show that they were still in the war, the British had mounted an attack into the Arakan, the narrow coastal strip of west Burma. Their goal was to capture Akyab Island, which strip of west Burma. Their goal was to capture Akyab Island, which had airfields that would be valuable for the support of future operations against Rangoon. Holding the island would also strengthen the defense of Calcutta. The area was lightly held. British plans were to send a reinforced division down the coast, while other troops advanced by short, amphibious hooks and a commando force swung in from the east. However, landing craft were unavailable--and the commandos were needed elsewhere. So the 14th Indian Division, under Major General W.L. Lloyd, was sent down the ninety miles to Akyab, plodding through mud and rice paddies flanked by jungle covered hills.

After a slow start the advance went well--until the 14th reached the towns of Donbaik and Rathedung, only ten miles from Akyab. Here the British and Indian troops became acquainted for the first time with Japanese log and earth bunkers, already unhappily familiar to the Allied troops in Papua, and here they were held up for a month while the Japanese brought in reinforcements.

Then the Japanese took their turn at counterattack, moving right across the jungle ridges which the British had thought impassable, striking at the division's rear and flank, and sending the British reeling back to the north. Now the tired, badly shaken Indian and British troops--many of them inexperienced and incompletely trained--began to crack. Many of "the troops that had been in action for the past weeks," recalled General William Slim, hastily called in to take command, "were fought out and could not be relied on to hold anything . . . [They] were untrained for the jungle and feared it more than they did the enemy." By May the Anglo-Indian troops were back where they had started--exhausted, racked by malaria, with morale at an all-time low.

To this dreary tale there was one hopeful footnote. In late 1942 Wavell had formed a large commando force called the Seventy-seventh Long-Range Penetration Brigade under Brigadier Orde Wingate, a brilliant eccentric and a veteran of irregular warfare in Palestine and Ethiopia. Wingate, with his magnetic personality, ascetic appearance, and far-away expression, was part visionary, part lunatic--but all soldier. His idea was that a relatively small force working behind enemy lines could cause damage out of all proportion to its numbers, confuse and demoralize the enemy, and wreck his communications. The Long-Range Penetration Brigade would work independently, in small groups, keeping in touch by radio and receiving supplies by airdrops.

Wavell had originally planned to employ Wingate's men in coordination with the Chinese offensives in north Burma planned for 1942-1943. Those offensives had long since been canceled; there seemed little point to sending in a diversionary commando force when there was now nothing to divert the enemy from. Wingate however, argued forcefully for the mission to proceed to forestall any planned Japanese offensive and test the theory of long-range penetration.

In mid-February 1943 Wingate's brigade of about 3,000 men--called "Chindits" after the griffinlike creatures which guard Burmese temples--crossed the river Chindwin and plunged into the jungle. Splitting up into seven columns, the Chindits attacked Japanese outposts and cut the north-south railway in more than seventy places. For three months they eluded the Japanese, covering over 1,500 miles. But the cost was high. Only about two-thirds of the force recrossed the Chindwin in May; many of the survivors were so debilitated they could never be used in combat again. One column of 1,000 men had returned with just 260. Sick and wounded had had to be left behind.

British commanders in India, viewing Wingate's exhausted and disease-ravaged troops, were inclined to write the experiment off as another costly failure. Yet the operation caught the imagination of the world. The Japanese, heretofore regarded as invincible jungle fighters, had been bested at their own game. Wingate's Chindits had demonstrated that British and Gurkha soldiers could also live and fight in the jungle and that, if supplied by air, they could be more mobile than the Japanese.

After the humiliating defeats in Malaya, Burma, and the Arakan, the news of Wingate's raid provided a sorely needed boost to British morale and self-respect. Correspondents proclaimed him "the Clive of Burma." "In the welter of inefficiency and lassitude which have characterized our operations on the India front," wrote Prime Minister Churchill, "this man, his force and his achievements stand out. . . . I consider Wingate should command the Army against Burma. He is a man of genius and audacity." With that, the prime minister summoned Wingate to London for a personal conference.

In the end however, the Chindit expedition proved most important not as a morale booster, but because it persuaded the Japanese high command to try something even crazier: a large scale invasion of India across the rugged Assam-Burma frontier to improve the Japanese hold on Burma and stave off further incursions. In the summer of 1943 planning began for an attack across the roadless mountainous frontier, an attack which would lead the Japanese to disaster.

Meanwhile, in Washington the argument over air power in China had swung in favor of Chennault and Chiang. Stilwell and the War Department pointed out that any air offensive which was strong enough to really hurt the Japanese would result in a Japanese ground offensive to wipe out the airfields supporting it. That was what had happened after Doolittle's Tokyo raid, when Japanese troops had rampaged through eastern China destroying every air base in sight. Nevertheless, the president was determined to go ahead. Backing for Chennault might not produce the great results promised--but it would keep Chiang happy and demonstrate American support of China.

At the president's order Chennault was given command of an independent air force, the Fourteenth, thus freeing him from serving as part of the Tenth Air Force under General Clayton Bissell, an old enemy. Some of Chennault's flyers had come to hate Bissell so much that at one air base a Chinese coolie who knew no English had been hired and carefully taught to shout "PISS ON YOU BISSELL!" at incoming Tenth Air Force planes.

Chennault's existing forces were also to be reinforced as quickly as feasible and to be allocated a guaranteed share of the Hump tonnage. Existing airfields were to be upgraded and new ones constructed.

All this still failed to satisfy Chennault, who complained that Stilwell was not giving him an adequate share of the Hump supplies. In April 1943 both Stilwell and Chennault were summoned to Washington for the TRIDENT meeting of the Combined Chiefs, which was to be held in May. Meeting with the president, Chennault was articulate and persuasive, while Stilwell was sullen and uncommunicative. "Vinegar Joe" disliked Roosevelt, disliked blowing his own horn--and probably felt resentful at having to explain the obvious to a rank amateur.

Whatever Stilwell might have said would probably have made little difference, for both Roosevelt and Churchill had by now decided that a full-scale campaign in Burma on the lines of ANAKIM was undesirable. Roosevelt liked Chennault's ideas better, while Churchill and the British chiefs had always believed the jungles of Burma the worst place on earth to fight the Japanese. Churchill favored bypassing Burma altogether and striking into the Dutch East Indies as a step toward retaking Singapore. As for China, the best course was to expand the air route across the Hump to support Chennault's air offensive.

The ANAKIM plan was thus quietly shelved and replaced by a scheme to build up the Hump route as quickly as possible. A much-abbreviated campaign into northern Burma alone was also included in Allied plans; its goal was to open a land route to China and thus shorten the flight across the Hump. Most of the anticipated increase in air tonnage was to go to Chennault, who was given an absolute claim on the first 4,700 tons flown in every month. A portion of what was left over would go to Stilwell to prepare the Chinese army for the campaign in northern Burma. Stilwell compared this arrangement to "trying to manure a ten-acre field with sparrow shit."

Actually, the situation was even worse than it appeared, for the TRIDENT decisions had been based on the assumption that the Hump air route would be able to carry a greatly increased load. Seven thousand tons a month was the target set for July 1943, and 10,000 for September. To this end the engineers and construction equipment earmarked for the Ledo road were shifted to upgrading and enlarging airfields and transport aircraft was rushed to India. Yet airfield construction soon lagged behind schedule due to heavy rains, difficulties with local labor, and bottlenecks in the movement of supplies north from Calcutta to the air-base sites in remote, undeveloped Assam. By July only 4,300 tons of supplies--not 7,000--got over the Hump; only 6,700 tons arrived in September. Since Chennault had absolute call on the first 4,700 tons over the Hump, little indeed would be left for upgrading the Chinese army--or anything else Stilwell might hope to accomplish.

Over the next few months Chennault's Fourteenth Air Force achieved little. His fighters inflicted heavy losses on their Japanese opponents, but they failed to achieve air superiority and were eventually driven from their advance bases in east China by unremitting Japanese air raids. Fourteenth Air Force bombers claimed to have sunk over 40,000 tons of enemy shipping during the summer of 1943, but the actual total was just a little over 3,000 tons. Many of the additional planes promised for the Fourteenth failed to arrive; those that did added to the supply problem by consuming oceans of fuel. B-24 heavy bombers could not be serviced at all in China: to attack Japanese targets they had to fly across from India carrying their own supplies, then return when these were exhausted.

Meanwhile Churchill and the British chiefs, reviewing the debacle in the Arakan and the general situation in India, and anxious to show the Americans that they were committed to a real effort in East Asia, decided to propose a new Allied command for Southeast Asia. General Wavell had shortly before been appointed viceroy of India; he was replaced as commander in chief, India, by General Sir Claude J.E. Auchinleck. Under the new arrangement Auchinleck would have no responsibility for operations against the Japanese in Southeast Asia. These would be entrusted to a new supreme Allied commander, who also had a mandate to develop air and land communications with China.

The British preferred to have the new Southeast Asia command set up along the lines of Nimitz's and MacArthur's commands in the Pacific. Thus, the Allied supreme commander would receive his operational direction from the British Chiefs of Staff, while general supervision over grand strategy would be exercised by the Combined Chiefs. The Americans, however, insisted on a command similar to that of General Eisenhower in the Mediterranean whereby the Allied commander answered directly to the Combined Chiefs, and was assisted by a deputy of a different nationality. The Combined Chiefs agreed upon a compromise arrangement at the QUADRANT Conference in Quebec during August 1943. The new commander was placed under the "general jurisdiction of the Combined Chiefs" on matters of strategy but retained the right of direct access to the British Chiefs of Staff. He would have an American deputy but his land, air, and naval commanders would all be British.

Selection of supreme commander caused even more trouble than defining the command. The British Chiefs of Staff nominated Air Marshall Sir Shulto Douglas. Douglas was heartily disliked by the Americans because of his habit of speaking "in derogatory terms of U.S. units and operations"--a habit which had on at least one occasion, nearly led to a fist fight. Churchill then turned to consideration of a general or an admiral; he finally hit upon the idea of nominating Vice Admiral Lord Louis Mountbatten, an officer highly thought of by all American leaders.

The U.S. Chiefs at Quebec enthusiastically concurred in Mountbatten's appointment as "Supreme Allied Commander, Southeast Asia" (SACSEA). Stilwell was appointed "Deputy Supreme Allied Commander," thus adding another to his chain of confusing and overlapping responsibilities. The British Chiefs were to oversee all matters pertaining to operations, but the Combined Chiefs retained responsibility for strategy and for allocating resources between Chiang's theater and Mountbatten's. Mountbatten's Anglo-American staff included Lieutenant General R.A. Wheeler as his G-4 and administrative troubleshooter and Major General Albert C. Wedemeyer as deputy chief of staff.

Mountbatten was only forty-two years old at the time of his appointment. Tall, handsome, a close relative of the royal family, he had distinguished himself as commander of a destroyer flotilla early in the war. (His exploits provided the inspiration for Noel Coward's popular move *In Which We Serve*.) Brought to London in late 1941 as chief of Combined Operations and a member of the Chiefs of Staff Committee, he had been the youngest vice admiral in British history.

A man of immense personal charm with a genius for public relations, Mountbatten was considered something of a lightweight by some of the more senior generals and admirals, who resented his swift rise to prominence. His new command was far from being the smoothly running Allied team which Eisenhower would soon command in Great Britain. American and British officers on the SEAC staff bickered endlessly over petty details, churned out endless operational plans which were subsequently canceled, and cursed the Dalhi weather and "the Wogs." American officers proclaimed that SEAC stood for "Save England's Asiatic Colonies."

Suspicion of British motives was widespread. *Life* Magazine reminded the British that "one thing we are sure we are *not* fighting for is to hold the British Empire together." Stilwell's political adviser, John Paton Davies, summed up the views of many Americans when he wrote that "British policy is naturally directed toward re-establishment of imperial rule over her colonies. Our policy is to cultivate friendly and politically disinterested relations with the peoples of Asia." He warned that "our present military association with the imperialist powers has created suspicion of American motives among peoples of Southeast Asia which, if uncorrected, will impair our relations with these people for years to come." The British for their part complained that the Americans could see "no role for SEAC at all except to cover General Stilwell's supply route." British strategists commented acidly on China's "inexhaustible capacity for absorbing resources without producing any concrete or timely result."

Although Stilwell and Mountbatten publicly professed admiration for each other, their behind-the-scenes relations were poor, sometimes hostile. Stilwell made no secret of his contempt for the British military effort in Asia; his conduct toward his "Limey" colleagues was often tactless and rude. Admiral Mountbatten claimed after the war that he had intervened on Stilwell's behalf when the generalissimo was about to sack him after a quarrel in October 1943; contemporary records show that the SEAC quarrel in October 1943; contemporary records show that the SEAC commander welcomed such a move. Indeed, Mountbatten was surprised and disappointed when Chiang relented.

At Cairo, in November 1943, the generalissimo met for the first and only time with Roosevelt, Churchill, and their chiefs of staff. Publicly, the Allies hailed the meeting as demonstrating China's new status as one of the great powers; privately, Churchill and Roosevelt were exasperated by Chiang's stubbornness, his seemingly erratic position on strategy, and the spectacular incompetence of his Chinese military staff and advisers. Roosevelt told Stilwell he felt "fed up with Chiang and his tantrums." According to Stilwell's chief of staff, General Frank Dorn, the president even suggested that the Americans in Chungking arrange for the Chinese leader's assassination.

Mountbatten came to Cairo with an ambitious plan to retake Burma and break the blockade of China. The plan included two separate operations, code-named TARZAN and BUCCANEER. TARZAN consisted of an offensive by the American-trained Chinese divisions from India; they were to attack eastward, clearing a path for the Ledo Road and capturing the important communications center of Myitkyina in northern Burma. A much larger Chinese force in Yunnan Province called "Yoke," or "Y Force," was to advance westward into Burma to link up with the American-trained divisions. These operations had already begun when Mountbatten arrived at Cairo. The British part of TARZAN was to be a combined land and airborne offensive into the north-central area of Burma around the towns of Indaw and Katha. In conjunction with TARZAN the British would mount BUCCANEER, an amphibious operation in the Bay of Bengal to capture the Andaman Islands, which would then provide a base for future landings on the Burmese mainland and for air operations in southern Burma and in Siam. How the capture of the Andaman Islands would help retake Burma or break the blockade of China was not very clear, but Chiang had long insisted on some British naval action in the Bay of Bengal. BUCCANEER was Mountbatten's offering, and assault shipping for the operation had already arrived in India from the Mediterranean.

All of these elaborate projects were soon reduced to little more than reams of paper. Returning to Cairo for a second round of talks after meeting with Stalin at Teheran, Churchill, Roosevelt, and the military advisers promptly scratched BUCCANEER off the list. Its assault shipping was urgently needed for the cross-channel invasion of France-- OVERLORD--which the Big Three had scheduled at Teheran for May or June of 1944. Shipping was also needed for supporting attack on southern France called ANVIL. At Teheran Stalin had promised that the Soviet Union would enter the war against Japan shortly after Germany was defeated. This pledge, Churchill argued, greatly reduced the potential importance of China in bringing about the defeat of Japan.

Some American strategists disputed Churchill's conclusion. But whatever they might think, the Cairo decisions marked a real change in American military policy toward China. Those decisions foreclosed the last opportunity for a major Allied offensive in China and the last possibility that Chinese armies would play much part in bringing about Japan's surrender. A January memorandum by the Army Plans Division on the "Future Military Value of [the] China Theater" acknowledged this new state of affairs, suggesting that henceforth the main effort against Japan would be made through advances in the central and southwest Pacific. China's main contribution would be as a base for Allied air power in support of those campaigns. Navy strategists still called for seizure of a port on the China coast, but it was becoming clear that such an operation would probably come only at the end of a trans-Pacific drive.

Whatever planners in Washington had in mind, Stilwell was determined to proceed with operations to open the way for the Ledo road. He had taken the cancellation of BUCCANEER calmly, never having believed much in its value anyway. But when Mountbatten's headquarters later proposed to cut short the long-projected campaign to retake north Burma and extend the Ledo Road, the American general was furious. Mountbatten's planners now favored an amphibious attack against Sumatra and Malaya in 1944-1945. To sell his new position to the Combined Chiefs, Mountbatten despatched a high-level mission called AXIOM to London and Washington, which presented the case for operations in Burma.

Although Stilwell was technically Mountbatten's subordinate, he despatched the counter-AXIOM mission without his superior's knowledge. He then gave an off-the-record press conference in Delhi to present his views. Those views did not remain off the record for long. A few weeks later *The New Republic* reported "some Americans believe the British are subordinating military strategy to the political aim of reconstituting her colonial empire" and that "the quickest way into China is to reopen the Burma road rather go around Thailand." The article closed with a warning about the "frankly imperialistic" group surrounding Prime Minister Churchill.

The British complained bitterly of "the reptilian activities of General Stilwell," while Vinegar Joe denounced the AXIOM mission's "fancy charts, false figures and dirty intentions." Predictably, Mountbatten's plans appealed to London; Washington--and particularly the Joint Chiefs of Staff--staunchly backed Stilwell. The result might have been the usual stalemate; but now, for the first time, developments on the battlefield, rather than at the conference table, began to exert a dominant influence on the war in Southeast Asia.

At the end of 1943, Stilwell had launched his long-planned campaign to reopen northern Burma. His objective was the town of Myitkyina and its airfield, a vital communications hub for the whole region. South of

Myitkyina, the Ledo Road could hook up with existing tracks which led to the old Burma Road into South China; Hump flights could use the shorter, safer, Myitkyina route.

To carry out his mission Stilwell had the three Chinese divisions (the 22nd, 38th and 30th) he had been meticulously training at Ramgarh. The greatest Allied asset was command of the air, an essential requirement for fighting in the trackless jungles and mountains which lay between Stilwell's forces and Myitkyina. The route of advance ran through some of the worst terrain in the world--"a rathole," in Stilwell's phrase--comprising three valleys, the Hukawng, the Mogaung, and the Irrawady. The valleys were an area of thick underbrush, impenetrable clumps of bamboo, and knife-edged elephant grass; and the intervening mountain ranges were worse. In such terrain troops could be resupplied only by air.

The area was held by one of Japan's best divisions, the eighteenth which had helped conquer Burma and Singapore in 1942. Stilwell's Chinese divisions outnumbered the Japanese and were tolerably well trained and equipped, but their commanders often displayed a lack of zest for combat. Well aware of these Chinese proclivities, Stilwell acted as his own corps commander in the Burma campaign, making his headquarters near the front, threatening, goading, persuading and even blackmailing his top Chinese officers into action.

The Joint Chiefs of Staff had been so impressed by Orde Wingate whom Churchill had brought with him to the Quebec Conference in August 1943, that they not only agreed to provide air support for a second and much larger Chindit raid into central Burma, but also to organize an American commando force to serve with it. This was the origin of the 5307th Provisional Regiment, an all-volunteer unit code-named GALAHAD. It was the first American ground combat unit assigned to the China-Burma-India theater.

The War Department intended that GALAHAD be composed of hardened jungle fighters. There were some of those, veterans fighting in the southwest Pacific, but there was also a good sprinkling of the bored, the restless, the adventurous, and the "misfits of half a dozen divisions." "We expected picked troops," wrote a medical officer with GALAHAD. "Instead, we found many chronically ill men. Many brave men came, but also numerous psychiatric problems as well as men with chronic distur-bances who believed they might get treatment if they could get away from their outfits." Because attacks of malaria in the Pacific "were given little more nursing care or rest than the average common cold at home," many Pacific veterans "volunteered in the hope that they would get hospital care." A strong motivation for some GALAHAD volunteers was the thought that assignment to a dangerous overseas mission ought to bring them home leave. It didn't.

Shipped to India with great speed and secrecy, the 5307th began wished to use the unit to spearhead his campaign in Burma. Mountbatten finally agreed, as he told Stilwell's chief of staff, "because it seemed to mean more to Joe than the bickering was worth." Wingate was less philosophical about the matter. He reportedly told the unit's temporary commander, Colonel Francis G. Brink: "Brink, you tell General Stilwell he can take his Americans and stick with his surprising command of colloquial American expressions." Stilwell appointed one of his best officers, Brigadier General Frank Merrill, who had accompanied him on his famous "walk out" from Burma in 1942, to command the unit. Reporter James Sheply of *Time-Life* promptly dubbed the force "Merrill's Marauders."

An even more unorthodox element of Stilwell's command were the Kachin Rangers, warlike tribesmen of north Burma who, unlike their hereditary enemies the Burmese, had sided with the Allies against Japan. Organized and trained by OSS detachment 101, squads of Kachins operated as pathfinders and scouts for the Marauders and other Allied units. "Often, we had a Kachin patrol with us and we never, if possible, moved without Kachin guides," recalled an officer in the Marauders. "The Kachins not only knew the country and the trails but they also knew better than anyone but the Japanese where the Japanese were, and often they knew better than the higher Japanese commands."

At the end of October 1943, elements of the Chinese 38th Division entered the Hukawng Valley of Burma. They promptly bogged down and were soon surrounded by the Japanese. Stilwell arrived at 38th Division headquarters and prodded the Chinese into action. Near the village of Yupang Ga they won their first victory over the Japanese in Southeast Asia. It was not a very big fight, Chinese casualties were high, and most of the enemy escaped--but it convinced the Chinese soldiers that they were a match for the Japanese.

Because the Japanese army in Burma was preparing for a big offense of its own against the British in Assam, its 18th Division was obliged to go on the defensive, fighting a delaying action against the advance of Stilwell's Chinese forces. Repeatedly Stilwell sent his numerically superior forces on wide swings to envelop the 18th Division, but the slow-moving Chinese could never quite close the trap. One Chinese regiment spent a week in what it called "preparations for attack." In February Stilwell determined to use the GALAHAD force, which had now joined him in Burma, to establish a block right across the Japanese line of withdrawal, trapping them between the Americans and the advancing Chinese.

The 18th Division commander, Lieutenant General Tanaka Shimishi, guessed what was happening. He decided to capitalize on the slowness of the Chinese to throw his entire force against the Marauders, who had established their block at the little settlement of Walawbun. He was confident of destroying the Marauders before the lethargic Chinese units confident of destroying the Marauders before the lethargic Chinese units could close up to help.

Dug in along a river, the Nampyek Nha, just east of Walawbun, the Marauders repulsed the Japanese attacks. Tanaka soon found himself in serious trouble. A force of Chinese tanks--the First Provisional Tank Group, commanded by U.S. Army Colonel Rothwell H. Brown--had advanced rapidly from the north, cut between two of Tanaka's regiments and began to fire on his division headquarters. Thoroughly shaken, the Japanese commander decided to give up his attempt to destroy the GALAHAD force. Instead he sought to move his division south to safety. In the confused fighting which followed, the Japanese lost heavily but still made good their escape.

Stilwell had once again failed to trap the 18th Division. But the Japanese had suffered another defeat: they lost over 800 men to the Marauders alone. General Merrill told his tired but exultant commandos: "Between us and the Chinese, we forced the Japanese to withdraw farther in the last three days than they have in the last three months of fighting."

Encouraged by these results, Stilwell resolved to send the Marauders on another long, enveloping swing to cut off the Japanese retreat to Kamaing, the central position in the Mogaung Valley, while the Chinese forces continued to attack from the front. Two battalions of Merrill's troops pushed their way south through the jungle to Inkangahtawng, about twenty miles above Kamaing, where they set up a block. The Japanese counterattacked so strongly that Merrill, concerned that his battalions might be decimated by the time the slow-moving Chinese came up, decided to pull his battalions out of Inkangahtawng into the surrounding hills.

Now the Japanese tried an envelopment of their own, sending a force north to attack the flank of the main Chinese drive. Learning of this move, Stilwell's headquarters ordered Merrill to take his men to the village of Nhpum Ga and cut the trail which the Japanese flankers would have to follow. For the already tired Marauders, the move to Nhpum Ga meant another exhausting trek through the jungles of north Burma; it also meant that they would have to conduct a static defense instead of the fast-moving, slashing attacks for which they were best suited.

At Nhpum Ga, Merrill placed one battalion on a hilltop near the village and another at Hsamshingyang three miles away to protect the airstrip, which was the Marauders' only means of supply and communication with the outside world. Merrill's men had barely time to dig in at Nhpum Ga when the Japanese came at them in force. There followed one of the toughest fights of the campaign, with the Marauders battling both to hold the village and to keep open the trail from the airstrip. During the first few days the Japanese pounded the Americans mercilessly with artillery and mortar fire. The attacking Japanese cut the trail from Hsamsingyang airstrip and captured the defenders' water hole.

Allied aircraft dropped enough water for the beleaguered Marauders to hold on. Gradually the two battalions narrowed the gap between them on the road between Nhpum Ga and Hsamsingyang, while the Japanese exhausted themselves in fruitless assaults. One night Sergeant Roy Matsumoto, GALAHAD's Nisei interpreter, overheard Japanese conversations indicating that the enemy planned to attack a small salient of the American perimeter. Warned by Matsumoto, the defenders withdrew from their salient and booby-trapped the abandoned foxholes. When the Japanese attacked they were met by a wall of fire from the waiting Americans. They dove into the foxholes for cover, only to set off the booby traps. At the height of the confusion, Matsumoto yelled "Charge!" in Japanese at the top of his lungs, bringing a supporting Japanese platoon to disaster as well. Early in April the Japanese abandoned their fruitless siege of Nhpum Ga and melted away into the jungle.

The GALAHAD survivors had been through two arduous jungle campaigns. Their ranks had been thinned by casualties and disease. The Army K-ration supplied to the Marauders as a routine diet was designed only for short-term combat situations and did not provide the necessary calories for an active adult. Among Merrill's men the average weight loss was over twenty pounds--and these men were already lean and hardened by arduous marching. According to the usual rules for jungle commando groups, the Marauders should have been relieved. But Stilwell had one more mission for them: the capture of Myitkyina, the great prize and objective of the campaign in northern Burma.

General Merrill had suffered a debilitating heart attack during the siege of Nhpum Ga. The Marauders, now down to somewhat less than half their original strength, were commanded by Lieutenant Colonel Charles N. Hunter. Stilwell's force, however, had been reinforced by two fresh Chinese divisions flown into north Burma; the remaining GALAHAD combat teams were also reinforced by Chinese units. Stilwell's command included as well the five brigades of Wingate's Chindits. They had been inserted deep into central Burma to operate against Japanese lines of communication and prevent attacks on Stilwell's flank. That March, Wingate himself had been killed in a plane crash. The Chindits, who had now been in the jungle for over four months, were in even worse shape than the Marauders.

Stilwell knew the Marauders were near the end of their endurance but he was planning a bold strike across the mountains to seize Myitkyina airstrip. For that task he would need a force he could count on to obey orders; only GALAHAD was available. So the hungry, tired Marauders, weak with disease, set out on their final mission. They crossed the 6,000-foot Kuman Mountains on an end run to Myitkyina accompanied by about 4,000 Chinese troops and several hundred Kachin Rangers. Less than three weeks later they emerged at Myitkyina and seized the airfield with little difficulty from a surprised handful of Japanese defenders.

Stilwell was exultant. "WILL THIS BURN UP THE LIMEYS," he wrote in his diary. Churchill cabled Mountbatten demanding to know how "the Americans, by a brilliant feat of arms, have landed us in Myitkyina."

Then things began to go wrong. Allied intelligence underestimated the number of Japanese in Myitkyina. The Allied forces at Myitkyina expecting to receive food, ammunition, and reinforcements on the first planes landing there, found that they carried an antiaircraft battery and aviation engineers instead. The Japanese rushed reinforcements to Myitkyina town; attempts by Chinese units to take the place ended in fiasco. The monsoon rains set in and the attempt to take Myitkyina settled into a long siege, reminiscent of Buna and Gona.

The Marauders, thoroughly "shot," in Stilwell's words, were being evacuated at the rate of seventy-five to a hundred a day. Their commander noted that as one company trudged onto the airstrip, "hardly a man could walk normally for fatigue, sores and skin diseases." One platoon suffered so severely from dysentery that the men had cut away the seat of their trousers so as not to be hampered in combat. Many believed the widely repeated reports that Stilwell had promised the unit would immediately be evacuated to rest camps in India upon the successful seizure of the Myitkyina airfield. Instead of being relieved they went directly into the battle of Myitkyina, along with American engineer units pulled off their construction assignments on the Ledo Road and "any other American who could carry a rifle." At one point Stilwell ordered GALAHAD personnel in hospitals--evacuated for fatigue and disease--back to the front.

Stilwell had little choice. He had repeatedly demanded that the British keep the tired Chindits, with their hundreds of sick and wounded, in the field; he was constantly pressuring Chiang for more Chinese units to commit to the campaign. Under these circumstances the American general could hardly afford to place himself in a position where he appeared to be overly sparing of his own troops. "While Americans were in the battle, the expenditure of Chinese troops at Myitkyina could not be challenged. And while he continued to fight at Myitkyina, the need for the British below Mogaung could be demonstrated." Yet Stilwell made things worse than necessary by his inadequate support for the Marauders, both physically and psychologically. Up to the battle for Myitkyina, "no member of GALAHAD had received a combat decoration, no member had received a promotion, a candy bar, a bag of peanuts, an issue of cigarettes, a can of beer, a bottle of whiskey, or a pat on the back by anyone."

Had the Japanese made a determined counterattack at Myitkyina, they might have swept the Chinese-American forces from the airfield. Fortunately, they overestimated the strength of besieging forces. Meanwhile the Chinese, in an unexpected display of skill and determination, had dealt their old antagonist, the 18th Division, a shattering blow, capturing Kamaing and driving the Japanese from the Mogaung Valley. This cut off one source of supply and reinforcement for the defenders at Myitkyina. By

Yet they fought on throughout the rain-soaked summer, while the Allied lines closed ever tighter around them.

Myitkyina fell on August 3, 1944. The cost was high but the rewards were substantial. A way had been opened for the Ledo Road. Engineers, laborers, technicians, and construction crews, following closely on the heels of the combat troops, were already clearing ground for the highway, gas stations, supply points, and motor shops along the route of the Ledo Road; they were building pipelines to carry aviation gas and motor fuel directly from India to China. Even before the fall of Myitkyina town, the Hump air transports, using the shorter, safer route via the Myitkyina airstrip, had increased the tonnage delivered to China from 13,700 tons in May to 25,000 tons in July.

While Japanese, Chinese, and Americans stubbornly fought it out in the sodden mud of Myitkyina, the decisive battle of the war for Southeast Asia was reaching its bloody climax hundreds of miles to the southwest around the towns in Imphal and Kohima on the Indo-Burmese border. Here the Japanese had launched their long-planned offensive, aimed at cutting off the British army in Burma and severing the line of communications through Assam which supported both Stilwell's army and the China air supply route over the Hump.

At first all went well for the Japanese. They followed their usual tactic of infiltrating around and behind British units, cutting them off from support, and forcing them to retreat. Yet the British now controlled the air and were able to shift men and supplies rapidly to threatened areas. At one point an entire division, complete with artillery and mules, was airlifted in eleven days.

Although badly outnumbered and cut off by the Japanese, the British and Indian troops at Kohima held out stubbornly until, just as the garrison appeared about to fall, a relief column spearheaded by the First Punjabi Regiment broke through with reinforcement and supplies. Further south, much larger British and Japanese forces were battling it out on the Imphal plain. The struggle developed into a bloody contest of attrition which the Japanese later compared to Verdun in the First World War. The British, abundantly supplied by air, gradually wrested the initiative from the Japanese, who had long since outrun their supply lines. By early July the emaciated survivors of the Japanese Fifteenth Army were withdrawing back across the Chindwin River into Burma.

Less than half of the Japanese soldiers who had set out for Imphal and Kohima returned. The Japanese military hold on Burma had been dealt a shattering blow and the way lay open for a British counterstrike to drive them from the country.

From Ronald Spector, *Eagle Against the Sun,* (NY: The Free Press, 1985), pp. 346-364.

Milton E. Miles

Chinese Pirates and the SACO Dragon

General Tai's emotions were mixed. He expressed amazement that the Chinese regulars should have retreated so precipitately from Changsha, but at the same time he seemed to have some satisfaction in being able to say that he had been "telling them so." I, on the other hand, felt ashamed that the United States had still found no way to combat the Japanese in China except with General Chennault's valiant few men and overworked planes. But despite the shock of the Japanese advance, General Tai was optimistic.

"Now we move ahead," he said. "The enemy is vulnerable at the back of the advance."

He wasted no time worrying about the water that had gone under the bridge. To him what had happened was merely another phase of a struggle that was already seven years old--a struggle in which there had been much fighting and retreating but also much infiltrating and boring from behind. And now, though still on a very small scale, we Americans could contribute to that.

Two groups of Americans--one under Joe Champe, and another under Ted Cathey--were already percolating as best they could through the advancing enemy in the hope of finding positions in the Japanese rear from which it would be possible to operate. During the confusion at Hsiangtan on June 14, I had sent my orders to Joe Champe and, despite the chaos that surrounded him, he had received them.

"Equip and start for Poyang Lake in Kiangsi," my message read, referring to a region some two hundred miles east of Hsiangtan and immensely farther by the route he would be compelled to follow, "leaving Cathey in Tungting Lake area, and proceed by any possible route before the Japs dig in so you can't move supplies through."

General Tai and I, some four hundred miles east of Hsiangtan, had already managed to slip behind the Japanese advance and we knew how open to infiltration the Japanese lines really were. Though it was often impossible to pass through the enemy lines directly, it was seldom that a way could not be found. Thus Champe, taking his four Americans and the twenty-five Chinese guerrillas he still retained, unhesitatingly went back up the Hsiang River to Camp Two. All his stores had been expended and about a hundred of his men had evaporated. Still, it had been in a good cause and he was now accepted by the Chinese military as an honored member of their corps who had been blooded in the defense of Changsha.

There were very few pickings left in camp--a few cases of explosives, some firing devices, and a small amount of ammunition--but he added two more Americans to his little group--Gunner Petrovskey and Aviation Machinist's Mate Schragel--and he also found William Hsing, who proved to be a gem of an interpreter.

When it came to trucks, Joe began to wonder if he hadn't been lucky in losing most of his guerrillas, for only three trucks could be found and they were out-of-repair culls that had been hidden away. They needed parts, and repairs and gasoline and oil, but all of this somehow materialized. Joe even managed to find two precious quarts of oil for his radio generator.

Cash money was a problem. Joe had none left and the same was true of Colonel Tong of the guerrilla force, though it was his job to pay all transportation expenses. So they went forty miles to Hengyang where they weathered two air raids while scrounging for dollars. Champe managed to persuade a money changer to dig up some buried treasure and, on Navy credit, he obtained a loan of $150,000 Chinese, though he was furious, two days later, when he opened the money packets and found that he had been outrageously cheated by the inclusion of a lot of "two-ballmoney"-- currency of the wrong issue that was worth only two-thirds of its face value.

Nevertheless, the soon-to-be-famous "Yangtze Raiders" were on their way. It is true that they numbered only thirty-six men in their broken-down trucks. And they still had to find their way through the Japanese advance. This, as might be imagined, had its problems, but despite their rattletrap equipment, their constant shortage of supplies, and the unpredictable route they had to follow, they managed to get through. They drove nine hundred roundabout miles to make good an actual distance of three hundred, and every mile was at least potentially a hazard because of bombing, enemy troops, lack of supplies, and destroyed or otherwise difficult roads. Help of any kind was a rarity. When a section of road seemed clear they scuttled along it as best they could. Here and there, where the opportunity offered, they loaded their trucks onto railroad flatcars so as to have them carried around enemy-held areas or sections of destroyed roads. And wherever they came upon a railroad there was one thing they could not understand. The railroad cars were all crowded with refugees who forever seemed to be traveling both ways--backward as well as forward.

One truck or another seemed forever to require repairs, but the Americans in the party wasted no time during these periods of delay. Gunner Petrovskey turned out to be a dedicated teacher. Richardson, the always useful pharmacist's mate, took his turn at teaching demolitions. In fact, by way of "class exercises" he and his "students" managed to ambush one Japanese train, to destroy several bridges, and even to damage a good-sized steamer.

The trucks, of course, were constantly providing instruction--too much of it, in fact. And Electrician Roberts, when not showing the Chinese how to make a proper circuit, was forever inspecting their rifles, checking their equipment, or retraining the soldiers in something or other.

"If I am going to fight beside these guys," he said, "they're going to be at least as good as I am."

Nor was he willing to confine his activities merely to the handful of men with whom he was traveling. Whatever Chinese soldiers they came upon were also subjected to his informal inspections and instruction. He paid no attention to the command of which they were a part, or even to the fact that they were sometimes intent on getting away from advancing forces of Japanese. On more than one occasion he had hundreds of men--perhaps, once or twice, even a thousand or so--sitting on the ground taking their guns apart and cleaning them. Having learned enough Chinese to be able to explain the damage that dirt might do to their weapons, he expounded at length while they cleaned their rifles and put them back together. And they like it.

Champe and his men made their way south through Hunan Province, finally entering the province of Kiangsi. There, in Kanchou, they stopped at a U.S. hostel and airfield. During all this time the Americans in this group had been so closely in contact with the Chinese that they had come to dress and even to look like them. At this airfield, in fact, they were almost unable to get in and the fly-boys found it difficult to believe that they had arrived by truck. Still, once they were able to identify themselves, their surprised hosts not only welcomed them but also led them to the showers, gave them cigarettes--which they had not seen for weeks--and even sat them down to an American meal.

"What's this?" Jo Champe asked when they led him to a table. "A fork?"

It was more than a year before they saw another one.

They left their battered trucks at Kanchou and headed down the Kan River by sampan. "What do we do now, skipper," the boys asked, "when we have a puncture?" But they did not have that problem very long. The area for which they were heading lay some two hundred miles to the north and, in order to bypass the Japanese, they had to make it on foot over narrow and little-known mountain trails.

The going was hard and for the first few days the Americans took great interest in the scenery in order to add to their rest periods. Each day they hired men at the villages through which they passed and so had help with the supplies and equipment they were carrying, but every man in the party was a carrier as well. Colonel Tong, a newspaperman in normal times, was as unaccustomed to this kind of walking as the Americans, but he kept busy even when the others were resting, for it was up to him to find them food, to collect the carriers they needed, and to locate places at which they could sleep--a task in which he was usually aided by the old imperial Chinese system that holds one man in each village responsible for the care of travelers.

The little mountain villages turned out en masse to see the first Americans who had ever come into their lives. Schoolchildren celebrated by firing firecrackers as the visitors passed. Magistrates made speeches. And on July 4, while they were still walking, teaching, and practicing, Colonel Tong helped them celebrate America's Independence Day by providing a veritable banquet of a breakfast--a meal that was especially appreciated because they had been subsisting so spottily along the way.

It was three months from the time they took leave of Camp Two before "Yangtze Raiders" finally reached an abandoned schoolhouse on the edge of their new area of operations. They had certainly come a long way around and had expended much energy. Still, they had not lost their sense of humor. As Joe Champe said, they "almost had the Japs surrounded."

They had no money. They had no supplies. And they had no students. But Colonel Tong was now in his home province and he promptly set to work to remedy their situation.

"As it happened," Joe Champe later reported, "we were lucky not to have brought men with us, for the men here fight well. They fight in defense of their own valley."

There was a fundamental guerrilla truth in this that we tried never to forget.

When Champe and his men started on their three-month journey, they left Ted Cathey and his small band at Hsiangtan where they were doing their best to find General Ho's column. In the confusion caused by the Japanese advance it was not easy to learn just what was going on. In fact, Cathey did very well even to locate the outfit for which he was looking and to bring his eleven Americans with him.

General Ho's column consisted of several thousand men, over half of whom had been trained at Camp Two, and their orders were to percolate through the one hundred thousand attacking Japanese. They also intended to prick the enemy in sensitive exposed spots in the hope of gaining time for the regulars of the Chinese Army to establish themselves in defensible positions somewhere back of Changsha.

Cathey's report of the first few weeks reads a bit like a custard pie comedy with Wild West trimmings. Doors were forever opening and closing unexpectedly, with guerrillas and then Japanese--or Japanese and then guerrillas--streaking through and not quite overtaking each other. Our heroes would be almost overpowered at one moment only to slip away on some lucky fluke at the next. Under such fantastic conditions it may sometimes have seemed that the guns that were going off were loaded only with movie ammunition--that the prisoners who appeared from time to time would quit presently and go off to the studio to pick up their pay--that the dead would get up and reassemble for another "take."

General Ho's headquarters group, with its newly arrived Americans, was caught in front of the Japanese drive like small logs swept along by a flood, and our boys split up to accompany different units. Then, for fourteen days, they skipped ahead--or hurried along parallel to--an army of ten thousand Japanese who marched in columns of about eight hundred each.

On one occasion three Japanese agents were flushed out of a house in which several of our boys had stopped to get a bite to eat. The weather was bad but even when it was raining and their blankets were wet, the Chinese often slept on the ground. Sometimes those who were more fortunate found a roof to shelter them and, when they could, they crowded onto the "kang"--the stone shelf at the end of the kitchen that was often heated by the smoke from the kitchen fire. Experience soon disclosed, however, that lice also congregated on these "kangs," so the Americans often chose to unhinge any available door in order to have a clean spot on which to unroll their sleeping bags.

At another time, a Japanese patrol found a farmhouse in which several of the Americans had taken shelter, and our men got away successfully on three minutes' notice. A few hours later they found another house, but the Japanese found them there, too, though again they escaped. Wet and half exhausted, they came upon a schoolhouse where they bedded down once more. But once more the Japanese appeared and this time the miss was so narrow that the Americans lost all of their belongings. It was after this experience that Ted Cathey asked somewhat plaintively for sleeping bags equipped with legs so that they, too, could run.

General Ho was a good commander--"wily," his colonels said. His troops were disciplined and seasoned, and they were paid from the sale of enemy supplies they captured. They always had two or three different spots selected at which they could gather in the event that they were forced to scatter.

Early on the morning following their three narrow escapes, the Americans reached another schoolhouse in a little village in which General Ho's constantly moving headquarters had momentarily been established. It was a few miles east of the path they thought the Japanese were taking but they had hardly more than arrived when guards reported the approach of several enemy companies. Because no Japanese had been expected, neither the people of the village nor the headquarters unit were able to move rapidly enough to make good their escape, and because the village magistrate needed time to move out with the village records and money, as well as with its highly valued supply of salt, he asked if a little time could somehow be gained.

General Ho, always willing to be as helpful as he could, obliged by making arrangements for a "fixed battle." Only a few guerrillas were immediately available but they were promptly ordered into position--six men for outposts, thirty men for the main line of defense, and twenty men in reserve. Carefully taking cover, that little handful of men, shooting carefully and at irregular intervals, held the line for three hours. But then, seeing that the Japanese were consolidating and were dragging up field pieces, General Ho ordered Cathey and the other Americans to escape with the machine guns they were manning.

"We don't want you captured," he told Cathey. "Take your men and hurry south to our next headquarters. Without you we can get away."

Cathey's little group wriggled off at an angle through the tall grass but just as they reached comparative safety a few hundred yards away they saw that the enemy had closed the gap through which they had escaped and had surrounded General Ho. Unable to offer any help, they hurried on with a twelve-year-old guide toward the next rendezvous, but on the way they met a messenger who told them that Dr. Coggins, with five sampans of supplies, had been captured by the same enemy unit from which they had only now escaped. Figuring that the Japanese troops were being kept busy for the moment by General Ho, Cathey asked for volunteers who would go with him back to the enemy headquarters in the hope of rescuing Coggins. They all knew the place, for it was there that they had earlier lost all their gear.

Just as they were perfecting their plan of operation, a runner came by with a letter from Coggins. He, it now appeared, was worrying about them! He had been making good time in the sampans and had even been using his bedsheet for a sail. But he and several Chinese had decided to walk for a time and, wondering how the sampans were getting on, had decided to inquire at the village. They had not yet reached it when they heard firing and saw scores of townspeople, some of whom were wounded, running out with the enemy after them. With that to urge them on, Coggins and his Chinese companions struck off by a roundabout route over the hills. On the way they learned that two out of five sampans had been sunk, though three, including the one with the medical supplies, were safe.

With that to report, Coggins and his Chinese companions made their way to the next "headquarters" where they finally met Cathey, and which General Ho also reached a little later. He and his men had shifted into civilian clothes and, with no more disguise than that, had walked out of the village and away from the Japanese. He had with them only five of his men, but he believed that he had actually lost no more than sixteen. The rest, he felt sure, would turn up in time. They did, too, though the last of them did not put in his appearance again for almost six weeks.

That night, incidentally, a group of General Ho's men went back to that captured schoolhouse and lobbed a few hand grenades at it so as to try their hand at "psychological warfare" and to disturb the enemy's sleep.

For almost three months this kind of warfare continued. Outnumbered by the heaviest kind of odds, and forever short of food, General Ho's force was frequently short of guns and ammunition as well. During all this time the little group of SACO Americans was scattered among the various

Chinese units--two men with General Ho, and two or three with each of his four colonels. They walked twenty-five to thirty-five miles a day and were seldom more than barely out of contact with the enemy. Fighting irregularly but more or less constantly, they worked with whatever Chinese units they had temporarily joined, slept with them, and ate with them. Their two daily meals of rice were often enough flavored only by weeds or the bark of trees, and their diet, by their own admission, made them both "leaner and meaner." But they "paid their way," and General Ho, the first Chinese general officer to take any SACO Americans into action, continued to do so until the end of the war. And other column commanders, envying his "score," decided that the Americans had something to do with it and so followed his example.

In this three-month period General Ho's fourth column had thirty-four actions in which 967 enemy soldiers were killed and 199 were wounded. And in those actions the guerrilla losses totaled only fourteen dead and ten wounded. Nor have I mentioned in this connection the surprising quantities of supplies they captured.

As I have said, General Ho's fourth column was made up, for the most part, of men whom we had trained, and an important part of the training had been our insistence on safety for the guerrilla fighters. "When trained men are lost," we argued, "there is something wrong." It was a new approach for the Chinese soldier, who had too often been sacrificed after having been persuaded that death in action was clear evidence of fearless bravery.

"That idea is stupid." our men insisted. "Find out how to do it more safely."

On our part, too, there was a gain, for Cathey--and others of us through his reports--began to see that all instructors needed "column experience" promptly so that they would not begin by underrating the little Chinese soldier, or feel too superior while they were teaching.

As a result of these developments, most of which were beyond our control, Unit Two had begun to divide, amoeba-like. Champe was in the Poyang Lake region, three months from Chungking by land travel. Cathey was north of Changsha, in the Tungting Lake area, three weeks distant if the traveler were fortunate. Camp Two, which had been active for so long, had turned its farmlike buildings over to its Chinese employees and had moved its headquarters unit to Hungkiang, near the Kweichow border two hundred miles to the west and south.

It took two months to make the walled military compound at Hungkiang sanitary and useful for our purposes, but even by then the Japanese had not completed their drive. Thus the unit at Hungkiang divided again, sending one group south to Nanning in order to instruct a new column which, though its men spoke Cantonese, had nevertheless heard what our courses of training had succeeded in accomplishing.

Camp Two, in fact, had started a kind of landslide, and from the fall of

Changsha until the end of the war we sent Americans into the field in ever-increasing numbers. Ultimately there were more than a thousand of us, working intimately with a hundred thousand guerrillas, with two or three hundred thousand plainclothesmen, with fourteen active guerrilla columns and innumerable saboteurs who came to be adept at following our patient, cooperative tactics.

Regularly we sent in reports of what they accomplished to the Intelligence Section of China-Burma-India Staff with the accounts of damage and casualties checked by Americans--checked and, I am confident, usually underestimated. Yet my wife regularly sent me newspaper clippings from home, all of which plainly indicated that only the Chinese Communist guerrillas were fighting the Japanese.

Even yet I cannot understand why word of what SACO was accomplishing was not given to American correspondents or, if it was, why it never appeared in the newspapers they represented.

For two weeks following the attack on Changsha, General Tai and I, along with those who had come with us from Chungking, rode our trucks east, south, and north from Camp Two. For a few days we had no idea that we were passing through a gap just ahead of the main Japanese advance. Consequently it was only with a maximum of good luck that we were able to make our way to the east for some three hundred miles, though by the very irregular route we took the distance was far greater. Actually, since leaving Camp Two, we had driven out of Hunan Province, in which Camp Two lay, had crossed the whole of Kiangsi Province, had entered Fukien Province, and had finally reached Kienyang, which lies no more than ninety miles or so from the coast. Even to me the place was familiar, for we had passed this way two years before on our way to Pucheng, which lay some sixty or seventy miles farther north.

We were well back of the Japanese "front" by now, but in Kienyang we had learned of unusual activities on the part of spies and paid assassins. Because of this we decided, like fugitives in a detective story, to change both beds and cars in the middle of the night. As we prepared to leave town, General Tai's clearly spoken orders were "On to Camp One," but a few miles out of the city the trucks in which our party was traveling stopped beside the road, leaving the other trucks to continue on their way while we headed off through the darkness toward Kienow. Whether or not we succeeded in throwing any trackers off our trail I do not know, but we surely managed to mix up the baggage.

It was at this point--though most unexpectedly to me--that General Tai declared that we would take a day or two off and go to see his mother.

No one--not even the Chinese--seemed to know very much about General Tai's family, and I had never imagined that he would open up any important phase of his private life to a foreigner. Already Eddie Liu had hinted that because we were ahead of time for an important meeting that was scheduled, the general might leave us at some time during this trip in order to visit his mother, but there had been no hint that we might be taken along. Eddie, in fact, had explained somewhat apologetically that the village of Pao An in which she lived was very poor, for it had recently been ruined by the Japanese. He added, too, that the general's mother--Lao Tai Tai or, literally, "the Old Mistress"--had only a small house, for she had refused to accept a new one her famous son had built for her because many of her neighbors had none. But now, to my surprise, we were all on our way to pay our respects, and even I was included as a friend of the family.

General Tai had been born in a valley in the southernmost portion of Chekiang Province, which adjoins Fukien Province on the north. The distance from Kienow was not great but rain began to fall as morning dawned and the miles seemed to grow longer as we made our way slowly over the rough irregularities of the muddy road. But after a time the sky cleared and, as the sun came out, we entered what I believe to be the most beautiful country I have ever seen. Rows and rows of pale green rice were reflected in the glassy smooth water of the paddies which were grouped on the level terraces that lay in broad and well-kept steps down the sides of the hills. Tung trees were in fragrant bloom, and the irritating characteristics of their tung oil were completely forgotten as we watched the lovely drifts of white blossoms. White flowers grew everywhere, and everywhere butterflies were flying among them.

In my relaxed mood even the rain was beautiful when it began again at dusk. And then, as the dusk grew deeper, we stopped in the gathering night at what seemed to be an entirely empty spot beside the road. There was no sign of a village that I could see. There was not even a house in sight, and the rain was drumming steadily on the tarpaulin that was stretched across the truck's curved metal supports.

"Here we are," said General Tai, climbing out into the wet, I heard shouts that seemed to echo from the hillsides, and saw burning torches that flickered high up beside the road in what I had assumed to be the sky. Then I dimly saw a series of sedan chairs in the rain as they made their way downhill toward us. Each chair was carried by six men and lighted by two "firemen"--one ahead and one behind--each of whom carried flaring six-foot torches that were made of thin plaited strips of bamboo.

Having given up the limited comfort of our truck for the cramped discomfort of the sedan chairs, we were hoisted jerkily up a goat path, with our chair-bearers taking turns with the lifting and steadying where the turns were sharp or the path was steep. And having reached the top, we found ourselves being carried through a "moon gate" that framed a cheerful white house with a red roof--a California-style two-story house that had four bedrooms. Built by Tai Li as a retreat for his mother, it was nevertheless unoccupied because she insisted that it was her duty to be farther down the slope among the villagers.

The house was lit with candles--red ones on tall pewter spikes that were supported by squares of Chinese characters that were intricately worked in the metal. "Long life and happiness," said Eddie Lin, translating the characters for me. And the red candles signified that we were honored guests.

Having cleaned ourselves and put on dry clothing, we had just seated ourselves at table for dinner when an old servant came in to report to General Tai that his son had arrived to pay his respects. The general grunted, and for more than an hour we went on with our dinner. It was only then that he announced that he would like to introduce his son, and sent for the "boy" who had been patiently waiting for his first visit with his father in fourteen months.

A man, not a boy, came to the door, stopping to bow low before making a respectful speech. Tai Li made a kind of whiffling noise in reply and introduced his son to me. The young man bowed almost to the ground and then started to retire. Disappointed, I asked General Tai if he couldn't stay for a while and when permission was granted he respectfully took a chair at one side of the room though there was an empty one at the table.

When I asked him how old he was, he answered me in English. "Thirty years," he said, and Tai Li added in Chinese, "Thirty-one counted in Chinese style." He was teaching, I learned, in the village high-school, was married, and had a son.

The conversation was constrained and the young man soon left. I had thought that Tai Li's occasional disparaging remarks about his "worthless son" had been pure Confucian oratory--mere customary expressions of worthlessness and uselessness spoken aloud about a child he adored. This is normal in China--especially where a first son is involved--and is supposed to protect him from the jealousy of evil spirits that may be listening. Actually, however, the general was deeply disappointed in his son, as I came later to understand. He thought the boy had been spoiled by his mother, and that he had not paid enough attention to his studies. He thought also that his own success had led the boy to depend on him for money and influence, instead of working energetically for himself. Nor was the general pleased with his son's marriage. General Tai's wife, I learned later, had asked on her deathbed that Tai Li promise to allow the boy to marry a pretty schoolteacher who, even at that time, had tuberculosis.

My own feeling was that General Tai was holding up impossible standards for his son. The young man was well above average in intelligence, and though he may have matured late there was no question about his courage and application. He had been attending a university in Shanghai when the Japanese occupied the city in 1939, and had not completed his course "although," the general said, "he was already twenty-five."

General Tai had sent him back to this lovely valley, partly to protect Lao Tai Tai, who refused to accompany her son to Chungking when the government later evacuated Nanking. Her duty, she insisted, demanded that she return to the village. Because General Tai's wife had died even earlier, Lao Tai Tai took the general's little daughter with her, and the son was accompanied by his wife, with whom he set up the village primary and intermediate schools at which both of them taught. As I learned more about the son I came to understand his difficulties and recognized that, despite his father's disappointment, the young man's accomplishments had been commendable and his success substantial.

Following our dinner we made an inspection of the house, for which the general had just paid $10,000 Chinese for repairs after the Japanese had peppered the place. "Costs are rising too quickly," he commented. "The house cost only $3,000 Chinese to build in 1936." Then he called my attention to some ingenious new windows that looked, I thought, like glassed-in holes. And that is what they were--holes caused by Japanese mortar fire that had been directed at the house because they suspected that the village's resistance had been directed from there. The general, proud of those holes and the reason for their existence, had refused to have them repaired. He had them framed, instead, and covered with glass.

Up to now I had been told no single word of the attack on the village, though it had taken place two years earlier just before General Tai and I had undergone the bombing of Pucheng together. At that time, I now learned, he had done his best to reach the village for the important seventieth birthday of his mother and, unable to reach the place because of the Japanese attack, had sent word telling them to resist. Because of this and her own unbounded courage, Lao Tai Tai, who had bound feet and could not walk well, had herself carried up to this house on the hill and directed the villagers from there. The whole village numbered no more than two thousand people, even counting the children, but Tai Li's son, perhaps with his father's example in mind, organized a small guerrilla detachment and, within about six months, killed most of the Japanese regiment. Hiding among the nearby hills, he led hit-and-run attacks that were ceaselessly repeated. The villagers were punished by the Japanese but they maintained so successful an appearance of ignorance that the enemy did not believe they could be responsible for the ever-recurrent trouble and, because the little hill village was not worth holding at so great a price, the Japanese finally withdrew. It was just before they left that they mounted a gun and turned it on the hilltop house, feeling, though they were never certain, that the trouble was being directed from there. Luckily the shells did not explode. They merely made the holes that General Tai had decided to preserve.

Once the Japanese had withdrawn, General Tai decided to build a new house for his mother, but she refused. "She told me," he explained, "that I was not worthy to be her son if I built her anything--even an office--before her neighbors all had roofs over their heads again." And he added--with some pride, I thought, despite the simplicity of his account--that because the village had given so fine an account of itself, Generalissimo Chiang Kai-shek had given it a decoration--the only village in China to be so honored.

The story differed only in detail from countless other small but spirited actions that were constantly taking place throughout wide areas of China. Nevertheless, it was a story of more than usual courage because the mother and the son of one of China's outstanding military leaders had not called on him for protection. Instead, they had covered their identity and had stayed to take part in the defense of their village. There is no doubt that the Japanese retaliation would have been horrible if these two courageous individuals had been taken and their identities had been discovered.

It was past midnight before our dinner was over and the general had finished his explanation, but then he apologized and left us.

"I must go," he explained, "and present my respects to my mother, who will doubtless spend the rest of the night telling me the things I have done wrong. And she will be right, of course."

Bright and early the next morning, Ward Smith, Eddie Liu, and I were up to see the view and, as the sun rose above the mountain back of us, Eddie Liu thoughtfully watched the light as it increased.

"The sun," he said presently, "has a much easier time of it than the moon."

"How's that?" I asked.

He wrinkled his brow for a moment.

"Because," he replied slowly, "at night when the moon comes over this mountain it has to make its climb in the dark."

As we stood on a second-floor balcony, we looked down into a lotus pool that had been filled to overflowing by yesterday's rains. The valley stretched out beneath us until it was enclosed by its circling hills and mountains. After the rain the air was clean and the sounds of the almost-hidden village were muted. Everything was so quiet and so restful that it seemed impossible that an elderly and determined little lady had once led the fight against a whole Japanese regiment from here.

As yet we had not met her. Even when we were taken to lunch at her village house she did not appear. The lunch was delicious and unusual but it was for men only and no lady was visible. But I wanted to meet her and I tried to think how I might go about it.

"General Tai," I said at last. "I have my camera with me. Couldn't we take some pictures of you with your family?"

He was usually willing to let me take his picture though he had formerly made it a firm rule to avoid cameras.

"Right away," he smiled. "There will be twelve."

The number surprised me. I knew that his wife had died in Shanghai in 1939, leaving him with a son and a daughter. In addition to these there was his mother, but even adding his son's wife and their son, twelve was more than I could account for. Still, I did not ask and presently a little girl came in and was ordered to pay her respects to me.

Instantly she was on her knees, preparing to bump her head to the floor in the formal kowtow. But Tai Li picked her up and, explaining that she should shake hands with foreigners, introduced his daughter. Dressed in a sweater and leggings, she was eight years old and was both pretty and friendly. She hung her head shyly when I spoke to her, but was fully in control of herself when she went to get Tai Li's grandson. He was four years old and as he entered he looked like a little old man with his fat tummy holding out his Chinese gown. He appeared almost overwhelmed in the awesome presence of his grandfather, but the little girl climbed happily onto Tai Li's knee and chattered brightly as well-loved little girls do the world over.

Now Lao Tai Tai appeared. Wearing the black bandeau of the married woman on her head, she was dressed in knee-length coat and pants made of well-worn local cloth, and her tiny feet were bound with strips of white. When I rose in order to be presented she looked me over with eyes that were as discerning as her son's and then flashed a smile that was remarkably like his. I could not speak her language but even through the words of an interpreter I felt her friendliness.

I thanked her for the excellent meal we had eaten and she said that she had prepared it herself since she was unwilling to trust the cook to feed such important guests. Then she brought out, as a present for my wife, two pewter caddies of tea that had been grown on their own land--Hsing Lung Diing, she called it, or "Real Dragon Well Tea." Raised only in this valley, which had been revered for its tea for a thousand years, this particular tea was so rare that not more than fifty or sixty caddies were produced in any single year.

Again I suggested using my camera, but before we could settle down to that task Lao Tai Tai ordered her famous son to put on his uniform.

"But Mother," he explained. "I never wear my uniform except for the generalissimo, or for some official and very important occasion."

"I like the uniform," Eddie Liu told me she replied, "and I am important on this occasion."

The uniform had to be pressed, for it had been packed for weeks, but once that had been done the general left to put it on and when he returned we were also joined by his brother, his brother's wife, and three children. But these, even when Tai Li's daughter was added, as well as his son, his son's wife, and his small grandson, made only eleven and not twelve as he had told me there would be.

Among the pictures I took was one fine close-up of Lao Tai Tai. Later when it had been blown up to life size, it became my New Year's gift to the general--a gift for which he promptly cleared a wall in his dining room in Chungking so that the picture could hand in a place of honor behind his chair.

Eddie Liu and I wandered down to the village of Pao An and met some of the heroes of the resistance, among whom the local butcher was especially prominent. Everyone with whom we talked spoke highly of the actions of Tai Li's son. To them he was a hero and I wished that his father would be a little more appreciative. But I learned no more at that time of Tai Li himself. It was not until some months later, on a lonely night when he was deeply shaken by the just-discovered dishonesty of a trusted friend, that I learned a little more of the heritage that had apparently conditioned him in his relations with his son.

His grandfather, it then appeared, had been a farmer who, with two brothers, had made a fortune from a roadside inn, but although he had accumulated so much wealth he had no son. By long-standing Chinese custom, of course, a son could be adopted, and in this case his brothers agreed that such a son would be permitted to share equally with their four natural sons.

It was as a result of this that Tai Li's father was adopted. Unfortunately, however, he turned out to be lazy, dissolute, and a spendthrift--a great disappointment to the family. His foster father, unable to control him, died. The two remaining brothers then did what they could to steady their adopted nephew but they too failed. In the meantime he had married, but his wife bore him no son and finally she, too, died, a disappointed woman. And now, with no son of his own to carry on the accepted filial duties to the family ancestors, he asked to marry again. But his foster mother, having suffered so much from his dissolute and incorrigible ways, refused to give her permission.

By now the whole village was concerned and a delegation of respected elders came to call on the old lady, respectfully importuning her to do her duty and permit her foster son to give her grandsons.

"Who in this village," she asked, "or in any village within gossip distance, would allow their daughter to marry our dissolute adopted scoundrel?"

Then she pointed to one of the committee.

"Your youngest daughter," she said, "is perhaps strong enough to straighten him out. Would you permit her to marry him?"

"The villager," General Tai told me, "was willing to sacrifice his daughter for such a cause, and my father's second wife is my mother, whom you have met. I am the eldest of three, the others being my brother and a sister. But my mother was never able to reform my father. I still remember seeing him in the family jail with irons on his leg and arm. My grandmother took me to see him as a bad example. She died when she was eighty-eight. My father died soon after, when I was not yet five. There was still plenty of money that he had not been able to squander but there was no respect for us in the family. By the time I was fourteen I had learned to dislike the whole clan, and I left home."

I understood him much better than most, I thought, for we had much in common. My father also drank too much. He died when I was 4-1/2 and

I ran away from home and a stepfather when I was fourteen.

The rest of his story came to me bit by bit. He went with a cousin to fight under a war lord--was wounded--almost died. When Sun Yat-sen advanced his ideals of government the boy discovered a cause that deeply moved him. He entered the Whampoa school founded by Chiang Kai-shek, graduated in its sixth class, and remained fiercely loyal to his teacher. In time he came to be a well-known aide of the generalissimo, but when that happened various members of the family started flocking around him in the hope of gaining favors. He never went back to the village of Pao An until his mother returned, but thereafter he made filial visits to it yearly though he was constantly importuned by relatives and villagers for money and soft jobs with the government. Already he had renounced his holdings in the valley so that the proceeds could remain there while he lived on his government pay, but the importunities never ceased. During a later visit Eddie Liu and I, who had been asked to stay at his mother's house, were kept awake most of the night by an elderly female who repeatedly screamed outside Tai Li's window. "Why don't you get my husband a job?" she shrieked. "Why don't you obey the rules of filial piety?"

The next day he got them all together.

"My father died a rich man," he told them, "leaving me the greatest land holdings in this whole valley. But I renounced my holdings and left them here for your livelihood. Living conditions are easy here. Food is plentiful. You want for nothing.

"I owe you nothing. I live on my government pay, and now have borrowed from the banks to live, for the pay is not enough. I have taken nothing from you but a few hams and some tea now and then. I will not give you money. I am not a son of this village, but am a son of the New China to which I owe my allegiance.

"I have a responsibility only to my comrades. They are suffering in this war. I must care for the families of our dead. If I have a family it is my thousands of comrades."

As we left the village of Pao An on that later visit, he was still fuming about declaring official war on the corruption that resulted from family demands.

"It must take four thousand years to cure," he said.

But now--in May 1944--we visited the village school. As is proper when important visitors arrive, the students were waiting in order to accompany us along the way with their horns and drums. And having arrived, graduation exercises were held for us to witness--a graduation that was carried out under a banner that bore eight characters--Loyalty, Filial Piety, Benevolence, Brotherly Love, Honesty, Chivalry, Peace, and Peaceful Negotiations.

These rules of Confucius had served for a thousand years to make the village tranquil and law-abiding. But each time Tai Li returned and attempted to introduce national patriotism as a larger concept of the family, and to advance the foreign idea of individual responsibility, the village was shaken to its very roots. Horizons were expanding. Good though the old principles were, they needed new applications. They should never be forgotten, but already they had produced Lao Tai Tai and her deeply loyal son, and other changes were already on the way.

I wrote Lao Tai Tai a note in order to thank her for her hospitality to a foreigner, and to express my admiration for one of her dishes--a very unusual soup. I also thanked her for the favor to my wife, who would enjoy the fine tea. And because my wife was also fond of cooking, I asked if it would be possible for me to have the recipe of Lao Tai Tai's very remarkable soup.

The soup, incidentally, was both delicious and unusual. It was like a thick cream soup, with chunks of vegetables and fish, and with small rice dumplings as big as your thumb.

A reply came promptly and I asked Eddie Liu to translate it and send it to my wife. I also suggested, when I wrote her next, that she had better practice that recipe--which I had not read--so that we would be able to honor Tai Li with a favorite dish of his mother's when he came to visit us in Washington after the war.

But Billy, having studied the recipe, wrote me saying that she would have to stick to spoon bread and apple pie for our guests. Then she added that perhaps I had been in China too long for, she pointed out, Lao Tai Tai's wonderful recipe began with "Take six octopi--".

Had I been too long in China?

I did not believe so. Still, I had been there long enough to have made a friend--the second most powerful friend one could then have had in that old land.

When I had been in Washington a couple of months earlier, Admiral King had given me important new instructions. "Be ready on the China coast," he had told me, "for Fleet landings possibly by December."

That had been in March 1944, and now it was May. It had been more than two years since I had first reached China, yet we still had nothing on the coast at all.

The Japanese drive that was still going on had come earlier than even General Tai had expected, and it indicated, we felt sure, that the enemy knew that their time was running out. But if we were to do as Admiral King expected, the time at our disposal was short, too. The problem was much on my mind--so much, in fact, that I had been having dreams of late-- dreams of racing hard--uphill--of being out of breath. Sometimes those dreams were so realistic that I seemed to feel the wind in my face, yet when I paused to look around I had not moved.

But now we were moving. We had a date with pirates, and pirates were a Chinese "natural resource" of which I had been conscious ever since

General Tai had first brought me to this part of China, and we knew that they could be turned against the Japanese. Now we were out to do it, though our destination was so secret that we did not even mention it by name.

If we could have afforded the weight of gas that was necessary to permit us to use one of our new planes we could have cut our travel time from two troublesome weeks to one long day. But that had been too much to ask. Therefore, we were now traveling on foot or on horseback, and we still had a five-hour trip ahead. Si Morris, who came from Texas, naturally thought he knew all about horses so he and Eddie Liu clambered aboard the shaggy ponies that had been provided, while I thrust myself into a sedan chair, my knees being temporarily out of commission because of a fall down a steep bank.

Tung Feng was our secret destination, and when we reached it we found it to be a pleasant temple compound with big trees and a rapidly flowing brook. General Tai had turned the place into a school for agents and, having established ourselves in the rooms we were given, we waited as patiently as we could for the representatives of two pirate bands to arrive.

In fair weather my room was delightful. It occupied a part of one wing of the old temple, and its beautifully carved woodwork and rice paper windows were unusually handsome and very Chinese. Unfortunately however, rainstorms were frequent and the driving rain melted those rice paper "windowpanes." At least on three occasions I had to sound "battle stations" in order to rescue my papers and bedding from drowning. "Speed," who had been my guard ever since General Tai, in Chungking, had first installed me in "Fairy Cave," would patiently paste in a new set of panes, but the next burst of horizontal rain would take them, too, and Speed finally had to solve the problem by using some of Ward Smith's typewriter bond. It let in less light than rice paper, but it was stronger in the rain.

The cookhouse was in the wing nearest to my room and the cooks apparently worked in shifts, quitting at midnight but returning to the job again about 3 A.M. After two noisy nights had left their mark on me, Eddie Liu reported the situation to General Tai who, characteristically, went boiling out to the kitchen but not with the idea of quieting the cooks. Instead, he summoned the camp commander, the architect, and the "chief of general affairs" and gave them orders to tear down the somewhat lacy bamboo screen between my room and the kitchen and to replace it with a thick mud wall. This, he felt sure, would "protect General Miles from the noise of cooks killing and frying chickens."

At three the following morning, consequently, the laborers arrived and their work began. The task was not a big one and they might very well have completed it in a day. The heavy rains, however, melted the new mud wall away almost as fast as it was erected, so a second wall--and even a third--had to be built. But it is only fair to say that even before the wall was finally completed, the noise of the cooks no longer especially troubled me. The workmen were fully twice as noisy, and successfully drowned out all lesser sounds. Thus everybody was disturbed each night except General Tai, who never appeared to sleep anyway, or at least I never caught him at it.

A dozen generals put in their appearance, their purpose being to clear the way for a five-division intelligence net with fifty coast watcher stations, an idea General Tai had accepted. As usual, a part of our work was carried out over the dinner table when all of us relaxed in the presence of good food and sprightly conversation. One prime dish, incidentally, consisted of very large frogs that are raised especially in that region. Cleaned and stuffed with rice, they are flavored with white wine and seasoning before being roasted. Each guest was served a whole stuffed frog, almost as if it were a squab except that the cook had arranged each frog very realistically on our individual serving dishes. My frog, I thought, appeared actually pathetic as it sat looking up at me. I ate it, for I had to, but I turned my mind to other things and don't remember how it tasted.

At another dinner we ate boiled fresh ham--a ceremonial dish that is usually reserved for the go-between who has arranged a marriage, or for the parents of the bride- and groom-to-be when they first meet. That dish naturally started a rash of mother-in-law stories which, I was interested to learn, are almost the same in Chinese as in English.

As my Chinese improved, I asked Eddie Liu not to interpret unless I asked him to, so as to permit the conversation to run along naturally. And thereafter it often seemed that the others forgot that I was not really "General Mei" at all. Certainly the table talk went more smoothly, and the "uncivilized" behavior of foreigners was often mentioned, with Americans not escaping their share of criticism by any means. I was interested to learn, for example, that my Chinese associates were much concerned about our treatment of the American Indian which, they now and then suggested, was much worse even than most "British atrocities." And the only excuse I ever heard offered for these shortcomings of ours was our "British blood"!

It was several days after we arrived when a tall cadaverous man with a straggly handlebar mustache put in his appearance. He wore rusty black Chinese clothes and a brown felt hat, and he gave the impression of having come to look us over. Certainly that seemed to be his idea, for he strolled about listening and waiting before finally telling us his business.

Perhaps I should have know him for what he was, for as a young lieutenant (j.g.) I had spent two years in China aboard the U.S.S. *Pampanga*, a river gunboat that often chaperoned oil barges up and down the West and Pearl Rivers between Hong Kong and Wuchow. We seldom had any trouble with the river pirates of that day for the *Pampanga*, compelled on one occasion to shoot her way out of a hold-up, had taken the top off the pirates' pagoda watch tower with her very first salvo and thereafter was well know as "the gunboat that shoots." Our first electric lights, which I rigged from a motorcycle engine, attracted much attention, and we later had a hot little "battle" during which our skipper took a shot through his cap. Another shot loudly rang the ship's bell beside me, and our stack was so riddled that for a time we had too little draft for our fires.

In times of peace, the coast pirates commonly exacted tribute from small ships that passed through narrow waters. Another idea was to send numbers of pirates aboard some one of the lesser passenger steamers as if they were ordinary passengers. Then, at some remote but previously agreed-upon spot, these "passengers" would assemble unexpectedly with arms in their hands in order to highjack the vessel from within, taking away all valuables and even, now and then, some passenger who might be held for ransom. They usually escaped aboard fast junks that had been sent to the scene of the crime ahead of time. This sort of business, in which many Chinese pirates were well versed, was obviously very similar to such guerrilla tactics as interested us now.

So far as war was concerned, Chinese pirates usually had little connection with it. Still, they heartily disliked Japanese interference and, as a result, they were about ready to work with us. General Tai, in fact, was concerned lest they jeopardize their usefulness by rushing openly to our side. We had no wish to see that happen for, while we had many uses for them, we were anxious to keep their efforts under cover so that they could continue to move with some ease among the Japanese along the coast. With this in mind I had already asked Washington for permission to work with them and to provide them with such supplies, weapons, and money as might be required.

General Tai, on his part, agreed to offer them both guns and training, for they would have to be trained to use such weapons as we could supply. The only guns with which they were familiar had originally been used during the Russo-Japanese War of 1904-5 and no ammunition for such weapons had been available for some time. The general was also willing to have them supplied with radios and weather instruments, which they would also have to be taught to use. As before, however, he flatly refused to permit us to "pay money for loyalty."

There were three important pirate leaders on the South Central coast of China. A certain Chang Kwei-fong had a fluid force known as the "Brethren of the Circle" that was said to number somewhere between eighteen hundred and twenty-five hundred, and his headquarters were on Tsungming Island off Woosung at the mouth of the Yangtze River. In addition to these, he also controlled some eighteen thousand operators who did many things, including smuggling and, probably, opium passing. So powerful was this somewhat vaguely organized outfit that it more or less controlled the coast throughout the three-hundred-mile section that extended fro Shanghai south to Wenchow.

Chang Yee-chow, on the other hand, had a somewhat similar organization of about four thousand men. His headquarters were said to be on Matsu Island, which lies a little way offshore near the port of Foochow, and his strip of coast extended north for some distance from that port. And in between the coastal sections that were controlled by these two lay a kind of middle ground where Tsai Kung, with whom we never dealt and who had only about five hundred men, served to keep his much greater pirate neighbors from poaching on each other's preserves.

Our fist grim visitor--he of the handlebar mustache--was a trusted member of the Brethren of the Circle. He explained that the leader of this organization--Chang Kwei-fong--had only to yell "Brother!" to have ten armed junks at his service. If, however, he were to yell "BROTHER!" there would instantly be a hundred. Then, carried away by his own eloquence, he assured us that "If he yells "BROTHER! BROTHER! BROTHER!" there will be twenty-five hundred armed junks ready for him to use!"

This particular visiting pirate, we learned, had made a long overland trip to reach us. He had traveled along many rivers and had passed through Suchow, which lies inland some forty or fifty miles from Shanghai. Chang Kwei-fong, he said, wanted to commit himself to General Tai. His people, we were told, were partly along the coast but were also along the Yangtze all the way up to Kiukiang in northern Kiangsi Province. Living ashore except when large operations were pending, they were organized as merchants, inspectors, and cargo carriers. Even the Japanese had moved into the island headquarters of the Brethren of the Circle near Woosung and had actually made Chang Kwei-fong a member of the Japanese general's staff. But Chang did not like the Japanese. They were bad for business. So he had sent his own chief of staff to organize a patriotic bicycle corps of women couriers in Shanghai. Some of the members of this organization carried collapsible bicycles with them and they could aid in transferring articles, information, or escaped prisoners if we wished.

This busy pirate chief of staff, incidentally, had already made contact with General Tai's Blue Shirts in Shanghai, and had also been the person who had convinced Chang Kwei-fong that the time was ripe for the pirates to give their help to General Tai's guerrilla forces. But now we learned--to my great surprise--that this energetic and influential chief of staff was not only a qualified junk master, but was also a lady pirate of established reputation!

As I thought about the problem that now confronted us I had to admit that I had learned very little as an undergraduate at the Naval Academy about doing business with pirates. And the Academy had been especially remiss in not having taught me anything whatever about *lady* pirates. So I wrote Jeff Metzel in Washington, asking for any available specialized information.

With my query on his desk, Jeff may have been a bit upset when he realized that there did not seem to be anything in Washington about the complications of working with active lady pirates. On the other hand, he hesitated for a time to take up his daily paper because the comic strip known as "Terry and the Pirates" had thought of so many operations that were remarkably similar to those that were actually engaging the attention of SACO at about that time. In fact, this coincidence soon began to be so noticeable that some of Jeff's higher-ups pointedly asked him if he was "leaking" any SACO information to Milton Caniff, the cartoonist who draws "Terry and the Pirates." If he was, they told him, it wasn't funny! Jeff actually had to write Caniff, asking him to soft-pedal the lady pirate for a time, especially where her Chinese operations were concerned. After all, the Japanese General Staff could read our funny papers, too.

At Tung Feng our visiting pirate--he of the brown hat and the handle-bar mustache--waited impatiently for two more days before representatives of the rival pirates' association kept their appointment. But finally two new pirate deputies arrived--short fisher-folk in black baggy pants and side-slit jackets that are characteristic of the Chinese sailing fraternity. And though the group they represented did much more of their work at sea than Chang Kwei-fong's group did, they nevertheless called their chief "General!"--General Chang Yee-chow.

This pirate leader, we now learned, was also paid by the Japanese, who even went a step farther. They rated him so highly that they had actually assigned a Japanese Navy captain and two ranking Army officers to his "staff." They were there, no doubt, to watch him, for though they paid him they questioned his absolute devotion to their cause. Still, they felt he could be useful, for a large number of pirate seamen were loyal to him, so they permitted him to wander about the coast at will and even to operate while they watched. What they failed to realize, apparently, was that there was plenty they did not see.

General Chang Yee-chow, I learned, had assisted General Tai before. More than a year earlier he had supplied our side with two thousand drums of gasoline that his men had salvaged from a Japanese tanker that had been sunk in his area by a U.S. submarine. And his representatives now reported that they had more than seven hundred additional drums that could be delivered. It even seemed that they were already counting on the eventual defeat of the Japanese and it may have been with that in mind that they were now so willing to declare themselves in favor of the Nationalist Government.

Our conference with these pirates was not only secret but was also both formal and correct. When General Tai introduced me he used my proper title. He was speaking in Chinese, of course, and it was the only time I ever heard him refer to me as "Brigadier General of the Sea." When that came out, our visitors rose and bowed low, which caused Eddie Liu to explain that they did not have much use for ordinary military people--that the only ones who really mattered were "sea people."

The proposition of both pirate groups was the same--a suggestion that they would capture the Japanese with whom they were working and that they would also take over all the Japanese-held islands and lighthouses in their areas. In return for this they wanted the promise that after the war they would be permitted to settle down with a little land, a little work in connection with the lighthouses, and with their names properly inscribed on the tax rolls of the government as loyal citizens so that "the Emperor will not be angry with us any more." It was fundamental Chinese family teaching--pay your taxes early and be rid of your troubles.

We convinced our pirate friends that the time was not ripe for openly casting off their Japanese masters. It would be better if they were to disguise themselves as Japanese sympathizers for a little longer. In the meantime we would set up training classes for their junior officers and enlisted men, would supply guns for their men and their ships, and would prepare those who were sent to us for the time when they could be of real use. We asked specifically for junk masters who could understand and speak Japanese, and who would work closely with our proposed coast-watcher stations. Such a group, properly trained and organized, would form a very useful mobile spy ring that could look into and report many activities along the coast.

For Chang Kwei-fong our plans included the manning of weather junks at sea north of Shanghai where there was a gap in our weather information. We also wanted to lay "couplets" of connected floating mines that would wrap themselves about Japanese ships in the channels leading to Shanghai. That was a very special operation, since ordinary floating mines would often miss the ships and go floating out to sea where they would become an added hazard for our submarines. And, fully as important but in another way, we wanted the help of his plainclothesmen and his corps of girl couriers to aid in the escape of such prisoners as we might rescue or "buy" from the jails in Shanghai.

General Tai's Blue Shirts were already specializing in such rescues, and after the war one of them told me how they worked.

"The Japanese magistrate, Noguchi," he explained, "was very helpful, whether he knew it or not. He had a Chinese wife who would pass us word that a stranger in Shanghai was captured and in jail. If we got this word within eight or ten hours, we could usually buy him out, but if he stayed there long enough for many papers about him to build up, he could be there forever.

"Every so often," he continued, "there would be O.S.S. men tangled up in Shanghai, or at least that is what they said they were. We spent a fortune getting *them* out. But the worst I saw was a Japanese who kept looking at me. I thought he was tailing me and had finally gotten my number. But he turned out to be an O.S.S. Nisei who was part Indian. It was stupid to send him in where the Japanese knew all their own. They caught him and shot him."

I had known that money was often used in Shanghai to "buy" prisoners back, and I often asked about it though I never got a bill. General Tai merely shrugged my questions off, saying that we'd let the Japanese pay for it in one way or another. It was not until later that I learned that smuggled counterfeit money was used.

Both pirate groups with whose representatives we conferred at Tung Feng promised to do all they could to rescue downed fliers promptly so as to keep them from falling into Japanese hands. They later proved very successful, too, actually picking up and sending back to us more than a hundred, all told. One of these was Don Bell, a correspondent who gratefully reported his rescue by "fishermen."

As our conference approached its conclusion, Chang Yee-chow's two representatives told us that they themselves would not be useful out on the coast after their return from this trip--that the Japanese would suspect them. They agreed, however, to stay in Foochow and communicate with us by radio, and told us that within a couple of months three hundred of their best men would "desert" and come to Tung Feng so as to be assigned to Camp Seven, the new training camp we were to set up. And we also began to plan another camp farther north--Camp Eight--for later arrivals.

The pirate delegates gave us detailed reports of their craft. Chang Yee-chow, they said, now had a total of eighteen junks. The Fourteenth Air Force had sunk two and had damaged two more during the past year, and we were implored to inform our pilots that these pirate junks were friends. We were unable to work out a recognition signal system because such craft had no radios and one junk looks very much like another. But we were able to specify certain home port bays that our men could learn to accept as "friendly territory" and which were to be passed by without bombing.

In discussing possible uniforms for the proposed pirate force we learned that they did not want to be called "soldiers" and that they preferred to dress in their own clothes. They were willing to consider our point of view, however, and agreed that while their men were at the training camps they would wear soldier uniforms.

When all the details of the agreement were worked out to the satisfaction of both sides, the pirate deputies rose and gave a signal. This had obviously been expected, for one of their followers promptly came in with a container of garlic water which the deputies gravely spattered about us. General Tai showed no surprise and before the formality was over I gathered that it was proper pirate procedure intended for the protection of our friendship from interfering outsiders. It was similar, certainly, to the idea that some of the coastal people of China have that garlic water will protect them from bullets. That these two ideas were related seemed reasonably clear when our visitors bowed, holding their bent arms close to their sides, and spoke their final words in unison.

"There will be no bullets between us," they said.

Before they left Tung Feng each of the pirate delegates gave me a small piece of carved ivory. The piece Chang Yee-chow had sent was a delicately carved little Chinese garden, and Chang Kwei-fong's gift was a miniature ivory cabbage complete with a carved worm. I hoped that this bit of realism would not prove to be significant.

Before we left Tung Feng the villagers told us about their local dragon which, like many other dragons, lived underground. Formerly, they said their valley had often been badly shaken by earthquakes resulting from their dragon's ecstatic lashings whenever a lady dragon happened to pass nearby. But they had corrected that by erecting one pagoda directly above their dragon's head and another above his tail. Because of the weight of these two structures he was fairly quiet now but, they told us, we must be very careful not to arouse him as we practiced detonations on their hill.

We listened gravely and with some sympathy. After all, we had made plans for a dragon of our own in the nearby coast--a dragon that must be free to move. Camp One was to be its head. Its heart would be a hospital that would soon be started nearby. Its eyes and ears would be the intelligence network and the many coast-watcher stations we were planning. Its body would be the three new camps we were about to establish. And its claws were to be the pirates and guerrillas these camps would train.

That was our plan, and though we knew that much work still remained to be done, we were confident. On May 30, after a full tumbler of warm White Horse whiskey for each of us "to celebrate your memories of your dead," we slid down the little river in a sampan which saved us three full hours over the upstream walk.

From Milton E. Miles, *A Different Kind of War*, (New York: Hawthorne, 1968), pp. 227-253.

Chapter 9

Algeria, Round II

In the wake of the fiasco in Indochina in the mid-1950s, French military leaders attempted to draw lessons that they could apply in their next counterinsurgent effort. The test came just a few years later in Algeria, and the French response was to create an integrated military strategy incorporating significant conventional and special force formations. Regulars were the assigned the role of *quadrillage,* which gave them the responsibility for garrisoning key areas, the principal "persisting" element in the counterinsurgency. French special forces, mainly the paratroops, became the *chasseurs* charged with raiding actions to hunt down the rebels. On paper, the approach looked good.

In practice, though, the *chasseurs* engaged in all manner of violations of human rights, creating both international opprobrium and dissent back in France. Though operationally effective, the unintended political consequences of their actions led to the unraveling of French policy. Algeria won its freedom, and the discontented paras engaged in *putschism* against their own government. Lartéguy's tale highlights, among other things, the need to think of special forces as having their own brand of civil-military relations, which may differ substantially from the manner in which other parts of the military relate to civilian authority.

Jean Lartéguy

The Leap of Leucadia

A week after Ahmed's arrest Si Lahcen and his band were driven off the plain and forced to take refuge in the mountains. The rebels had had to abandon their dumps and their hide-outs which were no longer secure. Information became scarce and supplies were no longer available from P——— where the whole political and administrative organization of the rebellion had been decapitated.

The headmen of the *douars* came up one after another to see Si Lahcen near the cave where he had set up his headquarters. They all had the same thing to say:

"Si Lahcen, we are aware of your courage and your strength, but take your band of *moujahidines* away from our *douar*, for the French are bound to hear about it sooner or later; then they'll burn down our *mechtas*, slit our throats and shoot your men."

Si Lahcen did his best to stem their panic. He ordered some spectacular executions, but the hundred or so men and women he had shot down or butchered could not wipe out the memory of the *mechtas* of Rahlem. The only remorse he felt was when he realized this massacre had been completely useless.

Sitting near his cave, with a blanket round his shoulders to protect him from the early-morning dew, he let himself be carried away by his memories.

His best friend in Indo-China had been Sergeant Piras, a lively, skinny little chap who had worked at every kind of job and read every book. He used to wink as he rolled himself a cigarette and he kept his tobacco in a sort of round metal tin.

Each time they ran across each other in the course of an operation, Piras would wink and ask him:

"Well, Lahcen, how's your destiny?"

If Piras had not been killed during Operation Atlante, he might perhaps now be fighting against him, disguised as a lizard. He imagined holding him in the sights of his rifle while Piras, standing like an ibex on a rock, took out his tobacco tin and greedily rolled himself a cigarette.

He would fire, but to one side, in order to scare him: Piras had been his friend. He realized all of a sudden that all his friends were in this army he was fighting against, whereas his own people, on the contrary, were alien to him and some of them, like Ahmed, disgusted him. Ahmed died as he had lived, not as a soldier but as a stool-pigeon. Captured, he had given away everything he knew.

A sentry came to inform him that a liaison agent, a certain Ibrahim, had just arrived from P————.

Ibrahim may have been fifty years old or he may have been sixty: his full beard was speckled with grey; he was dressed in European clothes, with a watch-chain stretched across his waistcoat, but on his head he wore a turban made of some sort of linen and his feet were bare. He was a wise, cruel and self-possessed man. For a long time he had been in command of the small group of killers who by night controlled P———— and the surrounding *douars*: it was a miracle he had not yet been caught when all his men had already fallen to the Frenchmen's bullets.

Ibrahim came and squatted down beside Si Lahcen and offered him a cigarette.

"What is it?" asked the rebel leader. "I told you to stay down at P———— — and reorganize your group."

"Si Lahcen, there's not a single lizard left in the town. They all disappeared in the night. They're hunting you up in the mountains and they know where you are."

"Who gave me away?"

"Yesterday evening they caught three of your *moujahidines* as they were leaving a *mechta* to come and join you. One of them preferred to die, but the two others talked."

"The lookouts haven't signaled any trucks on the road."

"The lizards are making war as we do; they've marched all night and are now less than two miles from your cave. As they advance they look under every stone and behind every bush to make sure there isn't a hide-out there."

"Do you think I can still get through by way of Oued Chahir?"

"That's the route they've taken. They're there already. I almost ran into one of their patrols which had laid an ambush and was moving up the river-bed at dawn. I hid under some branches and waited; then I took off my shoes and came up here, taking great care not to dislodge any pebbles."

Si Lahcen rose to his feet and, followed by Ibrahim who was still barefoot, he inspected his position. He could not have chosen a better one. He had encamped with his band on a sort of peak overlooking a little pebbly plain as flat as a glacis, an open bit of ground hemmed in by the mountains, into which his assailants would be forced to venture.

Behind him rose a sheer cliff, on his left was the crevice up which Ibrahim had climbed and which could be easily defended with a few cases of grenades. Only his right flank was vulnerable: it formed a fairly gentle slope bristling with natural obstacles, and led towards the west. But it was a narrow approach; with his machine-gun, his three F.M.s and his mortar it would be easy for him to foil the attack of an enemy who would be unable to deploy and would therefore be obliged to advance in file.

"We'll wait for them here," Si Lahcen decided. "If they want a fight, I'll take them on."

The sun had risen; it shone straight into Ibrahim's eyes, forcing him to screw them up, which gave him the rather sly expression of an old Berri peasant. He stroked his beard:

"*Allah-i-chouf.* Let me have a rifle."

Si Lahcen had about a hundred men at his disposal, the rest of the band having failed to join him. He made each one of them--and it was a difficult task--dig into a prepared position and build a little parapet of stones to protect himself. He gave orders not to fire unless certain of scoring a hit and to save ammunition, for they would have to hold out until nightfall before being able to withdraw towards the heights. He positioned the automatic weapons himself, gave each of them a definite mission, set up the mortar, then retired inside the cave. At the entrance to it he noticed a curious patch of sunlight which kept alternately appearing and vanishing.

Si Lahcen rummaged in his sack for a bar of chocolate. He pulled out a little leather case containing his Military Medal. He looked at this for several minutes. The ribbon was the same warm colour as the patch of sunlight.

Yes, he had certainly earned his medal out in Indo-China! The post overlooked the Red River. It was made of logs and the watchtower, soaring high on its stilts, looked like one of those stands which are put up in the middle of a vineyard when the grape is ripe.

The post commander was a lieutenant with a long neck and prominent Adam's apple who wore spectacles; every morning he would sadly ask:

"But why the hell don't the Viets attack? They can mop us up whenever they like."

The post was, in fact, completely isolated; it relied entirely on parachute drops; but more often than not a proportion of the containers fell into the river.

Lieutenant Barbier and Sergeant-Major Lahcen were in command of a hundred or so partisans and a dozen Europeans. The partisans had been suborned by Vietminh propaganda and were only waiting for a favourable moment to turn traitor. Wasted by fever, laid low by the damp climate, the Frenchmen were incapable of repelling a fresh attack. Lieutenant Barbier was no longer quite right in the head; he kept imagining that someone was going to murder him; at the slightest sound he would draw his revolver and fire it. He also killed all the house lizards, which bring good luck, and squashed them against the walls of his room, using his shoe as a hammer; it was a bad sign.

One night the Vietminh had landed on the bank of the river below the post. Another group had occupied the village. At four in the morning they had attacked from both directions, while the partisans mutinied.

Lieutenant Barbier had been killed in his bed. He usually woke up at the slightest sound but this time he had not heard his murderer approaching. Lahcen and the white men who were left had taken refuge in the central block-house; they had held out for six hours against a whole Vietminh battalion.

A *dinassaut* sailing up the river with its armoured barges had come to their rescue when they were down to their last hand-grenade. Lahcen had received a bullet in the lung and he still remembered the pinkish froth that had clung to his lips like toothpaste; but this froth had a sickly, salty taste: the taste of his own blood.

He had been evacuated to Hanoi by helicopter. He had been operated on straight-away and three days later, in a bed with snow-white sheets, a general had come to present him with his Military Medal and announce that he had been promoted. There were flowers on the table; the nurses wiped his face whenever he was too hot. Piras had come to see him, with a bottle of brandy hidden under his coat. Hospital regulations, just like the Koran, forbade all alcohol.

Lahcen had been happy; he was properly looked after, he was equal to the other Frenchmen; he had the same rights, the same friends. He laughed at the same jokes as his comrades. On his first night out some sergeant-majors like himself, but with names like Le Guen, Portal and Duval, had got him blind drunk in a bistro and had then dragged him off to a brothel.

Today, if he was wounded, he would not be entitled to a helicopter or to a hospital, and if he was taken prisoner he would finish up with a bullet in his head fired by Le Guen, Portal or Duvan, if any of them happened to be present.

To them he was nothing but a renegade, worse than a Viet. If the administrator of P——— had not brutally reminded him that he was just a desert-rat, if he had not stolen from him, then he would have stayed on the side of the French . . . or would he?

No, on second thoughts, he would have gone over to the other side just the same, to avenge a number of other injustices, to remind the French that the Algerian also was entitled to be treated with respect.

Two bursts from a F.M. and the explosion of three grenades interrupted his soliloquy. Si Lahcen slipped the Military Medal into his pocket and ran out of the cave. A platoon of Frenchmen approaching up the crevice had been well and truly engaged.

The group leader, Mahmoud, motioned Si Lahcen to come forward and showed him, a hundred yards farther down, the bodies of two paratroopers, pathetic little mounds of camouflage cloth, and, a little farther on, the wounded W.T. operator with his set attached to his back; he was signaling to his comrades who had taken cover behind some rocks.

"Just watch, Si Lahcen," said Mahmoud, "like hunting game . . ."

A paratrooper had rushed forward and was trying to drag the W.T. operator back, while his comrades opened up with all they had got to give him covering fire. The group leader calmly took aim. Hit full in the head, the lizard collapsed on top of his comrade.

"Would you like the next one?" asked Mahmoud.

Si Lahcen took up a rifle and finished off the W.T. operator. Then he turned back towards the cave. Information had just come in that on his right flank the paratroops were beginning to creep forward and were now holding the ridge overlooking the open ground.

Ibrahim came and joined him in the cave. Sitting cross-legged on the ground, he lit a cigarette, then drew his watch out of his waistcoat pocket; it was a big silver hunter which had been given him by his boss, a settler on the outskirts of P———. He was quite fond of him but destiny had willed that the *roumi* should be inside the armhouse with his wife and children when it was set on fire. He put the watch carefully back in his pocket.

"Ten o'clock in the morning, Si Lahcen, and it won't be dark till ten o'clock at night; it's going to be a long wait. They will have all the time in the world to send for their aircraft and perhaps some artillery as well."

"We could have made for the heights and then dispersed, but only at dawn and you arrived too late."

Si Lahcen sent for his five group leaders and told them his plan:

"We shall hang on until nightfall, then attempt a break-out at the weakest point of the 'enemy lines' and make for the riverbed." For technical words or expressions, Si Lahcen invariably used French and he took a certain pleasure in displaying his military knowledge in front of his subordinates. "We're cut off from the mountains ... Anyone attempting to surrender will be shot out of hand; the wounded will have to be abandoned. We may be attacked from the air, so dig in more deeply, and be quick about it ..."

The group leaders started to embark on one of those endless discussions during which no problem is ever solved but which provides an excuse for killing time and exchanging cigarettes, noble thoughts and, occasionally, insults.

Three mortar shells landed in front of the cave, putting an end to the *chikaia*. There was a scream from a man who had been wounded. The group leaders rushed back to their men who were firing like lunatics; their bullets whined and ricocheted off the bare rocks.

Another company was now doubling across the open ground under the spasmodic and therefore rather ineffective fire of the rebel automatic weapons. Si Lahcen gave orders for the mortar to fire, but the shells fell well beyond.

From the top of the peak the long files of soldiers looked like columns of clumsy, stubborn ants as they stumbled over the obstacles or vanished behind them and reappeared again. The Tyrolean rucksack which the paratroopers wore on their backs gave them enormous thoraces and spindly little legs.

Lying flat on his stomach outside the cave, Si Lahcen kept them under observation. The leading sections presently arrived at the foot of the peak and disappeared from view.

A reconnaissance plane appeared in the sky, little bigger than a fly and insistently buzzing like a fly. It turned and, growing larger, became a bird of prey whose savage shadow swept the rocks. In spite of his orders, the *moujahidines* fired at it, thereby giving away their positions. The aircraft appeared to be hit, it dipped one wing and swooped down towards the plain with the slow, graceful movement of a wounded sea bird.

A few minutes later two fighter planes roared over the ridge. On their first run they dropped some bombs which burst with an ear-shattering explosion, causing a hail of stones but no damage. On the second run they fired rockets and four men crouching in a hole were killed. One of them was seen to leap into the air, his back broken, like a wild rabbit that has just received a full charge of buck-shot.

Lahcen knew they would come in again and machine-gun at a low altitude. Only this time the aircraft would be vulnerable to F.M. and rifle fire.

One of the planes roared over the cave, firing all its guns. Burning-hot shell-cases rained down round Si Lahcen who was still lying prone at the entrance.

Then there was silence. Si Lahcen crept forward under cover of the rocks and inspected his positions. The machine-gunning had killed two of his men and two others were seriously wounded. The casualties had been hit in the stomach and there was no chance of their surviving. That at least was the opinion of Mokri, the medical officer of the band, who had studied two years at the Algiers Faculty.

For the whole of that day the two wounded men never stopped moaning and crying out for water; there was no morphine to give them. They were disturbing the morale of the band and suffering pointlessly, since they would have to be left behind in any case.

Si Lahcen drew his revolver, a Lüger, the one which the administrator of P——— used to keep on his bedside table, and deliberately, without the slightest emotion, put the two men out of their misery. One of them just had time to curse him before his brains were blown out.

The lull lasted an hour, then the position was pounded by the 81-calibre mortars. After a few bracketing shots they began to find their range. One of the F.M.s and its crew of three was wiped out.

Ibrahim drew his watch out of his pocket. It was only half past one in the afternoon.

Raspéguy was crouching cross-legged by the side of his transmitter, munching some stale bread spread with the army-ration meat-paste which tasted as though it was made of sawdust and shavings. In front of him was a large-scale map in a plastic cover on which he made a number of marks in red and blue pencil as each of his companies reported their position.

Major de Glatigny, who had just been with the mortars, came and sat down beside him.

"It doesn't look so bad," said Raspéguy. "We're closing in on them and the lads are sticking it out. What are the casualties?'

"Four dead and seven wounded. The dead are all in Esclavier's unit."

"What did they get up to this time?"

"Bucelier's group advanced along a defile almost right up to the rebel position. They thought they would be able to take it on their own and pushed ahead contrary to orders. Pinières, who went to their rescue, got a splinter in his arm but he refuses to be evacuated."

"Can he manage?"

"Yes."

"Then it's up to him."

"Merle's death was a great blow to him. He was engaged to be married to his sister and I think this death has put an end to the whole thing."

With a gesture of his hand Raspéguy indicated that all this was of no importance and belonged to the past. His only interest now was the rebel band which was caught in the net but was going to do its utmost to escape.

The colonel bent over his map again. The shadow of his cap concealed the whole of the top of his face.

"Glatigny!"

"Yes, sir."

"You are Si Lahcen, you're surrounded with a hundred or so men on a peak, with hardly any food supplies, water or ammunition. What would you do?"

"I shouldn't let myself be pinned down on the peak. In my opinion, Si Lahcen will wait till it's dark and then attempt to break out towards the river-bed and the valley."

"That's right, that's exactly what he'd do. But in which direction?"

"On his left flank. That's the easiest for him."

"No, along the ridge on his right, so that his men won't have too much ground to cover before coming up against our force and trying to dislodge them. His last chance is a swift, fierce hand-to-hand engagement."

Raspéguy unhooked his receiver and called up:

"Blue Authority from Passavant."

"Blue Authority listening."

"Well, Esclavier?"

"I had some difficulty getting Bucelier away. They were under fire but they refused to withdraw and abandon the bodies of their four comrades."

"The band is ours; you'll have it tonight; get ready."

A W.T. operator approached at the double.

"A signal from P———, sir, yes, from Colonel Quarterolles, it's urgent."

"Everything's urgent with him. Bring your set up here."

The operator lugged the "300" up to Raspéguy, who took up the earphones but held them out at arm's length, for Quarterolles at the other end was screaming as though he was being flayed alive:

"Send me the helicopter at once so that I can reach your position."

"The helicopter's being used exclusively for transporting the wounded, Colonel, and we've already got quite a number of wounded."

"This is an order."

"If you're so keen to get here, you can walk. That's all. Out."

And Raspéguy rang off, ordering the operator to cease all communication with P———. Then he turned to Glatigny.

"Men have been killed and more are going to be killed because of that fellow Quarterolles, and now he wants to come swanking up here in a helicopter, give a pat on the back to our boys who've been stewing in the sun for hours, who've had no time to eat, who've got no more water in their bottles, and ask them in a fatherly fashion: 'How goes it old boy?' when he himself has just left the lunch-table with a pint of beer inside him."

"He's still the garrison commander, sir. It's a serious business questioning the hierarchy of the army. In this particular case you're probably right! But at other times, at most times . . ."

"Jacques" (this was the first time that Raspéguy had used his Christian name, admitting him into his military family like Esclavier and Boudin), "don't you think I realize the danger? But if we want to win this war we have to shed all sorts of conventions. We are all responsible men and we stick together. What Esclavier and Boisfeuras did, which is condemned by every army regulation, has enabled us to get our hands on this band today. I don't like massacres and I don't like torture, but I feel it's you, myself, all of us, who slit those throats at Rahlem and who made Ahmed and his little friends at P——— talk."

"And God, sir?"

"Tonight Esclavier and his reservists will fight it out on equal terms with Si Lahcen's *fellaghas*. In this fight they'll settle their account with God or their conscience. Tonight they'll be making their confession to death. And we'll only intervene if they can't manage by themselves; but I know they'll hold out."

Raspéguy leant back against a rock and Glatigny had the impression he was withdrawing into himself, searching through his gory, painful and glorious memories for the strength to carry on with his war.

But Raspéguy was actually dreaming of a dark, stagnant lake, bristling with dead branches and reeds, streaked with slow-moving fish and exuding a slimy miasma. He lowered himself gently into these waters, tensing his stomach, contracting his nostrils, struggling against his fear and disgust.

The wireless began to crackle;

"Amarane calling Violettes. Send us up some more grenades; we're running short."

The hunt was on again, and the explosion of bombs and rockets echoed and re-echoed in the depths of the valleys.

Glatigny sat with his head in his hands, recalling the Méo highlands.

Night fell without a sound; there was no more firing. It seemed as
though the men had forgotten their quarrel and were taking advantage of
this peace and quiet to gather, friend and foe together, round a camp-fire
where, relieved of their burden of anger, courage and criminal actions, they
could confide in one another and talk about their homes, the ample,
welcoming bodies of their wives, their barns full of crops, sheep roasting
over glowing embers and the cries of children.

But all round the peak, oblivious of the magic of the night, the wireless
transmitters with their little orange lights were crackling louder than
crickets.

"Passavant from Blue: they're advancing on us now."

It was Esclavier's voce. Glatigny and Raspéguy remained glued to the
W.T.

Esclavier had posted his men half-way up the crevice, at the point
where it began to open out. They did not form an unbroken line, but were
scattered in twos and threes, crouching in holes or behind the rocks. They
were staggered in depth over a distance of more than two hundred yards.
Down in the river-bed Pinières's company stood in reserve.

It was pitch black, the moon was not due to rise for another hour.

A few pebbles had been dislodged, which had alerted the advance
posts, and immediately afterwards the *fellaghas* were on top of them,
yelling like madmen. The whole defile had been set ablaze, the F.M.s
firing long devastating bursts, the grenades exploding with a dull thud.
The mortars, meanwhile, lobbed over tracer shells which spun slowly over
the gorges and ridges, transforming them into a stage décor.

Bucelier found himself next to a machine-gun. It had just jammed and
the gunner was having difficulty inserting a fresh magazine. He pushed
him aside to take his place and was crushed by a body bearing down on him,
a body draped in a tattered *jellaba*. He felt a violent jolt in all his muscles,
while a blaze of light pierced and shattered the surrounding darkness.

"They've got me, like Bistenave," Bucelier reflected.

But he felt nothing, while his head remained enveloped in the sweat-
stained *jellaba*.

Then he heard some shouts, some words of command, the thundering
voice of Lieutenant Pinières. Some submachine-guns were firing in short,
sharp, angry bursts. He heard Santucci shout out:

"But where the hell is Bucelier?"

He was suddenly moved to tears because they were talking about him
as though he was still alive. Stupidly, he thought:

"It's good to have friends and not be dead in the midst of strangers, as
in a car accident."

The body on top of him was still soft and warm, but did not move and
smelt of vomit and urine. He called out and was astonished to hear the

strange voice which was his own:

"Here, here. It's me, Bucelier."

The *fellagha's* body was dragged off him and the sergeant looked up to see some stars shining indifferently in the sky, and then the faces of his comrades above him. Hands were feeling his body, but without hurting him, unbuttoning his camouflage blouse and loosening his belt.

"But there's nothing wrong with you at all," Esclavier told him.

The captain helped him out of his hole. Bucelier was covered in blood but he was not wounded. Whereupon he burst into a loud guffaw, a nervous explosion which ended up in a sort of hiccup. Esclavier put his arm around his shoulder and held him against him, like a lost child who has just been found again.

"You're lucky, you know, Bucelier. The *fellagha* who pounced on you was mashed to a jelly by a grenade thrown by one of his own friends. You'd better get down to the river-bed; the medical orderly will give you something to drink and if you think you can manage, you can come back afterwards. It's not over yet."

"Did they break through, sir?"

"No, but they're bound to try again. They lost thirty men in the process, though."

"And us?"

"A few."

Bucelier never forgot that display of affection, when Esclavier put his arm round his shoulder.

A quarter of an hour later the *fellaghas* attempted a second break-through. This time it was Pinières's company that bore the brunt. But Si Lahcen's men failed to come to grips, and the moon which had risen illuminated the gorge and the confused fighting that ensued.

As the *fellaghas* broke off the engagement, the lieutenant caught sight of a short figure behind them silhouetted against the sky; he was firing on the runaways with a submachine-gun to try and rally them.

Pinières picked up his carbine and, standing up, with legs apart, carefully took aim and fired one, two, three shots.

Si Lahcen fell to his knees and dropped his weapon, then rolled a few yards down the slope and his hands, which had been clenched, slowly opened. Pinières searched him and drew the Military Medal out of his pocket. In his wallet there was also his pension card and his last mention in Indo-China.

"There's something wrong about this war," Pinières said to Esclavier.

A few *fellaghas* who were well dug in still put up some resistance but at dawn they were dislodged from their positions. Five or six of them surrendered, the rest preferred to die.

The regiment withdrew from the mountains towards P———, bringing its dead back with it. Information had already reached the town about the death of Si Lahcen and the destruction of his band; the population knew that it had been a tough, relentless fight and that everyone had acquitted himself well.

As the paratroops fled past, some old *chibanis*, whose sons had probably been killed by them up in the hills, waved to them; on their grey *jellabas* they were wearing all their medals. It was not the enemy they were greeting but simply those who had had God on their side that day.

Next morning a religious and military ceremony was held in honour of the twelve men of the 10th Colonial Parachute Regiment who had been killed in the recent battle. Seven of them were reservists.

The coffins were loaded on to a G.M.C., coffins made of plain wooden planks whose thickness was laid down by Ordnance regulations, as was the diameter of the nails.

It was then Respéguy spoke, addressing himself exclusively to the reservists.

"You fought extremely well. You have paid a high price for the right to belong to us; so any of you who wish will be allowed to go on a parachute course as soon as we get back to Algiers. Gentlemen, I am proud of you and salute you."

And standing stiffly to attention, straightening his back and squaring his shoulders, Respéguy saluted the truck which drove off with the Ordnance coffins and the few hundred faces turned towards him, the mutineers of Versailles whose features were drawn with fatigue, but who felt happy, released by the fight from the bloody memory of Rahlem.

Then, accompanied by Major de Glatigny and Captain Boisfeuras, Raspéguy went off to take leave of Colonel Quarterolles.

"Colonel," he said, "I've got a present for you."

He produced Si Lahcen's Military Medal and put it on the desk, and also a sheet of paper folded in four and stained with rain and sweat.

"It's only a mention in dispatches from Indo-China, Colonel, but it earned Sergeant-Major Si Lahcen his medal."

Respéguy snapped to attention and read out the rebel's citation:

"Sergeant-Major Si Lahcen, of the Third Regiment of Algerian Light Infantry; magnificent leader of men, stalwart fighter, surrounded in a strong-point by infinitely superior forces, his officer being killed, he assumed command and although seriously wounded refused to surrender, withholding the attack for six hours until the arrival of reinforcements."

"It's the same Si Lahcen, Colonel, that Pinières killed, while he was trying to stem the rout of his men. It would have been easier to have kept him on our side."

"Ah, I almost forgot, Mayor; I think Captain Boisfeuras has also got something for you."

"It's a receipt for a contribution to the F.L.N.," Boisfeuras sneered.

"It must be a fake," said Vesselier.

"A receipt which isn't made out in your name but in the name of Pedro Artaz, the foreman on your Bougainvillées estate. I can't see how Pedro

Artaz, who earns 40,000 francs a month and has a wife and three children, manages to pay 400,000 francs every quarter out of his own pocket."

"I've also got a present,'"said Glatigny. "It's for Captain Moine. It's a letter from Ahmed to Si Lahcen which I found among his papers."

Puffing at an old cigarette end, Moine raised his head slightly and his little eyes betrayed the bestial hatred he felt for the handsome major who, with one foot on a chair, began to read Ahmed's letter:

'Brother Lahcen,
As far as Captain Moine is concerned, you needn't worry. He's drunk every night and owes 300,000 francs to the Mozabite, Mechaien. If he makes any fuss, we'll be able to blackmail him. But he's much too stupid, lazy and cowardly . . .'

"Here, take the letter, Captain."

Without moving, Moine stretched his hand out for it.

Colonel Quarterolles tried to change the subject:

"I've drafted a number of citations, for I must admit your men behaved admirably . . ."

Raspéguy replied with exaggerated courtesy:

"Colonel, I'm in the habit of rewarding my men, both dead and alive, myself, and I don't entrust anyone else with the task."

He saluted and withdrew with his two officers. Moine tore the letter up into small pieces, then ground the pieces under his heel and suddenly raised his head.

"I hope, sir, you're going to put in a report about the conduct of Respéguy's officers in P———. They tortured and liquidated Ahmed instead of handing him over to the proper authorities."

"But you've done the same yourself, Moine, countless times . . ."

"Yes, but I always made out a report which was counter-signed by the police; I was quite in order."

The regiment did not go back to the Camp des Pins straight-away, but wandered all over Kabylie to support the garrison troops whenever an important operation was undertaken . . .

The "lizards" marched through cork forests, in the indigo-coloured shade of the trees. The ferns bent and crackled under their jungle boots while flies, gorged on sap and plant-juice, came and settled on them as though dead drunk after a clumsy, faltering flight.

They toiled over the burning stones of the Aurès and Némentchas and, with parched throats, dreamt of the fresh springs of France half-choked by watercress and wild sorrel.

They ran their tongues over the salty sweat which dripped on to their lips. They marched, they laid ambushes, they killed rebels armed with sporting rifles or submachine-guns.

On 27 July they heard that the Egyptians had nationalized the Suez

Canal, which affected them scarcely at all since none of them had shares in the Company.

They went on marching or devouring the dust of the road in open trucks. One day they were sent off to occupy a series of little oases at the foot of the Saharan Atlas where they relieved a Foreign Legion unit.

Esclavier and his two companies of reservists set up head-quarters at V———, on the site of an old Roman camp of Cornelius Balbus. It was just outside the oasis, overlooking a broad expanse of sand-dunes.

The grove of palm-trees watered by *seguias* was cool and smelt of apricots. It was divided up into countless little grenades in which the *norias* of the wells made a gentle rattling sound. The women, unveiled, with tattooed faces, and adorned with heavy silver jewelry, smiled at the soldiers while the children, more persistent than the flies, ran after them begging for chocolate or offering them pleasures which the women of the oasis could not provide without a certain amount of danger.

The rebellion had not yet reached this area; the regiment took it easy and the officers spent their time calling on one another and showing off their palm groves with the pride and delight of owners. Raspéguy had left Boudin at Laghouat to attend to the administrative questions and supplies.

One evening almost all the officers had dropped in on Esclavier who, having taken over the legionaries' furniture, had the most comfortable mess. It boasted a refrigerator, a few fans and, on a whitewashed wall, a primitive fresco depicting the Battle of Camerone.

Glatigny had brought a gazelle which he had shot from his Jeep, Boisfeuras a case of whisky which he had ordered from Algiers, and Boudin had sent up a small barrel of Mascara wine. They had decided to make a night of it and had started drinking systematically to get drunk as quickly as possible; through drink they contrived to come to grips with the painful, unwelcome memories that dogged their footsteps, to grapple with them, and exhaust themselves in the effort so as to wake up in the morning with a splitting headache and their minds at rest.

They drank first of all to Merle and all the others who were dead, then to themselves, to whom the same thing might happen any day, to Si Lahcen whom they had had to kill, and to Colonel Quarterolles, Moine and Vesselier whom they would very much have liked to shoot. But as they got more and more drunk they began to forget Algeria and France and presently all of them were talking or dreaming of Indo-China.

At the same moment all the officers and warrant-officers of the French Army, all those who had known Tonkin or Cochin-China, the Haute-Région, Cambodia or Laos, whether sitting in the mess, lying in ambush or sleeping in a tent, were likewise aggravating their yellow infection by picking at the thin scabs that covered it.

Esclavier had never been able to bear drunken conversation for long and so went out into the cool, blue desert night. He wandered about the ruins of the Roman camp until he came to the edge of the plateau. Sitting down on the base of a broken column, he contemplated the infinite expanse of the sky and the dunes; he felt a shiver down his spine which was perhaps nothing more than the cold night air. To reassure himself, he ran his fingers over the column and touched the inscription that he had deciphered on the morning of his arrival: *Titus Caius Germanicus centurio III Legio Augusta.*

Twenty centuries earlier a Roman centurion had dreamt by this column and peered into the depths of the desert on the lookout for the arrival of the Numidians. He had stayed behind there to guard the *limes* of the Empire, while Rome decayed, the barbarians camped at her gates and the wives and daughters of the senators went out at nightfall to fornicate with them.

The centurions of Africa used to light bonfires on the slopes of the Saharan Atlas to make the Numidians think that the legions were still up there on guard. But one day the Numidians heard they were no more than a handful and they slaughtered them, while their comrades who had fled to Rome elected a new Caesar in order to forget their cowardice.

The centurion Philippe Esclavier of the 10th Parachute Regiment tried to think why he, too, had lit bonfires in order to contain the barbarians and save the West. "We centurions," he reflected, "are the last defenders of man's innocence against all those who want to enslave it in the name of original sin, against the Communists who refuse to have their children christened, never accept the conversion of an adult and are always ready to question it, but also against certain Christians who only think of faults and forget about redemption."

Philippe heard the yapping of a jackal in the distance and, closer at hand, the song his comrades were bawling out, as they rapped on their plates with their knives and forks . . .

He thought of the Communists; he could not help feeling a certain respect for them, as the centurion Titus Caius Germanicus had felt for the nomads prowling round his desert camp. The Communists were frank enough to say what they wanted: the entire world. They fought fairly and no quarter or pity could be expected. Did Titus Caius also know he would have his throat cut?

But Philippe felt hatred and disgust welling up against the people back in Paris who were rejoicing in advance at their defeat, all those sons of Masoch who were already getting pleasure out of it.

Titus Caius must have thought the same about the progressivists of Rome. The barbarians, like the Communists of the twentieth century, had needed those traitors to open the city gate to them. But they despised them and on the day of their victory they had decided forthwith to exterminate them.

A strange thought crossed the captain's mind: "Perhaps we could prevent the empire from collapsing by transforming ourselves into barbarians, by becoming males disgusted with all these females, by turning into

Communists."

As he rummaged in his pocket for a cigarette, Esclavier came upon a letter from the incestuous Guitte who refused to remain his sister by adoption. He had given her money and clothes, as he would a real sister; he had even paid the instalments on her small car. She had spread it abroad that it was perfectly normal for him to keep her since she was his mistress and was living with him.

Old Goldschmidt, who had heard these rumours, had given his daughter a severe reprimand in front of the captain. She had merely shrugged her shoulders and said:

"It was only to help Philippe. He's frightened of giving me a bad reputation; now that I've got one, what's he waiting for?"

Guitte had waited a few minutes, and since he had made no move, she had left the room; he had not seen her again before his departure. But she had just written to say that she had got a lover, which suited her down to the ground.

Mina kept sending him postcards from the Côte d'Azur where she had gone on holiday. There were photographs of grand hotels, naked girls on the beach, parasols and pedal-boats, regattas and water-ski championships. Philippe stuck them up in the mess; the second-lieutenants and cadets of the reserve came and brooded on these holiday pictures for hours on end.

How paltry everything suddenly seemed in the middle of this African night!

He heard a great crash; back there in the mess a table had collapsed.

Marindelle came out and joined Esclavier.

"They're dead drunk," he told him. "Dia made a bet he could jump over the table and landed right on top of it. Pinières has passed out in a corner of the room, stripped to the waist and covered in bandages. Glatigny is sitting back in his chair quietly smoking his pipe, while Boisfeuras is practising knife-throwing against the door."

"And Raspéguy?"

"He hasn't opened his mouth but keeps eating, drinking and cutting up his bread with his penknife. He's not very keen on these systematic binges. He thinks they're a waste of time, effort and breath."

"What about you, Yves?"

"I'm rather fed up."

"Your wife?"

"I don't love her any longer but I've got to get her out of my system; it'll take some time. There's some talk about the French and British intervening in Egypt. You know we're rather well in with G.H.Q. Algiers since that business at P———."

"I'm not very proud of that . . . We say we come out here to protect the Algerians against the barbarism of the F.L.N., and my men and I then go and behave like Ahmed's or Si Lahcen's thugs."

"We came out here to win, you know, and for no other reason. It's thanks to the example you set at Rahlem that we wiped out the best organized band in Algeria, thereby saving the lives of hundreds, maybe thousands, of men, women and children."

"When I went into the *mechtas* with a knife in my hand, I didn't think of that. I should like to be in a war which wasn't a civil war, a good clean war where there are only friends and enemies and no traitors, spies or collaborators, a war in which blood doesn't mingle with shit . . ."

Raspéguy came up behind tem.

"It's not a bad spot," he said. "We might have stayed here a little longer, but in a week's time we're going back to Algiers. We've just been posted to the general reserve."

"What does that mean, sir'" Esclavier inquired.

Raspéguy put a hand on each of the captain's shoulders, leaning heavily on them.

"It means we'll be the first to enter Cairo."

Two weeks later the 10th Colonial Parachute Regiment got back to its quarters in the Camp des Pins.

Before the reservists, who had just completed their six months' stint, were demobilized, Raspéguy insisted on putting any of them who wished through a parachute course. All the reservists who had taken part in the Rahlem business volunteered.

"I don't see how we can very well do anything else," said Bucelier.

He couldn't explain exactly why, but he felt it had to be done. Five or six soldiers who had been put off by the rigours of the training or the fear of breaking a leg just when they were on the point of going home, tried to get out of it. But their comrades did not give them a moment's peace until they too decided to jump.

One evening, at eighteen-hundred hours, during the daily Press conference at Government House, the Press Information captain of Area Ten announced that "the mutineers of Versailles" were going to do a parachute jump at the Camp des Pins a few days before being demobbed and that they had all volunteered for it. The journalists had been invited by Lieutenant-Colonel Raspéguy who was in command of the unit to which they belonged.

The spokesman who was at the meeting thereupon button-holed Villèle, his favourite butt.

"You'll be writing this up in the rag of yours, won't you, Mr. Villèle--that some reservists, Communists, have asked to do a parachute jump before leaving Algeria?"

"I'll see," said Villèle. "'I'm going out there and if it's true I'll certainly write about it."

He turned to Pasfeuro:

"Coming?"

They descended the broad stairs of the forum as far as the war memorial and went into a café where they ordered two anisettes.

"Had you heard about this story?" Villèle asked. "You know the whole Raspéguy outfit pretty well, don't you?"

He gave a slight sneer.

"Especially that fellow Marindelle."

"Some day, my fine friend, I'm going to bash your face in if you don't keep off that subject. No, I hadn't heard."

"Shall we go and have a look?"

"You said you were going anyway, do you need me as well?"

"No . . . but I think it'll be a good story. You could give me a lift . . . Let's meet outside the Aletti."

"Why don't you hire a car like everyone else?"

"I'm never in Algiers more than a few days at a time. Please let me pay for your drink."

Villèle could not help wondering what Pasfeuro's reaction would be if he knew that he put the cost of a car down on his expenses although the one he always used was borrowed from a friend. He had even managed to get hold of some blank Europe-Cars receipt forms.

In front of two or three generals, a handful of colonels and a dozen journalists, two hundred reservists led by Captain Esclavier launched themselves for the seventh time into the blue. Their parachutes floated in the air for a few moments. Pulling on their rigging-lines, they landed without mishap and received their brand-new paratrooper's badge from the hands of Colonel Raspéguy.

Then they marched back to their quarters and prepared for their departure. Bucelier, who had signed on again because he was now frightened of going back to France, watched them with a lump in his throat.

The rest of them were quits; they had done their jumps. But he wasn't yet, at least he thought not.

Colonel Raspéguy, Esclavier and Pinières went down to the docks to watch the reservists as they embarked on the *Sidi Brahim*; they remained there until the last moment when the liner cast off. While waiting for them at the bar of the Aletti, Pasfeuro, Villèle, Marindelle and Boisfeuras proceeded to get drunk.

It was after the fifth whisky that Boisfeuras mentioned the leap of Leucadia.

"I once knew an Englishman out in Burma," he said, "a crazy sort of chap who dropped into us one morning with some containers of gasoline meant for another unit which, unlike us, did at least have one or two vehicles. He was a specialist, but on Ancient Greece. Though he didn't have a clue about the Far East, he knew a great deal about Greece and her esoteric customs. All he could do was talk and I often used to listen to him.

"One evening, while the mosquitoes were busy eating us alive and we were trying to force a stew of monkey down our throats, he asked me:

"Do you know the origin of the parachute? I thought not. And I don't suppose you've heard of the island of Leucadia in Greece, either, have you?"

"He was a bit of a bore when he assumed his professional tone after whining all day:

"Well, it was at Leucadia that the parachute was born. At Leucadia there's a white cliff dedicated to Apollo-- Leucadia from λευκοσ, the Greek for 'white', as of course you know--a hundred and fifty feet high, from the top of which, in an extremely remote age, probably the proto-historical--that's to say some time between prehistory and history--they used to hurl people into the sea as a sacrifice to the Sun-god. They were either youths or young girls who had been charged with all the crimes of the community, like the scapegoat in Leviticus.

"At a later date the priests of Apollo used to look for volunteers among incurable invalids, criminals or victims of unrequited love, all of whom were much the same thing in the eyes of the Ancients. The unloved is a culprit, don't forget."

Marindelle almost upset his glass. "The unloved is a culprit!"

But Boisfeuras, punctuating his story with little sniggers, parodying the voice of the archaeologist-paratrooper, went on with his tale:

"They say that Sappho threw herself off the leap of Leucadia in a moment of despair. But which Sappho? There were two, one was a courtesan, the other a poetess. A woman who writes can't ever love, so it must have been the courtesan who did the leap.

"The priests humanized the leap, posted boats down below to retrieve those who had jumped from the cliff. But there came a time when no one was willing to take such a risk any longer; in the course of its development, civilization eliminates heroism. Those who were unlucky in love were more discreet or else were made to look ridiculous.

"So in place of those who wanted to redeem their faults, the priests themselves volunteered to jump, for a certain fee. They trained seriously, did gymnastics, strengthened their muscles, exercised their reflexes, and learnt how to fall. To delay their drop they fastened feathers, live birds and God knows what else on to themselves . . . in other words, the parachute.

"I knew all this when I dropped, and that's probably why I sprained my ankle. I was always the scapegoat up at Oxford; now I'm at peace at last."

Boisfeuras drained his glass, ordered another round and proposed this strange toast:

"I drink to the leap of Leucadia which Esclavier's two hundred reservists performed today to cleanse themselves of a fault which they thought they had committed."

"What fault?" Pasfeuro asked.

"Didn't you ever hear about the *mechtas* of Rahlem?"

"No," said Villèle.

He almost asked for further details, but his instinct warned him not to; this evening he was being barely tolerated.

"By the way," Boisfeuras went on, "I forgot to tell you what became of that English fellow. The gods felt that he had not cleansed himself sufficiently of his faults, or else those of Oxford University were too heavy by half. On his next jump he did a 'Roman candle' and smashed himself to bits."

From Jean Lartéguy, *The Centurions,* (New York: Dutton, 1960), pp.353-376.

Chapter 10

The Ultimate Rescue

This volume has dealt, thus far, only peripherally with the issue of rescues as special operations. The Trojan War was fought to rescue Helen, but Odysseus' commando operation was driven more by the desire to keep from having to give up the siege and face the humiliation of defeat. Rogers's raid on St. Francis did recoup one settler held prisoner, but it was hardly the main objective. Eaton's insurgency against the bashaw of Tripoli provided the coercive pressure needed to obtain the release of the American hostages held there, but his campaign can hardly be construed as a rescue attempt. Finally, the British commando raid on Tobruk included the goal of releasing prisoners being held there; but then, this raid sought to do a little bit of everything else, too.

This excerpt on Entebbe, drawn from General Chaim Herzog's memoirs, puts the rescue operation at center stage; and there is perhaps no better example of such clean execution of such a complex mission. Herzog's matter-of-fact prose contrapuntally heightens the wonder that the Israelis actually carried this mission off successfully, against all odds. The fact that the raiders suffered only one fatal casualty, their assault leader, remains a tribute both to their high level of efficiency and to Yoni himself, who exemplified all the finest traits of a special operations commander by leading from the front.

Chaim Herzog

The War Against Terrorism: Entebbe

Since the early 1950s, Israel has been subjected at various periods to terrorist attacks from across the borders, and has invariably reacted in reprisal raids. In 1968, the Palestine Liberation Organization launched its first attack against Israel overseas, by hijacking an El Al airliner flying from Rome to Tel Aviv and diverting it to Algeria. Thereafter, all aircraft bound to and from Israel, Israeli offices abroad and Israeli embassy buildings were subjected to attack by various components of the PLO--frequently aided by other groupings within the international terrorist community. An attack on Puerto Rican pilgrims in Lod Airport was carried out by members of the Japanese Red Army and, on numerous occasions, German and French terrorists bent on PLO missions have been apprehended in Israel.

The policy adopted by Israel from the outset rejected any form of compromise with terrorism, and was designed to stamp it out wherever it might appear. Thus, when terrorists hijacked a Belgian Sabena airliner, which was forced back to Ben-Gurion Airport in Israel in May 1972, Israeli commandos disguised as mechanics and ground attendants captured it, killed two Arab gunmen and saved 97 passengers. When children were taken hostage in a school in the northern Galilee town of Maalot in May 1974, the building was stormed by Israeli military units, despite the danger to the children: the terrorists were killed, but 22 children lost their lives. In an attack on the Haifa-Tel Aviv coastal road on 13 March 1978, when terrorists hijacked a bus, a battle ensued in which all but two of the terrorists were killed, as were over 30 passengers. In an attack on an Israeli El Al airliner at Kloten Airport in Zurich, an Israeli security guard stormed the Palestinian terrorists who were firing at the plane, killing one with his pistol.

The same pattern has characterized the instinctive Israeli reaction to terror throughout: compromise with terrorism would lead to an impossible situation. Every terrorist must know, when embarking on an action against an Israeli target, that he will in all probability have to fight his way out.

The Israel Defence Forces set up an élite unit highly trained in counter-terrorist activities. The policy guiding the Israelis on this issue was set out very clearly by Shimon Peres, who was the Minister of Defence in the

Government of Israel during the Entebbe hostage rescue operation in 1976. At a conference on international terrorism, he enunciated Israeli policy. He emphasized that there should never be surrender to terrorism, that Israel must have an elaborate intelligence system and an early warning system with properly trained people in order to nullify the terrorist advantage of surprise and indiscriminate attack. He emphasized the importance of fighting terrorism not only in the operational field but also in the psychological field. As he put it, "The tendency of terrorist groups to bedeck themselves with titles such as the 'Red Army' or the 'Liberation Organization' should not beguile us of our often-bewitched media . . . terrorist groups would be described in their true colours--groups which are impatient with democracy, which are undisciplined, corrupt in their attitude to life, and unable to free themselves from the domination of murder and hatred." He pointed out that terror has become international and must be fought internationally. The terrorists consider most free nations and peoples as their enemies; countermeasures must therefore be internationally co-ordinated.

The most dramatic reaction to international terrorism so far has undoubtedly been the Israeli operation that brought the release of 100 Israeli hostages who had been hijacked to Entebbe in Uganda in an Air France airliner.

On Sunday 27 June 1976, Air France flight 139, flying from Tel Aviv to Paris via Athens, was hijacked by four PLO terrorists after leaving Athens. Two of them, a man and a woman, were Germans, members of the Baader-Meinhof urban guerrilla organization; and two of them were Arabs, members of the terrorist Popular Front for the Liberation of Palestine. In the aircraft were 256 passengers and 12 crew members. Taking advantage of the lax security arrangements at Athens, the terrorists had succeeded in bringing on board guns and hand grenades. After being hijacked, the aircraft landed for refueling at Benghazi, Libya, and then continued south, landing at Entebbe in Uganda, where the terrorists were joined by additional Palestinian terrorists and by units of the Ugandan Army, who moved the hostages into the old terminal building at the airport.

Uganda Radio made known on 29 June the demands of the hijackers, which included the handing over of 53 convicted terrorists--40 held in Israel, six in West Germany, five in Kenya, one in Switzerland and one in France. Meanwhile, the Israelis had been separated from the other passengers and, in the course of the week, the non-Israelis were flown back to France. The Israeli Government was faced with the problem of achieving the release of the Israeli hostages, and a negotiating machinery was set up using intermediaries.

On the evening of 28 June, Lieutenant-General Mordechai ('Motta') Gur, the Chief of Staff, issued instructions to prepare immediately a paratroop force which would be ready to parachute into Entebbe, or arrive there across Lake Victoria, and capture the airport terminal, kill the terrorists and defend the hostages until arrangements had been concluded with the Government of Uganda to release them. But the Prime Minister, Yitzhak Rabin, refused to contemplate the operational plans presented to him, maintaining that they did not provide a complete solution to the problem. Indeed, at this stage of the developments, his general attitude as to the feasibility of a military operation was negative.

The Minister of Defence, Shimon Peres, took an entirely different view. In all the discussions, he emphasized the paramount importance of refusing to submit to the terrorists: their success in this operation would constitute a political and moral defeat for Israel of major proportions, and would constitute a most dangerous precedent for the future in the struggle against terror and hijacking. Apart from discussing the matter with the Chief of Staff, he discussed it in detail with the various senior officers directly involved. General Gur, for his part, emphasized the importance of success in such an operation and the catastrophic results of failure; unequivocally, he told the Minister of Defence that he would not recommend an operation unless he personally reached a conclusion that the risk was reasonable and that the proposal was feasible. On the Wednesday, the Israeli Cabinet met again on the subject, and the Prime Minister reiterated that, unless he received a proposal for a military operation backed by the General Staff, he would advise the Cabinet to accept the ultimatum of the terrorists and their conditions in order to bring about the release of the hostages.

Parallel to the planning efforts mounted by the General Staff, however, Major-General Dan Shomron, who was Chief Infantry and Paratroop Officer in the Israel Defence Forces (and who had commanded an armoured brigade in the Sinai during the 1973 War), had decided on Monday 28 June--without any instructions from above--to commence planning the release of the hostages in Entebbe. As soon as the separation of the Israelis from the other passengers had begun, he had recalled the selection process used by the Nazis in the concentration camps, and had given immediate instructions to his staff to begin planning. By Wednesday evening, his staff had already crystallized a plan on an airborne landing on the new airfield at Entebbe, movement in vehicles (adapted to the local background in Uganda) to the old airport, liquidation of the terrorists and release of the hostages. It became evident to the planners that it would be unrealistic to plan in terms of an operation designed to capture the airport entirely, because this could mean the killing of the hostages by the terrorists and Ugandans. The first strike would take place against the terrorists and the operation would develop from this central focal point outwards. The Air Force advised Shomron's staff that their Hercules aircraft could reach Entebbe, but that there would be a problem with refueling on the way back. The solution to this problem would be to refuel at Entebbe, using the existing fuel supplies and tanks at the international airport there.

On the morning of Thursday 1 July, the Prime Minister, by now under increasing pressure from the public and from the families of the hostages, asked the Cabinet for a quick decision approving the release of the imprisoned terrorists whose freedom had been demanded by the terrorists, in order to bring home the hostages. He made a similar appeal to the Leader of the Opposition, Mr. Menachem Begin, and the Chairman of the Defence and Foreign Affairs Committee in the Knesset, and received their approval. However, that same afternoon, Shomron was invited by the Chief of the Operations Branch, Major-General Yekutiel Adam, to come to the General Staff to present his plan. Present were Shimon Peres, the Minister of Defence; the Chief of Staff, General Gur; the Chief of the Operations Branch, General Adam; the Commander of the Air Force, Major-General Benjamin Peled; and the Assistant Chief of the Operations Branch, Brigadier-General Avigdor Ben-Gal. This was the first time the plan was presented in full detail. It called for a landing at Entebbe on Saturday 3 July at 23.00 hours, and for a "dry" rehearsal on the Friday evening using a model. The assumption was that, since the MiG aircraft of the Ugandan Air Force were parked in the old airport, there must be a tarmac taxiing runway leading from there to the new airport.

At the conclusion of Shomron's presentation, Shimon Peres turned to each one of those present, asking him for his views, what were the prospects for success, how many casualties he anticipated and whether or not he recommended carrying out the operation. There were those who opposed the operation; there were those who gave it a 50-50 chance. Shomron's reply was that there was one weak point--landing the first aircraft without arousing suspicion. If this were possible, then there was a 100 per cent chance of success. With luck, there would be no casualties. Should a fire-fight develop, he estimated that there would be ten casualties, and he recommended without hesitation that the operation be mounted. Peres indicated his approval of the plan subject to the final approval of the Cabinet, and ordered them to continue with all the preparations. As they rose to leave the room, Shomron turned to Peres and said, "I understand that I am to command the operation." Peres turned and looked at the Chief of Staff, and then said, "Fine. You are the commander of the operation." Shomron was given the authority to choose the units that would participate in the operation, and it was agreed that on Friday evening the plan would be tried on a model. On Saturday, they would take off from Sharm El-Sheikh at 15.30 hours for Entebbe.

In order not to give rise to any suspicion that a military operation was being planned, all the diplomatic negotiations in France and Uganda continued meanwhile, indicating that Israel would give in to the demands of the terrorists and make the necessary arrangements to meet these demands by Sunday 4 July. It therefore became imperative to release the hostages before this date. This consideration left Saturday night as the last possibility.

The units participating were assembled immediately, the telephone communications to and from their base were cut, and the men were forbidden to leave there. Two hundred highly trained personnel were assembled, most of them regulars, with battle experience.

Leaving open the involved problem of the landing at Entebbe (for which additional intelligence information was necessary), the General Staff laid down the general outline of the operation from the point of landing and allotted units and tasks. These would be:

1. A force to illuminate and secure the runway
2. A force to occupy the old terminal and release the hostages
3. A force to take control of the new terminal
4. A force to secure the airfield and destroy the Ugandan fighter aircraft
5. A force to evacuate the hostages from the terminal to the aircraft

In the course of the planning and preparation for the operation, considerable use was made of the photographs taken by Israeli Air Force personnel some years before, when they were training the Ugandan Air Force. (In one of the home movies that they studied, Idi Amin, the ruler of Uganda, arrived at the airport in a black Mercedes, accompanied by a Land Rover, and it was this that gave birth to the idea to look for a Mercedes car which would be used for deception purposes in the operation.) To this information was added intelligence collected by special interrogators who interviewed the non-Jewish passengers released by the terrorists, after their arrival in Paris. From their reports, a clear picture of the daily routine at the terminal was obtained: where they slept; where the various conveniences were located and how they reached them; what was the guard routine and in which rooms the terrorists live; the nature and character of the terrorists and their behaviour towards the hostages; the location of the Ugandan soldiers in the building and around, and their guard routine.

On the Friday, Israeli television broadcast a film that had been made by a foreign press correspondent, which showed the new terminal in Entebbe. From this they learned that the new terminal was a two-storey building. There were also photographs of the old terminal where the Israeli hostages were being held. The passengers who had been released described how the terrorists had placed boxes in the terminal; leading from each was a white detonating wire, and it was presumed that the boxes contained explosives. However, since information also indicated that Ugandan soldiers were stationed on the roof, the conclusion was drawn that the boxes were but a ruse to frighten the hostages, and that the building was not really wired for detonation.

As the intelligence material accumulated, General Gur decided that the operation was entirely feasible, and that he could recommend to the Minister of Defence that it be set into motion. At the same time, he issued instructions that he would command the operation from his headquarters at the General Staff, while the head of the Operations Branch, Major-General Yekutiel Adam, and the Commander of the Air Force, Major-

General Benjamin Peled, would constitute an advanced General Staff Headquarters in an aircraft flying over the scene of the operation. It was decided, too, that a second aircraft accompanying the advanced headquarters would include a fully-equipped field hospital; this was scheduled to land at Nairobi without any advance warning in order to set up a field hospital to deal with those hostages or soldiers who might be wounded.

Gur was very concerned about whether or not the aircraft could land safely in darkness until, on Friday, he and Peled flew in a Hercules to ensure that it was capable of a "blind" landing. The indications were that the weather would be good on the night of the operation, and that the night would be dark without any moonlight.

On the Friday, as exercises were carried out on a model, a debate was continuing in the Cabinet. The Prime Minister expressed serious doubts about the feasibility of the operation. Meanwhile, the Chief of Staff met all the commanders involved in the operation. He asked each one how he estimated the chances. All expressed the opinion that the mission was possible, and that the prospects of success were good. Gur addressed each one of them, asking them if they appreciated what the price of failure would be. However, he advised them that on the morrow, on the Sabbath, he would go to the Cabinet and recommend carrying out the operation.

On the Saturday morning at 08.00 hours, Gur presented his plan to the Minister of Defence, and then they together presented it to the Prime Minister. Gur opened his remarks by saying "I present to you a plan for execution this evening. The troops are on their way, and the entire operation is now in motion according to a pre-arranged plan." The Prime Minister gave his approval, subject to the approval of the Cabinet. Three hours later the final briefing of the troops took place. Take-off was set for 15.30 hours.

The plan was as follows. The first aircraft would land on the runway and disembark a unit of paratroopers, whose task would be emergency lighting of the runway in addition to the existing lighting arrangements. The aircraft would taxi rapidly to the end of the runway, and there the assault unit designated to take control of the two terminals would disembark. The unit under Lieutenant-Colonel Jonathan ('Yoni') Netanyahu, riding in two Land Rovers and the Mercedes, would move directly to the old terminal in order to release the hostages. The paratroopers, under Colonel Matan Vilnai, would move on foot to the new terminal and take control of it, the control tower and the refuelling tarmac. The commander of the operation, Major-General Dan Shomron, would disembark these two advance units together with his advanced headquarters staff.

The second aircraft would land seven minutes after the first, thus giving time to Netanyahu's force to take the old terminal by surprise and release the hostages. This aircraft would taxi to the end of the runway and disembark the remainder of the forces, including two armoured cars that would secure the immediate surroundings of the terminal and release the hostages. This aircraft would also carry Shomron's headquarters jeep in order to enable him to move rapidly between the units and control them as well as maintaining direct contact with the command aircraft circling above.

The third aircraft would land immediately after the second and would disembark two additional armoured cars for Lieutenant-Colonel Netanyahu's force and a unit of the "Golani" Infantry Brigade commanded by Colonel Orr, which would take control of the area linking two runways, would act as a reserve in the event of any untoward development in various parts of the airfield, and would assist the hostages to embark on the rescue aircraft.

The fourth and last aircraft would disembark the remainder of the reserve forces and a Peugeot tender for the rapid evacuation of the wounded. It would carry a medical team and also a refuelling team. This aircraft was ordered to taxi to the old terminal in order to embark the hostages.

It was envisaged that the critical elements in the operation would be the actual landing of the aircraft; the storming of the old terminal; prevention of the arrival of Ugandan reinforcements; and securing the runway in order to guarantee a safe take-off home.

At 15.20 hours, the Cabinet, still discussing the operation, authorized the 15.30 take-off; however, the actual operation was not yet approved. It was understood that, should approval not be given, the aircraft could be returned to their base. By 16.00 hours, all the aircraft were airborne, and it was after this by the time the Cabinet approved the operation unanimously.

After seven hours of flying, the force came within range of the Entebbe control tower. The operation had been planned so that the first aircraft could dovetail behind a scheduled British cargo flight, thus arousing no suspicion. Exactly as planned, they came behind the British aircraft as its captain was asking the terminal for permission to land. They flew in over Lake Victoria in a heavy rainstorm, and the approach for landing was made by instruments. Suddenly, the rain stopped and the skies cleared, and there before their eyes were the landing lights of Entebbe Airport.

The British cargo aircraft landed, and the first Israeli Hercules glided in immediately behind it without arousing any suspicion in the control tower. As they touched down, the pilot slowed according to plan, and the advance party jumped out while the aircraft was still taxiing. They doubled along the side of the airfield, placing goosenecks (mobile landing lights) ready to provide alternative lights for the three aircraft that were following, in the event that the airfield lights would be switched off. The aircraft taxied to a dark corner of the field without lights, the rest of the initial landing force disembarked, and the Mercedes car and the Land Rovers were rolled off. All around there was an atmosphere of quiet and peace. The only noise was that of the British cargo aircraft taxiing towards the terminal, which drowned the noise of the Israeli party. Major-General Shomron looked around and said to his men, "Boys, this operation is a success despite the fact that not one bullet has yet been fired."

The men mounted the vehicles, which drove with their headlights on slowly towards where the hostages were being held. The Mercedes led, followed by the two Land Rovers. The area was well lit up and there was no difficulty in finding the way to the objective. Approximately 100 yards from the control tower, two Ugandan soldiers came into full view in the Israelis' headlights. Netanyahu and another officer drew pistols equipped with silencers. One of the Ugandans pointed his rifle at the vehicle and called on it to halt. Netanyahu and the second officer fired at the Ugandan soldier from 10 yards range and hit him. Because of this unplanned encounter, the unit disembarked on the spot, some 50 yards from the terminal. One of the entrances to the terminal had been blocked, so the entire force entered by the remaining entrance instead of two entrances as had been planned. The point section broke into the hall where the hostages were lying, most of them fast asleep on the floor. A terrorist on the right of the hall opened fire and was killed. Two more terrorists--one of them a woman--were by the window on the left of the hall, and were shot by the leading soldiers. A fourth terrorist at the end of the hall was identified and shot. The hall was fully lit up and the terrorists were easily identifiable because they were all standing with weapons. They were completely taken by surprise.

From the moment that the Ugandan sentry had been shot outside the terminal until the four terrorists inside the terminal had been killed, only 15 seconds had passed. This speed with which the operation was carried out was undoubtedly the main factor in the initial success. One of the soldiers called out in Hebrew and English to all the hostages to remain lying on the floor--but one of the hostages, who in his excitement failed to obey the order, jumped up and was shot too. Lieutenant-Colonel Netanyahu followed the assault unit. He reached then entrance to the hall and paused in the garden before the entrance. Suddenly, fire was directed towards the attacking unit from the control tower. Netanyahu was hit by a bullet in the neck. Although evacuated safely, he died later.

The second aircraft had been scheduled to land exactly seven minutes after the first plane, thus giving an opportunity to the attacking forces to take the terrorists completely by surprise. As planned, the additional three aircraft landed, discharging their armoured cars. These drove to the terminal, with Shomron in a jeep. Inside the terminal, the assault units continued to mop-up and kill any terrorists or Ugandan troops that engaged them. Two European terrorists endeavoured to slip out of the terminal, pretending that they were hostages. A section commander called on them to halt when he noticed a grenade hanging on one of their belts. But they continued moving and were fired at, being blown up by the grenade, which detonated. Additional units searched and cleared the VIP lounges and the customs hall: 60 Ugandan soldiers on the second floor fled. In all, in the course of this operation, 35 Ugandan troops were killed. Thirteen terrorists were surprised, some of them in their sleep, and were shot dead at short range.

The Ugandan troops on the control tower continued to fire at the Israeli troops, as the hostages were being bundled out of the hall. The armoured personnel carrier with the force was directed to neutralize the control tower. This was done by means of concentrated heavy machine-gun fire and RPG fire. It was now possible, as aircraft number three taxied up to the vicinity of the old terminal, for Colonel Orr and two units with him to evacuate the hostages from the terminal. By the evacuating plane was the medical team which immediately began to treat the wounded. Loading the hostages, the wounded and dead took some fifteen minutes.

Meanwhile, as the shooting erupted in the old terminal, Colonel Vilnai was ordered by Shomron to move. One unit went directly towards the new terminal while a second unit searched the aircraft parking area opposite the terminal. The unit directed towards the terminal stormed the building, searched the entrance, the two storeys of the building and the roof. According to their instructions, the troops were ordered not to fire at the Ugandan troops in the new terminal unless fired upon by them. All Ugandans were to be allowed to flee, but fifteen Ugandans who surrendered were locked in one of the rooms and warned not to leave. Within fifteen minutes of the commencement of the operation, Vilnai's force had taken control of the new terminal, and the Peugeot tender arrived with the refuelling equipment. At this point, Vilnai and the captain of the leading aircraft (who was the squadron commander), recommended that the refuelling should not be done in Entebbe. Shomron accepted their recommendation and asked for permission to take off without refuelling from GHQ advanced headquarters, which was flying above in a Boeing 707. Permission was given: instructions were issued not to refuel in Entebbe but instead to do so in Nairobi.

The first aircraft had landed at 23.01 hours; at 23.58 hours--57 minutes after the commencement of the operation--the first aircraft loaded with the hostages took off from Entebbe in the direction of Nairobi. Forty-two minutes later, the last aircraft left after one of the final units to leave the airport had set fire to eight Ugandan Air Force MiGs by machine-gun fire. Shomron with his headquarters remained with the rearguard unit and took off with it in the last plane to leave.

The aircraft landed for refuelling in Nairobi Airport, and thereafter made their way back to Israel, to arrive to a joyous and victorious welcome, having accomplished one of the most electrifying, imaginative and universally applauded rescue operations in history. Back at his control headquarters at the General Staff in Tel Aviv, General Gur, the Prime Minister, the Minister of Defence and members of the General Staff drank a toast to those who were winging their way back from Entebbe.

This had been an operation with a high risk factor. It was not planned in order to capture territory or to cause casualties by use of concentrated fire: it was planned to release hostages under guard, and in such circumstances the use of concentrated firepower would have been futile, and indeed counter-productive. Such an operation had, of necessity, to be highly sophisticated, like using a sharp stiletto instead of a sledgehammer, and was therefore a highly involved operation. Speed was of the essence, because any hesitation would have cost the lives of Israeli hostages. The force was up against between ten and thirteen trigger-happy terrorists stationed amongst the hostages. Around the whole force were hundreds of Ugandans. The main problem had been to release the hostages alive. This guiding fact influenced the entire plan and mode of operation. Furthermore, the operation had no safety margin. In the field of battle, if an attack does not succeed, then one tries again or moves to another sector. If one battalion fails then another one is thrown into the battle. Artillery support and air support can be added at will. But there is always a margin of safety. In an operation such as that at Entebbe, all elements are interdependent. The slightest error, the slightest lack of co-ordination, and the whole structure is liable to collapse like a pack of cards. This lesson emerged in the ill-fated United States attempt to rescue their hostages in Iran in 1980. Such operations leave little or no margin for security.

The planning had been carried out under the most difficult circumstances, because there were a large number of unknowns. All the subsequent stories about agents in Uganda and on Lake Victoria are complete fabrications and without foundation. The operation at Entebbe was the culmination of years of training for such eventualities on the part of the counter-terrorist unit and the other commando units that accompanied it, and testimony to the fact that the Israel Defence Force leaves nothing to chance. All eventualities are thought out and planned for well in advance, so it was possible to plan and execute such an operation at very short notice. The rescue at Entebbe was a resounding blow to international terrorism, and gave rise to a new resolve, both in the United Nations and elsewhere, to fight this dangerous phenomenon and to emulate the Israeli example.

In the debate at the United Nations Security Council, in which an unsuccessful attempt was made to condemn Israel for carrying out the rescue operation in Entebbe, the author of this book, who represented Israel, said:

"It has fallen to the lot of my small country, embattled as we are, facing the problems which we do, to demonstrate to the world that there is an alternative to surrender to terrorism and blackmail. It has fallen to our lot to prove to the world that this scourge of international terror can be dealt with. It is now for the nations of the world, regardless of political differences which may divide them, to unite against this common enemy which recognizes no authority, knows no borders, respects no sovereignty, ignores all basic human decencies, and places no limits on human bestiality.

"We come with a simple message to the Council: we are proud of what we have done, because we have demonstrated to the world that in a small country, in Israel's circumstances, with which the members of this Council are by now all too familiar, the dignity of man, human life and human freedom constitute the highest values. We are proud not only because we have saved the lives of over 100 innocent people--men, women and children--but because of the significance of our act for the cause of human freedom.

"We call on this body to declare war on international terror, to outlaw it and eradicate it wherever it may be. We call on this body, and above all we call on the Member States and countries of the world, to unite in a common effort to place these criminals outside the pale of human society, and with them to place any country which co-operated in any way in their nefarious activities . . ."

From Chaim Herzog, *The Arab-Israeli Wars,* (New York: Random House, 1982), pp. 365-376.

Bibliography

Arquilla, John. "The Strategic Implications of Information Dominance." *Strategic Review,* 22/3:24-31 (Summer 1994).

Asprey, Robert. *War in the Shadows: The Guerilla in History.* New York: Morrow, 1994.

Barnett, F.R., B.H. Tovar, and R.H. Shultz, eds. *Special Operations in U.S. Strategy.* Washington, DC: National Defense University Press, 1984.

Beaumont, Roger A. *Military Elites.* New York: Bobbs Merrill, 1974.

Beckwith, Charlie and Donald Knox. *Delta Force.* New York: Random House, 1983.

Bekker, Cajus. *The Luftwaffe War Diaries.* New York: Doubleday, 1967.

Billington, James H. *Fire in the Minds of Men: Origins of the Revolutionary Faith.* New York: Basic Books, Inc., 1980.

Blassingame, Wyatt. *The French Foreign Legion.* New York: Random House, 1955.

Brodie, Bernard. *Sea Power in the Machine Age.* Princeton: Princeton University Press, 1944.

Carell, Paul. *The Foxes of the Desert.* New York: Bantam, 1962.

Catton, Bruce. *The Civil War.* New York: American Heritage, 1961.

Cohen, Eliot. *Commandos and Politicians: Elite Military Units in*

Modern Democracies. Cambridge: Harvard University Center
for International Affairs, 1978.

Collins, John M. *Special Operations.* Washington, DC: National
Defense University Press, 1994.

Cook, Fred. *The American Revolution.* New York: American Heritage,
1959.

David, Heather. *Operation Rescue.* New York: Random House, 1971.

Davis, Burke. *Get Yamamoto.* New York: Random House, 1969.

Des Brisay, Thomas D. *Fourteen Hours at Koh Tang.* Washington,
DC: Government Printing Office, 1975.

Dupuy, R.E. and W.H. Baumer. *The Little Wars of the United States.*
New York: Hawthorne, 1968.

Gazit, Shlomo. "Risk, Glory, and the Rescue Operation." *International
Security,* 6/1:111-135 (Summer 1981).

Glines, Carroll V. *Attack on Yamamoto.* New York: Orion, 1990.

Graves, Robert. *The Siege and Fall of Troy.* New York: Doubleday,
1962.

Grimble, Ian. *The Sea Wolf.* London: Blond and Briggs, 1978.

Hart, B.H. Liddell and Robert Graves. *T.E. Lawrence to His Biographers.* New York: Doubleday, 1963.

Herzog, Chaim. *The Arab-Israeli Wars.* New York: Random House,
1982.

Joint Chiefs of Staff. *Publication I, Department of Defense Dictionary
of Military and Associated Terms.* Washington, DC: Government Printing Office, 1979.

Jones, Archer. *Why the Confederacy Lost.* London: Oxford University
Press, 1992.

Just, Ward. *Military Men.* New York: Alfred A. Knopf, 1970.

Kedourie, Elie. "The Real T.E. Lawrence." *Commentary,* 64:49-56
(July 1977).

Kelly, Francis J. *U.S. Army Special Forces, 1961-1971.* Washington
DC: Government Printing Office, 1973.

Kelly, Ross S. *Special Operations & National Purpose.* Toronto:
Lexington Books, 1989.

Lartéguy, Jean. *The Centurions.* New York: Dutton, 1960.

Lawrence, T.E. *Seven Pillars of Wisdom.* New York: Doubleday,
1926.

Lodwick, John. *Raiders From the Sea.* Annapolis, Maryland: U.S.
Naval Institute, 1990.

Lord, Walter. *Lonely Vigil.* New York: Viking, 1977.

Lowell, Thomas. *Raiders of the Deep.* New York: Doubleday, 1926,
1935.

Mack, John E. *A Prince of Our Disorder.* Boston: Little, Brown, 1978.

McRaven, William. *Theory of Special Operations.* Novato, CA:
Presidio Press, 1995.

Meyers, Jeffrey, ed. *T.E. Lawrence: Soldier, Writer, Legend.* New York: St. Martin's Press, 1989.

Miles, Milton E. *A Different Kind of War.* New York: Hawthorne, 1968.

Monsarrat, Nicholas. *The Cruel Sea.* New York: Alfred A. Knopf, 1951.

Porch, Douglas. "Bugeaud, Galliéni, Lyautey: The Development of French Colonial Warfare." In Peter Paret, ed., *Makers of Modern Strategy: From Machiavelli to the Nuclear Age.* Princeton: Princeton University Press, 1986.

---------. *The French Foreign Legion: History of the Legendary Fighting Force.* New York: HarperCollins, 1991.

Richter, Melvin. "Tocqueville on Algeria." *Review of Politics,* 25:361-93 (July 1963).

Roberts, Kenneth. *Northwest Passage.* New York: Doubleday, 1936, 1937.

Rowan, Roy. *The Four Days of Mayaguez.* New York: Dutton, 1975.

Ryan, Paul B. *The Iranian Rescue Mission: Why It Failed.* Annapolis: Naval Institute Press, 1985.

Sachar, Howard. *The Emergence of the Middle East, 1914-1924.* New York: Alfred A. Knopf, 1969.

Schemmer, Benjamin F. *The Raid.* New York: Harper and Row, 1976.

Spector, Ronald. *Eagle Against the Sun.* New York: Free Press, 1984.

Thomas, Lowell, *Raiders of the Deep.* New York: Norton, 1924.

Thomson, G.M. *Sir Francis Drake.* New York: Morrow, 1972.

Tolstoy, Leo. "The Raid." In *The Cossacks and the Raid.* Trans. by A.R. MacAndrew. New York: Signet, 1961.

Trevor-Roper, Hugh. "A Humbug Exalted." *New York Times Book Review,* November 6, 1977.

Vandenbroucke, Lucien S. *Perilous Options: Special Operations as an Instrument of U.S. Foreign Policy.* New York: Oxford University Press, 1993.

Walker, Greg. *At the Hurricane's Eye: U.S. Special Operations Forces From Vietnam to Desert Storm.* New York: Ivy Books, 1994.

Wilson, Jeremy. *Lawrence of Arabia.* New York: Macmillan, 1990.

Index